MODERN GREEK LESSONS

MODERN GREEK LESSONS

A PRIMER IN HISTORICAL CONSTRUCTIVISM

James D. Faubion

PRINCETON UNIVERSITY PRESS

PRINCETON, NEW JERSEY

LIBRARY OF CONGRESS CATALOGING-IN-PUBLICATION DATA

FAUBION, JAMES D., 1957–

MODERN GREEK LESSONS: A PRIMER IN HISTORICAL CONSTRUCTIVISM /
JAMES D. FAUBION.

P. CM. — (PRINCETON STUDIES IN CULTURE/POWER/HISTORY)

INCLUDES BIBLIOGRAPHICAL REFERENCES AND INDEX.

ISBN 0-691-09473-X

ISBN 0-691-00050-6 (PBK.)

1. ATHENS (GREECE)—CIVILIZATION.   I. TITLE.   II. SERIES.

DF920.F38   1993   949.5'12—DC20   93-15480   CIP

THIS BOOK HAS BEEN COMPOSED IN BITSTREAM ELECTRA

PRINCETON UNIVERSITY PRESS BOOKS ARE PRINTED
ON ACID-FREE PAPER AND MEET THE GUIDELINES FOR
PERMANENCE AND DURABILITY OF THE COMMITTEE ON
PRODUCTION GUIDELINES FOR BOOK LONGEVITY
OF THE COUNCIL ON LIBRARY RESOURCES

SECOND PRINTING, WITH CORRECTIONS,
FOR THE PAPERBACK EDITION, 1996

PRINTED IN THE UNITED STATES OF AMERICA
BY PRINCETON ACADEMIC PRESS

3   5   7   9   10   8   6   4   2

To W. R. D.

FOR THE FOUR WALLS,

AND ALL WITHIN THEM

CONTENTS

ACKNOWLEDGMENTS

MY RESEARCH in Athens was funded by a grant from the ITT International Fellowship Foundation. I am grateful for the foundation's support. I am also grateful for the support and the guidance offered me by the staff of the American Educational Foundation in Athens, whose members were exceptionally kind and assisted me far above and far beyond what their duties warranted. I would not have been able to go to Greece at all were it not for the sponsorship of the Academy of Athens's Center of Social Research. I would like to express my thanks to the director of the center, Ghrighoris Gizelis, for the advice and the contacts with which he provided me; to Eva Kalpourtzi, who arranged my association with the center; and to Iliana Andanakapoulou, who with Ms. Kalpourtzi listened to my ill-formed ideas, to my ramblings, and to my complaints, and treated me with more patience and tolerance than I deserved. Thanks, too, to Akis Papataxiarchis and to Marina Iossifidhi, both of whom should know that an apology, too, is implied.

I owe an unaccountable debt to the many Greeks who allowed me into their homes and into their lives. Some would prefer to remain anonymous; I deliver my thanks to them without naming names. Others, I trust, will not mind if I thank them publicly: Dhimosthenis and Andiklia (and Ino!) Aghrafiotis; Mariella Dhoumani; Andreas Ioannidhis; Margharita Karapanou; Nikos and Maro Saravanos; Elissavet Spiridhou; and Ghrighoris Vallianatos.

Modern Greek Lessons would never have been written without the encouragement, the gifts, and the coercion of many American colleagues and friends. For the photographs that accompany the text, for much else besides, I thank William Dall. For their insights and their support, I would like to thank Robert Bellah, Stanley Brandes, Jill Dubisch, Stephen Foster, Mia Fuller, Victoria Mukerji Gorsia, and Herbert Phillips. For her tolerance, her judgment, and her faith, I would like to thank my editor at Princeton, Mary Murrell. Thanks, too, to Brian MacDonald. I owe a more elaborate debt to three others. Weber's diagnosis of the inevitable unbrotherliness of scholars fails to apply; they are all exceptions to the rule. Michael Herzfeld read an earlier version of the manuscript assiduously and generously, and I credit him with many emendations, many refinements, and much inspiration. Samuel Danon—a cosmopolitan of precisely the stripe that I have in mind in much of *Modern Greek Lessons*, raised in Greece, trilingual in Greek, in French, and in English, now a professor of French language and literature at Reed College—has presided over my translations, and has improved them all. Paul Rabinow has been a mentor—in the time-honored and most encompassing sense of the term—from the beginning and still today; an advisor, a critic, and, above all, a friend.

PREFACE: TERMS AND DEFINITIONS

SIX YEARS AGO, I set out to investigate in Greece what Marshall Sahlins had already been exploring in eighteenth-century Polynesia, Renato Rosaldo among the Ilongot, and Richard Price among the Saramakas: the cultural and institutional context, the intellectual ordering, and the practical expression of a certain "historical consciousness."[1] Sahlins, Rosaldo, and Price had successfully undermined the theoretical cogency of positing any Great Divide between peoples without, and peoples with, history. But they had not undermined, had instead only confirmed, the cogency of a suggestion that Lévi-Strauss had made, and repeated, before them: that the relation between past, present, and future, the ontological and existential significance of the flow of events, must receive some definition in any passable view or vision of the world; and that definitions vary from one place and time and civilization to another. In *The Savage Mind*, Lévi-Strauss conflated views of the world with societies and, ever the binarist, casually grouped all societies under one or the other of two dichotomous indexes. Some societies, willing to recognize in change only a subordinate but in permanence the ultimate reality, were accordingly "cold." Other societies, convinced of the ultimate reality of change and committed to furthering it, were "hot."[2] Lévi-Strauss later corrected his conflation, and even ventured to reshape his discrete scale into one more continuous. Not everyone was satisifed. Rosaldo continued to see even in Lévi-Strauss's emendations an invitation for the Great Divide to reenter anthropological theory through an analytical back door.[3]

I saw something of greater interest. In *The Savage Mind*, the distinction between "cold" and "hot" had served more than a classificatory, a purely academic end. It had also served a polemical end, and served it, I think, effectively enough. The distinction paved the way for a diagnosis of the limitations of the program for a "historical anthropology" that Sartre put forward in the *Critique of Dialectical Reason*. The diagnosis may not have been fair in all respects, but its basic thrust was on the mark. Lévi-Strauss was correct in arguing in the closing chapter of *The Savage Mind* that Sartre's anthropology was grounded in a view of the world so "hot" that it could not begin to countenance the legitimacy, the rationality, the "authenticity" of views even slightly more lukewarm. He was correct in pointing out that Sartre had taken the ultimate ontological and existential reality of a contingent and mutable universe for granted. Though he did not, he might also have pointed out that Sartre was far from alone. Among the classical social theorists, only Durkheim had made an anthropological object of human conceptions of time and change. But not even Durkheim had bothered to treat his own evolutionism as a social fact, and so to put it anthropologically into focus. Like Marx and Weber, he was guilty of overlooking what Lévi-Strauss had brought to light: the characteristically Western and characteristically modern tenor of views and visions of the world radiating for all their differences a similarly high degree of "heat." But were our prevailing portraits of modernity not, then, seriously incomplete? Were they perhaps in need of fundamental revision?

What I found in Greece led me to conclude that our prevailing portraits of modernity were in need not simply of revision but of a counterbalance, of the portraiture of "another modernity," a modernity for which "heat" was not a forgotten or secondary but rather a central principle. In *Modern Greek Lessons*, I have pursued revision and the task of constructing that counterbalance hand in hand. I have begun with a piecemeal collection of curiosities, of ostensible anomalies, of artifacts and activities ostensibly neither "traditional" nor modern. I have sought gradually to articulate an interpretive framework within which those pieces might all coherently come together, their anomalousness diminish, and their proper modernity emerge in a clearer light. Throughout, I have understood modernity much as Shmuel Eisenstadt has recently recommended: not as "the ultimate endpoint of the evolution of all known societies" but rather "as one specific type of civilization which . . . originated in Europe and which has spread . . . all over the world."[4] I, too, have rejected evolutionism and have attended to diffusion even though I have stopped short of returning to diffusionism. I have referred to "modern systems" and have understood them, with Eisenstadt, as systems at once institutionally and ideologically distinct. I have not, however, identified modernity as a property only of those systems, much less of anything so global, so total as a "civilization." I have instead followed Weber in identifying it first and, primarily, as the property of a type of praxis. Weber located modernity—or at least its dominant, northwesterly modality—in the practice of what he came to call "formal" or "technical" rationalism." I have located its Greek modality, the "Greek modern," in the practice of what I have named "historical constructivism."

Defining a Practice

Talk of practices has grown too fashionable, too glib, and more doctrinaire than it need be. Especially since the publication of Bourdieu's *Outline*,[5] it has also become entangled with a reductive materialism that has robbed it of much of its diagnostic force. Throughout *Modern Greek Lessons*, I have followed Bourdieu in understanding practices essentially as habitual actions, the manifestation of those "structured and structuring dispositions"—those habitus—through the acquisition of which human beings

erywhere become social beings, each with characteristic tastes, and sentiments, and presumptions, and goals.[6] Bourdieu has argued, quite rightly,
that practices simply do not admit of perfect formalization, of the sort of
"mechanical modeling" that Lévi-Strauss once declared the cardinal standard of any "adequate" anthropological analysis.[7] Every disposition, no matter how structured, still bears the particular stamp of the particular being,
one of a potentially infinite number of beings, in whom it is embodied.
Every practice comprises a potentially infinite array of particular actions,
each one of which can be interpreted only relative to the particular features
of the particular situation in which it unfolds. Bourdieu's argument is hardly
original. One can find it in Aristotle's *Nicomachean Ethics*.[8] One can find it
in Geertz.[9] It entails in any case that the analyst of practices is always in the
face of a potential infinitude of variables. Mechanical models can accommodate only a finite number of variables. The analyst of practices is thus
condemned to be a mere "statistician."

So it goes: but Bourdieu has gone further, proposing that practices are not
simply unformalizable but also fundamentally informal; that they may be
wrought with reference, but never fundamentally in deference, to rules or
norms. The proof that Bourdieu adduces is just this: that practitioners often
enough violate the "official" norms of their practices with virtual impunity;
that they often enough violate them not to suffer the sanctions but instead
to reap the rewards of their deviance.[10] The conclusion he draws is that all
practices are at base strategic; that whatever else they may appear to be and
whatever else those who are engaged in them might believe them to be, they
are all at base simply different manners of the seeking of the maximization
of capital—symbolic, or material, or both. Bourdieu's "brutal"[11] reduction of
practices to exploits pays little heed to the native's point of view. For Bourdieu, the native is virtually always more wrong than right. The same reduction may appeal to our modern, Western cynicism, and especially to that
cynicism—superficially populist but in fact profoundly elitist—that would
pronounce all values equal and all values equally illusory.[12] Our own, "native" point of view might, of course, be correct. But Bourdieu's proof of it is
exceptionally weak. Some practitioners do, no doubt, violate the "official"
norms of the practices they pursue, at times with impunity, at times only to
reap greater rewards. But even those practitioners can do so only exceptionally. The practitioner who violates the official norms too often or too
regularly is likely to be labeled not clever but incompetent. The clever, the
"masterful" practitioner knows that official norms can be violated only so
often, and knows that some norms are more violable than others. Nor does
the master simply know that some norms might occasionally be violated; he
or she knows, too, that mastery can be established and maintained through
their occasional violation. Practical mastery is in this respect just as normatively governed as practical competence, even if the norms of the former

might call for the occasional violation of certain of the norms of the latter. Might practical mastery and practical competence both still be reduced to strategies for the maximization of capital? They might be, but only at the cost of overlooking that the ends that practitioners pursue might and often do have other rationales than the simple rationale of profit. They might be, but only at the cost of overlooking that the pursuit of certain ends could and does, in certain circumstances, have a more cogent rationale than the pursuit of many others: of overlooking as a consequence that not all values are, independent of circumstance, quite so illusory as they might seem.

In *Modern Greek Lessons*, I have resisted reduction and tried to preserve instead a multidimensional analysis at once of practices and of the ends and values toward which they are directed. Throughout, I have treated all practices—historical constructivism among them—as having three constitutive dimensions. The first of those dimensions is precisely the dimension of normativity. Even purely strategic action is, of course, "normative" in its way. Even it is governed by some principle of maximization—whether of capital, or of profit, or of subjective utility. But I would, *pace* Bourdieu, follow both Durkheim and Weber in regarding strategic action as a practice only when its governing norm is collectively ordained and collectively sanctioned. As both Durkheim and Weber recognized, "rationalism" is of sociological interest, and of sociological consequence, only once it has become a social fact. As Weber especially recognized, rationalisms are themselves of variable principles; and one might add that not even all modern, occidental practices are rational in any of the diverse respects that Weber specified. The normativity of practices distinguishes them only from some (but by no means all) types of "affective" or emotionally motivated conduct. All practices impose upon those who would pursue them minimal norms of competence. I have not assumed, however, that all impose additional norms of mastery. Nor have I assumed that all, even of those practices that warrant a distinction between mere proficiency and full-fledged mastery, demand of the master even the occasional violation of any norms whatsoever.

I have treated all practices—the practice of historical constructivism among other practices that I have addressed in *Modern Greek Lessons*—as having also a teleological dimension. Nothing controversial here, really: theorists of practice from Aristotle through Bourdieu have agreed that practices are always directed toward the realization of characteristic types of ends or values even if they have agreed on little else. They have consequently agreed that practices are never purely "expressive"; all are "instrumental." Practices are, however, necessarily iterable. Not all instrumental actions meet the same criterion. I might, for example, undertake on some rare occasion to break into an automobile in which I happened to have locked my keys. I would call upon my scant knowledge of engineering, and I might even succeed in achieving my aim. My actions would be instrumental, but they would not betoken a practice. I would be pursuing only a particular end, not the properly iterable, properly practical end of breaking into whatever automobiles happened to be locked with their keys inside them when the occasion demanded. I would not deserve the title of "locksmith" (or "car thief").

Whether practices and practitioners might be defined exclusively by the ends (or values) they pursue has remained a matter of debate from Aristotle forward. Aristotle seems to have thought that practices had a third constitutive dimension, a methodological dimension that set them apart from actions and activities equally instrumental but procedurally only hook-or-crook. I would concur, but would also underscore Aristotle's own proviso: even the most methodical of practices retain, and must retain, an element of procedural hook-or-crook. Even the most methodical of practices unfold in particular circumstances and aim at the realization of particular instances of iterable ends. Even the most methodical of practices consequently retain an element of improvisation that no amount of procedural systematization could possibly dispel. Bourdieu may hold to an even stronger, a more radical position: that practices have, in the ultimate analysis, no methodological systematicity whatever; that they are instead strictly improvisational. The position would be more plausible were practices indeed all (in the ultimate analysis) simply so many strategies for the maximization of capital, free of the governance of (any other) norms. Throughout *Modern Greek Lessons*, I have maintained a position much closer to Aristotle's than to Bourdieu's.

Modern and Countermodern Practices

My position may be closer to Aristotle's even than to Weber's. Weber presumed that the "irrational gap" between the intelligible and the sensible domains was the source of the incorrigible informality of any science that treated human action. The same gap—or something like it—would seem to be one of the sources of the incorrigible informality, at least of the pedagogy of any science whatever.[13] It could certainly be one of the sources of the informality not just of pedagogy but also of every other human practice, whose executors are inevitably constrained to project their plans and schemes upon an "empirical manifold" that, as Weber might have put it, never permits of "total comprehension."[14] When he turned, however, to the analysis of technical rationalism, Weber sometimes forgot his neo-Kantian epistemology. Or perhaps he purposefully left it behind. He might have thought that he had found—in the early Protestant compulsion systematically and single-mindedly to make of life a controlled, experimental proof of salvation—the precursor of a practice that would finally succeed in transforming the sensible into the intelligible, the human into a merely "functional" domain.[15] Technical rationalism was for Weber an instrumental practice with a peculiarly dehumanizing twist. Its governing norm was the norm of "calculability"—the requirement that those ends alone should be sought, could rationally and legitimately be sought, the means to which were subject to precise empirical determination.[16] The norm was incompatible with the pursuit not simply of otherworldly salvation but also of any end, any value whose transcendence rendered it empirically vague. It was incompatible, too, with any action colored even slightly by hatred or love, malice or compassion, by any motive too unsystematic in its manifestation or too particular in its object to allow of abstract accountancy. Technical rationalism had as its end the maximization of subjective utility, but only so long as subjects restricted themselves to desiring mundane and effectuable ends. It was a strictly methodical practice. Its masters might take, might even be obliged to take, (calculable) risks that merely competent practitioners would disdain, but neither its masters nor the merely competent could dare to be stylists. All alike were constrained to be automata.

Weber was right to identify technical rationalism as ascendant, indeed as dominant, in the modern Occident of his time; wrong to suppose that it had overcome the informality to which all other human practices are heir. He was right to regard it as the hallmark of modernity in his place and time; wrong to regard it as the hallmark of modernity *tout court*. Had he more carefully attended to the implications of his broader analytical program, he might have recognized at least the latter mistake. In his religious sociology, Weber hinted that men and women arrive at the threshold of modernity not when they arrive at technical rationalism but rather when they meet up with a problem, at once theoretical and practical in its implications. For Weber, the line of the religious—the metaphysical and existential—threshold of modernity was drawn when the existence of the "cosmos of tradition," an "ethically and somehow meaningfully oriented cosmos,"[17] came into doubt. It was drawn, in short, with the posing of a problem: how to live, how to proceed, if the existence of the ethically ordained cosmos can no longer be trusted? Weber acknowledged the two great practical responses that the problem has inspired in an analysis of the difference between what he spoke as the "ethic of conviction" and what he spoke of as the "ethic of responsibility." The ethicist of conviction declares the absolute, the cosmic validity of his or her evaluative principles *in spite of all* who would doubt. The ethicist of responsibility embraces his or her principles, in deference not simply to those who would uphold other principles but also to the memory, the passing, of the ethically ordained cosmos itself.

In *Modern Greek Lessons*, I have developed Weber's hints and suggestions not simply for my own but for what I have argued to be far broader comparative purposes. I have insisted throughout that modernity is not one but many things: but that the many things it is and might be are all practical responses similar in type if not in content to the same problematical threshold. I have not assumed that the ethically ordained cosmos, once cast into doubt, must remain in doubt. On the contrary: "tradition" is far too resilient, and human beings far too resourceful, for that. I have not assumed, either, that the existence of the ethically ordained cosmos comes into doubt for all members of a social collectivity in precisely the same manner at precisely the same time. Once again, quite the contrary. I have not assumed, but have nevertheless proposed, that an ethic of conviction is a less "adequate"—a less realistic, and less adaptive—response to the problem of the undermining of the ethically ordained cosmos than any ethic of responsibility (or at least, any that I know). Weber proposed the same. I have most often spoken of the ethic of conviction that prevails in Greece as "culturally classicist"—a label that highlights its tendency not simply toward absolutism but also toward what Geertz has called nationalist "essentialism."[18] I have sometimes spoken of it as "countermodern." I think that label, too, a just one, but hope that I would not, in applying it, foster the impression that its referent is either rare or always reprehensible. I have spoken of ethics of responsibility as "modern," but with similar circumspection. An ethic of responsibility informs the practice of technical rationalism, but I think no better of technical rationalism than Weber did. An ethic of responsibility also informs the practice of historical constructivism, the virtues of which I have tended to emphasize, but the shortcomings of which I have not sought entirely to ignore.

Cultural Classicism and Historical Constructivism Compared

Over the past several years, Michael Herzfeld has developed a penetrating and by now virtually exhaustive analysis of nationalism, and nationalist essentialism, in Greece.[19] In *Modern Greek Lessons*, I have focused on a more moderate and more "relativist" current of thought and action but have also tried to show that both currents, essentialist and relativist, have taken shape in very much the same objective circumstances. The founding fathers of the contemporary Greek state declared their independence from the Ottoman Empire in 1821. Neither their declaration nor the eventual instauration of the state would, however, mark the establishment of stable, much less impervious, national boundaries. Greece's boundaries have since become more fixed, though many natives have continued to believe them threatened. The natives are nearly right. Greece last suffered military invasion during the Second World War. But its borders were easy enough to cross long before the war, and they have remained just as easy to cross, just as permeable, up to the present. The entire history of the Greek state has been a history of importations and irritations. Tourists are only the last of a long train of "outsiders" who have confronted local residents with "alterna-

tives." They seem, as yet, to be less consequential, and certainly more benign, than the venture capitalists, the "political advisors," and the secret
operatives who have accompanied and preceded them. "Insiders" of various
sorts have had their impact as well. The diaspora has sent a fairly constant
stream of persuasive emissaries to Greece's territories. Returning guest
workers, returning expatriates and exiles, returning travelers have carried
exotic and attractive souvenirs back with them. No wonder, then, that the
cosmos of tradition has given way in Greece to a cosmos declared from all
sides to be "disorderly," even "chaotic."

Greece's essentialists have rarely undertaken actually to restore the cosmos of tradition. They have undertaken instead to restore or to uphold—
failing that, to impose—a corpus of "traditions," the inviolability of which
might at least keep utter chaos at bay. They have almost always searched for
their traditions in the local historical past, whether distant or more recent.
They have almost always treated the past as a domain not of contingencies
but rather of what Herzfeld has called "eternal verities,"[20] of customs and
characterological exemplars and collective identities written (sometimes
quite literally) in stone. The colonels who sat at the head of Greece's last
military junta, in power between 1967 and 1974, cultural classicists and
essentialists to a man, found their eternal verities in the still living and dur-
able past of Orthodoxy, even though their theological sophistication was
minimal at best. Their Greece was accordingly a Greece of, and for, "Greek
Christians." So, in their eyes, it would have to remain, whatever other diversity it might allow, and whatever other changes it might tolerate. Their
historical sensibility was far from "cold." Ardent traditionalists, they were
also ardent enthusiasts of industrial development and technological modernization. They were quite convinced that, without fear of inconsistency,
they could be both at once.

Greece's historical constructivists have pursued not restoration but instead reform and reformation. They have taken from the cosmos of disorder,
a cosmos of fragmentation and flux, at once a provocation and an inspiration. A world in pieces might be an unsettling world, but it is also a world of
sheer potential, a world that might be given form, ordered or reordered, if
only its pieces could be put together, anew or again. For historical constructivists, a metaphysics of chaos has itself become normative. So, too,
however, has the project of converting the potential into the actual, the
partially actual into something more inclusive, more comprehensive, more
complete; the world that might be, must be put together, anew or again.
The world as a whole, of course, would be a vast and daunting object with
which to grapple. The historical constructivists whom I have addressed in
Modern Greek Lessons have concentrated upon more modest and more
manageable objects, most of them already more or less actual. Whatever

their object, they have sought at once the direction and the materials of reform in a temporal domain, a domain of things past and present but of things always and only contingent. Historical constructivists put just such things to reformative use. Hence, their pragmatics is a pragmatics "of history." But they have not sought, as a rule, to extract from history even the remains of eternal verity. Nor have they supposed, as a rule, that their own reforms might somehow transcend the contingent, the "unnecessary" nature of the stuff out of which they are built. For all their convictions, they have remained "responsible."

But not responsible positivists. I have devoted considerable attention in *Modern Greek Lessons* to the interiors of apartments and homes, the exteriors of public buildings and monuments, to literary works, to fashion, and costume, to a variety of other artifacts in the creation of which historical constructivists have had an unmistakable hand. I have devoted considerable attention, thus, to what used to be grouped together under the rubric of "material culture." The rubric is nevertheless doubly misleading. It is misleading first of all because historical constructivists have had a hand in the creation and reformation of a great variety of less material things such as gender roles or "style"—none more fundamental than collective and individual identity. The rubric is even more gravely misleading because the "raw materials" with which historical constructivists have worked, whatever their purposes, have never been "material." The stuff of historical constructivism has never been just "one damn thing after another"—the concrete and strictly particular events of "empirical history." It has always been instead what I have called concreta—those "agglutinations" of reference and sense that would, were historical constructivists *bricoleurs* and the logic of their practice the logic of myth, more properly be called "signs." Concreta are not "signs" because their significance is not given, or is given only as potential. Historical constructivists differ from *bricoleurs* not simply because the logic of their practice differs from the logic of myth but also because their significative universe is inherently "open."[21] The practice of historical constructivism is precisely analogous to the practice of *bricolage*, however, in one crucial respect. The superordinate aim of both, the aim that in Aristotle's terms "includes" all others, is synthesis, the combining or recombining of disparate "parts" into coherent amalgams, if not precisely into "totalities" or "wholes."

Masters of historical constructivism might be distinguished from the merely competent by their greater "daring." They tend to reach farther afield for their raw materials; and they tend to have a special attraction to both materials and reforms that the merely competent—not to mention "cultural classicists"—might regard as too sacred to permit of manipulation. Like all practitioners, masterly and competent historical constructivists alike must have command of the crude logic of means and ends. But they must have command of much more. Not only the concreta with which they work but the specific ends they pursue are "significative": objects, entities, states of affairs, and activities that bear meaning. Historical constructivism is, then, a practice of *significative* reform or reformation, though a practice whose reforms can and often have had immediate and direct repercussions on institutions and behavior. Its methodology consequently cannot be reduced to the sheer logic of means and ends, the logic of rational decision and rational action. Its methodology and its teleology both demand powers of judgment quite different from, quite beyond those that would enable its practitioners merely to determine the relations among causes and effects. Historical constructivism requires of those who would practice it the further power to judge and to maintain semantic and connotative coherence from one reformative step to the next. It requires of those practitioners, whether merely competent or truly masterful, the capacity at once to preserve and to make meaning, whatever other ends they might seek to realize. It consequently requires of them a certain poetical know-how, a skill at figuration and refiguration, that demands not instrumental but rhetorical analysis.

Semiotics and structuralism both have provided us with a rich diagnostics of signs, symbols, and texts, but with astonishingly little in the way of a diagnostics of either figuration or refiguration, of either the making or the remaking of meaning. They have consequently left us with only the crudest apparatus for treating the significative dynamics of which the practice of historical constructivism affords only one of many examples. They have too often left us instead with the impression that "cultural change," significative revision, is always radical: a breakthrough of the "imagination," a reaction to contact or some other strange encounter, a quasi-mechanical outcome of the operation of outside forces. Whatever its causes, though, and however reactive it may be, cultural change is rarely if ever a change of whole cloth, and significative revision almost always a poetically disciplined process. The revisions of historical constructivists are no exception. In diagnosing them, I have borrowed heavily from Harold Bloom's "practical poetics," a theory of the making and remaking of meaning that underscores the importance not of texts but rather of the relations between them.[22] Bloom formulated his theory first in order to illuminate the dynamics of the practice of versification and verse criticism in England and America from Milton forward, but soon applied it to a much wider array of revisionary practices, only some of them "poetical" in the stricter sense of the term. It has proved a useful approach to historical constructivism not least because it treats actors suffering from a productive malaise very similar to the malaise from which historical constructivists suffer themselves.

Bloom's poets are victims of the "anxiety of influence," the subliminal terror that the visions of their precursors might be so overwhelming as to rob them of the poetical individuality, the originality that they are obliged to attain.[23] Some historical constructivists are victims of precisely the same anxiety. All of them are victims of an "anxiety of indefinition," a pressing if still largely subliminal suspicion that nonsense, or insufficient sense, is all that has been made of this or that piece or part of the world in which they live. Bloom's poets have no choice but to be sensitive to the historical past; the norm of originality under which they labor imposes it upon them. I argue in *Modern Greek Lessons* that a certain sensitivity, at once to the significative primacy of the past and to the fragmented diversity of the past and the present, is for all intents and purposes imposed upon anyone who would not simply reside but also "dwell" in contemporary Athens. I have argued further that the Greek engagement with historical and civilizational diversity—not always a willing engagement—constitutes the fundamental motor of a political system at once burdened and fueled by sempiternal crises of identity and legitimacy. From the Greek "politics of crisis," the Greek threshold of modernity derives. Historical constructivists are perhaps no more sensitive to diversity, no more sensitive to the crises it has induced, than their countermodern antagonists. The historical constructivists' "poetics of reform" in fact runs parallel to the cultural classicists' "poetics of restoration" just until it reaches its rhetorical conclusion. Bloom's theory offers a terminology precise enough to capture its tropological movement from start to finish.

Bloom has proposed that poetic revision is always "dialectical," but its dialectic tropological rather than logical. He has classified tropes, or figures, into two types. Irony, metonomy, and metaphor are "tropes of limitation," figures that undermine the poetical sufficiency of extant visions—literalist or fictional—by exposing their referents to be more, or less, or other than what they seem. Synecdoche, hyperbole (or litotes, its understated contrary), and metalepsis—the reversal of cause and effect, or of any temporally defined relations of priority and posteriority—are "tropes of representation," figures that replace extant visions with visions of new objects, whether parts of previously extant (but no longer literal) wholes, or wholes of previously extant (but no longer independent) parts.[24] Every dialectic needs a third term, of course, and Bloom has one: "substitution." He has suggested that revisionists who set out from irony reach their rhetorical telos in a substitutive synecdoche; that those who begin from metonomy reach their substitutive telos in either hyperbole or litotes; that those who begin from metaphor reach their substitutive telos in metalepsis. Bloom has further proposed that revisionism follows a dialectical sequence: from irony to synecdoche; from the conversion of synecdoche into either hyperbole or litotes, from the conversion of either hyperbole or litotes into metaphor; and from the conversion of metaphor into metalepsis.[25] Neither historical constructivists nor cultural classicists consistently follow Bloom's sequence.

Some begin their refiguration with metaphor; others begin with irony, but take no intervening steps. All, however, seek in one tropological way or another to arrive at metalepsis. And well they should: metalepsis is the historically sensitive trope par excellence, the only trope in Bloom's catalog that revises history itself.

But not all metalepsis is the same. Bloom distinguishes two kinds: "introjective" and "projective." Both refigure apparent or presumptive historical priorities. Both thus refigure what has already been figured; both are "tropes off of other tropes," and both effect a reversal of the priorities represented in the tropes off of which they turn. Each, however, moves in a contrary direction, and moves against contrary tropes. Introjective metalepsis effects a reversal of the prioritization of the future, or present, over the past. It opposes the figuration of either the future or the present as the telos of the past. It opposes the figuration of either the future or the present as the "completion" or perfection of the past. Introjective metalepsis instead locates the imago of both the future and the present in the past. It is the master trope of the "traditionalist," of cultural classicism, and so of nationalist essentialism, at least in Greece. Though not inherently pessimistic, it tends to be the master trope of every modern, occidental vision of the historical process as a process of "decline." Projective metalepsis effects a contrary reversal. It overturns the prioritization of the past over either the present or the future. It opposes any epic or exemplary figuration of the past, any figuration of the past as the exclusive standard of the present or the future. It is thus "antitraditionalist" but not necessarily "antitraditional." As the master trope of historical constructivism, it constitutes not a rejection but instead a reincorporation of the concreta of the past into the present. To be sure, it also constitutes a redetermination of the concreta of the past in the light of the present. Hence, the poetical antagonism between "countermoderns" and "moderns" in Greece.

Cultural Classicism, Historical Constructivism, and "Greek Culture"

The antagonism between countermoderns and moderns would be enough in itself to preclude the identification of either as the bearers of "Greek culture." Since the same antagonism at once reflects and reproduces profoundly divergent understandings of community, divergent ethics, divergent ways of behaving and being in the world, it might even warrant the identification of two "Greek subcultures." The ethnographic record compiled by my predecessors and colleagues may warrant the identification of many more than just two. Talk of "subcultures," however, presupposes that each "part" belongs to a common "whole," that the members of each "part" at once act and exist within a common "web of significance." Neither the ethnographic record nor my own research supports such a presupposition. On the other hand, neither supports the contradictory supposition that all in Greece has come unraveled. I argue in *Modern Greek Lessons* that most Greeks, rural and urban, of the lower and of the middle and upper strata, continue to share common political values and a common political orientation. I also argue that most, though by no means all, Athenians share a common "urbanity," more or less refined from one citizen to the next. If not all Greeks, most Athenians share a common "awareness" of the historical domain, past and present, even if they do not share either the same experience of it or the same response to the problems that it poses. Most Greeks share certain cultural "traits." The webs of significance within which they act and exist are nevertheless plural.

Should one talk instead, then, of several "Greek cultures," all of them perhaps different members of the same "civilizational family"? That would be no more fruitful and, in the end, even wider of the mark. It would run the risk of casting as static, even as immutable what is in fact neither. It would run the risk of conjuring boundaries in their actual absence. It would run the risk of underestimating not just the permeability of the broader field of potential and actual signification but also the interaction among players positioned diversely at once within that field and on its sidelines. To talk of either cultural classicism or historical constructivism as "cultures" might further highlight the poetics only at the expense of obscuring the very real institutional entrenchment of both. Worst of all, it would obscure at once the poetical and institutional powers of both. Cultural classicism and historical constructivism are practices learned and transmitted from one generation to the next. The practitioners of each share a common project, if not always precisely the same symbolic system. So far, both practices do indeed sound more or less like "cultures." But cultural classicism and historical constructivism are in fact metacultural. For both—as for anthropology, it should be added—culture itself has become an object, one among many objects of practical reflection and practical (re)figuration, of restoration or of reform. Both make and remake sense, of "culture" and from culture. Both have their own master ends and master tropes. Both have their own teleological and poetical discipline. Both have their own practical norms, but the practitioners of both characteristically act within and through a similar institutional framework. Organizationally, both might most accurately be spoken of as "regimes" for the production and reproduction of signification. I speak of both as "regimes of signification" throughout *Modern Greek Lessons*.

How, then, best to speak, best to think of *Modern Greek Lessons* itself? I would like to think that it is a contribution to the anthropology of ethics, to the anthropology of modernization and modernity, and to the anthropology of Greece. But it is certainly not an ethnography; its comparative scope is too broad, and its descriptive focus too narrow. It is not even an "ethnology," for it neither compares nor describes *ethnē* ("cultures"). Perhaps it is a "praxology," a study at once comparative and descriptive that has at its centerpiece one of many modern and metacultural practices. The term at least derives from perfectly good Greek.

MODERN GREEK LESSONS

INTRODUCTION

FOR THE TIME BEING: SOME NOTES ON THE
MANNERS OF MODERN LIVES

C ONSIDER A MAN: slim, balding slightly, soft-spoken. When I encountered him, in the early autumn of 1986, he could have been no
more than forty-one or forty-two years old. In Greece, he was well
known. In spite of his age, he already had an established seat in the Vouli,
the Parliament. Intermittently, he also appeared on the rosters of one or
another of the government's ministries. He was named Yiorghos after
his grandfather, an important diplomatic liaison during the internecine
struggles that had rocked his country in the late 1940s and prime minister
in the early 1960s. The younger Yiorghos belonged to what was, in 1986,
Greece's majority party: the Panelliniko Sosialistiko Kinima, the Panhellenic
Socialist Movement, or PASOK. His mother, Margaret, led the largest of
Greece's feminist organizations. His father, Andreas Papandreou, had held
the prime ministership for some five years running and was at once chief
and founder of PASOK. Even among many of those who would never consider voting for him, Yiorghos was acknowledged to have been born not
simply to politics but for them. He was perhaps a somewhat too favored,
somewhat too prodigal son, at least in the more meritocratic of reckonings.
He was unquestionably the heir apparent to the most resilient and most
charismatic leftist dynasty in the postwar period. But like his father, who
had been chairman of the Department of Economics at the University of
California at Berkeley in the later 1950s and early 1960s, he was cultivated
and well trained. He held a doctorate, in sociology, from the London School
of Economics.

On 3 October 1986, he talked before a small group of scholars and staff
assembled at the Athens offices of the American Educational Foundation. The conference was gestural in part: a show of goodwill in the face of
American threats to withdraw support of the Fulbright Fellowship program. The speaker could not in that respect have been more ideal: his English was impeccable; his temperament little inclined toward nationalist apologetics; his signature causes based for the past several years upon an
articulate conviction in the virtues of social and cultural cross-fertilization.
Introducing himself, he stated that he "would have had difficulty returning"
to Greece from abroad had he not felt that the country "could be changed."
His subsequent remarks were similarly ambivalent, similarly worldly, sim-

ilarly colored by a preoccupation with reform. He described what he declared to be "the Greek paradox": that his fellow citizens, who seemed willing only to revile the government "bureaucracy," were also disposed to regard themselves as utterly dependent upon it, to expect of it as they would never expect of themselves the procuring and provisioning of goods and services more or less as desired, more or less on demand. Explaining the paradox, he focused upon more than a century of poorly checked administrative centralization, of exclusion and disenfranchisement. He called, as many postwar Greek leftists have also called, for localism and the greater democratization of mechanisms of participation. He emphasized the need to inculcate a less fragile, more consistent ethos of self-reliance. The theme returned when he offered to respond to queries from his audience. Asked what "most kept him awake at night," he told of his worries, his perplexity over how to "get people to take things into their own hands."

He spoke, in vaguely Millsian terms, on the position of women. He gave an estimate much higher than the official one of the percentage of rural women still unable to read and write. Asked about the achievements in which he took most pride, he cited the recent expansion of remedial and vocational instruction for adults. He referred as well to his efforts to alleviate some of the problems suffered by generations younger than his own. He mentioned a program that could provide would-be entrepreneurs with the technical and financial tools necessary to launch small businesses; and another that could provide budding artists with opportunities to pursue and display their work. Above all, he was determined to slow if he could the persistent emigration—of ambition, of talent and intellect, of sheer numbers—that Greece has been witnessing even since the earliest days of its independence. He was seeking ways, he said, in which to encourage diaspora communities to maintain a sense of unity with their homeland; ways in which to encourage at least some of those who had gone away to reestablish themselves. The *agendum* had some measure of its motive in the simple pragmatics of state interests: among other things, defense (against Turkish attack, or so it was feared) demanded a larger standing army, he said, than the resident population could comfortably sacrifice. It had some measure of its motive, however, in what must have been more intimate, more self-reflexive, more personal experiences and visions: like the nation's youth, he said, the Greeks of the diaspora were "valuable" for their "critical perspective on society," for their attraction to and familiarity with "other ways of life," for their "marginality." He reiterated the point. It was precisely that "marginality," he said, that he hoped could be put in the service of the "transformation," of the "betterment" of Greece.

Registering Doubt: Toward a Definition of the Threshold of Modernity

A mere face in the crowd that October day, barely settled into my stay in the field, I did not seek another meeting with Yiorghos Papandreou, who departed from the Educational Foundation offices almost as brusquely as he had arrived. I saw him again only on televised news broadcasts and in two or three journalistic *photo-reportages*. The circle to which, soon enough, I gained an introduction, the network of colleagues and acquaintances to which I would subsequently become most closely bound, included one or two social activists, but no one who could properly be deemed a career politician. Its members were for the most part academics, writers, artists, civil servants, and liberal professionals. Few were as illustrious as the younger Papandreou. All had much in common with him, even so. Some were, some were not technical specialists. All, however, were acknowledged "experts"; all could consequently be counted, with Papandreou, among a sociocultural elite, notable less for their material wealth, and less simply for their "power" than for their "distinction," their stylistic and intellectual authority. They might derive their eminence, their particular right to be heard and heeded, from one or more quite disparate sources: the charisma of blood or office; the proof of achieved credentials; the secular grace of "talent" or "genius." They shared neither a singular point of view nor a singular style of life. Many of them nevertheless shared a disarming cosmopolitanism, especially disarming for its wavering, its insistent melding of loyalty to place with a seemingly irresolute *dépaysement*. Yiorghos Papandreou was by no means the last of the Greeks I encountered whose local engagements were informed by an undercurrent of distance, of worldly remove; by no means the last whose missions, ethical or moral, owed their definition not to the dogmata of psychological or ethnic "essences" but rather to the counterdogmata of "doubt."

"Doubt" glosses the demotic *amfisvitisi*, which one contemporary dictionary defines variously as *enandioloyia yia kati* (the raising of objections about something); *filonikia* (quarrelsomeness); *amfivolia* (uncertainty); or *andirrisi* (dissent). *Amfisvitisi*—not quite a "total social phenomenon" in Greece but not an institutionally specific phenomenon either—had and surely continues to have much the same place in the life of Yiorghos Papandreou, and in the lives of my native circle, as it has in *Modern Greek Lessons*. For them as for the "praxology" they have inspired, it is at once an ethical, a moral, and an intellectual point of departure and return. It is hardly an anthropological novelty. Contravening political and social commentaries, some of great eloquence, some brutally admonitory, are among the most familiar and widespread genres of what Maurice Bloch has called "traditional oratory."[1] Rather more cerebral disputations are recorded even in Bateson's *Naven*. If quarrelsomeness is not, then quarrels are, needless to say, no less universal than the prohibition of incest. Systematic or methodical "uncertainty" is perhaps of a more restricted provenance. Its most vigorous carriers—one thinks first of the classical sophists, or of the Hellenistic Skeptics—are within what we now have little alternative but to characterize, if in the broadest of senses, as "Western" horizons. Against that narrowness, however, which is in part the outcome of a rather recent institutionalization of our civilizational boundaries, one might do well to reiterate, with Geertz, a Weberian analytics of the religious imagination. If "bafflement, suffering," or "a sense of intractable ethical paradox," sufficiently intense or sufficiently sustained, may indeed be "radical challenges to the proposition that life is comprehensible and that we can, by taking thought, orient ourselves effectively within it,"[2] if such radical challenges cannot but lead to a "sense of deep disquiet,"[3] then "doubt," at least in its more primordial of modalities, can be no more "Western," and no more of a human rarity, than religion itself.

Nor is dissent original to the Europe and America of the 1960s. But not all *amfisvitisi* is, of course, the same. We would be in error to equate the oppositional import of a Tshidi headman's complaints about the irresponsibility and licentiousness of his royal superiors[4] with the oppositional import of, say, Lord Devlin's complaints about the legalization of homosexual conduct[5] or Reverend Jerry Falwell's complaints about the banning of prayer in public schools. All alike might strike us as similarly conservative. But the headman can rest his conservatism in a cosmos the ethical order and moral content of which are beyond doubt, and which he can consequently trust his Tshidi listeners to take for granted. Neither Devlin nor Falwell can trust their own listeners nearly so far. We would be just as much in error to equate the suspicions of the early Skeptics with the *soupçon* of such latter-day deconstructionists as Richard Rorty or Jacques Derrida. Even the Skeptics' successors, from the Roman Stoics through Descartes, remain confident that the fundamental design of the cosmos is moral in principle. Neither Rorty nor Derrida can agree. The failure of such equations may not compel us to posit any Great Divide. But it does, as Weber himself recognized, compel us to posit a great difference: between those doubts, those problems, and those problematics that coherent cosmogonies and cosmologies can go some way toward assuaging and those doubts, those problems, and those problematics that arise only once the cosmos has been declared ethically and morally neutral, God declared dead, and men and women declared—with a finality that they would be "irrational," would be "fools" to deny—to have nothing from which to proceed but their own devices.

In the third chapter of *Modern Greek Lessons*, I argue at length that

Weber's insight still leads to the most practicable definition of the ethical and moral "threshold" of modernity we might have. Granted, his insight may be imbued with a romantic pathos that we would do better to avoid. It surely has romantic roots. Some century before the publication of *The Protestant Ethic*, Friedrich Schiller had registered the occidental turning from a "naïve" to a "sentimental" sensibility, the former confident of both the transparency and the timelessness of its visions, the latter confident of neither. Reiterating the same turning and enlarging upon it, Weber focuses upon that rather vague and extended juncture at which values began to lose their self-evident facticity and world views to devolve into "ideological perspectives." He might or might not agree that the juncture is also one at which commodities began to become fetishes and producers alienated from the products of their labor.[6] For Weber, whose understanding of modernity is not as intimately tied to the economics of capitalism as many of his readers assume, the fetishization of commodities and the reification of labor are in any case only two facets, at once catalysts and outcomes, of a process of much longer duration: of rationalization itself. Scientific socialism and interpretive sociology are two others. For Weber as for Durkheim, modernity is most intimately tied to systemic differentiation. For Weber, however, modern systems are not simply the most complex. Nor are their ambivalent Durkheimian hallmarks—organic solidarity and anomie—as basic as another: their lack of integration. Though they might be strikingly (or frightfully) efficient, Weber's modern systems are nevertheless those in which the values that govern economic and political and various other spheres of action have been rationalized so far, have become so distinct and so autonomous, that they preclude being reconciled. The threshold that emerges with what Weber sometimes thinks of as their "lawful" dissonance is thus altogether negative. It marks the end, if it ever existed, of any genuinely mechanical moral unity. It marks the end, if it ever existed, of any genuine moral innocence. Weber mourns the passing of both. We need not share his grief. We cannot, I think, do without his diagnosis, which manages to do justice to the earlier insights of Marx and the contemporaneous insights of Durkheim without falling prey to the disingenuous positivism of either. We cannot do without his dark conclusion that, having arrived at the threshold of modernity, we are left either to cleave "irrationally" to a cosmos whose ethical and moral preordination has become both antiphysical and antisocial, or to resign ourselves "rationally" to a life beyond and without it.

Weber's modern systems are not, however, unmitigatedly secular, not systems from which either religion or religiosity have been banished. Modern systems might, modern systems still do have countermodern inhabitants, who would insist upon their transcendent faiths even in the face of the most ardently earthly of detractors. But the (pro)modern inhabitant, too, might have his or her faith: if not self-consciously and proudly irrationalist, if not otherworldly, still transcendent in its way. Consider at once the ontological scope and the ontological ground of that *amfisvitisi* with which Yiorghos Papandreou and my circle were so preoccupied. Papandreou likely fashioned himself a skeptic, a questioner of "his" society and "his" culture; certainly he fashioned himself as nothing less, though neither as anything more, in his October lecture. Many of my circle would be quite correct in fashioning themselves as questioners *tout court*. Among them, *amfisvitisi* ranged freely over the entire spectrum of human institutions, human pursuits, and human affairs: from haute cuisine to imperialism; from populism to psychoanalysis; from air pollution to erotica. But it also had its inhibitions. I met, in Greece, no real nihilists. I met and worked instead with "troubled optimists." They had no more trust in the immanently moral and immanently meaningful cosmos of traditional or premodern soteriology[7] than would Rorty or Derrida. They had not, however, yet resigned themselves to imprisonment within that mechanical "iron cage," the immanent meaningless of which so horrified Weber. The world in which they continued to live, a world that warranted and required a vigilant *amfisvitisi*, a world that allowed but also demanded reform, was less cage than "chaos." Its distressfulness, its ominousness, lay precisely in its unmitigated contingency. My circle was fond of a couple of slogans that I at first dismissed as mere clichés. "In Greece," I would regularly be told, "anything is possible." "In Greece," I would frequently enough be told, "*everything* is possible." Neither slogan was in fact a cliché at all. Both rather have the air of tenets, of first principles. Both invite immediate and direct comparison with the *principium* that Robert Bellah locates at the heart of every modern faith: that reality is not a single, but an "infinite possibility thing."[8]

Getting There and Being There: Modernization and Modernity in the Plural

Should such a comparison, such a convergence really surprise us? Perhaps not: Greece, after all, is not a new but a rather old European state, Athens a vast and by no means sheltered metropolis, and the Athenians of my circle for the most part a very sophisticated and up-to-date lot indeed. But the suggestion that some Greeks, some Athenians at least are every bit as modern as anyone else is curiously out of accord with a notable body of social scientific opinion. Is it simply that no one so far has bothered to "study up"? Not that, I think: my project may be something of an oddity, but my contact is far from the first, and my contacts far from pristine. Nor are foreigners alone in finding fault, or finding trouble, with the very idea of a "modern Greek." Native sociologists—members of the very stratum to which, to my mind, the idea most readily applies—frequently have troubles of their own.

I reserve space for a more extended commentary on such indecisiveness for later chapters. Here, I merely remark that it strikes me as being at once sound and misguided. It virtually always rests on the entirely accurate observation that the Greek "system" is in many respects incommensurable with any other, the Greek case in many respects unique. It virtually always rests as well, however, on the entirely mistaken presumption that every modern system is, in both its origins and its operations, a mirror image, every modern personality an attitudinal and behavioral clone, of every other.

A presumption very similar to the latter informs Daniel Lerner's *Passing of Traditional Society*.[9] On the other hand, it has less of a place in Bellah's study of Tokugawa Japan,[10] and comes under convincing attack in Reinhard Bendix's "Tradition and Modernity Reconsidered."[11] That this presumption remains in such favor cannot, then, be due to its having admitted of no analytical alternatives, much less to its having proved itself of remarkable analytical virtue. That it remains in such favor may instead be due, more than anyone or anything else, to Weber himself. His definition of the threshold of modernity may for its part be of a negative sort. It may merely define a problem. It certainly implies nothing at all precise about the conditions under which such a problem can be guaranteed to emerge. It isolates only a very few of the general properties that modern systems and their modern inhabitants might be expected to manifest. Whether or not it invites, it certainly allows us to suppose that both passages to and positions beyond the threshold might be indeterminately plural, that both modernization and modernity might consequently be not one but instead very many things.[12] An open-ended definition, it is nevertheless imbedded—even buried—in the developmental reckoning of a particular system, a particular case of such apparent "world-historical significance"[13] that it had to be treated as paradigmatic. The sheer intellectual force of that reckoning has understandably bewitched even the most sober of readers, Parsons among them. It has very often bewitched me.

In the second part of *Modern Greek Lessons*, I argue even so that Weber's reckoning—comparative, of course, but in the end a reckoning only of the modernity of the capitalist core of the Occident at the turn of the twentieth century—has numerous shortcomings. We can, I think, still accept his genealogy, at least in outline; though impelled by developments in the arts, in the sciences, even in military strategics, modernization at the core of the Occident still appears to have had its most urgent impetus in that great conjoining of Protestantism with an ascendant bourgeoisie. The conjuncture has, however, no exact counterpart in Greece, which has yet to be touched by anything resembling a Protestant reformation and the social structure of which has long been slanted not toward economic but instead toward political values.[14] Extrapolating from both the historical and the ethnographic record, I suggest in my fourth chapter that modernization in Greece must for all its economic catalysts hence be approached primarily as a political transformation. It is only tangentially a matter of the transformation, much less the "rationalization," of what Parsons would call latent motivations. On the contrary, Greeks in the present continue with their ancestors to place a categorical premium on the seeking and securing of both personal and collective sovereignty. What has changed, what has indeed dissolved, is rather the cosmos of performative ideals—in a phrase, the "political script"—by which the quest for sovereignty was traditionally given direction and traditionally constrained. With its dissolution, not even bureaucracy has been able to function as a performative alternative; it has functioned more often simply as one more tool in the sovereigntist's bag of ideological and tactical tricks.[15] In the long run, it has functioned no more effectively than any other. It, too, has come, and gone, and come again. Modernization in Greece has accordingly been marked by an institutional instability notably more extreme than modernization farther west. The threshold of modernity has loomed as a threshold not simply of doubt or critique but of politicoethical crisis. Beyond it, both "legitimacy" and "identity" have seemed to many foreign and native observers alike always already undone.

Beyond it, however, there are still ways positively and productively to live, manners of living that can direct us among other things to the shortcomings not just of Weber's reckoning of modernization but also of his reckoning of modernity, even at the core of the Occident. There is much to recommend his central conclusion: that modernity at the core is both parent and child of a technical rationalism, a mentality bound to rules and procedures that in Bismarck's Germany no less than today would compel us to justify not merely our choice of means but also our choice of ends in the light of an overarching norm of "calculability."[16] In the light of that norm, magicians still might pursue their craft and penitents still seek some station in a heavenly paradise, but only as absurdists, one and all. In its light, experimental scientists, bureaucratic functionaries, and capitalist accountants appear the most perfectly "reasonable men." Are they, however, the only modern men and women we know? Weber himself knew others—the mystical poet Stefan George among them—but feared them a vanishing breed. He has been proved wrong. If our rules and procedures have come to dominate us, they have not, even at the occidental core, come as yet altogether to determine us. If proceduralists, *sine ira ac studio*, enjoy a special prestige, they must still share their prestige with an ever growing number of nationalists, ethnicists, regionalists, and various other doctrinaires, at once angry and zealous and eminently capable of putting science and bureaucracy and capitalism in the employ of what at first sight seem quite antithetical taskmasters.[17]

Gerth and Mills have observed that Weber failed to foresee the rise even of the most malign, but also the most bureaucratized, of modern nationalists: the German Nazis. Their observation is, however, only partially correct.

If Weber overlooks the currents that, even in his day, were beginning to lead to Hitler, he is still well aware both of our lasting urge to value and of our lasting susceptibility to the "charismatic." His lapse, relatively minor, instead consisted of his having despaired of uncovering anything other in the Occident's future than a long train of Hitlers. His modernity is a Kantian agency come unglued. It is an existential schizophrenia: of moral forms that no longer tolerate any ethical content; and consequently, of needs and interests and passions that might lose their essential privacy only to become the stuff of blind fanaticism. With his diagnosis, Weber's prognosis has been so often confirmed that it must stand largely intact. Among his contemporary readers, Habermas surely goes too far in insisting that the lifeworld that seems to have come to an end with the capitalist appropriation of Protestant "methodism" in fact still survives. But Habermas is right to assert that Weber—too much the Kantian in this regard—has no conceptual room for the intersubjectivity that would allow him to acknowledge even those remnants of the lifeworld that have retained their potency. In retrospect, it can only be astonishing that the most wide-ranging of sociologists had so little to say about the sentient body, which has served since the eighteenth century as the common ground not simply of an occidental politics of health but also of an occidental politics of liberty, of security and well-being. In retrospect, it is even more astonishing that someone who portrayed himself as making merely a modest contribution to historiology should have had nothing whatever to say about the substantive matter with which historiology is concerned, about those significative concreta of the past and present that have served, at the core of the Occident and virtually everywhere else, as the common ground not only of nationalists and ethnicists and regionalists but also of their more cosmopolitan cousins.

The concreta of the past and present—to which I shall refer simply as "history"—provide my Athenian circle with the largest portion of those raw materials that give ethical substance, if for each member of that circle a somewhat individual ethical substance, to what all share of a distinctly cosmopolitan moralism. Focusing on the origins, the setting, and the practical realizations of that moralism, I attempt in *Modern Greek Lessons* to supplement Weber's hermeneutics of technical rationalism with the hermeneutics of another modernity, another way of being modern, which appears to come the more fully into its own the farther one moves away from the Occident's core. Whether or not it turns out to be a success, the attempt itself seems to me all the more urgent as more and more of the world's peoples find themselves not simply at modernity's threshold but too often pushed abruptly and unceremoniously beyond it, at best imperfectly aware of the diversity of alternatives they have available. It seems to me even more urgent as the unification of Europe puts some of those alternatives that have already been worked out at a greater risk than ever of being lost or suppressed. Hence, I betray one of my many biases. I am no more fond than

Weber of technical rationalism, and believe the historically grounded cosmopolitanism of my Athenian circle to have much, ethically and morally, to recommend it. I am, then, a neoromantic, and a neoromantic very much in the American tradition. *Modern Greek Lessons*, a text written like all others for and against its own place and time, should be read accordingly.

Might I, in the furtherance of my biases, simply have stayed to reflect upon and write about those neoromantic impulses now prevalent, and by which I am apparently affected, at home? I might have, I suppose: but as Bourdieu has remarked, practitioners can never really know what they are doing until they get away from what they are doing. Had I not gotten away and gone to Athens, I would never really have known how very truncated and distorted my North American exercise of a historically grounded moral imagination in fact remains. I would certainly never have known what such an exercise might achieve if given—as it is given, to many at least, in Athens—freer reign. Might I have done even better, though, to travel to a much more distant, a much more exotic locale? I suspect not: the "margins of Europe" are distant enough to allow for an escape from North America, but not so distant that they fall altogether outside that single part of the world in which modernity may properly be regarded at once as endemic and endogenous. Many Parsonsians have held that modernity might, like all "proper systems," be detached from its original milieu, that a hermeneutics of modernity is and should be "essentially generalizable." I follow Shmuel Eisenstadt and the other contributers of *Patterns of Modernity* in rejecting such a position, which seems to me to rest upon a grave misunderstanding of the sort of generalities that the social sciences have to use. Theoretically and methodologically, *Modern Greek Lessons* is most closely aligned with Eisenstadt's collection and with two other less scientist monographs, one of which I had the opportunity to read in draft shortly before I departed for the field, the other of which I read in print shortly after I returned. Like Paul Rabinow's *French Modern*,[18] like Michael Herzfeld's *Anthropology through the Looking-Glass*,[19] my own text seeks not to abstract but rather to stretch, to broaden one of the most salient of the occidental core's motifs of self-reflection in order to render it of greater comparative, and so of greater anthropological, service.

Studying Up and Writing Up: The Fashions and the Fashioning of the Greek Modern

Out of all the margins of Europe, Athens has accommodated my ambitions perhaps better than any other. I still know of no other place in which history past and present has been so dominant an ethical concern; no other place in which history past and present has been at once so productive a moral bur-

den and so compelling a modern object of sociocultural re-creation. I came
to Athens not knowing, however, but instead upon having made an educated guess about what I might encounter. I based my guess not solely, not
even primarily, on ethnographic documents. I relied instead on several other
sorts of documents, worth mentioning here because their traces are everywhere in the document that I have composed. I am not Greek and had not
visited Greece before 1986, but had my first acquaintance with an artifact of
what I would now call the "Greek modern" more than a decade before,
when at the too unripe age of sixteen I read Kazantzakis's *Zorba*. I read most
of the rest of his oeuvre soon after, as soon indeed as I could get my hands
on it, and have continued to "read Greek" ever since. From Kazantzakis I
nevertheless took a very long backward step. My later undergraduate and
early graduate studies were primarily concentrated in philosophy, and especially in the philosophies of Plato and Aristotle. Beginning in 1981, I applied
myself to learning ancient Attic. Two years beyond that, when I entered the
graduate program in anthropology at Berkeley, I presumed that my dissertation would rely more heavily on Sally Humphreys and Louis Gernet than
on scholars of the "neo-Hellenic." Fortunately, my antiquarianism rapidly
gave way to the excitements of the experimental moment. Paul Rabinow
helped me devise a curriculum that permitted me not simply to keep up my
interest in philosophy but to turn it into an investigative advantage. Various
modalities of the historical consciousness, various modalities of historically
grounded ethical and moral and intellectual practice had already been made
ethnographic objects in Oceania and South America.[20] Herzfeld's *Ours
Once More*[21] had proved that they could also be made an ethnographic object in Greece, and made one without the result degenerating into a mere
documentation of survivals. I sought a teacher of demotic, and found Maria
Kotzamanidou, who has enabled me to make my way even through much
(not all!) of Kazantzakis's eccentric prose with only occasional resort to a
lexicon. In the seventh chapter of *Modern Greek Lessons*, I treat one of
Kazantzakis's most gifted literary successors, Margharita Karapanou, whose
two vibrant and violent novels merit special consideration for being virtual
manifestos of the generation that came of age in 1974, when the military
junta that had seized power eight years previously finally fell.

Literature, particularly the literature of Kazantzakis and Karapanou,
might seem to occupy a rather rarefied domain, far removed from the mainstream of everyday life. Indeed it does: but that makes it perhaps all the
more exemplary of Greek moderns themselves, for whom a certain social
and cultural view from afar is less a luxury than a practical necessity, and
who are consequently likely always to be few in number. They are not, however, a cadre of aesthetes. For all their literary virtues, for all their beauty,
the oeuvres of neither Kazantzakis nor of Karapanou are mere objets d'art.
The specific norm that presides over the production of both is less the norm

of aesthetic sublimity than of revelatory originality. The signatures with which both are inscribed at once constrain and permit them to express a subjectivity that they serve also, in part, to define. However rarefied its domain, literature thus functions for Kazantzakis and for Karapanou as a technology not simply of beautification but also of self-creation. It proves to be only one among many of the self-creative technologies to which Greek moderns have avail. They take from language many, if not all their raw materials; but even language, though long favored as an index of Hellenicity, provides only some of the concreta of the past and the present upon which Greek modern invention depends.

Modern Greek Lessons proffers no exhaustive inventory, whether technological or historical. I aim instead at isolating and illustrating some of the most representative characteristics of a dynamic field: its background and foreground; its perturbations and its most enduring significative patterns; the qualifications and the qualities of its current master players. With my treatment of Karapanou, I group two others of roughly equal length. The first explores Greek modern self-creation more eclectically. It features a woman whom I call "Maro." Strictly speaking, Maro is a fiction, a composite of five actual members of my Athenian circle, a summation of sorts of their common condition and of what is common in each of their responses to it. She is, however, no more typical than any one of them; or rather, she is typical precisely in her cultivated atypicality. Maro incarnates the existential anxieties of a cadre for whom socialization and culture both have become subject to *amfisvitisi*, a cadre for whom the socialized and acculturated self is consequently only a "rough draft" of its more "authentic" imago. As Karapanou does, Maro, too, incarnates the still only partially realized existential hopes and dreams of a generation that came of age in an era—the era of the Papadhopoulos junta—with whose collective tendencies and collective resolutions it has set out implacably to break. The last of my treatments explores self-creation writ even larger. It addresses what might, for lack of a better term, be called psychosocial reformism. Its particular subject is "the homosexual," one of the postjuntan generation's most novel beings and the cause célèbre of an ongoing "liberation movement." If not a summation, "the homosexual" is at least an indicator: of the junta's provision of a "creative catastrophe" from which both self-examination and cosmopolitan tolerance have acquired an almost missionary vigor; of the significative challenges that both that vigor and that cosmopolitanism have faced; of the significative formulas that both have deployed; and of the broader social impact that both have made.

Modern Greek Lessons begins, however, as many precedent monographs have also begun: by setting the scene for its dramatis personae. Its initial chapters are accordingly devoted to the painting of a highly selective portrait of Athens itself. The portrait does not amount to an urban ethnography; I lived in the metropolis long enough to walk almost all its streets but intimately to know only a minority of them. Nor does it strive toward ethnographic holism. Quite the contrary: if culture is not always a thing of shreds and patches, it has become one in Athens. Tourism has encouraged its commodification. The historical self-consciousness and anthropological virtuosity of many of its inhabitants—those of my circle among them—have encouraged its virtually continuous reconceptualization and reordering. Socially and culturally, Athens reflects the influence of many and disparate guiding hands, an influence that a presumptive holism would only disguise. My portrait instead intentionally leaves disparities unresolved; it is intentionally "anecdotal." My intentions are twofold. On the one hand, I seek to adduce a particularly insistent empirical provocation for raising again the issue of the relation between "tradition" and "modernity." On the other hand, I seek an exterior simile for the interior dilemmas and dispositions of those that I know best. My Athens, if not the only one, is thus not an irreal one, either.

Athens's topographical and toponymical uniformities are likely to seem anything but uniform to the urban North American—at least at first sight. The metropolis has not one center but rather a complicated nest of them. It lacks a neat division between "uptown" and "downtown." It has not a single numbered avenue or street. All its avenues, all its streets instead bear names. Some of those names—Hermes, Athena, Homer, Sophocles—might be recognized even by the least informed. Others—Soutsos, Voukourestios, Paparighopoulos—ring a bell only for the cognoscenti. It is not uncommon for two or more streets lying in different districts or neighborhoods to bear the same name. The local past dominates the local present in Athens; the metropolitan skyline grants pride of place not to commercial skyscrapers and towers but to two ancient points of reference: the Acropolis and Mount Likavittos. Not all even of the local past wins a representation equal to what actual events might warrant. Classicism prevails. Byzantine themes and revolutionary allusions are closely second. Very little is left, however, either to record or to recall the long centuries of Ottoman domination; even less to record or recall the briefer Catalonian or Venetian occupations. A capital city, Athens had in 1986 and 1987 some eighty foreign embassies; but it had remarkably little of the sort of long-established and well-organized cultural and ethnic enclaves typical of New York or San Francisco. In spite of the penchants of its sociocultural elite, it was not a cosmopolis. It had class-based and status-based enclaves, however, the more exclusive of which revealed a cultivated taste—some natives would call it a "mania"—for foreign goods, and foreign services, and especially for foreign styles, those of Paris, and Milan, and London prominent among them.

Thus, in brief, the ambient echo of what has become of culture itself: a restricted but still "disintegrated" multiplicity that constitutes for my circle as for other Greek moderns the primary experiential stimulus of self-creation; of creation *tout court*. The multiplicity of Athens might be stimulus enough for those who have found their vocation in architecture or in urban planning. The contemporary metropolis is amply endowed with their showpieces. It was, however, the multiplicity, the antitheses of the human being that most stimulated Kazantzakis, who for all his adamant Hellenicity spent most of his life outside of Greece. It is the multiplicity, the antithetical pushes and pulls of her own human being and her own human condition that urge Karapanou toward a Manichaean ontology, but also toward a far more private gnosis. It urges her contemporaries toward other ontologies, and other gnoses. The precise ethical and moral and intellectual bearings of Greek modern creation might, then, vary considerably from one case to the next; but its provocation is a constant. So, too, its end: Greek modern creation does not have its consummation in a resignation to multiplicity but has it rather in synthesis. It could be labeled Hegelian, except that its attendant attitude is less philosophical than practical. It might occasionally appeal to theory, but it remains a fundamentally pragmatic exercise, a pragmatics of history, the results of which are meant to be no more historically definitive than they are meant to be historically impartial.

Take one example, an example that I offer in the fifth chapter of *Modern Greek Lessons* as a prototype of sorts, long predating the works and lives of my Athenian circle but of more practical consequence—so far at least—than all of their works and lives combined. It is the original brainchild of Adhamandios Korais, a notable man of letters and even more notable Hellenist during the era of Greece's reclamation of national independence. His invention: katharevousa, so-called purist Greek, an utterly artificial dialect made of ridding the going vernacular of most of its Turkish "corruptions" while supplementing it with what it had lost of the cases, the suffixes, and the stems of its more ancient linguistic predecessors. Quite the synthesis indeed: it was soon elevated to an official status, and remained the *modus dicendi* of the Greek government for more than one and a half centuries, until 1975. Populist pedagogues have rightly disparaged its institutionalization, which effectively left command of the discourses of law and bureaucracy in the hands of a highly educated few. Still, Korais cannot himself entirely be held to blame. His intention—Greek modern *avant l'heure*—was simply to provide his Greek-speaking contemporaries with an effective bridge to their linguistic past, and so to provide them with a means of making a bridge between the past and the present. Granted, he exaggerated and overrated the continuity between the two. Korais was not, however, backward-looking. Katharevousa became more and more Atticizing the more it became not his own invention but the invention of others. He would have had little praise for the arcane and increasingly static scribery that his philological successors made of it. His katharevousa was heuristic and was meant to change as change was needed; the katharevousa of his successors degenerated into a weapon of exclusion.

The teacherly Korais was too much a man with a mission to be reduced merely to a "technical rationalist." How, then, to come to terms with him? Promising leads come from an emerging school of "conceptual historians," among whom Hans Blumenberg is especially instructive. Like Weber before him, Blumenberg is disturbed by present-day technocracy, which rightly or wrongly he sees as a cancerous deformation of an earlier ethic of craftsmanship.[22] His modern Occident is not, however, merely or inevitably a technocracy. It is also a place that permits, with unprecedented license, the indulgence of curiosity about the world and all that is in it. It opposes to Platonic perfectionism an aesthetics of discovery and world disclosure; to classical teleology the idea of "infinite progress." It opposes, to the ethical quietude of both antiquity and the medieval era, "self-assertion": "an existential program, according to which [one] posits his existence in an historical situation and indicates to himself how he is going to deal with the reality surrounding him and what use he will make of the possibilities that are open to him."[23]

What the self-assertive agent loses, for Blumenberg as for Weber, is the guidance, at least the immediate guidance, of intellectual, ethical, or aesthetic absolutes.[24] What he or she gains, to Blumenberg's mind at least, is the liberating opportunity of a self-definition unconstrained by any cosmic controls.[25] The self-assertive destiny, for better and for worse, is not delivered; it must rather be made. The meaning of the self-assertive life, for better and for worse, is not decided in advance; a temporal and situational matter, it must rather be devised a posteriori. The modern institutionalization—intellectual, ethical, and aesthetic—of the hiatus between the universal and the particular, between possible worlds and the actual world, between life and the individual's passing being, is tragic for Weber precisely for the infinite existential imperfection that it implies. The modern, the Faustian hero is, for Weber, who and what he is precisely for his never being able to be complete. He can die "weary"; he cannot die "sated."[26] But compare Blumenberg's assessment:

> The cosmos of the ancient world and of the metaphysical tradition—in other words: the belief that one is confronted . . . with what is already "finished" . . . that all one can do is either adapt oneself to this world or violate it, determining thereby nothing but one's own happiness or unhappiness—this cosmos proves in retrospect to be precisely what Nietzsche was to call "the most crippling belief for hand and reason." As a Romantic principle, the avoidance of evidence of completion is only the reflex in the aesthetic realm of the radical transformation of the concept of reality into the concept of an "open consistency," of something that remains outstanding and at man's disposal, that offers to *define* rather than to *take over* self-assertion's unending task.[27]

Though extracted from events at the core of the Occident, Blumenberg's parameters reach—further than Weber's—to the ethical horizon of the Greek modern. Not even they, however, quite arrive at its cardinal regulative idea: synthesizing the concreta of the past and present into one or another more integrated historical unity is not quite the same thing as making progress, much less making it ad infinitum. The former is restitutive; the latter may well be constantly disruptive. Synthesis has its rationale in the principle that things are all in pieces; progress, in the principle that things could always be better than they are.

The idea of progress is, if not ancient, still premodern; but it begins to acquire both its modern semantics and its ethical primacy at the core of the Occident only in the period of the French Revolution. Only then does it become the ethical byword of a class of citizens determined to pin their hopes no longer upon kings or the church but instead upon a malleable and manipulable future.[28] The idea of synthesis per se is certainly ancient and may, as Charles Stewart has recently suggested, play a signal role in the Orthodox reception of pagan and littler religious traditions from the patristic period forward.[29] It begins to acquire both its modern semantics and its ethical primacy in Greece, however, only at the beginning of the nineteenth century, and initially only from without. Present-day Greece was, at the turn of the nineteenth century, still largely an Ottoman colony. Those sovereigntists—some from the indigenous gentry, many from the diaspora bourgeoisie—who were championing its independence were desperate for the support of the Great Powers: Russia, Great Britain, and France. They could have resort to a variety of pragmatic selling points. The rhetoric of legitimacy was, however, less flexible. It imposed upon irredentists the demonstration of ethnohistorical entitlement. The romantic ideology of statehood had it—still has it—that rightful claimants to a sovereign territory were those whose "racial" forebears had, by first settling it and cultivating it, made it their own. It demanded more: by the beginning of the nineteenth century, those Greek nationalists who were courting the favor of the Great Powers were already obliged to inscribe themselves into a developmental matrix that had its instauration in the Athens of the fifth century B.C. and its culmination in Republican Paris. They were obliged, in short, at once to revivify the classical past and to reveal its continuity with an ostensibly "orientalized" present.[30] Their claim of kinship with the European community of nations could stand on nothing less.

As might be expected, the task was assigned to, or taken up by, those men who, like Korais, had amassed sufficient philological and folkloric knowledge and sufficient ideological fluency most persuasively to effect it. Looking in from without, looking back, we might be tempted to regard it as having required nothing more than the stitching together of a sort of state window dressing, a pretty curtain to pull over the uglier physiognomy of realpolitik. It is clear, however, that even the most dispassionate of Greek intellectuals took the task from its outset to imply not simply a political but a far more personal challenge. Or rather, it implied the latter because it implied the former: the legitimation of the ethnos was inseparable from the legitimation of the self. So the first of what would gradually become modern Greece's politicoethical crises came hand in hand with the obligation to propose an historically synthetic solution. Perhaps because the crisis itself was quite so personal, the obligation soon lost its exteriority. Even Korais appears already to have internalized it. His descendants—among whom my circle should be counted, in spirit at least—would grow up with it, "forgetting" its origins precisely as they would expand its purview. Historical synthesis would accordingly become an imponderable, an increasingly deepset aspect of the elite habitus. There is, however, less reason to believe that it has also become an aspect of the less privileged habitus. Not even historical synthesis can be identified as that "Greek culture" that the holistic ethnographer would seek to describe. It would in any event be a metacultural disposition even were it pervasively shared; customs and mores belong like all other concreta of the past and present to its repertoire of practical resources. Its impact is, as I hope to show, remarkably wide; wide, however, at least in part because its carriers, those most richly endowed with what Bourdieu calls "symbolic capital," are also those whose tastes and opinions are most likely, if not to dictate, still to set the standard for all others. They are my "historical constructivists," and they are at the head of one of Greece's leading industries of both cultural reproduction and cultural reform; one of its leading "regimes of signification."

Projective metalepsis, the figurative telos of my circle of historical constructivists, also defines the style of a great many artifacts that might be found scattered all about Athens. Those artifacts are indeed so characteristic of Athens that the trope itself has become the theme of the second, and more comparative, of my ambient chapters. I am well aware that so "literary" a treatment of the urban landscape might strike some of my readers as fuzzy-headed, even intentionally obscurantist. I grant that *Modern Greek Lessons* is not an "easy" monograph. "Praxology" or not, it is a descriptive and analytical experiment, a very blurred genre, an exploratory writing not of culture but of the aftermath of culture. It is—in what I dare to put forward as a stab at ethnographic realism—as lacking in what we now like to speak of as "closure" as the people, the activities, and many of the anecdotal incidents on which it dwells. It may be obnoxiously ethereal. But I hope that my reconstrual of Greek modernization might at least stir up a small breeze within the doldrums in which the Circum-Mediterranean ethnology of modernization is currently stalled; that my rendering of the Greek pragmatics of history might at least provide some small empirical corroboration of the thesis that modernity is not ineluctably technocratic; and that my spelling out of the historically constructivist poetics of reform might at least hint at a coherent apparatus, a more unified analytical framework than we yet have, for addressing both sociocultural continuity and sociocultural change.

I am enough of a neoromantic to hope for more. I make, in what follows, frequent enough allusion to a "hermeneutics of domination," though a hermeneutics not nearly so systematic as either Foucault's or Bourdieu's. My trifling is purposeful. The human beings about whom I write, though exercising domination, are not, even in the ultimate analysis, motivated solely to accumulate and invest their capital. They are not, even in the ultimate analysis, illusionists who profess to ethical and moral commitments only to deceive others, or, if nothing else, then only to deceive themselves. They are not such beings in part because I do not render them such beings. My anthropology consequently lacks both the apocalyptic shock and the scientific scorn of which Foucault, occasionally, and Bourdieu, more constantly, are such masters. My anthropology is perhaps no more, no less immediately falsifiable than theirs. I suppose that I could be content were I understood simply to have proffered a plausible critique or rethinking of some part of social and cultural theory; among other things, that is precisely what I have intended to do. But I persist in the belief, perhaps self-deceiving and maybe even self-destructive, that a sustained reflection on the Greek modern can do more than score a few paltry academic points. I persist in believing that a sustained reflection on another, a historically constructivist modernity, can force us to confront and to reconsider what "we," we "occidentals," have long distorted and suppressed in reflecting upon the modernity that we allegedly know so well. Is historical constructivism the way out of the iron cage? It would be appallingly naïve to declare that it is, or even that it might be. Would it be as naïve, however, to suggest that it could serve as a fruitful incitement for the further "testing of our historical limitations" and hence, as Foucault would have it, for our further "enlightenment"?

Enough of "us." What might a sustained reflection on historical constructivism teach, what might it offer to the Greeks themselves? Any response I might offer is likely to sound more like a dictating of terms than anything else. I hope in any event that it does not offer them yet another example of American "shallowness." They have already had enough of that. I hope that, if nothing else, it offers some of them a springboard, an opportunity to "talk back." I would not consider Modern Greek Lessons a complete failure even if my Greek colleagues uniformly disparaged it. I would consider it a complete failure only if they were entirely, and blithely, to ignore it.

PART I

REVIEWING ATHENS

1

MODEL IMPROBABILITIES:
ATHENS AT FIRST SIGHT

"I have also thought of a model city from which I deduce all the
others," Marco answered. "It is a city made only of exceptions,
incongruities, contradictions. If such a city is the most
improbable, by reducing the number of abnormal elements,
we increase the probability that the city really exists.
So I have only to subtract exceptions from my model,
and in whatever direction I proceed, I will arrive
at one of the cities which, always an exception, exists.
But I cannot force my operation beyond a certain limit:
I would achieve cities too probable to be real."
(Italo Calvino) [1]

I ARRIVED AT Athens's Ellinikon Airport in September of 1986, relieved after having spent a tense layover in what was then an East bloc
country to find the customs agents unbothered by my passport and
bored with my luggage. I had carried along little more than clothes and a
Blue Guide. I had been chosen from among my cohort of Fulbright appli-
cants to receive a privately endowed fellowship. I was consequently on my
own, though I had been assured that the local Amerikaniko Ekpedheftiko
Idhrima, the American Educational Foundation, was prepared to offer me
whatever aid it could. A colleague at Berkeley had succeeded in securing
temporary lodgings for me at Kalamaki, a comfortable suburb near the airport, the residents of which were thoroughly accustomed, if not all equally
well disposed, to tourists and other foreigners. I had a letter of introduction
to the Academy of Athens's Center of Social Research, the director of which
had graciously agreed to sponsor my stay. He would provide me with the
initial entrée into what would become my "circle." I was, however, as much
a *ksenos*, a "stranger," to him as to everyone else. Both my project and my
presence were abstract. So, too, my expectations: the Greece I knew was a
Greece of novels and poems, of historiographies and ethnographies, of the
occasional television documentary and coffee-table picture book. The
Athens with which I was most familiar was an Athens long past: the home
of Thucydides and Plato. I did not believe that I would find it intact in the
present. But I was not at all sure what, precisely, I would find in its place.

The Center Does Not Hold

In *The Ancient City*,[2] Fustel de Coulanges set out to show the secular reformers of his day that the ancient *poleis*—Athens among them—and the
urbes that they so admired were not cities at all like nineteenth-century
Paris, and not cities in which they would actually want to live. His efforts
were impeded by an archaeology that had not yet dug deeply enough definitively to prove his case. Recent scholarship indicates that even with the
evidence he had, he might better have reached conclusions antithetical to
some of those he drew. Neo-Marxists are inclined to accuse him of having
underestimated class conflict; neo-Weberians, to accuse him of having mis-
construed despotism as devotionalism.[3] Though frequently betraying an
egalitarian bias that can, as Louis Dumont would remind us,[4] lead to interpretive distortions of its own, their complaints have considerable merit.
Fustel was too ready to infer what men and women believed from what they
said and how they behaved. But what he achieved should not be forgotten.
He managed—no small feat—to do genuine anthropology: to render a way
of life, if perhaps a way of life too probable to be real, plausibly human
without dismissing the profundity of its differences from the ways of life
that his readers could be presumed to lead. He managed as well to endow
social thought with one of its most precise and enduring conceptions of
what Max Weber would later call the "urban community."[5] The cities about
which Fustel wrote were neither quaint nor backward, but they had not yet
lost all their traditional air. They had not yet become merely demographic
or administrative conglomerates. They were still "religious associations,"[6]
established with the lighting of sacred fires and the adoption of a coterie of
tutelary deities. They were organizationally complete. Citizenship had not
yet become merely a legal formality. It still rested upon a profession of loyalty and faith that mollified the competition among both adversarial classes
and adversarial estates. If not quite self-enclosed hierarchies, Fustel's cities
were still largely autonomous collectivities. For all their complexity, they
still had their cultures, overarching and well-bounded "designs for living."
They were still wholes. So Fustel represented them, and so he designed his
text: like the cities it includes, *The Ancient City* is a scholastic *summum* in
Panofsky's precise sense—an all-encompassing totality composed of homol-
ogous and systematically interrelated "parts and parts of parts."[7]

At the turn of the nineteenth century, Athens might still have had
enough of a culture, might still have been enough of a whole, to satisfy the
scholastic. It was not, however, the city it had once been. It had become a
minor Ottoman colony, a sleepy village of some five thousand souls.[8] Its
inhabitants kept their homes close to the Acropolis, as their predecessors
had done. But the Parthenon had been converted into a mosque, complete
with a minaret. The Areios Pagos—meeting place of the ancient assembly—

was empty and overgrown. The agora, where Socrates had pursued his inter-rogations and poisoned himself in a prison cell, lay buried beneath a thriving Turkish neighborhood. The Attic plain had been given over to the cultiva-tion of grains and olives.

By late 1986, Athens had become quite another thing again: an object lesson in the inadequacy of all totalistic and insular conceits, if not at first sight in what might improve or replace them. Perhaps it had regained some of its former glory; it certainly had no Greek rival. But it was no polis, either. It was instead the seat of a national government, of occidental business, and of an international network of diplomatic principalities. It was home to the majority of the intellectual and artistic establishment; but home to many others besides. The sleepy village had grown into a metropolis with a popu-lation in excess of three million. The Attic plain, virtually bereft of its for-mer agriculture, overrun with highways and apartment buildings, held a population of perhaps two million more.[9] The Parthenon was undergoing its latest and most meticulous restoration. The agora was exposed, and open to visitors. Traffic was fierce. The atmosphere was often foul. Unemploy-ment was often high. By 1987, Athens, had no real slums, no ring of shanty-towns, very little homelessness, very little visibly abject poverty. But without a constant influx of imported goods and imported currencies, its citizens would have had next to nothing to eat, and even less with which to occupy themselves.

Dismiss it all as being beyond the ethnographer's ken? Not a wise strat-egy, especially in a region whose "prevailing human order" is, as Braudel puts it,[10] an order "dictated by" its urban leviathans. Subdivide it into more manageable units? A prudent strategy, and one that the majority of Athens's ethnographers have so far pursued.[11] But it offers a poor vantage from which to consider the wider metropolitan tableau in which natives and sojourners alike must, after all, find and maintain their bearings. Seeking a better, at least a more stereoscopic vantage, one might simply take a funicular, or climb, up the slope of Mount Likavittos. Approaching an elevation of some nine hundred fifty feet, it is Athens's highest. In the ancient era, its summit was graced with a temple honoring Helios, the sun god. After the advent of Christianity, and still today, it is graced with a shrine dedicated to Saint George. Likavittos is notably higher even than the table rock of the Acropo-lis, which looms unobstructed on the southwest skyline. Municipal ordi-nances, though evidently liable to occasional subvention,[12] prohibit the erection of towers and skyscrapers that would spoil the view. Athens's only skyscrapers—two or three, depending on how one reckons them—are tucked into the lowest parts of the Attic basin. Around Likavittos, around the Acropolis, rooftops are low. From the summit of Likavittos, one looks down upon a metropolis that, like the Acropolis itself, is predominantly angular and off-white. (See Plates 1–3.) It has one great patch of green: the confluence of the National Garden and the Ardhittos Wood. From the sum-

PLATE 1. Athens from Mount Likavittos: the National Garden, lower left; the Acropolis, right of center.

PLATE 2. Athens from Mount Likavittos: the Attic Plain today.

PLATE 3. An alternative vista: Athens from Lofos Strefi, the Acropolis at left.

mit, only the Plaka—a tourist's mecca, rich with restaurants and tourist shops and the ruins of the agora—appears something of an exception: a sociohistorical palimpsest, a stratigraphic tracery, not of everything that Athens was, but perhaps of everything that, in a rather more felicitous world, it might have been. Directly above the Plaka, on the highest of the Acropolis's inhabited slopes, Anafiotika reflects the architectural conventions of the Cycladic islanders after whom it is named (Plates 4, 5). Anafiotika spills into traces of neoclassical "rhythm,"[13] of Doric understatement, Romanesque pomposity, Byzantine interiority, Constantinopolitan sumptuousness, provincial privatism, and contemporary kitsch (Plates 6–12) that even those Athenians who are ill-disposed toward such elegant but more westernized of Athenian neighborhoods as Kolonaki—where, after three weeks in suburban Kalamaki, I spent the rest of my tenure in the field—are likely to find agreeable, and agreeably "Greek," enough.

Fustel's ancient cities may have made for an even more diverse stylistic tableau. They allowed, however, of far less directional ambiguity. Topographically, they may have contained numerous points of reference. Symbologically and institutionally, they contained, in the ultimate analysis, only one, to which all others led. Fustel's "religious associations" always had a temple at their center, home and homage to a patronal deity. In ancient Athens, the Parthenon—the "Virgin's Apartment," built for that daughter of Zeus to whom Aeschylus credited the conception of juridical democ-

PLATE 4. "Traditional" architecture in Anafiotika.

racy—should have reigned supreme; the companion temples that stood with it on the Acropolis, a sort of attendant court. Other precincts may have been busier: the agora; and the more distant city gates, site of Pericles' funeral oration and a cemetery called Keramikos, "ceramic," for the pottery whose manufacturers practiced nearby. Fustel could not, through his monological lenses, see those precincts as anything but tangential. For him, the sacred was central; the ancient city's architectural materialization of its profession of faith, its centerpiece.

PLATE 5. Anafiotika below, the Acropolis above.

One might argue that the Acropolis remains Athens's centerpiece, even if what it now materializes is not civic unity as much as a westernizer's myth—not altogether false, but very much an artifice—of genetic coding. When I first toured it, on a clear and blustery October morning, I was nearly overcome. The Acropolis was, I thought (and creature of my socialization, continue to think) an incomparable flower of human spirituality. It did not look, however, as it had during the Periclean era, or the Hellenistic era, or any era, for that matter, preceding the modern one. It would surely have

PLATE 7. A lane in the Plaka: tidy blend of neoclassicism and romanticism.

been less prepossessing to me were many of its past adornments and excrescences still in place. The wooden roofs and pigmented surfaces of most of the structures have of course disappeared, even though traces of paint remain on several of the statues kept in the museum that has been chiseled into the plateau. The Parthenon, dedicated in Periclean Athens to the Olympian goddess of wisdom, was rededicated in the Byzantine era to Saint Sophia (her name is the Greek term for "wisdom"), later to the Virgin Mary.

PLATE 8. Bits and pieces of Europe: "eclectic" architecture in the Plaka.

It acquired then a bell tower that the Ottomans would later convert into a minaret. But the minaret has disappeared.

In 1687, the Parthenon was a warehouse for Turkish gunpowder and armaments. The Venetian Admiral Morosini ordered his fleet's cannons to fire upon it. In the ensuing explosion, eight of the Parthenon's northern columns, six of its southern columns, and the bulk of its cella were demolished. Shortly afterward, Morosini attempted to remove the horses and chariot of Athena from the devastated building's western pediment; the statuary fell,

PLATE 9. Almost Venice, almost Paris: romanticism in the Plaka.

and shattered. In 1787, the Comte de Choiseul-Gouffier removed a section
of the remaining friezes. In 1801, Lord Elgin removed numerous marbles
from the Parthenon and the nearby Erechtheion. The "Elgin marbles" are
now on display in the British Museum. Greeks of late have adamantly been
seeking their return, so far to no avail.

The first of many sculptural and architectural restorations was begun in
the 1830s. Othon, imported from Bavaria to serve as the first king of independent Hellas, ordered it done. Leo von Klenze, a famous Bavarian de-

PLATE 10. Synthesizing traditionalism and neoclassicism: an elegant Plaka home.

signer whom Othon summoned to be his state architect, supervised it. The current restoration, by no means rushed, supported by the European Economic Community and a variety of corporate and private contributors, is clearly the most careful, the most ambitious, and the most desperate: airborne hydrocarbons will, if unchecked, completely erase the more delicate of the surviving outdoor reliefs by the year 2000.[14] The principles that guide the project are extremely restrictive. They countenance little of what existed before the sixth century B.C., even less of what was erected after the fourth. Yet it would be a mistake to identify those principles as classical, even as classicizing. Classicism was more committedly exuberant, and coloristically far more indulgent. The monuments today instead suggest a striving to realize in stone the laconic sobrieties of an exquisite *écriture blanche*.

On the other hand, they are not yet fully modernist. They retain too many echoes of transcendence. The rules of comportment that any visitor to the plateau is asked to observe are, in their way, quite explicit: one should re-move nothing, however incidental it may seem, one should keep to the demarcated paths, one should refrain from touching the museum pieces; but one should also be quiet, be respectful, conduct oneself with a solem-nity befitting that of the environs. A placard reporting Athens's liberation from the Nazis and singularly left untranslated from the Greek tells of two

PLATE 11. Studied modernism in the Plaka.

compatriots who raised the Hellenic flag on "this sacred rock"—a phrase, it might be added, to which foreigners would probably be more genuinely and consistently receptive than the current Hellenes themselves.

Virtually transcendent, nearly mythic, the Acropolis is even so not altogether either. It is caught, as perhaps no other artifact is quite so inextricably caught, in the ambivalence of a civilization—not just westernized but, in this respect at least, ardently Western, ardently "occidentalist"—that prides itself on its capacity to deconstruct, to see through the veridical pre-

PLATE 12. High above the Plaka: history under construction.

tensions and timeless aura of myth; but cannot abandon the myth of an unadulterated origin to which all its claims to inimitability might be referred. The Parthenon especially, whose apparently perfect proportions are in fact only an assiduously calculated optical illusion, has in both discourse and in practice gradually been fashioned into a virtual wellspring, a seminal paradigm of the occidentalist's eagerness to become the measure of all things.[15] In the process, it has been brought ever nearer the verge of being reduced to a simulacrum, a mere copy of itself.[16] But no one has dared—not

PLATE 13. From the agora: the Erechtheion, left; the Parthenon, right.

yet at least—push it so far as to put its radical particularity into question. Emblem of a relentlessly "temporal regime," it could not, like the Australian churingas, simply be discarded and done over were it to wear out. It could not, like the proverbial ship, slowly be replaced "plank by plank" and remain the same thing it was. No genuine occidentalist could tolerate such inauthenticity.[17] All restorers have accordingly had to cope with at least some degree of hostility. The latest restorers are importing the new marble they need from the quarries where the old was mined. But the gesture is not universally regarded as adequate (Plate 13).

No doubt with the Acropolis above all in mind, geographer Jean Gottmann characterizes Athens as a "historical hinge": but for whom? The "British Hellenists"[18] had rediscovered Athens long before Greece's independence. By the end of the nineteenth century, a small band of native enthusiasts had joined them. In 1813, the Filomouson Eteria, or Society of the Friends of the Muses, was launched in Athens with the aim of collecting whatever antiquities it could find into the first "Greek" museum. But Richard Clogg points out that little was done to put "so ambitious a scheme into practice before 1821."[19] Nor did the scheme emanate from the Greek grassroots. It was the inspiration instead of a nationalist intelligentsia, educated abroad and eager to appropriate for its own purposes the historical rhetoric of revolutionary France and America.[20] The masses shared the same political hopes but were less interested in the intelligentsia's particular strategies—in fact, obligatory strategies—of legitimation. Consider the comment of the revolutionary Greek "social bandit" Nikotsaras upon being compared with Achilles: "What Achilles and such like fairy tale are you talking about? Did the musket of Achilles kill many?"[21] The Athenians of my circle fall for the most part somewhere in between the members of the Filomouson Eteria and Nikotsaras. One of the more casual of my acquaintances once remarked to me that he would not mind if the Acropolis were simply "torn down." His contempt, however, was directed less at the monuments themselves than at what they could not help but recall to him: a syndrome of symbolic domination that has left Athens what another of my acquaintances would speak of as a "cultural colony."

A troubling centerpiece, the Acropolis now lies just south of what most contemporary Athenians, and most contemporary road signs, identify as *to kendro*, "the center" of the metropolis. On a map, it has the shape of a triangle, formed by the intersection of Leoforos Athenas (Athena Avenue), Leoforos Ermou (Hermes Avenue), and Leoforos Stadhiou (Stadium Avenue). As often as they might refer to it as "the center," Athenians might also refer to it as the *emboriko trighono*, the "commercial triangle." It is an exceptionally and sometimes exasperatingly fast-paced conglomerate of banks and offices, department stores and boutiques, shops and way stations. During the Christmas season, it is closed to all but foot traffic. In the past few decades, several of its interior streets have been transformed into permanent pedestrian malls; in the course of my stay, several more were marked for a similar fate.

Pedestrians are in need of their special spaces, in which both to walk and to breathe. Roughly 750,000 private cars are registered in and around Athens,[22] almost twice as many per square mile as are registered in Los Angeles.[23] On Sundays, between July and August, on holidays and in holiday seasons other than the Christmas season, for the duration of busmen's strikes, all are free to circulate wherever their owners might drive them. On ordinary business days, however, only half are allowed entrance into what the local Department of Transportation has declared to be its own "center": inclusive of the commercial triangle but extending far beyond it. The regulation, reminders of which are printed in all the major daily newspapers, is recent. Most of the members of my circle, several of whom owned cars, seemed to approve of it. Most everyone else seems to obey it regularly enough, if only to avoid the penalties of noncompliance. Few would dispute its rationale. Athens has become spectacularly overcrowded, air pollution ever graver.

Add to the metropolis's two contemporary centers yet a third: Omonia Square. It is situated at the confluence of Athena and Stadium avenues, hence at one of the commercial triangle's junctions. Like the triangle, it dates from the era of Othon's reign. Its past—more on which in the next chapter—and its present are both somewhat checkered. When I asked my native acquaintances after their city's "real" center, most of them named

Omonia. Their responses reflect the intentions of the capital's nineteenth-century master planner: the same von Klenze who supervised the first restoration of the Acropolis.[24] They reflect an official line. I am less certain that they reflect more spontaneous intuitions. Some of my acquaintances—the more populist and bohemian of them—adored Omonia, which tends to be as bustling at three in the morning as it does at three in the afternoon. Other of my acquaintances told me that, from the early 1960s forward, they never bothered to go to Omonia anymore. I was warned of my pocket being picked; more subtly, of sights better left unseen. Syntagma Square, opposite the contemporary Parliament and another corner of the commercial triangle, might suit them better as "center" and hangout both. Syntagma is, however, usually mobbed with tourists. It is their center, at least. Omonia is seedier, if not quite so seedy as New York's Times Square. It attracts provincial "hicks," who have not yet become fully competent in capitaline etiquette. It attracts prostitutes, female and male. Polite company might not mention, might not even be aware, that a popular "gay bar" and a "gay bath" operate seasonally at its perimeters. Wanting to direct the foreigner to a more presentable locale, polite company might pass over Omonia entirely for Kolonaki: my home away from home, and the current metropolitan center of "high style."

Named after a "little column" that continues to stand beside a still operative waterworks, Kolonaki was barely sketched out at the turn of the century. Its two squares—one known officially as Filikis Eterias but less officially as Dhexamenis (after the waterworks), the other known simply as Kolonakiou ("of Kolonaki")—are now restful and well tended. Its panoramas are among the most envied, and its numerous art galleries among the most watched. It has its quotum of opulent mansions, though far fewer than such distinguished suburbs as Kifissia and Psikhiko. *Polikatikies*—"multiple residences," apartments—the ground floors and basements of which may hold not simply galleries but also antique and gift shops, piano bars, and architectural offices, are more common. Leases and rents are, by most local reckonings, very expensive. With its advocates, Kolonaki also has its detractors. My address there not infrequently met with ironical smiles and well-meaning exhortations. I was cautioned, particularly by the culturally more anxious, that I would, once settled, run the risk of speaking only in my native tongue, and of taking away at best a distorted image, not only of contemporary urban mores but also of contemporary Greeks. Kolonaki is home away from home to many foreigners, and the site of many foreign establishments and enterprises (Plates 14–16). It has more "gay bars" than any of Athens's other numerous districts—all of them, however, very discreet.

Athens's other districts might not be able to boast of Kolonaki's chic. But each might, at least to its more permanent residents, be considered a minor center in its own right. Each tends to conform, in its size and in its cogency, to a principle that must be labeled "presociological" or "protosociological."

PLATE 14. Not in Greek: a lane in Kolonaki.

PLATE 15. The class of commerce in Kolonaki.

PLATE 16. Italian chic in Kolonaki.

The Athens Center of Ekistics—of the "Science of Dwelling"—renders the principle one of the "minimization of the consumption of energy."[25] Its implication: that people are inclined, at least in Athens, to perform the preponderance of their activites—productive and consumptive—in the arena closest to their doorsteps. There were 286 such arenas in Athens in 1962.[26] Should the metropolis continue to grow at its past rate, some 1,450 could be expected to be in place by the end of 1992. So far, each of those already in place has accumulated roughly the same share of services and facilities. If protosociological in their emergence—an apparent product of demographic density—most have come to be endowed with that barest but also most basic of cultural identities: a common appellation, a title of, if not always a title to, one's own turf.

An Urban Community?

Is Athens, then, a "vast collection of little villages," as a native social scientist once suggested to me? If the image thus evoked is one of "the traditional," it is surely misleading. If it is one of fragmentation, it is more apt. The ancient city may have been divided by class, by estate, by occupation, by gender. But Fustel was more correct than many of his successors have granted in arguing that it was still joined together in what Durkheim would later call a "church." Classical Athens had four annual civic festivals, all of them religious in the strictest sense of the term; all reenacted the tie of one citizen to another, and of each citizen to the presiding gods. Two were devoted to Dionysus, and featured dramatic contests at which the plays of Aeschylus and Sophocles among others would have been performed. The wealthy were eager to finance the expenses of production; in peaceable times, they had few better means of increasing their portion of honor. Male citizens made up an obligatory audience. Alien dignitaries, perhaps even women might have attended as well. The greatest of Athens's festivals, the Panathenaea, was even more embracing. Men, women (its most indispensable functionary was the priestess of Athena, selected from the daughters of one of the city's most noble lineages), and children, all but slaves had a place in its grand procession.[27] Its organization was hierarchical, but hierarchical as both Fustel and Dumont would understand it: an orchestra of pieces ranked with reference to a synergistic whole.

Athens today is the site of an Orthodox cathedral known simply as the Metropolitan or the Metropolis. Its archbishop has, since 1864, been the primus of Greece's official church. Orthodoxy is international in its past, and Greek Orthodoxy maintains many international affiliations at present. It nevertheless has a plethora of decidedly local expressions and local variations; its god and its saints, a corresponding plethora of local aspects.[28] The Metropolitan Cathedral would, however, appear to have been designed at once to incorporate and surpass them; it is constructed from the remains of seventy-two earlier churches and is the outcome of the contribution of four different architects[29] (Plate 17). It is a national, not merely a civic cathedral—the embodiment of a national but of neither a civic nor any longer of a civil religion. During the long centuries of Ottoman domination, Orthodoxy provided the basis for social, if not for "ethnic" identity. The Ottomans, committed by Koranic principles to some measure of religious tolerance and attracted to the managerial efficiency of the *millet* or "religious community," in fact did much to promote the solidification of an Orthodox "bond."[30] In the years immediately preceding independence, members of the Orthodox clergy were among Greece's most vigorous freedom fighters.

The precedent they set can still be revitalized when the occasion warrants. In the late spring of 1987, Greece hosted the European Basketball Tournament. For the first time ever, it also saw its team victorious, besting in the final a prodigious and much larger Soviet adversary. Statements of congratulations and pride from the heads of both church and state were broadcast over the same evening's late news. Thousands of revelers flowed into Omonia Square. Among the songs they chanted was one whose lyric was a simple "Oh, Madonna, Oh, Madonna." Some of them paid obeisance

PLATE 17. Multiplicities: the Metropolitan Cathedral, foreground; an office complex, midground; the Acropolis, background.

to the Greek flag. Others danced in the square's fountains. In their midst, a small group of pallbearers marched about with a shroud-draped coffin on their shoulders. Out of it rose a pale and impassive young woman, dressed in white muslin, polysemic icon of the Virgin and a reanimated Hellas herself. In her right hand, like a protective talisman, she held the Orthodox cross. Next day, the city's newspapers were filled with proclamations of the *thriamvos*, the "triumph," *kata loghou*, "against reason," of the *elliniki psikhi*, the "Greek soul."

The journalists may have had no tongue in their cheeks. The pallbearers, though, were aware of the joke that they were perpetrating, of which the church was less the medium than the butt. Especially among the young, the church is notorious for its conservatism. Its reputation is not wholly deserved, but not wholly undeserved, either: many of its leaders actively favored Greece's monarchs, and many of them even guardedly favored the Papadhopoulos junta. It has its leftists as well. In any event, its lack of political neutrality has, in the long run, not served it particularly well. In the past few decades, it has largely lost its former capacity to stand as an untrammeled representative of the nation or the state, either one. Its strengths are still real. Constitutionally, it is separate from the state. Juridically, however, the two are still virtually equal. Constitutionally, freedom of worship is guaranteed. Juridically, however, the church has exclusive dominion over its officers and its territorial holdings. Until very recently, it also exercised certain authorities that have long been secularized in more northerly and westerly regimes. Not until the administration of Andreas Papandreou did it lose the exclusive privilege of marrying its members. The same privilege was extended to other churches as well. But not until the Papandreou administration did Orthodox and non-Orthodox alike have the option of being married by a civil magistrate in a purely civil ceremony.

The church continues to work in provisional concert with the state. It continues, for example, to champion the late Archbishop Makarios's campaign for the unification of Greece and Cyprus—with fewer reservations than Makarios had himself. With the rise of Papandreou's proudly secular socialism, it has nevertheless found itself more and more at odds with the state, and has proved quite willing to wage war against what it has regarded as untoward secular encroachments. Its army has remained large and potent. In 1987, the Papandreou administration undertook to pressure the Orthodox prelacy into redistributing some of its real estate. The prelacy agreed to compromise. But the same administration also undertook to pressure it into ceding jurisdiction over the parcels redistributed.[31] The prelacy refused. The struggle that ensued was without precedent. Billets appeared throughout Athens proclaiming the inviolability of the church's corpus, insisting upon the observance of the constitutional letter, and inviting the faithful to a demonstration before the Parliament's front doors. The demonstration was the largest the metropolis had seen for several years. Participants arrived in busload after busload from towns and villages all over the mainland. They were peaceful, but unyielding. So, too, were those who had provoked them.

Officially, at least, the vast majority of Greeks remain in, if perhaps not of, the church. National statistics on religious affiliation, presumably taken from the attestations demanded of anyone who applies, as everyone must, for his or her *taftotita* or "identity card," are representative. Ninety-seven percent register an Orthodox baptism. Two percent, residing largely in Macedonia and the Dodecanese, register themselves as Muslim. Catholics number about fifty thousand. The *dhiamartiromeni*, the Protestants, are too few to mention.[32] For all its capitaline ecumenicalism, even Athens shows few signs of deviating from the norm. With the Metropolitan Cathedral, it has countless other Orthodox churches and shrines. On the other hand, it has only a single synagogue. It is home to multidenominational St. Andrew's, whose reverend delivers his sermons in English; to four Churches of Christ, at least two of which minister in English; five Evangelical churches, one practicing exclusively in German, two others offering counsel in English; one First Christian church, with services in Greek and in English; one Pentecostal church, whose services are exclusively in English; one Lutheran Swedish Seaman's church; two Anglican churches, St. Paul's and St. Peter's; some fifteen Roman Catholic churches, at least one performing the Latin rite and several with liturgies in French or in Italian; one Mormon church, serving in Greek; and a single mosque, located on the roof of the Caravel Hotel. A bookstore called O Pirinos Kosmos ("The Fiery World") supplies esotericists of less routinized persuasions.[33] Over three-quarters of Greece's national holidays have an Orthodox stamp. Athenians have a further opportunity to take heed, or take advantage, of the anniversary of the name day of Dionysios the Areopagite: widely believed to have been converted by the Apostle Paul, the city's first bishop, and an early martyr in whose memory, or with the excuse of whose memory, most businesses close. Until recently—or so, in what might have been an instance of what Herzfeld calls "structural nostalgia,"[34] I was told—Athenians would congregate en masse in the Plaka to celebrate Carnival. Carnival in the Plaka is still a notable but by no means a citywide affair. Many Athenians continue to attend religious services at Christmas, and most at Easter. (One of my native friends once told me that Christmas was imported from "the north," but that Easter was an "indigenous" holiday; hence its greater appeal.) On the eve of Easter, the shrine of Saint George on Mount Likavittos is the focus of a favorite remnant of civic ritual. Near midnight, thousands of celebrants ascend an easy network of serpentine esplanades to its patio. When they arrive, they light the candles that they have brought, announce to those around them that *Khristos anesti,* "Christ is risen," expect in response the same declaration or the declaration that *alithos anesti,* "truly He is risen," and wend their way, in a liquid and glittering trail, down into the city again.

Contemporary Athens's other civic or quasi-civic rituals, such as they are, are equally elective, but no longer religious even in their allusions. One might describe them as almost campish: historical or garden clubs, for those who have the appropriate interests and social credentials; support for the local soccer team, for those who do not. There are other alternatives: a ballet, a civic theater, an opera, a symphony, a book fair, and two "cultural festivals." Attendance at the Athens Festival, reinaugurated in 1987 after a lapse of more than a dozen years, is a matter not simply of choice but of good luck: of being able to procure time or time off, and of being able to procure tickets. The festival's staff prefers to import musicians and dance troupes from Europe and America. Tourists, flocking to the picturesque precincts of the restored Theater of Herodes Atticus and the new Amphitheater of Saint George, constitute a significant number of the typical audience—or at least they did when I was there. The Athens Festival—in the years preceding the Papadhopoulos junta, among the most glamorous events in all of Europe—lasts throughout the summer. The late spring of my tenure in the field brought a one-day gala, replete with music and sports and food. It may have convened for the first time ever in 1985 or 1986. It did not draw great crowds in 1987. Its banner was an imperative: "Love the City!" Meant to rejuvenate metropolitan pride, it was marred in 1987 by the death, sensationally and pointedly pondered in the local press, of a long-distance runner.

Another gala—more violent in my witnessing of it—needs a more elaborate exegesis. In the late 1960s, Greece appeared to the more conservative of its commanders to be poised to succumb to the interests of the majority coalition of its parliamentary leftists and, in succumbing to those interests, to be teetering on the brink of communism. King Konstandinos II—an ardent conservative and the last king of Greece—consequently gave his support to a coup d'état conceived by the generals of his army. The coup was, however, preempted by Colonel Papadhopoulos, who executed, in alliance with a bevy of lieutenants versed in what NATO strategists had taught them, a blockade of Athens's major thoroughfares on 21 April 1967. The junta thus entrenched, which at the very least benefited from virtually unqualified American aid, became infamous for its paralegalism and for its willingness to resort to torture. In the middle of November 1973, a group of students occupied Athens's Polytechnic Institute, set up a radio transmitter, and broadcast an appeal for revolt. On the seventeenth of the same month, many of those students were shot during a government reprisal. The junta survived until July of the following year.[35] The seventeenth of November has since become the most explicitly activist of any of Greece's national holidays. Formally, it is labeled "Polytechnic Day"; less formally, "Anti-American Day." The protests that it invites have sometimes been not merely violent but anarchic. The "Seventeenth of November" also serves as the moniker for a terrorist band, originally organized to hunt down some of the junta's "collaborators" but more recently responsible for the bombing of tavernas frequented by American military personnel and for the assassination of a few native capitalists as well.

After Culture: Dialectics of Objectification and Internalization

The ancient Greeks may have been the first to engage in what Niklas Luhmann has called sociocultural "self-thematization": a conscious if sometimes self-serving consideration of the lineaments of their way of life, of what made them different from those around them.[36] With Herodotus, who roved far and wide through North Africa and the Near East in search of an explanation for the unique fortitude that his fellow Greeks had displayed in resisting Persian encroachment, it amounted to a compendious, anecdotal ethology. With Pericles, at least as Thucydides portrayed him, it amounted to civic chauvinism; Pericles' systematic glorification of the Athenian way of life against its various Greek counterparts was based less in scientific curiosity than in imperialistic concupiscence. Even at its most chauvinistic, however, sociocultural self-thematization has always departed, if only for the sake of argument, from two provisional axioms.

One of them, the axiom that there is more than one way to live a life, has informed every utopia from Plato's Kallipolis forward. The other, the axiom that each way is contingent in both its origins and in its pursuit, each as much a contingency as the next, has been the cardinal tenet of conservative and progressive and radical reformists, hence of both sociocultural conservation and sociocultural recomposition, from Solon to my circle of his distant dispositional descendants. The conditions of the ancient dawning of the latter axiom are by no means patent. The conditions of its contemporary reinforcement are patent enough.

Walk along Athena Avenue: to the ethnographically informed pedestrian—to this one, anyway—it has a tangibly Greek aura. It is a place of family businesses. It has cobblers and brassworkers, leather, and clothing, and hardware shops. It has an array of sidewalk kiosks, most of them offering the same sunglasses and cigarettes and newspapers and minor souvenirs. It owes its particular restlessness, however, to an abundance of other commodities. Its several confectioners are well known for their selections of roasted legumes and nuts, of the intensely sugary fruit pickles called *ghlika koutaliou*, "spoon sweets," and of khalvas, an originally Anatolian dessert made of semolina and almonds the textures and flavors and aromas of which differ, like those of French butters, from one region of production to the next. Its two largest delicatessens, both well supplied with local sausages and olives and cheeses, directly face each other from opposite curbs. The verbal jousting, the agonistic self-advertisement in which the proprietors and employees of each customarily engage, can also be sampled at the *laikes aghores*—"popular markets" that convene weekly in various of the city's residential districts and in Attica's outlying demes. The *dhimosia aghora*, a "public" and much grander market, convenes virtually daily at the intersection of Athena and Euripides Avenues. Fruits, vegetables, and flowers are available along an open-air concourse. Winter produce arrives largely from the greenhouses of Crete and the southern Peloponnese;[37] more diverse summer produce arrives from throughout the country. Meat and fish mongers, often more than a hundred, have their stalls and counters inside a vast arcade, completed just after this century's turn and resembling with its tall iron vaults and glass-paneled ceilings Paris's Gare de l'est. In the past fifteen years or so, its two or three round-the-clock cafés, long serving early breakfasts and late lunches to tired buyers and sellers, have also come to be patronized, after the theater or cabaret, by a better-rested clientele. They retain their well-tried menus: mutton chops fried with garlic; *stifadho*, a spiced beef and onion stew; and *patsas*, a glutinous tripe soup favored as a digestive. On Athena Avenue, traditions are continuously on parade. They can be watched. They can be bought and sold. Transmuted into a nostalgic panoply of petty luxuries, they can be consumed, tasted, literally eaten.

Move to a less mundane locale: the antiquarian—this one, anyway—might risk noting certain similarities between the ancient Keramikos cemetery and the First Municipal Cemetery, even though the former lay just beyond the ancient city's and the latter lies well inside the contemporary metropolis's boundaries. The sculptures and stelae of Keramikos are no more, no less ostentatious than those of the First Municipal, where several generals of the War of Independence and several of the last century's most prominent financiers and philanthropists have their graves. Effigies are still popular at the First Municipal, and can be made to order at nearby stone-carvers' ateliers. But their mien is quite different from those of their ancient counterparts; to some observers, quite comic:

> The giant figures, some nearly eight feet tall, stand as stiffly as any archaic *kouros* or *kouri* [sic] but they appear wildly, bizarrely funny. Perhaps this is because they are fully clothed, and in fairly modish modern dress at that. Somehow one's eye is not affronted by a seven-foot-tall naked youth, but is when it falls upon a giant marble school child complete with short pants, long socks and a pious expression, or on a housewife—still in her apron—being led off by an angel.[38]

The law decrees that burials must now be completed within twenty-four hours after death. It still licenses the secondary burials that have been studied in the Greek countryside.[39] Mourners at the Municipal Cemetery must be prepared to mingle with others who have simply come to enjoy the cypresses, the laurels, the cut roses, and the view of Mount Himettos. They must be prepared as well to mingle more and more with ethnographers, with bemused journalists, with amateur photographers arriving and departing on chartered buses.

How much have ethnographers themselves been responsible for putting even unwilling Athenians on a cultural stage? How much have they been responsible for inducing in the merchants on Athena Avenue or in the popular markets quite so self-conscious a sense that they are indeed "agonists," and that in being agonists, they are indeed being "Greek"? How much have they been responsible for inducing in the mourners at the Municipal Cemetery quite so self-conscious a sense that their manners of expression might be comic curiosities? Ethnographers should not overestimate their own impact. They are, after all, relatively few in number and relatively rarely read. On the other hand, they belong together with the journalists, with the authors of guidebooks and the directors of tours, and the droves of other participants and observers from whose selective gaze Athenians have been less and less able to hide. If not always intentionally, they belong together with all the other agents and patients of a late capitalist market in which tradition itself is, as Baudrillard suggested some two decades ago, just another commodity.[40]

Too much of neoromantic sanctimoniousness is, however, inappropriate. If the foreign gaze is one from which Athenians are less and less able to hide, the foreign presence is one that they have learned, for all their victimization, to put in its place. Germans, for example, suffer under materialistic and anal-retentive stereotypes. They are quietly mocked for wearing socks with their sandals. The French have immediate prestige. Frequently mistaken for a Frenchman myself, speaking French badly, but weirdly enough to pass, I could get better services at the post office and at the National Library than many natives, and certainly better than Americans could typically hope to have. But the politesse was double-edged: Athenians make an effort to put forward a better, a less haughty and condescending impression, than the French stereotypically leave. The English are regarded as passionless; *ekhoun dhiskolies*, "they have difficulties," are constipated. No foreigners are more identifiable, and none more vulgar, than Americans. The stereotype is quite precise: "Americans" are tall; they are fair, and they are *khazi*, "stupid" or "silly." Curators at the National Picture Gallery circulate stories of American tourists inquiring during the course of their guided tours whether the icons on display date from before or after the time of Christ.

Foreigners of all kinds are morally suspect. They are "loose"; their behavior should not be emulated: such, at least, is the official position. Foreigners do not, however, usually come to Athens as tourists either to brandish their exoticism or to impose it. They do not come to Athens as they might to New York or to San Francisco to indulge in lavish entertainment or to explore the colorful eccentricities of Chinatowns, of Little Italies or North Beaches, of Christopher or Castro Streets. They come instead for the sun, for the sea, and for moussakas and spanakopita, folk and retsina, rusticity and antiquities. Supply in concert with demand, they usually find them, though find them intermingled with a great many copies and pseudomorphs that they might not always be able, or even want, to set to one side. Tradition, genuine and spurious, sells well in Athens to natives and tourists alike. Athens has it all: sea sponges and souvlaki, gold chains and silver bracelets, breasted ewers and the aluminum *tamata*, "pledges," stamped with burning hearts and cattle and smiling children and automobiles and offered in thanks for answered prayers at Orthodox altars. Athens has ouzo and aromatic Metaxa cognac, Hadrian's Arch—now badly eroded by those ubiquitous hydrocarbons—and the Sacred Way, Thracian furs and *amanedhes*, "songs of despair," on cassette. The airport gift counter keeps a stock of satyrs, grasping gargantuan penises in their hands, for those in need of last-minute trinkets.

Athenians have caught on; they have as acute and as objective an eye for culture and its uses as anyone else. The ethnographer is likely to find himself a step behind—and, if he is a romantic, even a neoromantic, find himself slightly disappointed as well. Seeking "key symbols," condensed incarnations of still latent proclivities and projections, he might take initial heart in Athens's hundreds and hundreds of errant cats, some of which are owned, but most of which are not. They are particularly common in the metropolis's finer and more charming neighborhoods, especially in Kolonaki and the Plaka (Plates 18, 19). They lounge in alleys, under cars, on porches. They rummage through trash, spar and mate noisily, bear seemingly endless litters of timid young. All quite natural: but like the behavior that comes naturally to Bali's fighting cocks, the behavior of Athens's cats figures into a substantial repertoire of bawdy jokes, serving as a farcical epitome of a humanity writ small and reduced to its most elemental, its most bestial, its most self-absorbed. Cats offer a continuous display of the political animal at its rawest: dominating and submitting; exercising sheer might and exercising subtle cunning; surviving and dying. Feline theater is interactive: the men and women who attend it also enter into it. It is virtually Homeric: cats are heroic; actual men and women their somewhat capricious, more sovereign gods. Cats have their fate: to be kicked sometimes; to be coaxed and coddled at others; to be loved sometimes; to be shunned and abused at others. They may receive charity: matrons frequently leave them table scraps on curbs and doorsteps; outdoor diners in the Plaka may toss them what they do not wish to eat themselves (Plate 20). But cats cannot count on anything: some grow fat; others, victims of misfortune or their own weakness, starve.

Feline theater, genuinely microcosmic, also has its more pastoral side. Cats, occasional victims, are also inhabitants and inheritors of a good and gentle Greek earth. Pastoral cats frequently find their way onto postcards and calendars, where they could hardly be portrayed as less troubled, less desperate, or more at peace. They bask in the crisp luminescence of cliffside terraces. They sleep against the backdrop of an indigo Aegean. They lounge with their kittens on the whitewashed domes of humble Cycladic shrines. Their stripes and calicoes harmonize with the intense enamels painted onto simple wooden shutters and with the bright dyes of airing quilts. The darker underbelly of the feline condition sells poorly. But local entrepreneurs have discovered that pastoral cats sell quite well. There may, even so, be a bit of sarcasm in the title of one calendar available at most Athenian kiosks. There is surely no more primitive innocence in it than there is in dropping by at one of the cafés in the public market for a sobering bowl of *patsas*. The title declares, not in demotic but in English, that "Greece . . . is cats."

The guiding hand of the consumer's market can, however, act more subliminally, act as much upon its entrepreneurs as with them. It has led, among other things, to an alternative definition of the seasons. Summer continues to impose itself, throughout the Circum-Mediterranean. In

PLATE 18. Part of the scene: some of the Plaka's cats.

PLATE 19. *La condition humaine*: more of the Plaka's cats.

PLATE 20. Among the denizens of a Plaka *ouzeri*.

Athens, schedules of work and leisure in spring and winter and autumn as well defer to the heat of summer afternoons and the freshness of summer mornings and evenings. Summer darkness brings people out of doors: to their balconies, often draped during the day with drying clothes; to open-air coffeehouses and cinemas. Winter keeps them inside. Summer is a season of vacations and of exodus. Fall and winter and spring, milder in Attica than anywhere else in mainland Greece, are seasons of return. Bars and restaurants closed in June often reopen in October, and remain open until their proprietors leave again, seeking brief peace or better profits in the islands. On so vague a series of divisions, however, another more precise one has come to supervene. It resolves into a simple dichotomy between a "high" and a "low" season. High season begins, by convention, at the Orthodox Easter. Low season begins in middle or late October, with the first chilling rains. Both have a certain meterological motivation; but both make more basic allusion to the flow and ebb of tourists.

Consider hours of business: they vary, throughout Athens and throughout Greece, with the kinds of merchandise sold. *Khromata* ("colors," hardwares) are offered from about 7:30 A.M. to 3:00 P.M. Monday through Saturday. Butchers and fishmongers close slightly earlier, but open again on Tuesdays, Thursdays, and Fridays from 5:00 until about 8:00 P.M. So, too, with bakeries. Groceries and greengroceries maintain comparable schedules, but usually do not open until 8:00 A.M. Haberdashers and stationers, among others, open at 9:00 A.M. Wine and liquor stores often open at 7:00 A.M.; their second rounds last from 5:00 until 10:00 P.M., not simply on Tuesdays, Thursdays, and Fridays, but on Saturdays as well. *Zakharoplastia,* "sweet shops," and *periptera,* "kiosks," are often open continuously, even on Sundays, and may not close until well after midnight. The same is true of many of the businesses advertising themselves, usually in bold letters and always in English, as "tourist shops." Tourists are often discouraged by so blatant an indication that many, many others have been there before them. But the advertisements are not meant, as a rule at least, to spoil anyone's fun. They are rather meant to inform or to persuade patrolling gendarmes that the shops' owners have procured an official license allowing them to keep their doors open when others must close.

Not only many bars and restaurants but also virtually all of Athens's indoor cinemas shut down entirely in summer. Christmas and Carnival provoke other alterations. Any synopsis of the whole must take numerous variables into account. The customary divisions of the Greek day are paramount, but not all the natives to whom I have spoken agree on their precise delimitations. Everyone I know is in accord about *to proi,* a period of work from about 6:00 A.M. to about 2:00 P.M. Some define its aftermath as *to mesimeri,* "midday," the duration of what is usually the largest of repasts. Others include *to mesimeri* in *to apoyevma,* "the afternoon"; but even those who do might not be in accord about its end. For some, the afternoon ends, with the customary siesta, shortly after 5:00 P.M. For others, it extends into the period of work that follows. After the afternoon comes *to vradhi,* "the evening." No matter when it starts, it is marked by another repast, and ceases around *ta mesanikhta,* "midnight." After midnight, *nikhta,* night itself, begins, and lasts until morning comes again. The distribution of sacred days and holidays has its own importance. The variant periodizations of the Julian and the Gregorian calendars have theirs. So, too, the costs of heating and air conditioning; the local semiotics of production and consumption, commodities and expendables; the politics of profit. Too many variables to encompass within a proper system, perhaps, but not so many as to prevent normalization: the hours of "tourist shops" and virtually all other businesses are, in Athens and throughout Greece, matters of law. In 1987, Athens's musicians took to the streets to express their displeasure at the strictures inflicted upon nightclubs.

There are not so many variables that the impact of a more northerly and westerly industry is altogether obscured, either: stereotypically tardy Greeks have evidently begun to watch their clocks, and to watch them rather carefully. They have evidently begun to work, or at least to be active, much longer. Charles Bigot, a fellow in the nineteenth century at the predecessor of the Institut français d'Athènes, observed that "all circulation" in the city he was studying came to a stop "from eleven in the morning until four in the afternoon."[41] Native employees of contemporary foreign enterprises, most of which are open from 9:00 to 5:00, could hardly keep their jobs were they to follow so placid a pace. But Athenians of all occupations have cast off, or considerably abbreviated, what must have been the only *mesimeri* or *apoyevma* their urban predecessors knew. Not a single Athenian of my acquaintance was aware—none, at least, remarked to me—that so severe a contraction of quotidian relaxation had ever occurred at all. Compared with the American "lunch hour," the Athenian midday meal still seems marvelously luxurious. But like deprivation, luxury, too, is experientially only relative; hence, perhaps, its manipulability in the absolute.

Toward Exclusivity: Civilization and Cultivation

It would, however, be a mistake to deem late capitalism—a highly indefinite phenomenon in any case—the only motor of either the commodification or the disestablishment of "culture." There are other motors: the politics of distinction, of what Pierre Bourdieu calls "cultural consecration,"[42] perhaps the most powerful of them; a politics in which Athens long ago bested all its urban rivals. The capital's size alone is indicative. It now boasts some 40 percent of Greece's total population.[43] Thessaloniki, Greece's second largest metropolis, can claim only 5 percent. Thessaloniki is home to an important segment of the fashion industry and to an important segment of the artistic avant-garde. But Athens has a far greater concentration of the artistic higher brow. Both Thessaloniki, in Macedonia, and Rethimnon, in Crete, are homes to distinguished and reputedly "radical" universities. The University of Athens is considerably more conservative. But like its neighbor, the Academy, it has far greater prestige. Greece has myriad museums, two of the finest of them in Olympia and Delphi. But Athens has the National Archaeological Museum and the National Picture Gallery. Athens, of course, has the Acropolis Museum, and the Parthenon.

In the drive to accumulate ever more cultural capital, Athens does not march through the touristic era unopposed. More and more outlying Greek municipalities have begun to nurture movements toward *topiki aftodhiikisi*, "local self-administration." The idea and the practices of "local self-administration" were first disseminated thoughout the countryside by the Communist resistance during the Second World War. The idea of it, at least, has been a prominent element of leftist platforms ever since.[44] It has been the theme of some impressive regional revivals: in the port of Kalamata, for example, though as much has been owed there to the talents of a dynamic and charismatic mayor. But not all the champions of "local self-administration" have been mere regionalists. Not all have been antagonistic even to governmental centralism. Many of them have sought only to resist capitaline acquisitiveness. Only, though, with limited results: like corpulent and greedy primates elsewhere, Athens continues to exert "too much authority" over its weaker satellites, and to hoard "too many" goods and services and other desiderata for itself.[45]

Its hoarding of cultural desiderata is, however, highly selective, as all connoisseurship must be. Jean Gottmann remarks that all capitals "tend to create for and around" themselves a certain kind of "built environment," heavy not only with pomp but also with hauteur.[46] Athens is no exception. It does indeed have something of everything stereotypically and incidentally "Greek." With its archaeological museums it also has ethnographic and "laic" museums. Its tolerance of free-floating vulgarity is, however, only minimal. In Greece's other, lesser cities, in many of its provincial villages, one can, for example, still stumble across parlors in which men might dance, singly or in provocative pairs, to the tunes that they have solicited some dilapidated house trio to play. In Athens, to my knowledge, only one remains. An acquaintance characterized it as "very underground." Past councils have put a more official end to a variety of other popular diversions. Milkmen once held an annual ceremony at the Temple of the Olympian Zeus; but since 1961, the ceremony has been banned.[47]

Cultural connoisseurs are unlikely ever to see their aims altogether realized. From the Acropolis to Omonia Square, at its centers and even at its outskirts, Athens nevertheless offers ample testimony to the persistence of their efforts. Their tastes might vary, but are with very few exceptions more notable for what they all have in common. They run, with very few exceptions, toward the "Hellenic." The attribute is, in its way, as exclusivist as any ethnic essence. It is not, however, limited to the classical. Hellenic Athens has room for yacht clubs, for the importations of Kolonaki, even for such allegedly "English-speaking ghettoes" as the rich suburban hamlet of Ghlifadha. It has room—so it seems—for a great deal of technological kitsch. It has little room for Turkish neighborhoods, even less for China-towns. It can embrace Poseidon's temple in Sounion and the graffiti that Lord Byron is rumored to have carved upon it. It can cope with architectural neoclassicism of the Bavarian or the Parisian sort. It copes better with austerely functional apartment buildings than with flamboyant palm trees. It has avenues dedicated to Homer and to Hesiod, to Euripides and to Sophocles, to Athena and Hermes and the ancient Stadium, to Saint Dionysios and to former kings and queens. It even has an avenue dedicated to Constantinople: Leoforos Konstandinopoleos, however, not the "corrupt" Leoforos Istanbul.

Even if Athens were to become perfectly, consummately Hellenic, it would consequently still have something of an irreducibly plural effect. It would be an occidentalist capital; but it would retain a local character, corresponding to a more local understanding of the Hellenic itself. Local, but not ancient: for several centuries after Emperor Constantine founded "The City"—so his grand port is still known to contemporary Greeks—Byzantine Christians called themselves Romii ("Romeotes"). In the thirteenth century, however, the knights of the Fourth Crusade laid siege to what they saw as an irredeemably apostate Constantinople no longer in rightful possession of the myriad Christain *sacra* it held. The Orthodox hierarchy fled with a substantial flock southeast to Nicaea. Leaving Constantinople behind, they left all allusions to Roman citizenship behind as well.[48] The "Hellenes" of early Byzantium were its lingering, infidel pagans. But their ancestors had also inspired the theologies of the first Orthodox fathers. The Nicaeans, hating the Catholics and ignoring the pagans, began in their exile to refer to themselves as "Hellenes": truer Christians and conservators of the Septuagint Bible, the truer Christian Word.

The majority, especially of the less privileged classes of Greeks, persisted in referring to themselves as Romeotes until well into this century. But one should not overlook the Nicaean precedent for a sense of the "Hellenic" that evoked less of secular humanism than an Orthodoxy branded "oriental" in both the Catholic and the Protestant West. The Nicaean "Hellas" was not as much the occidentalist's ethnic polity as a devotionalist brotherhood. Hellas thus conceived has always had its share of muscular advocates: the patronal gentry;[49] the lower and middle cadres of the petty bourgeoisie, and, above all else, the church.[50] Their victories have at most been partial. Occidentalists—most of the earliest of whom came from the *grande bourgeoisie* or from one or another outpost of the diaspora—have seen most of their pet projects to fruition. The design of Greece's regulative apparatuses is not (literally) Byzantine but Franco-Belgian; the design of its educational apparatuses Franco-Germanic; the design of its several constitutions influenced by French, American, and even Swedish models.

Hellenic Athens is in any event a mixture, an Orthodox and an occidentalist capital at once. Not all Greeks favor just one of the two aspects of its "Hellenicity," nor indeed just one of the two aspects of Hellenicity as such. Some accept both in the spirit of poetic inconsistency. Others accept both, but argue now as in the past for the possibility of reconciliation. Konstandinos Paparighopoulos, professor at the University of Athens in the later half of the nineteenth century, was among the first to undertake a demonstration that the "history of the Hellenic ethnos" could be narrated without interruption from the *Iliad*, through the Septuagint and the writings of the neo-Platonist church fathers, to the literate journalism of his own day.[51] He, too, has a contemporary capitaline street named in his honor, even if he did not succeed in convincing every one of his readers of his position. A discriminating Hellenist, he also left something out: the very vulgarity that contemporary Athens also tends to shun. But not all of even the most discriminating of Greeks, not all of even the most discriminating of Athenians, think the vulgar—the popular—quite so deserving of avoidance.

Neither the early nor, to be sure, the most elevated of Byzantines provide the model for what is presently conceived of as Romaic. The "folk"—humble, miscegenetic, part Anatolian, part Balkan, part Cycladic, part Minoan, pious but pious very much in their own way—do better. The "folk" indeed persisted in calling themselves "Romeotes" in spite of Nicaean and later nationalist disapproval. Athenians today refer to themselves officially, regularly, though still not exclusively, as Hellenes. Among the Athenians of my circle, the contrast between the Romaic and the Hellenic no longer has much conversational appeal. But the elite still know the Romaic when they see it. Poets still resort to it in their most intimate lyrics. Thus Yannis Ritsos, in his semiautobiographical *Isos Na'ne ki' Etsi* (Maybe it's even so):

> Then Miss Esmerelda let out a moan that the whole cemetery roared back, and the stone and wooden crosses stirred again over where we were, and the marble maidens fluttered their eyelids over the gravestones, and as if all of Romiosity [*Romiosini*] were crying, from centuries beyond, for all its ancient, ancient tortures, a song welled up from the entrails of the blind Esmerelda—
>
>> The sky blackened, my heart blackened, myriad sorrows, black sorrows like grains of sand, and I have neither a stone to stand on, nor a branch to sing from, I have only Charon to accompany me, alas, alas, alas . . .[52]

No mention of Hellenicity would serve as well. Only Romiosity is evocative of a unity not of an intellectual but of an experiential and sentimental temper. Hellenicity inheres in the warrior and the statesman and the scholar; Romiosity in the illiterate fisherman, the impoverished shepherd, the unillustrious dead and their mourners.

There is a term in demotic that approximates the anthropological sense of "civilization": *i politia*. There is a term for "the civilized": *to politismeno*. Both have their evident perlocutionary force. The manager of the Kolonaki apartment building in which I lived, for example, delivered a note to his tenants one morning reminding them that as *politismeni anthropi*, "civilized persons," they would surely want to deposit their trash on the sidewalk for collection only after dark. He reminded them as well that they would surely want to deposit it only in sturdy, neoprene bags, and not the flimsy substitutes, difficult to tie and easily raided by roaming cats, that they had been saving from their trips to the grocery store. Not so, of course: but within twenty-four hours everyone had complied—myself, I might add, among them. Romeotes would have scoffed at or been bewildered by the advice. But we were not Romeotes. We were Hellenes. We had to prove it.

Greek has, on the other hand, no particularly current term for "culture" in its ethnographic or anthropological sense. Academicians sometimes use the obvious barbarism *koultoura*. But *koultoura* cannot escape, in Greek, from the bad habits of the *koultouriaris*, the "dandy" or "fop." One contemporary author has defined a periphrastic usage: *politistiko morfima*, literally "civilizational formation." His defense of it is exquisite;[53] but relatively few natives have either read or accepted it. The Romaic is nevertheless a cultural, not a civilizational attribute. The tradition it now denotes is an irremediably Little Tradition. To the more rigorous of Hellenic purists, it can often denote something even worse: an unsavory melange, a bastardization of Greek by other, baser compounds, with no cultural integrity of its own.[54] Perhaps the purists are even correct: the Romaic is indeed a mixed bag, a hodgepodge. It is leftover and degraded fare, and if not entirely banished from Athens, at least rigorously suppressed.

But precisely in its degradation the Romaic has its populist and lyrical poignancy. The Hellenic has virtually none. Romeotes may provoke the disgust of the adorants of the classical, both Greek and foreign.[55] They may offend with their uncouth comportment the sensibilities of the more refined. But Hellenes are not altogether spotless themselves. They are vulnerable in their way to the reproaches of a Romaic countercritique. Allies of the West, they often look suspiciously like the West's handmaidens. Dismissive of Romaic vulgarity, they often look suspiciously like fanatics of artifice: comportmental, but linguistic and cosmetic as well. The Romeote may be a mongrel; but he at least pretends to be nothing more than what he is. The Hellene is perhaps not all pretense. But he does put on his airs. Not even in Athens has Romiosity, though suppressed, been entirely silenced.

Hellenes and Romeotes have in fact tended in the long run to rebut one another less by rejecting than by incorporating one another, so much so that they no longer constitute real but instead ideal types. Any adequate analysis of the actual content of contemporary Greek *politia* needs a third type in addition: the Phanariote. Named for the Constantinopolitan district of *fanaria* or "streetlights" in which they resided, the Phanariotes were among the most fortunate of the Greek-speaking Christians of all those who lived under Ottoman rule. By the seventeenth century, they were the principal executives of the Sultanate's *noblesse de robe*. Their authority coalesced and crystallized as Greek more and more became the lingua franca of the empire. Many of the Phanariotes claimed descent from the bereft Byzantine aristocracy. Most in fact were traders "who had accumulated their wealth . . . in the Aegean, in the Danubian principalities and in Russia before they settled in Constantinople and extended their activities to the political and administrative field."[56] They can themselves hardly be deemed either traditionalists or modernizers. They were socially quite conservative. But they were also at least as cosmopolitan as any of the diaspora bourgeoisie: thoroughly European,[57] but Levantine and easterly in the same breath. They were at first ambivalent about the Greek revolution. When they concluded that it was inevitable, they came to its side. They were not among its finest soldiers. But they were able to serve the new state well. They knew how to administer. No one else did.

Like the *grande bourgeoisie*, the Phanariotes soon learned to transform the charisma of office into a charisma of blood; they soon learned the art of passing posts of state service to their heirs. Politically astute, they were rarely actively partisan. Konstandinos Tsoukalas recognizes them as "harbingers of a ruling cadre of Greek-speaking Christians," but points out that they were also isolated from the "illiterate masses of Greek-speakers and Slavic-speaking Christians" alike.[58] Precisely in their remove, both from partisan politics and from the masses, they embodied a refinement of which any contemporary sophisticate must still take heed.[59] Even more than the bourgeoisie, the Phanariotes established the most enduring single criterion of contemporary sophistication: a worldly education.

Ernest Gellner has argued that formal educational apparatuses, productive and reproductive of that "literate high culture" so crucial to the cybernetic needs of the industrialized world system, have become even more constitutive of the modern nation-state than the monopolization of legitimate violence.[60] He has argued further that the same apparatuses tend, with the advance of industrialism, to become even more basic than the mode of material production in the nationalist and statist infrastructure.[61] His arguments carry considerable diagnostic force for Greece. What Tsoukalas notes of the past century holds even more rigidly in this one:

> The weight of the school as an institution among the other subsystems that collectively form the social mechanism and that effect its reproduction had, indeed, special importance. The distinctive function of the Greek school consisted chiefly in its role as a social "divisor" within the field of upward social mobility.[62]

A catalyst of social mobility, the school has also been one of the securest means of procuring social and symbolic "dignity" and, with them, both social and symbolic power. It may well be the securest means. The hypothesis would account in part for the enormous lengths to which the petty bourgeois especially often go in seeing to the schooling of their sons and daughters. Add to this the fact that not just capitalism but the economy of distinction, too, is world-systemic, that Greece is no more at the core of the former than it is at the core of the latter, and one might further account for the lengths to which Greeks of all classes go to send their children, either to foreign-speaking preparatory academies in Athens—the Lycée français d'Athènes and the Amerikaniko Kolleyio are particularly chic[63]—or to foreign colleges or universities, or to both. Had Greece somehow been absorbed into the world-systemic core, would the Phanariote precedent be less relevant, polyglossia and polymathy less compelling ideals than they presently are? They might all well be; but natives of all classes nevertheless con-

tinue to regard them less as conditional than as categorial. Due in part to
Phanariote precedent, however, distinction remains not purely a matter of
achievement. The culturally elect, the genuinely *politismenos anthropos* is
still presumed to be *evyenis*: "polite," but more accurately "well bred." The
evyenis is presumed always to be *politismenos*. A case in point: at the elegant
Plaka apartment of a well-known Athenian hostess, I found myself one afternoon in the midst of a conversation concerning the slights and vexations
that natives too often inflict on even the most well meaning of foreigners.
The American acquaintances whom I had accompanied, in the country to
study local musical traditions, were relating an especially unpleasant encounter with a famous Greek songstress, to whom they had been sent for
instruction and advice. Our hostess was appalled at what she heard. A native
friend of hers, who happened to be present, was also appalled. "But isn't she
from a good family?" he asked. "I thought she was from a good family."

Our hostess did not know. But her friend at least knew that election ought
to be transitive, that civilized mothers and fathers ought to give issue to
well-bred daughters and sons. The transitivity of election flows backward as
well: prestigious heirs can confer laurels retrospectively on their ancestors.
It flows laterally: one consanguine gains or loses from the gains or losses of
another. In all of this the past is more decisive than the present, and the
male more decisive than the female.[64] The parvenu who cannot claim a
distinguished father or grandfather stands on somewhat thin ice regardless
of what he or she has achieved. The declassed can rely upon the election of
their fathers and grandfathers to cushion their own fall. Not eternally,
though: distant by more than three degrees, eminence weakens, and must
either be performatively renewed, or renounced.

The ethnographer is thus back in his, or as often in her, own waters—or
so it seems at first sight. Whatever its Phanariote precedent, the arithmetic
of *politia* seems plainly enough to rest in a matrix well known to scholars,
not of ancient but still of rural and "traditional" Greece: a bilateral kindred
of limited extension with a similarly limited patrilineal bent.[65] In traditional
Greece—by most reckonings—such kindreds are the channels through
which property and names and reputations all flow. Even in traditional
Greece, both material and symbolic capital can be achieved. The acquisition
of the latter—"honor"—appears to be a local obsession; the loss of it, also
achieved in its way, no less of one. *Plus ça change . . . ?* The question deserves a carefully considered answer, which I reserve for my fourth chapter.
Here, I would merely submit that if kinship remains, even for my Athenian
circle, a more entrenched channel of the flow of capital than it allegedly
does in more purely meritocratic and technocratic welfare states, its depths
are less normative than rhetorical. One of the most refined and well-edu-
cated women of my circle once confided to me that her "cultural memory"
(she delivered the phrase in English) of such things as *la parenté* (she deliv-

ered the phrase in French) had become very thin. Though she continued to care devotedly for her ailing sister, she disparaged almost everything that kinship in Greece has traditionally controlled—especially the conduct of daughters. One would have thought that she had little reason for her forgetfulness; she was from a very "good family." She had, however, married a handsome and brilliant villager, whose father was at once a "peasant" and an inveterate gambler.[66] Only a few of the other members of my circle mentioned his humble beginnings, and then only to insist that they had no interest in them. Many of them nevertheless considered him "too hungry." Their criticism was in some respects justified. But hunger aside, he, too, was a member of my circle, and not only as a consequence of hypergamy. His kinship could be used against him but, in the end, not altogether effectively. It was only one variable, one ploy in a far more complicated game.

Such a game is not restricted to Athens. Ernestine Friedl observed it in rural Greece several decades ago and has provided an incisive description of the condition to which both the more upwardly mobile and the more downwardly mobile of its players are typically reduced. Up-to-date in theory, the condition is merely one of "lagging emulation" in fact,[67] and one for which ruralites and rural migrants to Athens are especially notorious. The stereotypic *vlakhos*, literally a "peasant" but figuratively a bumpkin, wears dull, ill-fitting sportscoats and heavy, polished black shoes that even proletarians would eschew. The proletarian knows better: he dresses in a jacket and jeans. The peasant spends his money in Athens on useless and showy luxuries—for example, English soaps. The proletarian is austere. The peasant carries a large wad of paper money in his pocket, rolling the bills off at every transaction. Only the more bohemian and populist of Athens's intellectuals now humor him, and "slap" bourgeois propriety, by doing the same. But even the most bohemian and populist of Athens's intellectuals know how to cross a street. The peasant, insufficiently *politismenos*, does not: he jostles, he pushes, he challenges moving cars, believing himself accomplished all the while.

The peasant is the butt of uncharitable jokes and the cause of frequent complaints. I occasionally found cause to complain about him myself. The members of my circle—even the most bohemian and populist—were generally in sympathy with my tantrums. They agreed that Athens was not always humanly the most pleasant of places. Several of them nevertheless insisted that things used to be different, that only since the 1960s had the metropolis become quite so overrun with people who "did not know how to behave."[68] They were far too civilized to mention that I was also part of the problem. Rural immigrants are not the only ignobles who have swollen the contemporary city's streets. Tourists and other foreigners have arrived with them, and in ever greater numbers. They are not "peasants," perhaps; but they can be irritatingly incompetent all the same. They "do not know how to behave," either. No more than peasants are they "real" Athenians. But who, or what, are the latter?

In the absence of an urban culture, there might still be a conventional repertoire of practices, fluency in which distinguishes the insider from those who merely fill the rosters of the census. New Yorkers have one repertoire, San Franciscans another; Athenians also have one of their own. Exclusivist, it is not as elitist as the constituents of cultivation. The upper classes are not its only arbiters. Nor is it a matter of nativity; the born-and-bred Athenian is not necessarily the "real" one; and even the immigrant, at least the Greek immigrant, can become one with time. I made only the barest progress toward becoming one myself. I was reminded daily of how little progress I was making. Like all comportmental practices, those that go with being a real Athenian do not allow of perfect formalization. They cannot be followed but must rather be embodied. No surprise, then, that even the most self-consciously real of Athenians have difficulty articulating just what it is that makes them quite so real. What is worse, any two of them might not always agree that the other is quite so real as he or she believes.

In the waning, for example, of a dinner that I hosted one evening, I was quietly advised, by a guest of somewhat extreme and chauvinistic opinions, that another at my table was perhaps not actually "from Athens." His predilection for strips of raw onion was not "really" Athenian; above all, his "accent" suggested a Thessalonikean upbringing. Whether or not he knew it, however, the accuser was mistaken. I had learned, independently and some long time before, that the accused was the scion of one of Athens's most rooted and most distinguished families, and was told that he would (as indeed he did) make the perfect informant; he was an insider's insider. So real Athenians may have a taste for raw onions, and may even have an "accent," after all. But they should not, as the man accused had himself informed me sometime earlier, beckon a stranger from whom they are seeking directions or the time of day with a "psst." Elsewhere, the summons is quite acceptable. In Athens, it is not quite Athenian enough. I asked him later whether he might, because of the way he spoke, ever be confused with a Thessalonikean. *Borite*, he answered; "it's possible."

La parole, then, is an ambiguous diacritic. Usage varies within Athens by class. I was once reprimanded by a member of my circle for having acquired what she described as a *petit bourgeois* and "ugly" pronunciation of certain demotic verbs. I had, in fact, arrived in Athens with the pronunciation she preferred; I had altered it after having been informed—once by a waiter, another time by a teacher of Greek as a second language at the Hellenic-American Union—that I sounded "archaic" and that "Greeks didn't talk that way anymore." Usage varies by region; but a few of my acquaintances tolerated the suggestion that a real Athenian might speak with a slight regional twang, so long as all of his or her idioms were adjusted to metropolitan frequencies. Insiders must know the current frequencies. They should also know the best places—rarely the most expensive, and preferably not yet discovered, and so "ruined," by tourists—to eat and to drink. They should know the boundaries of Athens's various districts and as many as possible of the streets within each. They cross streets with special finesse: the light need not be taken into account; the *trokhonomos*, the "traffic policeman," and the actual flow of automobiles, are more crucial. Insiders, real Athenians, know when to shop: the array of business hours must be committed to memory; so, too, the maxim that being earlier at the fishmonger's or the greengrocer's is always better than being later. They know how to expedite their proceedings at the post office: to ask, at the outset, whether they are standing in the appropriate line; only afterward to wait. They know the worth of maintaining a friendly rapport with their butchers and electricians. They know how, in properly agonistic fashion, to barter at the delicatessen, and the appliance store, or at the weekly outdoor market: first, feign only the mildest of interest in a product; then, object to the price sought and walk away; negotiate only when called back. They know how to get the attention of their waiter after having seated themselves at a taverna's table, and—arcane art indeed—how to get his attention again, when they wish to pay their bill and leave. Their savoir faire—of which I have only scratched the surface—is not so thoroughly a matter of exceptions and incongruities and contradictions that it passes altogether beyond comprehension.[69] But to the North American who has come to expect signposts at every crossing, universal graphics to guide his every interchange; to the North American who has come to take for granted and even to find relief in the rigorously shallow impersonalism of his own postcultural urbanity—to that North American, real Athenians are, like the metropolis in which they live, only a few steps away from being too improbable to be real at all.

2

REMEMBERING AND REMODELING:

THE METALEPTIC METROPOLIS

> . . . wandering amid broken stones, three or six thousand years,
> searching in collapsed buildings that might have been our homes,
> trying to remember dates and heroic deeds;
> will we be able?
>
> *(George Seferis)* [1]

M Y IMAGE, my sense of city life was not, when I arrived in Athens, merely bookish. I was raised in a very small American town, but had moved on, in my later adolescence, to Portland, Oregon, to which I have since returned. I had spent a year in Chicago, visited New York and Washington and Los Angeles. Before leaving for Athens, I had lived for about three years in San Francisco, where I had passed many of my younger summers; once back in America, I would live there for another three years. My small town had never appealed to me. I had become an urbanite with a vengeance. I had developed a passion for crowds, for noise, for subways, for easy anonymity, even for Californian jadedness. I had not expected Athens to be altogether like San Francisco. But I suppose that, my anthropological training notwithstanding, I had not expected it to be nearly as different as it turned out to be. Athens resembled Fustel's ancient city no more than it resembled a modern American metropolis—even San Francisco, the "most European" among them.

The Disciplinary and the Undisciplined City

In *The Practice of Everyday Life*, Michel de Certeau writes of a "utopian and disciplinary city," an unabashedly functional city, the regulative ideal of the modernist planner, and "the machinery and the hero of modernity."[2] The disciplinary city produces "its own space." Within it, "rational organization must . . . repress all the physical, mental, and spiritual pollutions that would compromise it."[3] It is designed, it works to substitute "a nowhere, or . . . a synchronic system, for the indeterminable and stubborn resistance offered by traditions."[4] It drifts toward becoming a "universal and anonymous subject" of its own kind. The disciplinary city is de Certeau's New York, which "has never learned the art of growing old by playing on all its pasts." Instead, New York's "present invents itself, from hour to hour, in the act of throwing away its accomplishments and challenging its future."[5]

Real New Yorkers might smile at such exaggerations. Real San Franciscans might think them on the mark, but little applicable to their own urban milieu. Even the latter would be deceiving themselves, and not simply because earthquakes have done much to erase what might otherwise have been preserved. De Certeau's disciplinary city is not defined by its content but rather by the norms that govern the arrangement, the grading, and the alteration of its content. The disciplinary city is formalist; its matrix—fundamental if mutable—is the orthogonal grid. It is a progressivist and technocratic city; it is constantly being improved, enhanced, bettered, functionally refined. It is systemically a forgetful city. For the progressivist technocrat, neither the past nor the present are ever quite as perfect as the future might be. Both are eminently liable to be sacrificed for the perfection they lack. In New York as in San Francisco, older buildings come down to be replaced by others, structurally more sound and functionally more dense. Those that survive—so long as they survive—are deemed worthy of preserving not because they are unique but because they are stylistic paradigms: exemplary forms and formalizations of historical particularity. The visitor to San Francisco's Fisherman's Wharf twenty years ago would barely recognize it were he or she able to return to it today. Everything that was shabby about it before has been gentrified in strict accord with the most forward-looking of middle-class tourist families' tastes: disciplinary and utopian par excellence.

De Certeau contrasts his disciplinary New York with an antipodal Rome. The contrast between New York and Athens is, however, even more extreme. The latter city has its share of progressivists. During my stay, the Parliament and civic leaders announced plans for "seven great public works," the expansion of the metro rail system among others, all of them "improvements" of the metropolitan infrastructure and "enhancements" of the quality of metropolitan life. But in Athens, traditions are particularly tenacious; particularistic "pollutions" crop up everwhere. At the southern terminus of Athena Avenue, for example, sits Monastiraki, "The Little Monastery." It has the form of a standard Byzantine basilica. It dates from the tenth century, was restored in 1911, and was throughout 1987 being restored again. It lends its name to a nearby train station, to a variety of tavernas and shops, to the immediate vicinity—a bustling if somewhat vaguely defined mercantile conglomeration at the northern edge of the Plaka. Tourists favor the Plaka. They visit the vicinity of Monastiraki as well, but natives come to it less for its sights than for its used bookstores and its several purveyors of inexpensive clothing, shoes, cookwares, rugs, and small appliances. The atmosphere is humble and weathered. Most of the signboards that hang outside its shops remain in Greek, though even here some offer transliterations into Roman script, or translations into English.

Monastiraki, the edifice itself, is now a church. In past centuries, it was perhaps rather isolated. Settled now, however, at the juncture of Athena Avenue, Hermes Avenue, and three lesser streets, it is engulfed in a mundane blizzard of casual urban exchange and interchange. Its frontal plaza is a place of profit and contact: vendors hawk breads and pastries from wheeled carts; people meet, though rarely linger there (Plate 21). The exterior foundations of its central nave are barely separate from the pavement. Nor is its situation any longer exceptional. Slightly to the east of it, a smaller basilica, dating from the eleventh century and known as Kapnikarea, sits quite literally in the middle of Hermes Avenue (Plate 22). The asphalt circle within which it rests is some meter higher than its own base; a small stair allows access to its door. Most people simply take its presence for granted. Is it that Greeks are not compelled to keep the sacred and the profane carefully separate, each in its own particular place? As a rule, perhaps;[6] but Athens's councillors once devised a plan to transport Kapnikarea from the middle of Hermes to a more serene and dignified location. To be sure, they never executed it. Perhaps their principles were idiosyncratic. More likely, they lacked financing, and those who succeeded them were more interested in devising plans all their own.[7]

The planning of the capital has been subject to a variety of political "pollutions" even from its advent. When Ludwig I insisted that his son, Othon, be installed in Athens, the Hellenic Council of Ministers was at first reluctant to grant his wishes. They had chosen the Peloponnesian port of Nafplio as the new capital of independent Hellas, and so of the throne. Ludwig, however, was too enthusiastic an archaicist to have much taste for Nafplio's Venetian over Athens's classical aura. The Regency accordingly intervened on his behalf, and promptly solicited plans for a new and neoclassical Athens. Stamatis Kleanthis won the initial contract.[8] A Greek, Kleanthis had nevertheless trained in Germany and drew his blueprints in collaboration with a German colleague. His Athens had far more in common with Ludwig's Munich than with the village it was intended to replace. A triangle—considerably more vast than the "commercial" one, but in rough accord with the rather bent figure formed by the intersection of contemporary Hermes, Stadium, and Piraeas avenues—was its structural fulcrum. An elegant, Vitruvian geometry informed it throughout.

Local residents, however, found Kleanthis's Athens barely tolerable at best: some, because it was simply too "foreign"; others, because its grandiose and regular proportions paid far too little respect to extant properties and estates.[9] The Regency once again bowed to pressure, retaining Kleanthis's blueprints but asking Leo von Klenze to emend them. The architect not just of Munich's Glyptothek but also of St. Petersburg's Hermitage, von

PLATE 21. Monastiraki today.

PLATE 22. Knee-deep in asphalt: Kapnikarea.

Klenze had studied in Paris, traveled widely in England and Germany, and cultivated a great fondness for the picturesque. A neoclassicist, he was also a romantic. His most memorable buildings reveal a preference for more "primitive" Greek over Roman orders; and a penchant for syncretism that H.-R. Hitchcock describes as "distressing to purists but wonderfully symptomatic of the ideals of the age."[10] His Athens is, however, most notable for its modest pretensions. It retains a skeletal triangle; but it lacks the complement of hubs and radials that Kleanthis had provisioned. Still a city of grand avenues, von Klenze's Athens has fewer and narrower avenues than the original upon which it was based. Still a regular city, it has far more room for minor, "Mediterranean" irregularities than its original would have made.[11]

Mannerisms and compromises: these are, in the judgment of at least one native architectural historian, the "seeds" of all of Athens's "unhappy futures."[12] The historian has his technocratic point; but von Klenze should not suffer the brunt of it. He should not, at least, be blamed for forcing his northerly and very fashionable ideas of urban order upon a population at once politically exhausted and culturally insecure. Like Kleanthis before him, he was no doubt sincerely convinced that the Greeks needed a properly "European" capital to call their own. He was no doubt thrilled at the prospect of devising one for them. What better place, after all, to carry out a program at once neoclassical and romantic than Attica itself? Like Kleanthis before him, he was in any case simply fulfilling the wishes of his royal admirers and patrons. Nor can von Klenze entirely be blamed for having catered to those many private parties who banded together to protect their interests against any too categorical a right of eminent domain. His influence could not have been any match for theirs. But the seeds that, willingly or not, he planted have continued to grow. Athens remains even today as deeply etched with mannerisms as any of its "colonial" sisters farther east or south.[13] Hitchcock indeed observes that "the new capital of remote Greece possesses more, and on the whole more impressive, Romantic Classical buildings than do Vienna and Budapest, capitals of the Austro-Hungarian Empire."[14] Planners today are only slightly less obliged than von Klenze to accommodate or do battle with private parties who "always," or quite often, "end up imposing their own laws."[15]

"Unhappy," perhaps: but von Klenze's blueprints—not the last to have been offered,[16] but the last and only comprehensive blueprints ever to have been put into material effect—deserve more praise than the technocrat is usually willing to award them. Granted, they now seem short-sighted. Granted, they do not amount to genuine structural emendations of their prototype. Kleanthis drafted a plan for a capital that could comfortably have been home to 600,000 residents. If not even he anticipated that it would someday be home to five times that many, he did at least sketch in the radial vectors of what might have been a more guided expansion. His Athens was prepared to go beyond its triangularity. Von Klenze's Athens was not. Its structural limitations should not, however, overshadow its symbolic liberalities. However much a neoclassicist and however much a romantic von Klenze may have been, his "corrected" capital has—not so unhappily, after all—never quite become either one. It has never been altogether deprived of its interstices, and consequently of its intimate indefiniteness. Von Klenze's Athenians, cramped though they be, have nevertheless been left with symbolic breathing spaces that Kleanthis's Athenians might not have been able to claim. They have been left with organizational and orientational alternatives—not very disciplined, but then Foucault and de Certeau both have taught us how very perilous the virtues of discipline are.

Another example of the same: the Athenian *dhimos*, or "township," includes well over two thousand avenues and streets within its boundaries. Not a single one is numbered; every one bears a name instead. Traffic in Athens consequently never proceeds "sequentially." Movement is never confined or channeled through arithmetical grids. Even the compass is too impersonal: places in Athens are never merely "west" or "north" or "east" or "south"; they, too, all have their particular names, some knowledge of which is practically essential. What would be intolerable in a disciplinary and utopian city is quite common in Greece's capital: several different streets might have the same name, with nothing but the districts through which they pass to distinguish them. There are, for example, two Tsaldharis Streets. Named for a statesman of the interwar period, leader of the Populist party, one runs through the Filopappos district, in Athens's southwest quadrant. The other runs through the Pangrati district, in the metropolis's southeast. Their case is far from unique; it is in fact only one of many. An Odhos Ayias Sofias in the northwestern Attiki district is matched by another, again in Pangrati. An Odhos Armodhiou, again in Attiki, is matched by one in the Averof district. There are two examples of Odhos Vrilissou (east of Averof and south of the Ilissia district); two of Odhos Dhoreliou (one near Mount Filopappos, and the other again in Pangrati); two of Odhos Thisiou (again in Filopappos, and in the Plaka); two of Odhos Korai (in the central city and, still again, in Pangrati); two of Odhos Metaxa (likely not the interwar dictator, Ioannis; the Metaxas family is large and diversely famous); two of Odhos Paparighopoulou (between the green space known as the Pedhion Areos and the Neapolis district, and again in the Plaka); two of Odhos Smirni (again in different districts). There are three examples of Odhos Soutsou (all, again, in different districts, likely remembering the poet Panayiotis Soutsos among others).

The explanation? Many of Athens's outlying districts were once distinct municipalities. All have been gradually absorbed into the metropolis's ever widening perimeters. Their streets retain their original names, perhaps, in order to memorialize a former independence; they retain them, perhaps, simply from oversight or "undisciplined" nonchalance. The confusions they must occasionally produce are likely minimal. Even for the uninformed, Athens is surprisingly navigable. The Acropolis and Likavittos are always available as references. Most smaller streets lead sooner or later to open squares. Some centers are more central than others. Every place has its own particularity, but a particularity rendered manageable enough by the relative abstraction of the relation between one location and the next.

The Plural City and the Homogeneities of Athens

The disciplinary city can accommodate pluralities—of religion, of ethnicity, of class, of status—almost ad infinitum. Its grid is content-neutral. Within its "nowhere," little "somewheres" might always be inscribed. A pure space, it is in principle divisible without limit. New York and San Francisco both are exemplary of a disciplinary city's practical potential, even if neither is perfectly utopian. San Francisco's Nob Hill, Telegraph Hill, and Pacific Heights owe their exclusivity in part to particular features of the natural landscape. But even in San Francisco, the natural landscape is no more than a secondary determinant of the content of a place. Accident is primary: the only arbitrariness that formalist discipline can countenance; the only arbitrariness to which it can genuinely be indifferent. Athens, on the other hand, may be a vast collection of protosocial or inchoately cultural little villages. It holds a plurality of places of class and of life-style, the more exclusive of them revealing the consistent attractions of ruins, of views, and of shade. But its homogeneities are far more striking. Scholars of pluralism occasionally note it as an extreme: its various sociocultural shreds and patches notwithstanding, it revealed in 1986 and 1987 virtually none of the internal institutional divergences that have become so common, and so consequential, not just in metropolitan America but in metropolitan Africa and Asia as well.[17] Though it has its share of cosmopolitans, Athens itself was, during my stay, neither a structural nor a cultural cosmopolis; and even if one sometimes heard Ghlifadha described derisively as an "English-speaking ghetto," greater Athens had no true ghettoes, whether religious, ethnic, cultural, valuational, or even gustatorial. Until very recently, it has had virtually no "foreign restaurants."[18]

In part, capitaline homogeneity is a more or less mechanical product of the broadest of world-systemic and geopolitical trends. In the past, the Turks settled in what is now Greek territory with other Levantine and Circum-Mediterranean peoples. In the past, Bulgarians and Albanians joined them. But migration has in the long run flowed far less toward Greece than away from it.[19] Imperialism and colonialism have left France and Great Britain and the United States with large minority populations, but left Greece in the mid-1980s with very few.[20] The economic brilliance of the Occident's centers, though presently tarnished, has continued to attract Africans and Asians and Europeans—Greeks among them—long after colonialism's end. The relative economic obscurity of the Occident's semiperipheries had left Athens relatively ethnically simple. Virtually no Africans resided in it while I was there. Those who did were either diplomats or domestics. Virtually no Asians resided in it, either. Those who did were, for the most part, either diplomats or restauranteurs. In 1987, Athens had three *kinezika estiatoria*, "Chinese restaurants," two of them owned and managed by Chinese. Since my departure, I have learned of an influx of immigrants from the Philippines, most of whom have sought work as domestics. The gypsies have been a presence—a visible, a sometimes maligned, but a hardly countable presence—for a very long time.

If macrostructural dynamics have thus regularly discouraged the entrenchment in Athens of those sociocultural pluralities that they have with as much regularity encouraged elsewhere, more irregular events have conspired not simply to discourage but altogether to eliminate them. In the past, there were more than a few Turks in Athens, and still at the turn of the century some 300,000 Turkish-speaking Muslims living in independent Hellas. Today, almost no Turks live in Athens, and only about a third of the former number in Greece as a whole. Their diminution is historically due to what is appropriately known as the Mikroasiatiki Katastrofi, the "Asia Minor Disaster."

Constantinople—"The City"—fell to the Ottomans in 1453. It remained the object of many Greeks' fondest irredentist dreams for more than four hundred years. The object, indeed, of more than mere dreams: the Meghali Idhea, the "Great Idea" of a Greece that would rule over all the lands of late Byzantium, had become something of a state obsession by the 1850s. It survived the many critics who took it to task at the inglorious end of the 1897 Greco-Turkish War. It survived the "Split"—a civil war of sorts, launched in late 1915 by the founder of Greece's contemporary Liberal party, Eleftherios Venizelos, against the supporters of his king, Konstandinos I.[21] It had a reflorescence shortly later, once Venizelos took control of a reunited government and Konstandinos fled into exile. By 1920, a Greece that had devoted much of its diplomatic and military energy to irredentist expansion could claim most of the northern Epirus, most of Thrace, virtually all of the Heptanese and the Dodecanese as its own "once again." Anatolia and Constantinople were, however, still in Ottoman hands. Venizelos thought the time for a campaign had come. Several religious and ethnic minorities in Thrace opposed it. Royalists and anti-Liberals opposed it even more strenuously. Venizelos acted nonetheless. His impulsiveness cost him the election of November 1920. The objections of the Allies notwithstanding, Konstandinos was called back by a public referendum a month later.

The Anatolian campaign inaugurated by Venizelos did not, however, cease when Konstandinos returned. It intensified instead. The Allies grew increasingly disturbed. Great Britain vacillated; France soon shifted its support entirely from the Hellenes to the Turkish adversary. Late in the summer of 1922, the Greek armies that had infiltrated Anatolia were definitively expelled. Their commanders in chief were humiliated. Konstandinos was sent away for a second time, largely pro forma, and his son, Yioryios II, given for a short while the vacant throne. In 1926, Yioryios would himself be dismissed to Sicily. In 1935, however, he, too, would return.[22]

The Asia Minor Disaster came to an official close in 1922 with the Treaty of Lausanne. The Meghali Idhea was officially, though by no means actually, brought to a close with it. The animosity that has informed more contemporary relations between Greece and Turkey was only given new fuel. Even in disgrace, Greece lost more than it wanted to gain, but far less than the Turks thought it should lose. Venizelos was in fact among those who negotiated for his fellow Hellenes terms markedly more favorable than realists had expected to emerge. The treaty left Greece with most of Thrace and many of the Aegean islands; if none were gained, very few of the territories that were Hellenic by 1920 were actually lost. But the treaty included a provision, ratified in 1923, the severity of which could not be ignored. It prescribed the "exchange" of the some 1.3 million Greek Orthodox residents of Anatolia for some 350,000 Muslim residents of Greece.[23] Most of the Orthodox refugees who lived through the exchange came to Athens. In 1920, the capital was home to some 385,000 people. By 1926, it was home to nearly 600,000. The refugees who had so swelled the population typically arrived with little more than their elegance—sometimes prodigious—and their labor to sustain them. Most would endure both economic and social hardship for the next two decades. For all the hardship it brought, the resettlement is still sometimes asserted to have had its "beneficial side." Both foreign and native historians sometimes mention with approval precisely its homogenization of a citizenry that had been of too many faiths and too many tongues.[24]

Even after the resettlement, Athens was not yet altogether one. Though Thessaloniki was home to more, the capital was itself still home to a sizable number of Jews. But what the Treaty of Lausanne left unfinished, the German occupation managed nearly to see done. The Germans did not pause long after the failure of Mussolini's bumbling attempt to invade Greece at the beginning of the spring of 1941. Only a month and a half later, Hitler's troops summarily crossed the Macedonian frontier. Only a few weeks after that, they secured an armistice with the collaborationist General Tsolakoghlou, who soon found himself in Athens at the head of a puppet government. Yanis Yanoulopoulos reviews the course of the three and a half years that followed:

In the absence of any industries or raw materials that could be useful to their war-machine, the welfare of the local population was of little consequence to the occupying authorities. A heavy importer of grain, Greece was to suffer severely from the trade blockade that the Allies were maintaining on enemy-occupied territories. In the harsh winter of 1941–2 nearly three hundred thousand people died from starvation. Fortunes were lost in desperate attempts to buy food and new fortunes were made in the thriving black market. Thousands of city dwellers made their way back to the villages from where they originally came . . . to scrape a living off the land.[25]

But thousands of villagers also came to Athens. Yanoulopoulos suggests that Germany's interest in Greece was "solely strategic."[26] Perhaps so: but it was not solely military. Greece held the original relics of the occidental aesthetics of identity but also of the Nazi aesthetics of power.[27] Villagers and city dwellers alike were well aware that Athens would be very unlikely to be bombed either by the Allies or by the Axis. Fewer Greeks were aware, however, that the Germans were pursuing the Final Solution as vigorously in their homeland as they were in Budapest and Warsaw. The local Holocaust is still poorly documented.[28] Approximately seventy thousand Jews were transported from throughout Greece to concentration camps in Balkan and Slavic Europe.[29] Perhaps more than twenty thousand were transported from the capital alone. Very few returned. A friend has estimated that some five thousand Jews live in Athens today. I suspect the number, served by a single synagogue, to be much smaller.[30]

Not all discrimination, not even all violent discrimination, has, however, come from without. In 1847, a vigilante mob ransacked the home and property of a certain Don Pacifico. A Jew and also a British subject, Don Pacifico complained to his consul. The British government immediately demanded that Greece offer formal apologies and adequate material compensation to the victim. Woodhouse recounts that Lord Palmerston, then the British foreign secretary, demanded much more: compensation for the historian George Finlay, a piece of whose Greek property had been confiscated by the king; and two small islands off the western coast of the Peloponnese.[31] The king, Othon, scoffed at Palmerston's ultimatums until he found that the British fleet had blockaded Piraeas. Diplomatic maneuvering led, to the delight of many Greeks, to a falling out between Great Britain and France. But Greece did not win. Othon was finally forced to yield.

Anti-Semitism—sometimes more of a catalyst than a spoiler of pluralism—also played a role in determining the alliances and antagonisms that led to the Split between the Venizelists and the Royalists.[32] Though not specifically anti-Semitic, racism continued to inform the interwar period, especially in the immediate aftermath of the Asia Minor Disaster. One native political scientist has observed:

The almost complete ethnic homogeneity that came to pass with the exchange of populations remained, essentially, more promise than reality. The "Hellenicity" of the refugees itself was put into doubt by the native-born with such characterizations as "Turk's spawn" [*tourkospori*] and "yogurt-baptised" [*yiaourtovaftismeni*]. The racial chasm had indubitably genuine manifestations. . . . It was enough for anyone to make note of the refugees' typical last names, as well as their language, which for many was not even Greek.[33]

In part because of its association with the Nazis, racism in contemporary Athens is somewhat taboo. It exists but is conversationally in the worst taste. An upper-class native acquaintance once commented to me, during a comparison of Greek and American society, that his compatriots were generally quite racist, as racist as mine, but that it was far more polite to confess, over an Athenian dinner table, to having committed some perverse sexual act than "to having seen a 'negro' on the street." Other native acquaintances were prepared to deny that Greeks were racist at all, though largely on the basis of the same point of manners. The truth lies somewhere in between. Taboo notwithstanding, a certain racist imagery manages to find expression from time to time in self-situating reflections, particularly those of the relatively declassed and relatively declining sectors of the old bourgeoisie. As such reflections go, these can be surprisingly systematic: an indication above all of the perduring persuasiveness of the charisma of blood.[34] Taboos notwithstanding, racists do not always restrain themselves: least of all in front of what they presume to be a sympathetic stranger. A fragment from among my earliest field notes:

> I was approached on the beach this afternoon by an elderly man. He ostensibly wanted a cigarette. I said that I would be glad to give him one. Alerted by my accent that I was not Greek, he asked me where I was from. He was not satisfied when I told him that I was from America. "No," he said in English, "but who are your ancestors?" He was amused at the variety of them. "A mongrel," he said. He told me that he was an Athenian, that his family was one of Athens's most established. He was disappointed that I did not recognize the surname. He asked how long I was visiting; he was delighted that I would be staying several months. Had I been to the Acropolis, or the National Museum? No, I had not yet been to either. "You must go," he said. "You must. We Greeks today, we are nothing. Our own ancestors did everything. There is nothing left. We cannot rival them. No one can rival them." He asked me if I spoke French. Yes, I said, a little. So we spoke together briefly in French. He said that he often traveled to Paris and to Berlin, where he had several friends. He had, he said, probably the best collection of music in Attica. He had never been to America. He had never particularly wanted to go. He evidently held the place in considerable disdain. He suggested that our political choices displayed a great deal of "naïveté." "You have many 'negroes' in America, don't you?" he asked. I said I

supposed so. "How many?" I said I wasn't at all certain—perhaps thirty million. He was visibly horrified. "I must be honest with you," he said. "I do not like them. They use drugs, and they steal." I suggested that the stereotype was far from just. "Well," he said. "Well, I just do not like them."

The ugly child—so Dumont would argue[35]—of individualistic ideology, racism is always in need of a compendium of differentia. But its pluralism is always exclusionary. It neither has nor wants anything to do with the commensual promiscuity of that rather prettier, though rarer, child of individualistic ideologies: cosmopolitan "decadence."

Neither, for that matter, does what the Greeks call *o ethnismos*, "ethnicism" or "nation(al)ism,"[36] with which so much of European and romantic racism has long been intertwined, want anything to do with decadence. Nationalism is perhaps not always racist. But Michael Herzfeld has recently reminded us that the imagery of peoples and cultures and histories, once transformed into the essentialism of a People, a Culture, and a History, is the very stuff of which oppressive license is, in the era of the nation-state, all too often made.[37] Herzfeld has also reminded us that the same essentialism is an altogether too familiar product of anthropological practice itself, a product all the more dangerous for the stamp of professional authority that, anthropologically pronounced, it usually carries. In Greece, not simply anthropological but a wide variety of other (would-be) social scientific practitioners have been among the most influential and politically self-conscious of nationalists from independence forward. Herzfeld himself has offered extensive analyses of some of their more curious contributions: katharevousa, that entirely artificial "purification" of demotic that, purged of Turkish influences and brightened with ancient syntactic and semantic paradigms, remained Greece's official language until 1975; and "traditional literature," carefully interpreted or carefully amended to disguise its "oriental" and highlight its "Homeric" flavor.[38]

Hence the close association between nationalism and the "Hellenization" of Greece. Not all Hellenizers have, however, been such ardent ethnic purists; not all of them, as I have already pointed out, such ardent occidentalists, either. Many of them have been quite willing to give the mongrel Romaic its due. Not even the most cosmopolitan of them can, even so, properly be described as pluralists. Like Romeotes themselves, Greece's Hellenizers have proceeded in accord with a principle of an entirely different kind. Americans are familiar with the idea of "the melting pot." Once considered fondly, it has since given way to the pluralist glamor of "cultural diversity." Necessity made into a virtue, perhaps, but a virtue of which Greeks could be expected not altogether to approve: if not enthusiasts of the idea of the melting pot, they are inclined to view the utopian and disciplinary version of the cosmopolis with suspicion. Socially, culturally, and stylistically, they reveal a taste for multiplicity, but not as an end in itself. They aim primarily at another end: assimilation.

Hellenes and Romeotes might sometimes adopt one another's habits merely to blunt the force, each of the other's scorn. But the rhetoric of assimilation in Athens today is imbued with a moral ardor that precedes all calculation. Some dozen years ago, when residents of the capital witnessed the first of several subsequent public "homosexual" rallies, they were exhorted above all to recognize the evils of *gettopiisi*, "ghettoization." Athenian journalists continued during the term of my fieldwork to denounce ghettoization not simply in Greece but in the rest of Europe, in Africa, and of course in the United States. The social isolation that ghettoization institutionalizes is in local disrepute for the social marginalization and social disenfranchisement to which it so often leads. It is, whether elected or inflicted, in disrepute as well for the existential diminution that it so often implies.

Greeks may have begun to acquire their penchant for assimilationism during the period of the Ottoman domination, when as members of one *millet* among many others, they were themselves often relegated to ghettoes. Some may have acquired it during a sojourn abroad: often profitable, the life of the enclaved *gastarbeiter* is rarely an altogether fulfilling one.[39] On the other hand, the penchant has not been built upon the basis of negative experience alone. Assimilationism has also had more seductive, and more determinate precedents. As Charles Stewart notes, Orthodoxy has been a vigorously synthetic religion from the patristic era forward.[40] Recall, too, the eclectic Phanariotes, who must be given pride of place in any genealogy of good contemporary Greek taste. Neither purists nor purgers, the Phanariotes seem instead actively to have sought out the curios of ostensibly discordant civilizations—but only in order that their assimilative amalgamations might be all the more inimitable.

Their sensibility has had a notable impact on urban architecture. Von Klenze was, of course, something of an assimilationist himself. From a neoromantic as from a Phanariote point of view, his convictions appear exceedingly narrow. Many of the natives who witnessed his capitaline plans put into effect thought them excessively narrow as well. Many did not wish to see the Acropolis plateau altered; many of them complained that the "demolition" of its "Turkish and Frankish structures" would destroy the very picturesqueness that its remodeler was supposed to adore.[41] Von Klenze was, however, able to count on the support of several of his most illustrious native colleagues. One of them, Lissandros Kaftanzoghlou, had been trained at the Ecole des beaux arts in Paris in the immediate aftermath of the "neo-Grec" movement that had burgeoned there,[42] and so "did not hesitate to unveil Romantic classicism" of the Bavarian and Parisian sort "as *Hellenic* architecture, thus emphasizing the convergence of the archaic with the contemporary."[43] He called upon his fellow professionals to move, with von Klenze, *epi to ellinikoteron,* "toward the more Hellenic." The phrase is not demotic but Attic. Its archaism corresponds to another: Kaftanzoghlou's imperative "faith in the ancient forms," and his admonition "to approach their perfection without deviations."[44]

Kaftanzoghlou's mission was aggressive. It conjured an Athens whose special legitimacy and special distinction would lie in its being even more "formalist," even more "perfect" than its counterparts farther west. On the other hand, the mission was not his own. It came from the west, and it had as its end the fashioning of the Athens that Europe required: a literal *locus classicus,* an urban museum of origins that had their final expression elsewhere. Kaftanzoghlou seems not to have been even dimly aware of the extent to which his "faith" served others more than it served the Greeks. He certainly did not foresee that so many of the Greek intelligentsia would, near the turn of the twentieth century, come to regard his sort of highmindedness as part and parcel of both political and cultural dependency. As the century turned, local architects accordingly left a rigid occidentalism behind for more complex, more Phanariotic doctrines of composition.[45] From that time forward, they began to conceive of Athens's "proper style" in accord with more variable axes: the first formal, differentiating the "high" from the "vernacular"; the second substantive, differentiating among the ancient, the Byzantine, and the "eastern" or "oriental." The matrix has proved quite capable of accommodating the most austere, at least, of the components of functionalist modernism. Perennially stringent demands of thrift have, in conjunction with the easy availability of cement, further contributed to the proliferation of the tidy and simple office and apartment complexes in which most Athenians now work and live. Such unfrivolous complexes might look quite garish in Paris; but they manage to look quite "Mediterranean" on the Attic plain[46] (Plate 23).

The same matrix has, in theory, also allowed for the aesthetic rehabilitation of "Anatolia." But the Phanariotes notwithstanding, the Near East provides Athens with only a few occasional grace notes; the Far East, with virtually none at all. The metropolis's taste-makers are largely content to confine their intrigue with the Turkish or the Japanese to the interiors of their homes. Governmental tolerance of the non-Western has waxed and waned.[47] During my stay, it was slightly on the upswing, though with very little spatial effect. In the past, especially during periods of strife with the Turks, it has had definite lows, the effects of which have been far more clear. Athens was in 1986 and 1987 a far less Anatolian place than it used to be. Von Klenze's purgation of the Acropolis started the trend. The unearthing of the agora continued it. Excavations of the agora began rather late, only in 1939, during the regime of Greece's "benign" dictator, Ioannis Metaxas. Like so many other sponsors of Athens's narrower Hellenization, Metaxas was

PLATE 23. Functionalism, plain and simple.

authoritarian, indeed quasi-fascist, and deeply conservative. The precincts of the agora had, however, been ceded to the American School of Classical Studies almost a decade before he came to power, during the more republican if no less grandiloquent administration of Eleftherios Venizelos. Financing for the expropriation was provided by a grant of some twelve million dollars from the Rockefeller Foundation.[48] What vanished, once work got underway, was more or less all of Athens's surviving Turkish quarter. A prominent native, K. E. Biris, who was active on the Athens Planning Commission from 1925 to the mid-1950s, lamented the destruction:

> The archaeologists are, by their very methods of operation, bent on shattering the tradition and continuity of Athenian history. With their demolitions . . . they have made a desert round the Acropolis, thus creating an altogether false picture historically. For never has the city of Athens been reduced to so deathly a condition—a wasteland stripped even of its ruins. The living palpable form of the historic town has been wiped out; in its place the chilling picture of its precursor's underpinnings and foundations—a sight that may interest the specialist but does not stir even his own heart. The excavations have obliterated the reality of the city's development in time, leaving a void for our eyesight and our feelings. We shall never be able to see anything but the relics of the ancient town on the one hand, and, on the other, the office blocks and apartment buildings of the new, as if Athens had no intervening, no continuous life.[49]

During the same period, between the two world wars, the palm trees that adorned Omonia Square were felled under the order of officials who found them "too African."[50] Roughly concurrently, a Memorial to the Unknown Soldier was built along the frontage of Othon's former palace, which had become the new home of the Parliament. Its endpoints were marked with Delphic omphaloi. Its bas-reliefs and calligraphy were carved in unreserved Ionic severity. It has been guarded by *evzones*, "well-girded" soldiers dressed in traditional Greek costume, ever since.

The Second World War brought all excavation and renovation to a halt. Afterward, however, and even in the midst of civil turmoil, the Americans returned to the agora, and succeeded not long after in reconstructing the ancient Stoa of Attalos, which opened as a museum in 1956. Biris for his part was so impressed with the Stoa that he entirely changed his mind about the worth of what had been razed to recover it. American archaeologists have continued to labor on the agora more or less apace from 1956 forward. Their labors were approved with considerable zeal by the Papadhopoulos junta. The junta's officers were, like Metaxas before them, committed not only to the instauration of a "'healthy' and 'disciplined' political order,"[51] but also to industrialist economics, to Orthodox pieties, and to a notoriously nebulous rightness of mind that disposed them not merely to spatial censorship but to censorship of other sorts as well. School textbooks were rewritten at the colonels' command; admission to institutions of higher education was made conditional upon the passing of certain ideological examinations. The colonels also had a profound hatred of the Turks. They professed great love of the Classics. The names of the inlets at Piraeas—Tourkolimano ("Turk's harbor") and Passalimani ("Pasha's harbor")—were officially replaced during their regime with more ancient appellations.

Since the junta's fall—or better, because of the junta's rise and fall—the propriety of the vernacular has been redeemed, and the banned usages revived again. But greater Athens remains narrowly Hellenic even so. Since Greece's entry into the European Community, the capital's responsibility to the greatest of its pasts, its identification with that past—these have, if anything, become even stricter. Many Athenians were quite pleased and many remain quite pleased that their city was chosen over Paris or Berlin or London to be the first of the community's annual "cultural capitals." Athens's economy enjoyed a brief boom as a result. But the choice also cast what had become a fragmented, frantic, effectively posturban metropolis once again into the ancestral role that it had played for Europe some two centuries earlier, and that it has in some measure continued to play all along. Perhaps it has been forced less than the rest of Greece to play the "humiliated oriental vassal" at the same time. Six of one, half dozen of the other? In a sense: for, as Michael Herzfeld remarks, "the two roles might seem incompatible, were it not for the fact that both imply inferiority to the 'true' European of today."[52] If, however, assimilationism continues to be affected by Greece's various dependencies, it has not been crushed by them. Athens is still somewhere, someplace. But where precisely? What sort of place?

A Poetics of Urban Form

Even if ancient cities had never actually existed, some genuine ethnographer would sooner or later have invented them. They are perhaps less places than processes, but processes that have sloughed off or suppressed the contingencies of their beginnings and arrived at that sort of homoestasis or dynamic equilibrium that has always lent itself so readily, so naturally, to functional and organic analysis. They have histories like all places and processes. They might even retain a few irreducibly temporal tokens of their past. The poetics that prevails in ancient cities is, however, no more temporal than the poetics that has prevailed so long over the methodology of "genuine" ethnographic description itself. On the contrary: both share a master trope that is notable above all for its essential synchronicity. Both favor synecdoche, the imagery of elements and totalities, parts and wholes. Both—so Fustel first demonstrated—are made for one another.

Pluralism, especially "ethnic" pluralism, was with good reason among the earliest inspirations for an anthropological critique of genuine ethnographic description. In the Burma highlands, in the hinterlands of the Near East and of Southeast Asia, it proved to be less dynamic than fluid, and less fixed and permanent than contextual and situational. It was also "strategic," and strategies, as Barth saw and as Bourdieu has also emphasized, are always temporalizing.[53] Not simply in rural but also in urban settings, pluralism has been among the most compelling empirical impetuses for the development of an ethnography of "practices"—de Certeau's among them—to which the poetics of synecdoche hardly does justice. But on the other hand, it has not as yet inspired an actual descriptive revolution. Even ethnographers of practices have continued often to return to the "systems," the "organic unities," that they seemed to have left behind. First, perhaps, blame the world: pluralism might have forced more far-reaching alternatives were ethnic and religious differences, differences of class, differences of status and style of life not all quite as prone to compartmentalization and spatial bureaucratization as they have proved under disciplinary and utopian pressures virtually everywhere to be. Blame, however, the stronghold of anthropology's poetic tradition as well: the synecdochic representation of Lebanon, once considered a hallmark of "plural" and "modern" unity, has turned out to be no more realistic and no more informative than the synecdochic representation of Los Angeles would be today.

Hayden White has called upon historians to explore rhetorical alternatives to the rather limited tropological array embedded in historiography.[54] A similar call is by now also familiar, perhaps all too familiar, to anthropologists, some of whom have responded to it, with decidedly mixed results, and many of whom have resisted it, either in the currently fashionable name of "pure critique" or in the currently less fashionable name of "scientific conservatism." I understand the call as one made in the name of something so currently unfashionable as realism, of "getting it right."[55] Ethnographies may be *fictiones*, they may on occasion even be pure fictions. But so are human actions and human creations, metropolises among them: symbolic things, things made and, in however roughshod a manner, made or found meaningful in the process, even if not always as meaningful, as aesthetically coherent and complete, as they might be. See their tropes, see the tropes toward which they aim, and you do not perhaps see them for all that they are; the paradox of unintended consequences among others serves as a hermeneutical reminder of the inevitable partiality of all social reportage. But report the tropes incarnate or executed in human actions as you see them, and you have at least a first, or primary, reading not simply of mental but also of material events. Report the tropes incarnate in or aimed at in human creations, metropolises among them, and you have at least a first, or primary, reading not simply of a mental but also a material "configuration," however short of a "culture" it may be. Rhetorical analysis is thus not merely ideal-typical. As people imagine, as they are constrained by precedent or circumstance to imagine, so they behave. So they are.

The ancient city is a city of synecdoche, and so a city whose parts are always less than and never quite adequately representative of the whole to which they belong. It has its modernist counterparts. Le Corbusier's Chandigarh, commonly considered an urbanist failure, and Brasilia—sometimes disparaged as a utopianist fantasy, sometimes praised as a consummate melding of natural background and architectural artifice—are among the most prominent.[56] Beijing, indeterminately classical or modernist, should also be mentioned. Are there metonymic cities that, designed as or tending toward a whole, nevertheless allow of a partitive or "reductive"[57] representation? Savannah is perhaps the most exact illustration: a city of "cells of . . . family houses," which make up larger cells of squares and related blocks.[58] De Certeau would approve of Edmund Bacon's characterization. Savannah, writes Bacon, is "highly disciplined," focusing "in icy sharpness" its architect's command of "expression in the third dimension." It is an orderly interspersing of residences and parks. "The total effect," as Bacon puts it, "is an interaction between the two patterns, the gridiron web of streets dividing the basic units, and the web of green spaces and their green links which overlies the geometry of the streets."[59] Its design allows for growth both by accretion and by extension. The Savannah River provides it with a picturesque frontage; the riverine forest with a whole cloth out of which it has continually been cut and recut from 1733 forward. A realization of Vitruvian principles in the New World, it is saturated with temporality, though with a temporality apparently deprived of any structuring influence. Savannah's homes reflect the evolution of architectural taste through more than two centuries. But its skeleton is geometrically invariable.

The design of Savannah is not entirely unique. Many of the planners of North American cities, including those who designed San Francisco,[60] have incorporated it, even if they have not rested with it. Numbered avenues remain one of its most explicit, and most reductive, legacies. Its rhetorical opposite is not Athens but cities far more unorganized and unplanned, cities of the unexpected, cities of surprise and irony that rarely make their way either into essays on the "urban community" or into essays on the normative orders of urban form. The occidental imagination, sociological, literary, or touristic, tends to regard such cities as quite literally outrées: beyond the urban, purely exotic, provocatively mystical. It has persistently found a watershed in the Circum-Mediterranean, especially in older Cairo and Alexandria. It has inclined as well toward the Far East, especially Bangkok and Rangoon and Jakarta. A justified inclination? Perhaps: on a "primary" reading, the major cities of precolonial Africa and Asia lack and lack precisely the regularity of political and administrative design that has been the hallmark of occidental (of occidentalist) urbanization. One finds no "city-states" very much east, nor very much south, of the Mediterranean. One does not, as Weber recognized, find their natural urban legacy very much east or south of the Mediterranean, either. The borders of the sea offer a mixture; but planning has historically migrated not as much toward the east or the south as toward the north and the west, at least before the colonial era.

The pluralist city may, like Savannah, be rigorously planned, or at least rigorously organized. It may, like New York, have a discernible, indeed even a monumental center. On the other hand, it may be as "disorderly," or its order as piecemeal, and inscrutable, as any city of surprises. But the cosmopolitanism, social or cultural, that distinguishes the pluralist city, whether as a matter of principle or as a matter of fact, cannot in the end be read as either metonymic or ironic. Cosmopolitanism, whether realized as a figure of thought or as a figuration of urban space, is tropologically sui generis. The cosmopolitan city is dominantly metaphorical—if of nothing else, at least of itself. Metaphor, as Harold Bloom has observed, is like irony and metonymy a "trope of limitation." It neither represents nor reconstitutes meaning, but instead "curtails it," typically through "the endless perspectivizing of dualism, of inside-outside dichotomies."[61] New York is patently enough a city of ever proliferating dichotomies (only a few of them specifically "ethnic"). Los Angeles generates dichotomies even more rapidly. The presence, the interiority of the "first great post-modern metropolis" is (but is not) "neo-Hispanic." It is (but is not) "Mediterranean." It is (but is not)

"Pan-American"; is (but is not) "Pan-Pacific"; and so on. Whatever the clarity of its administrative boundaries, the unclarity of its stylistic and symbolic boundaries is irresolute. In some measure like all its pluralist sisters, the metropolis that is some of so many different things is condemned (or free) simultaneously to be none of them at all.

Kenneth Burke has argued that synecdoche, metonymy, irony, and metaphor are the four "master tropes," those tropes under which all figures of speech or thought or action can ultimately be subsumed.[62] But can they accommodate the figurations of contemporary Athens? The question presupposes that a metropolis no longer an "urban community," no longer commensurate with the ancient city that it has replaced, nevertheless demands or invites tropological accommodations of some kind. Does it? No longer a city of synecdoche, it has not evolved into a metropolis dominated by ironies, either. Many of my Athenian acquaintances were, to be sure, prepared to label the capital, indeed Greece as a whole, both "disorganized" and "chaotic." But Athens's actual structure is not quite either one. If it has outstripped and superseded the quite disciplined geometry of von Klenze's blueprints, it has carried closer to fruition the idea of a historical capital and capital of history that those very blueprints quite explicitly contained. Athens is not plural in the manner of New York or of Los Angeles or even of Paris. On the other hand, it often appears, both structurally and toponymically, to be dominated by the proliferation of dichotomies quite similar to those that dominate any metaphorical cityscape. It would be more perfectly analogous with New York or Los Angeles or Paris were its dichotomies still at base cultural, its assimilationism still at base a cultural syncretism, and its assimilationists at base cultural pluralists turned inward. Many of its multiplicities are of course "cultural"; but like its disorderliness, they too are subject less to a spatial than to a more fundamentally historical, a temporal registry. The occidental and the oriental, the European Hellenic and the Nicaean Hellenic, the Hellenic and the Romaic, the civilized and the vulgar, the "foreign" and the "native," the pure and the impure: view Athens as a place, and all these grand and antagonistic metaphors of difference appear to constitute the urban bedrock. View Athens, more appropriately, as a process, and they prove, if by no means superficial, still subordinate to another; they are all conditioned by the contrariety of the past and the present.

None of Burke's master tropes is more than accidentally related to the contrariety of the past and the present; none is imagistically or expressively dependent upon it. Seeking to account for the distinctive character of romantic poetics, the first poetics to require historical sensitivity because the first to require its practitioners to be original, Harold Bloom supplements Burke's list with two further tropes: hyperbole; and that finalizing figure, the poetic *summum* of romantic revisionism, metalepsis.[63] Athens is not, of course, a poem. It is not a work of art. Like most other cities, it is a thing of too many and too discordant authors to be either. It is by no means "monotropic." But seeking to give some account, some positive primary reading of the dominant tropology of a city itself reborn and set again into motion at the height of romantic nationalism, a city that has passed from the romantic to the neoromantic without any significant modernist interlude in between, I can do no better than to adopt Bloom's supplement as my own.

Hyperbole is for Bloom the trope of transcendence, of overreaching and surpassing, the trope of the romantic sublime. Architecturally, it is the trope of monumentalization: the transformation of the ordinary into the larger than life, of the particular into a paragon. At first sight, Athens seems extravagantly hyperbolic. Monuments appear to be everywhere: from the Acropolis to Venizelos Park, which has a statue of its namesake some ten feet tall. I was consequently surprised when one of my well-traveled acquaintances remarked upon the joint American and Soviet "obsession" with monuments, casting his own tradition as "other" in the process. Initially, I dismissed him out of hand. But once again, the native was right. Athens has its array of grand statuary. It has its architectural extravagance. Its monuments are nevertheless vulnerable, and most have succumbed, to the more constant and prevailing assault of historical particularization. Washington is a true city of hyperbole. Even its most modest historical memorials tend, often quite rapidly, to assume the transcendent character appropriate to the icons of a "civil religion." In Athens, the trend goes in reverse. In that metropolis, at once nostalgic and dissatisfied, even the most sacral of monuments, even the Acropolis, have come to assume the status of museum pieces. They are robbed of their status as paragons, an essentially atemporal status, the more that they are exposed as representatives merely of a time past. Dated, transformed into metonymic shreds and patches, they tend all to fall victim sooner or later to what Bloom speaks of as metaleptic "meta-reduction": the diminution of a totalistic figure into partiality and partitivity.[64]

Metalepsis is thus not just one trope among others. It is the master trope of the historical revisionist, the "revisionary trope proper," as Bloom would have it. Its message is always that what was thought to be whole is really only a facet of some more encompassing perspective or picture. It thus exposes the whole that it reduces to a part as itself a trope, a figure passing for a literalism. Hence its own operation as a "metatrope," as a play on what is already a play, of speech or thought or action; a play that overcomes other plays by revealing them—but also, potentially, by revealing itself—to be neither primordial nor timeless, to be "mere" tropes. Bloom argues that romantic poets—*poiētes*, "makers"—deploy tropes consciously or unconsciously as defenses against those anterior visions that would compromise the originality, and so the essential individuality, of their own creations. They direct their tropes against their creative precursors—but allude to them and so memorialize them in the process. Hence the source of the systematic continuity, the irrevocable tie to the past, in what is nevertheless an enterprise of persistent innovation. The poetics that has metalepsis as its rhetorical *summum* accordingly allows us to define a tradition that at first sight appears to be marked by nothing but "continuous rupture."[65]

As defense and as innovation both, metalepsis may be either introjective or projective. Introjective metalepsis sacrifices the integrity of the present "to an idealized past." It absorbs the present into the past, and so has the effect of renovating or renewing the past. Literarily, it involves the "substitution of [historically] late words for earlier words in an anterior trope."[66] As a figure of social and cultural action, it most often involves the use of contemporary, of "modern" tools in the repairing or the reinvigoration of "tradition." Projective metalepsis executes a "distancing, a projecting of the past," and so an identification either with a new present or a yet unrealized future. Literarily, it involves the "substitution of early for late words." As a figure of social and cultural action, it involves the use of the shreds and patches of traditions in order to enrich, to fill out the present or the future.

Talk of metalepsis, of introjection and projection, risks not just obscurantism but interpretive self-indulgence; but the risk is one that I am prepared to take. From the next chapter forward, I argue that the *summum* of what Bloom refers to as his "practical poetics" maps with astonishing precision the rhetorical force and flavor not of the Greek "genius" nor of Greek "culture" but rather of some of the most striking habits and penchants of the socially and cultural elite cadre to which my Athenian circle belongs. Bloom is less concerned than I am to distinguish between metalepsis of the introjective and metalepsis of the projective variety. Literarily, the difference between them may not be altogether momentous.[67] Culturally, it marks a difference of considerable import. Introjective metalepsis is the rhetorical *summum* of a historical essentialism—a "cultural classicism"— that has persistently been a part of nationalist discourses in Greece from the revolutionary period up to today. Projective metalepsis is the rhetorical *summum* of a distinctive relativism—a "historically constructive" relativism— long favored by Greece's sociocultural elite and long opposed both to essentialism and to its collective realization. For the remainder of this chapter, I simply add some finishing touches to the review of an urban setting that at once reflects and reinforces the latter's antithetical thrust.

A Poetics of Athens

Whether introjective or projective, metalepsis departs from a gap, a *hiatus irrationalis* between the past and present. The *hiatus* does not, however, separate significative equals. The past always has priority, even if its priority is, for the projective metaleptician, only prima facie. If not supreme, the past has, in Athens as perhaps in such other historically burdened and historically rich metropolises as Istanbul,[68] an advantage over the present, an advantage that might be more serviceable or more onerous from one situation to the next. It has, to be sure, been put to service, sometimes far too naïvely and with little ultimate success. The rather lugubrious affair of Athens's bid to host the Centennial Olympics of 1996 has been a recent and well-publicized case in point. The bid was no doubt undertaken with an eye to profit. But it was deeply infused with a historical rhetoric, the righteousness of which was in most local minds incontrovertible and entirely prior to merely pragmatic considerations of any sort whatever. Other competitors may have had more serviceable facilities; Athens had the original stadium, the marble foyer and seats of which were installed by Herodes Atticus in preparation for the games of A.D. 144. Other competitors may have been able to make better provision for the security of visiting athletes; but the stadium was the site of the opening ceremonies of the revived games of 1886 and was ready to be the site of them again. As in Herodes' time, its tiered rows had been restored to a brilliant white; now, however, it was equipped with an electronic scoreboard emblazoned with six interlocking rings.[69] Athens was for quite some time regarded as the "sentimental favorite" in the competition. But it was finally passed over in favor of Atlanta. The deciding committee, whose significative priorities were evidently an inversion of the Athenian committee's own, cited precisely what was not supposed to matter: greater safety, better facilities, better hotels.

The past in Athens is an analogue of the "stressed morpheme." It is "marked." The present, less so. Consider Odhos Xenias, whose name derives from the Attic term for hospitality, especially when shown to a "stranger guest." It runs through the neighborhood known as Ilissia, after the now underground river Ilissos. It is only a few blocks long, a convenient shortcut between Queen Sophia Avenue and Asia Minor Road. It is lined with trees, rather busy in the morning and evening rush hours but placid during the rest of the day. It has a few shops: a hairdresser's; a pharmacy; others selling teas, vintage apparel, potables. Its apartment buildings rent reasonably and are generally well maintained. Their balconies are more often adorned with potted plants than with drying laundry, their residents more often than not solidly, though unostentatiously, *astiki*—a demotic term sometimes meaning "urban," sometimes "middle class," and sometimes "bourgeois."

I know Odhos Xenias well, but only because a gracious couple, who befriended me and whom I visited quite frequently, lived on it. Otherwise, I doubt that I would have become familiar with it. It is a "perfectly ordinary street": attractive, but not charmed enough to pique the interest of tourists; tidy, but neither homely nor dandyish. It has no antiquarian pull—no memorials, no plaques, no remains, not even a little Byzantine shrine of its own. It has no antiquarian reminiscences at all. It has no reminiscences even of the Asia Minor Disaster, or of the resettlement of the refugees by whom it must once have been trod. Its course is flat and quite straight. Likavittos, the Acropolis: these are far away. It has its sensibility, but the sensibility only of the simple present, not yet either Oriental or Occidental, Hellenic or Romaic, High or Low, Pure or Impure. It is "perfectly insignificant."

Nothing on Odhos Xenias has as yet found its way into any of Athens's museums, of which the Ethniko Arkheoloyiko Mousio (National Archaeological Museum) is the largest. From the middle of the preceding century, laws have prohibited the export of antiquities beyond the Greek border. Since about 1890, the National Museum has housed most of what has been locally excavated not only by the Greek Archaeological Society but also by French, British, German, and American teams. It was enlarged considerably before the Second World War. It displays finds from throughout the country. Outlying regions are, however, likely to be possessive of their masterpieces; there are, accordingly, archaeological museums not just at Olympia and Delphi but in Epidaurus and Iraklio as well. There are other archaeological museums in Athens: on the Acropolis, at the agora, at Keramikos. The Ethniki Pinakothiki (National Picture Gallery) shows Greek iconographic and pictographic works from slightly before El Greco forward. The Ethniko Istoriko Mousio (National Historical Museum) ranges over culture and politics from Byzantium through early independent statehood. The Byzantine Museum's collection is kept in a decidedly Florentine villa, designed by Stamatis Kleanthis and the salon in the preceding century of the flamboyant Duchesse de Plaisance. The collection includes religious art and artifacts produced from about A.D. 400 to 1750. The Mousio Benaki was formerly the estate of Immanouil Benakis. It includes a spectacular Persian parlor, artifacts of diverse quality from the protogeometric period forward, and a large collection of traditional costumes: a testament to the eclecticism of Benakis' own connoisseurship. The Polemiko Mousio (War Museum) was "erected during the dictatorship to demonstrate the prowess of Greek arms through the ages": thus, the *Blue Guide*.[70] The Theatriko Mousio dates from an earlier period, and has a different purpose. Several other repositories, historical and ethnographic, are accessible only to researchers. In virtually all cases, exegetical placards are rare. Handbooks or docents are essential. The elegant Goulandris Museum of Natural History can be visited in suburban Kifissia. But there is no museum of science and industry in the metropolis; no public planetarium; no museum of modern art.

Athens's museums must supply what the touristic economy demands. But its toponomy, the product of planners and councils, is much more its own, and its toponymic biases revealing enough. For all its simple presence, even Odhos Xenias has a name that recalls the theme of the *Odyssey*. The sheer present, a present not built out of one or another past, a present without reference to the local network of pasts, is at its Athenian best something about which nothing can be said. It is at worst a monstrosity, an abomination. Much of Greece's past is now housed in Athens. But Greece's past does not belong to Athens so much as Athens belongs to it. Hyperbolic Washington is a metropolis of both monuments and museums, some of them devoted to American history, others not. Athens is a metropolis of memorials and museums, the overwhelming majority of which are historical. But it is itself the grandest memorial and museum of them all. It is not in the best array. It reveals little concern for systematic chronology. It reveals no lessons in evolution, in development, in progress. The past in Athens repeats itself, intersects itself, is entangled with itself. But this much is clear: the past in Athens is, literally and figuratively, a presence.

Between the alpha and the omega of the metropolis's avenues and streets, a vast temporal digest unfolds. In some instances, the past is mythical: with Leoforos Ermou (Hermes Avenue), one finds Apollonos (to Apollo) and Mouson (to the muses). But such allusions are rare. Athens reveals a consistent preference for the real. Navarino (for the great sea battle at which the Ottomans fell) runs through Kolonaki; so, too, Omirou (for Homer), and Dhimokritou (for Democritus), and Solonos (for Solon); so, too, Themistokleous (for Themistocles) and Kleomenous (for the Spartan general about whom Thucydides wrote). The metropolis still has its Iera Odhos, its Sacred Way. Its path, connecting the Keramikos district with Eleusis (now Elefsina), mimics the path of the ancient Sacred Way. But its mimicry largely stops there. Just west of the cemetery, it now allows access to the *gazi*, the "gasworks," a startlingly graceful wrought-iron relic of fin-de-siècle industrialism, presently languishing. Beyond the *gazi*, a less idle row of foundries and warehouses and garages stretches to the university's Botanical Gardens and Agricultural School. Beyond them, there are very few palpable mementos of what Hellenistic pilgrims must have seen, however distorted or faint they may be. Virtually all the shrines that the pilgrim Pausanias recorded in the second century A.D. are gone. Only remnants of the anciently celebrated olive groves survive. The river Kifissos now flows in an artificial canal. Salamis (now Salamina) has become a harbor for supertankers as well as other classes of both merchant and naval ships. An oil refinery operates on the Attic coast at Aspropirgos. Past the monastery at Daphni, Eleusis itself is in ruins. But not its memory.

Athens has an Odhos Rangavi, a Rangavis Street. It runs through the Averof district, which grew up hastily and dispassionately in the years after the Second World War and immediately ensuing Civil War. Averof the man was one of nineteenth-century Greece's great philanthropists. An old battleship bears his name. A statue of him stands in front of the stadium, the restoration of which he helped fund. Alexandhros Rangavis was a nineteenth-century lumiere. He is the author of a historiography and a topography of ancient Athens. His observations of the Othonic city have been published as a four-volume memoir. He is more particularly known as an essayist, a poet, and the founding editor of *Takhidhromos* ("Postman"), one of the period's most respected newspapers.[71] His contributors wrote in French, in German, and in katharevousa.

Rangavis Street leaves from the southeastern side of the Pedhion Areos, the site among other things of a military academy for whose construction Averof yet again paid, and runs unintriguingly for two kilometers or so. The culturally belated, the literary epigones of more glorious precursors, are not, it is true, always assigned to such marginal vectors of the urban grid. But counterexamples are nevertheless rare. Odhos Paraskhou (for the early nineteenth-century poet Akhilleus Papaskhos) is also in the Averof district. Soutsou (presumably for the poet Panayiotis Soutsos) takes up three short blocks in Kolonaki. Ghalanou Sofokleous, on the other hand, and Evripidhou are both near Omonia, and by no means obscure. Isiodhou (for Hesiod) is brief, but borders the palace built for Greece's monarchs a few years after Othon's quarters became home to the Parliament. There is a street in the Vathi district named after Victor Hugo, and one in the Plaka named after Lord Byron. There is a Miller Street in Keramikos. Could it be named after Henry Miller, who spent several years among a literary troupe that included the Nobel laureate George Seferis? I was never able to secure an altogether trustworthy answer. But it is noteworthy, even so, that there is no street memorializing Seferis himself; none, for that matter, remembering the poets Palamas, Sikelianos, or Cavafy.

How far can money buy what less material endowments cannot? Consider Leoforos Singhrou, which runs southwest from the Temple of the Olympian Zeus. Less avenue than highway, its several lanes can barely hold all the cars and buses going to or coming from the jumble of suburban *dhimi* now amassed down the Attic coast: Kallithea, Nea Smirni, Palio and Neo Faliro. Its route is a staccato of billboards and companies, with an occasional gaudy nightclub or gritty cookery fitted in here and there. Andreas Singros himself was originally from Chios. He brought with him an almost outlandish family fortune. Among Athens's nineteenth-century patrons and benefactors, he surpassed even Averof. With his aid the Evangelismos Hospital, still one of Athens's largest, acquired its finishing touches. The Dhimotiko Theatro (Municipal Theater) opened in 1888, was once known as the Theatro Tsinghrou [*sic*]. The Filakes Singhrou, a prison, opened some two years before, and an Erghostasio Aporon Yinekon (Workplace for Lost Women), another of Singros's projects, one year after that.

Much more readily than mere wealth, service merits toponymic appreciation. Leoforos Filellinon (Philhellenes Avenue) is with Leoforos Singhrou one among many examples. It recalls a more external generosity. Greeks under the Ottomans were not capable of freeing themselves on their own. Some families had grown wealthy during the subjection, but even among the willing, far too few to fund a countermovement for which plausible hopes of victory could be entertained. At the end of the eighteenth and early in the nineteenth centuries, internal resistance was largely the doing of *kleftes*, "thieves," literally, who had taken to the hills, survived on plunder, and were at first regarded by other Greeks with understandable distrust. They were heroized by nationalistic folklorists only after the actual war,[72] which was in fact won with substantial outside assistance. The logistical contributions of the Filiki Eteria, a covert "Friendly Society" organized by three Odessans but based in Constantinople, were in most historians' judgments paltry.[73] The society's propagandistic contributions were more fruitful. Not least, it succeeded in disseminating the somewhat wishful idea that Russia was an enthusiastic champion of the liberationist cause. It is the society after which one of Kolonaki's squares is named.

Greek freedom fighters also benefited from romantic Europe's fervent pursuit of a less feudal and more secular symbology of identity than it ever had or ever needed before. Orientalist flirtations were left behind; what has somewhat cynically been called "Hellenomania" flowered instead.[74] It had its focus, of course, primarily upon the Hellenes of the fifth and fourth centuries B.C. But a variety of philologists and aestheticians and anatomists labored sedulously to certify the raciocultural Hellenicity of the pagans' putative, Orthodox heirs. Its thrust, however, was by no means merely theoretical. With the goal of recovering the soils and relics of Civilization from its barbarian purloiners, the more doughty organized a secular crusade. Lord Byron was merely one of thousands of "philhellenes" who marched forth. He died—of illness, alas, not in battle—at Mesolonggi in the spring of 1824. Nor is Lord Byron the only foreign philhellene to have been accorded an Athenian street. The Frenchmen Didot and Chateaubriand, for example, have theirs; so, too, does the Italian Count Santarosa. Leoforos Filellinon itself runs roughly parallel to an avenue named for Othon's queen, Amalia. It covers a few blocks from Saint Paul's, the Anglican church, to Leoforos Othonos (Othon Avenue), at the southern border of Syntagma Square. It is infused with Syntagma's present concerns: travel, tourism, banking. Buses wait along it to transport ticketed passengers to Olympic Air flights leaving from the Ghlifadha terminal.

The abecedary ends with Odhos Oriyenous (Origen Street), which extends for no more than a quarter kilometer, sloping diagonally down the north face of Mount Likavittos. The theologian after whom it is named, a Gnostic and the first great advocate of the Christian embrace of pagan wisdom, was formally anathematized by Justinian's still unified church in A.D. 553.[75] Does he find his way into Athens's toponymy because his sins have been forgiven or forgotten? Or have they merely paled, and the brilliance of his philosophical and religious genius outshone them? Does Odhos Oriyenous run opposed to the supremacy of the Orthodox Word? In favor of the visionary over his detractors? Does it suggest, however obscurely, that a synthetic imagination is, in the end, everything?

Weights and Measures: The Greater Past over the Lesser

Athens's toponomy presents a tangle of pasts, but in the tangle three are most salient: the ancient, the Byzantine, and the national. Three pasts, three "Hellenic civilizations," as dictator Metaxas liked to call them: the Dark Ages that began with Constantinople's and ended with the Ottomans' fall grow darker every day. The ages of the Catalonian and Venetian occupations grow darker with them. Athens is not merely "for the record." Its various foreign curators, from von Klenze on, have evidently been no more obsessively antiquarian than the rest of its citizenry. Minute details are left for scholars and the writers of guidebooks to accumulate. What remains standing in the metropolis, what remains inscribed in its avenues and streets, is a more selective and more exemplary history. No "pure science" here: the prevailing mnemonics has a moral cast to it. In the Municipal Cemetery and elsewhere, remembrance is always honorific: forgetfulness sometimes charitable, often admonitory.

Secular patrons win civic immortality along with the sacred ones; Singros and Averof are as permanently dyed into the metropolis's toponymic fabric as Saint George, for example, or Saint Dionysios the Areopagite. Foreign patrons merit more occasional mention: Didot, Santarosa, Lord Byron, the army of "philhellenes." Founding fathers and the church fathers are recalled in equal numbers; Kolokotronis, a general in the independence movement, with Patriarch Ioakeim. A few other military men are honored: Kleomenes with Alexander the Great, who gives his name and title to a hasty thoroughfare that runs throughout Keramikos. Paleologhou, after one of the last Byzantine emperors, runs briefly through the Vathi district to the Peloponnesos train station. The Greek nation's kings and queens and princes and princesses are not neglected. On the contrary: many of them have far more prominence posthumously than they had while they were alive. A discomfiting assemblage, Greece's imported royals, many of whom made every effort to see that their names were imbedded into the metropolitan landscape long before their reigns were complete. Why should they be humored? Perhaps because of their charismatic blood, perhaps because they have provided the nation with an incorrigible link to a Golden Europe. At present, they are remembered for little else.[76] Othon retains his avenue in spite of his having been sent into exile. Olga, the wife of Yioryios I, retains hers in spite of her alleged treasons. Konstandinos I was one of the figureheads and certainly one of the agents as well of the Split between an "older" and a "newer" Greece. But now, the park dedicated to his archadversary, Venizelos, has its frontage along the avenue named for his wife, the queen Sophia.

Absurdist? It would be, were the history etched into Athens a history of actual persons and places and things. But the pasts of Athens's present are neither biographical nor *événementiels*. They are instead the pasts of *arkhes*: indeed of "principles," but also of "leaders," or "origins"; secular and sacred patrons, founding fathers and church fathers, generals and kings and republicans alike. Those who embody precedent share their pedestals with those who set it, no matter how incompatible the precedents might be. Partisans rise above their biases in retrospect when and only when they are the first to have them. Venizelos would have been far less likely to have a park of his own had he not introduced Smithean liberalism to Greece; the royals would not be so often recalled were there anyone else who could fulfill their linking function. Athens pays homage as well to the *arkhes* of spirit, to Greece's great civilizers: Homer, Hesiod, Sophocles, Socrates, Aristotle, even the minor poets Paraskhos and Soutsoss, even Rangavis. The belated must wait their turn. In the century to come, there will probably be some street named or renamed for Seferis. Papaskhos will not last forever. Seferis has won the Nobel Prize. He is virtually a culture hero. Athens must find room for him sooner or later.

Weights and Measures: Historical over Formal Organization

But an Avenue of Victor Hugo? Not *per impossibile*, of Henry Miller? Athens retains broad strokes of an arbitrariness that de Certeau's utopian and disciplinary city could not allow. Greece's capital has outstripped the monumental and geometric plans to which its Teutonic designers intended it to conform. It has left them behind. No one since has made any concerted effort, either, to impose upon Athens the even more "logical" and more purely recursive plans that designers would come, in the twentieth century, to impose upon metropolises expanding further west. Zoning is remarkably casual. Commercial and residential architecture intermingle; so, too, the workplace and the home.[77] The commercial triangle is well supplied with apartments. Industrial complexes, though more common on the city's outskirts, are often in the midst of or at least next door to apartment complexes. The central squares attract more businesses than residences. Around them, however, shops and offices often share their addresses with private flats—an arrangement that seems to perturb virtually no one.

But about what, beyond the prominence of the relatively abstract presence of history itself, are Athenians "clear"? Who, after all, knows of Origen? What Athenian knows, for that matter, the precise biography of Queen Sophia, or of Dionysios the Areopagite; of Herodes Atticus, or Themistocles, or Rangavis, or Singros? What Athenian knows that Alexandhros Soutsos and the poet Soutsos are different but related men? Or knows the references and connotations of the names of a hundred other streets that I could not even begin to explicate? Who has, or even cares to obtain the sort of

information about the Temple of the Olympian Zeus that the *Blue Guide*
provides for tourists?

> Scanty remains of a small early shrine have been discovered with vaults beneath
> having an exit through a subterranean passage to the Ilissos. This may account
> for the tradition that a temple was founded there by Deukalion over the chasm
> through which the waters receded after the flood. Pausanias relates that in
> commemoration of this event an annual sacrifice of flour mixed with honey was
> thrown into the cleft. Peisistratos seems to have been the first to undertake the
> construction of a temple on a grand scale, possibly, as Aristotle suggests ("Poli-
> tics"), to keep the people too busy to indulge in plots. Work ceased before the
> stylobate was complete when Hippias went into exile and much of the masonry
> was used in the Themistoclean wall. . . . In 197 B.C. Antiochus Epiphanes, king
> of Syria, resumed building to a new design by Cossutius, a Roman architect,
> who substituted the Corinthian for the Doric order. Work was again inter-
> rupted at the entablature stage and put back further in 86 B.C., when Sulla
> carried off some of the shafts and capitals to Rome for the Capitoline Temple.
> The honor of its completion was reserved for Hadrian who dedicated the tem-
> ple in his second visit to Athens, c. A.D. 130 and set up a chryselephantine
> statue of the god within the cella (a copy of that by Pheidias at Olympia), as
> well as a colossal statue of himself. Cyriacus of Ancona (c. 1450) noted 21
> standing columns with their architraves. In 1750 the Turkish governor con-
> verted one to lime for the construction of a new mosque; the great storm of 26
> October 1862 overthrew another.[78]

Some Athenians bother to rival the *Blue Guide*. Some—specialists, experts,
historical and cultural virtuosi—know and care to know considerably more
than others.

Metropolitan savoir faire does not, however, require either historical ex-
pertise or loric virtuosity. It does not even require the internalization of any
of the various weights and measures, any of the various *arkhes* inscribed
toponymically or architecturally into the Attic landscape. Real Athenians do
not have to be aware that Tsaldharis was the leader of a now defunct political party. They do not have to accept a contextualism that grants significative priority to the specificities of time over timeless space. They do not, in
the end, even have to accept the significative priority of history itself. Neither the toponymy nor the architecture of Athens imposes upon those who
reside in the face of it or within it a determinate lifeworld, a normative
"*congregatio corporum*" or "*universitas rerum*."[79] Neither imposes any precise understanding of the relations among self, and society, and this and
some other world. Athenians are free to come to their own understanding,
chacun à son goût.

But free, on the other hand, within limits. Athenians need not accept the
arkhi of history, but they must do more than merely make note of it. Sooner

or later, they must adapt to it. Sooner or later, they must adapt above all to the ponderous ubiquity of the past. Anyone who hopes not simply to reside but also to "dwell" in Athens, actually to "be" there, need not embrace the past. Anyone who hopes to dwell in Athens must nevertheless come to terms with it, must make something with and out of it: thus the normativity of the metaleptic act, or enterprise.

What, though, to make of it? That is indeed the question: for Athenians; for many other Greeks as well. It would be a simpler question were the past itself more uniform. Athens was in 1986 and 1987 no longer ethnically plural. It was no longer religiously plural. It was no longer as historically multiple as it once was. But it still preserved a variety of pasts, none of them with indisputable priority over any of the others. It was a "Hellenic" metropolis, yes, but with myriad qualifications. The preclassical, the classical, and the postclassical predominated. The ancient had a détente with the Euro-national. The Byzantine provided a secondary, the Cycladic, the vernacular, the folk provided tertiary syncopations. The spectrum was not exhaustive; it was not, to repeat, merely for the record. But it was still quite diverse: too diverse to meld into a single tonality, even at its farthest horizons. Were it a utopian and disciplinary city, synecdochic or metaphorical, Athens would perhaps have been more monotone. But it was not that sort of city. It still had its irreducibly separate wavelengths.

The preclassical, the classical, and the postclassical predominate. But that solves little: the problem of making something out of a multiplicity of pasts neither begins nor ends with a quantitative ranking of civilizations and styles. It does not even end with a qualitative ranking. Judging the Acropolis beatific or the French Revolution a milestone is not enough. The metaleptic task of making something out of a multiplicity of pasts also requires that the beatitude of the one or the world-historical import of the other be brought into some informative rapport with the present and with the future. That might be all. But Athenians do not live in isolation from one another, and the uses to which any one of them puts the past, whether to define the situation of the present or to provide direction for the future, inevitably impinge upon the uses to which others put it, upon the definitions at which others have arrived, and upon the directions that others would care to establish for themselves. The results have not always been as respectful of the priority of the past as either genuine antiquarians or introjective metalepticians might hope.

We have encountered many of those results already. We have encountered them in the melange of past and present, native and imported temporalities that come together in the current schedules of business and leisure. We have encountered them in the equally diverse melange of local and international manners that make up the savoir faire of the real Athenian. We have met one of their prototypes in the cultivated eclecticism of Phanariotic style, and some of their most coherent material expressions in the

Benakis Museum, and in the Metropolitan Cathedral. We have met the grandest, if not the tidiest, of such results in meeting the metropolis itself: an urban museum, but a projective museum that, from the Acropolis to Monastiraki, from Omonia to Syntagma Square, from the gasworks to the waterworks of Kolonaki, refuses to be determined by its multiple pasts precisely by accommodating them all. But let us conclude on a more intimate scale. Let us go to Odhos Khatzimikhali (Khatztimikhalis Street): it is in the Plaka, and like many others nearby, it winds narrowly and none too purposefully from one somewhat arbitrary crossing to another. It is relaxed, and rarely taken by cars. Among the more palatial of the buildings along it is the former villa of Angeliki Khatzimikhali, who undertook with an adventurousness common among the young upper-class women of her day to spend several years with the Sarakatsani, compiling as she did perhaps the most meticulous and painstaking report of the material culture of any Greek-speaking people ever produced. Among other things, she provided the ethnographic precedent for John Campbell's *Honour, Family, and Patronage.* Later in her life, she put together an illustrated and similarly thorough volume on regional costumes.

The Khatzimikhalis villa was designed shortly after the First World War by Aristotelis Zakhos, and is often considered the best of his "neo-Byzantine" creations still standing in Athens. It is a magnificent reconciliation of Romanesque curves and Cycladic planes (Plates 24–26). Like many other of the Plaka's grandest homes, it has been ceded to the state. It houses an Institute of Popular Arts. But Angeliki's daughter, Ersi, more than seventy years old, continued to occupy its basement during my stay in the field. She welcomed visitors from abroad. Her French and her English were both excellent. She spoke to me, during our single meeting, of plans for an American tour. The devaluation of the drachma had, however, forced her to postpone it. She was devoted to her mother's memory, and to many of her mother's interests. But she was not a researcher. She was a painter, and had in her older age become something of a Greek Grandma Moses. Her primitivist tableaux hung in her rooms side by side with works that she had collected or been given: some impressionist; others abstract. Her floors were covered with ornate Turkish carpets. Her furniture was solid, wooden, "Greek provincial." Her parlor was a barely navigable curiosity shop, full of marble chess sets and statuettes, brass cauldrons and salvers, books and journals, glass vases and ceramic plates and bowls, willow baskets and amber beads. She kept a television sputtering in the background. She had a huge writing desk in the midst of everything. In a January 1986 issue of *Andi,* "Contra," a respected leftist journal, she published a eulogy for her late brother, Nikos. He had been imprisoned during the junta. Ersi wrote that he was a "fighter," and that he had been *aghnos,* "pure" or "chaste." He was a well-known architect. Ersi wrote that "he made no money, did not want to make money. His work was his being. He could not betray his being."[80]

PLATE 24. Romanesque, Anatolian, Cycladic: the Khatzimikhalis estate.

Nothing nouveau riche about the Khatzimikhalis family. Ersi's own demeanor, her own interiority hearkened back like the rooms in which she lived to the busy, somewhat rustic, remarkably tolerant and collectivist gentility of a patronal past in which the Hellenic and the Romaic had not yet drifted apart, and were consequently not in need of being drawn together again. But let it be noted: the effect was very much of her own devising.

Ersi was not the only descendant of Greek gentility whom I would find to

PLATE 25. Neo-Byzantine details: the Khatzimikhalis estate.

have leftist sympathies. Several other of the members of my Athenian circle, of similar descent, shared them. No surprise, really: they have all been somewhat declassed, and the declassed typically sympathize with the dominated. Just as importantly, though, their sociopolitical heritage is of a hierarchical, and so of an inherently collectivist cast. With democratization, that heritage has been transmuted more coherently into socialist than into liberal bourgeois partisanship even when the resulting political consciousness is, by the strictest of Marxist standards, plainly false.[81] But Ersi's leftism was, like the

PLATE 26. Intimate synthesis: the Khatzimikhalis estate.

leftism of many of the members of my circle, also a projective and metaleptic metatrope. The trope off of which it played was that metaphorical
Hellenicity given substance and currency by the more nostalgic sectors of
the petty and the most industrialist sectors of Greece's *grande bourgeoisie*.
Ersi's interior spaces played off the same Hellenicity, in favor of a present at
once satirical of the nostalgist and touched by the nostalgist's specters. We
shall meet many more of her comrades—not always political as much as
poetic comrades—in what follows.

PART II

ANOTHER MODERNITY

3

CROSSING THE THRESHOLD: NOTES ON
CONFLICT AT A CERTAIN GREEK AIRPORT

ICHEL BUTOR, searching after the Second World War for the
genius of the Mediterranean imagination, found himself quite
disappointed with ununiform Athens: "At the beginning of the
nineteenth century, there was nothing at the base of the most famous
acropolis of all but an infinitesimal village, and the capital that has grown up
around it, although it certainly lies on the same ground as the ancient city,
is in no sense an extension of it, but something completely different, a
modern Mediterranean city which has no more relation to it than the Alexandria of today has to that of the Ptolemies."[1] Butor has not been alone in
judging the Greek capital modern, and modern at the expense of its past.
The mainstream of social scientific opinion has, however, been contrary.
Natives agree with foreign scholars: politically and economically, Greece is
a "premodern" country; Athens itself, if not secure in the habits of its past,
is not entirely free of them either. The consensus has a relatively exact theoretical basis. Keith Legg: "political motives rather than social and economic
change were responsible for the initial mobilisation"[2] of the Greek citizenry
as a citizenry. Political motives have, with few exceptions, continued to
dominate both social and economic changes ever since—throughout the
country, a fortiori in Athens. The pattern is the precise reverse of the pattern that Parsons claims essential to the development of any "modern industrial system."[3]

The story might end there, and Athens's many "oddities" simply left in
the same peripheries and margins to which they have already been assigned.
But a term is missing: rather than "culture," call it "meaning" or "signification." Parsons is willing to grant the "significative domain" at least a limited
independence from the politicoeconomic, but in *Structure and Process*
treats only its contribution to the integration of modernized political and
economic systems.[4] Anthropologists from Geertz[5] forward have by and large
been more far-reaching. But very few have abandoned Parsons's presumption that "significative modernization" and politicoeconomic modernization should ultimately be reconciled, one with the other. Very few have
abandoned Parsons's essentially Weberian presumption that significative and politicoeconomic modernization move, in the long run at least, in
the same directions: on the one hand, toward formal rationality; on the

other, against substantive particularism toward an ever more refined moral universalism.

On the one hand, Athens is not significatively devoid of all formal rationality. On the other hand, it is not a utopian and disciplinary city either. On the one hand, Athenian savoir faire is "largely disburdened of all religious and metaphysical mortgages."[6] The pasts that provide it with its stylistic underpinnings and its citizens with their existential raw materials are multiple. On the other hand, they are limited; Athens is not a comprehensive Museum of Man, "uniting all differences" within its boundaries.[7] It is neither an ancient city nor even a very traditional one. But is it yet modern? If not all Greeks, might Athenians be modern? If not all of them, at least some? "Significatively," if not in altogether every respect?

These questions come easily to self-secure occidentals, who do not really have to worry about their outcome. But ask them, as a self-secure "occidental," to a Greek. Ask them at least, as I did, to a sampling of highly educated and thoroughly urban Greeks. They can be doubly awkward. One must first of all search for the proper term. There are several candidates, none of them entirely suitable. A *neoteros anthropos* is, in demotic, roughly a "modern person." But *neoteros*, which often translates as "recent," is simply the comparative of *neos*, "young" or "new" or, by an intriguing connotative extension, "violent" or "strange." *Neoterikos* is closely cognate. The nominal neuter plural *neoterika* appears now and again on shop signs. It denotes the latest designs in furniture and appliances, synthetic fabrics, plastic tumblers and vinyl shoes. One sometimes see advertisements announcing *iper-neoterika*, "hyper-" or "ultramodern" items, for sale. Goods advertised as *iper-neoterika* are, however, often only *neoteristika*, "trendy," even "cheap," even "pseudomodern." The verb *neoterizo* suggests discovery, pathbreaking, social and political progressivism. The noun *neoterismos* suggests a striving for reform, or for originality, or even revolution. In the plural, *neoterismi*, it also appears on signboards, typically referring to "gadgets" or "novelties." *Neoterikotita*, morphemically "modernity" but sometimes only signifying "modernism," is an exceptionally recent coinage, first formally introduced into public print only a few years ago.[8] It is by no means current, nor as yet even easily cognized, by nonspecialists, or for that matter by specialists either. Most sociologists in Greece have contrasted and continue to contrast *paradhosi*, "tradition," with *ekmodernismos*, a hybrid devised of a demotic prefix and suffix and an imported romance root and glossing none too clearly into English as either "modernization" or the horrific "modernizationalism." *To moderno*, "the modern," is again linguistically exotic, though heard, and seen in print, frequently enough. From it, *modernikotita*, "modernity," rarer but still understandable, derives. Both terms circulate primarily, however, in the phraseological fields of the fine and plastic arts; neither as yet circulates neutrally outside of them.

That there is no demotic term at once general and current enough to gloss, without significant roughness, as "modernity" does not, however, imply at all that Greeks, particularly educated and urban Greeks, are any more confused about or ignorant of what modernity is than educated and urban speakers of English. Demotic terms, however partially suitable each separately may be, nevertheless govern jointly more or less the same denotative and connotative universe as the English catchall does itself. In both demotic and English the sterotypy is approximately the same. In both, the modern is about the rule of the new, the original, about change and progress, about fashion, technology, functionality, and so on. In both languages, scientists and critics have further elaborations and interpretations to offer. Greek scientists and critics in any case rarely hesitate to resort to some other language besides demotic when they feel they have cause. Most are fluent in English or French—in one or the other of which I had many of my most "serious" conversations with my Athenian circle—or if not those, then in German or Italian.

Translation is always awkward; but troubles that arise when translating queries about Athenian or Greek modernity from some other living language into demotic can be overcome. Troubles that follow upon their translation can be less tractable. To what extent is Athens modern? To what extent are Greeks? Is it not worth pursuing what natives themselves might have to say, what their conclusions might be? Is it not at least ethnographically standard? Of course it is. But natives have reason enough to suspect ethnographers of bad intentions, and reason enough to suspect investigators of modernity of the worst. Occidentals can be confident enough of their modernity to be critical of it. People long accustomed to having themselves placed at the margins of the Occident, so long accustomed that they often place themselves there, are less likely to be familiar with modernity's critics than with its "progressive" and "enlightened" missionaries. They are, at least, less likely to be able clearly to discern them from their opposites: from a distance, especially from an enforced distance, missionary and critical voices meld into a more harmonic chorus, their counterpoints into a prevailingly positive refrain.

To what extent is Athens modern? To what extent are Greeks? These queries need not be, but they often sound rhetorical. Why ask them, if not to add to the various dichotomies with which Greeks already labor—East versus West, Romaic versus Hellenic, Inner versus Outer, Early versus Late—an even more exasperating one: between "tradition," whatever that might be, and modernity itself? Why ask them, if one doesn't already know the answers to them, and know the answers to be negative? Why ask them at all, if not to suggest underhandedly that Greeks are not quite modern enough? Why ask them at all, if not to challenge through the back door the validity of the Greek present?

Uncertain Replies: If You Can't Beat Them, Join Them

Why indeed? Relatively few of Greece's external and occidental observers actually do bother to ask. Most make up their minds at first glance, and most are willing to declare their determinations quite openly. Determinations vary. Political scientists, however, generally agree with ambassadors and business people and other lay experts that neither Greece nor Greeks are "quite modern."[9] Some, but not all see the opinion as an indictment. Perhaps it is not. Still, there is very little rhetorical difference between being "not quite modern" and being "not quite modern enough"; little rhetorical difference between that and being just plain "backward." It is hardly surprising that many Greeks should react defensively even to the barest suggestion that they might be "backward." It is, however, more surprising that so many should so deeply suspect that they really are "backward."

But many do, some of the most prominent of contemporary academics and intellectuals among them. Many in fact devote their entire careers to making their suspicions more rigorous and to putting them into print. The most vituperative and most elaborate indictments of the validity of the Greek present came, until the end of the last century, largely from without; but they have come, since then, at least as often from within. They have in fact come, of late, to be something of a scholarly obsession. Or at least to seem like one: very soon after my arrival in Athens I was introduced to a professor at the university who announced to me that "everything written in Greece in the past fifty years" had been written "about modernity." When I asked for clarification, he retreated from the hyperbole. "A great deal of important scholarship," he said, had been focused on untangling "the failure of the Greek Enlightenment." True enough: one need only survey the titles in any of the metropolis's serious bookstores.

The junta was a special inspiration. Konstandinos Tsoukalas wrote his *Greek Tragedy: From the Liberation to the Colonels* in exile, and originally published it in English. Since the junta's fall, it has found its way back into Greek. A plethora of other monographs, similar in tone and in theme, have joined it. Many of them address the "flaws" of a political system that could never rise above clientelism far enough to nurture true and stable parties.[10] Many more address the flaws of an educational apparatus designed less to produce an informed citizenry than an elitist and cybernetically removed cadre of legislative and administrative "masters."[11] Critical histories of state building share center stage with critical histories of the invention, adoption, and entrenchment of katharevousa. Some are explicitly leftist. Virtually all are explicitly censorious and exhortatory. Virtually all remain topical: an indication that the intelligentsia not only sees the past in the present but also fears its repetition in the future; an indication that the junta itself lingers as a specter not only of ruthlessness but of some social darkness out of which Greece has yet securely to emerge.

Perhaps these new, scientific tragedies are heuristic. Perhaps they even effect a salutary catharsis. But they are poor therapy for any Greek complex of "inferiority" or "fallenness" or degradation.[12] At best, they are enactments of it. At worst, they are merely the latest in a long, long line of irritations.

Uncertain Replies: If You Can't Beat Them, Avoid Them

Not all Greeks are quite so bleak about their past, and not all quite so concerned that they might fail to be "modern enough." Not all even of the intelligentsia are tragedians. Some are pastoralists, who care less about Greece's modernity than about its still living "traditionals." They have two or three favorite "tribes." The smallholders and fishermen of Mytilene are popular for their dialect. They supposedly retain usages phonetically and morphemically closer to ancient Attic than any of the rest of their compatriots. The Cretan shepherds are popular for their alleged ethnic purity. They are, as Michael Herzfeld notes,[13] important figures in the "self-image that Greeks," some Greeks at least, "present to the outside world." The transhumant Sarakatsani are popular less for their ethnic purity than for their alleged Mediterranean primitivity. Greece may or may not be modern; but the Sarakatsani are for many pastoralist hermeneuts less modern than even the most traditional of Greeks. They are, for some, so unmodern that they are other than Greek.[14]

Pastoralism is not yet particularism, but Greece has its share of particularists, academic and journalistic, as well. They introduce into the contemporary discourses of self-imagination not further reflections on Greece's potential or actual modernity but doubts about the cogency of the idea of modernity itself. They can be remarkably insightful—but not always. I cite a single example:

> The polar clash between "modernization" [eksingkhronismo] and "tradition" [paradhosi], if not missing entirely, takes entirely different forms in western European societies [than in Greece]. If the juxtaposition of new and old created in many circumstances extremely bitter political and cultural disputes, the problem never assumed the catholic character that we encounter in Greece. In the majority of European societies, the new sprouts over the old, and modernization respects traditions and lays over them the bases of its perpetual evolutionary course. Tradition is understood as the substratum, and modernization as the process of its alteration and rationalization. In Greece, in contrast, the very meaning of tradition is problematic.[15]

The closing assertion could hardly be more correct; in Greece, the meaning of tradition is, as we shall soon see, indeed problematic. But the rest could hardly be more incorrect; and asserted by a scholar otherwise of such acuity, it can only be regarded as defensive. In Greece, "modernization" and "tradition" do not always clash. Sometimes, they do: but in no more bitter and in no more catholic a fashion than in "western Europe" or, for that matter, anywhere else.

For all its errors, the argument nevertheless has a strategy. The strategy is common, and it is even effective, as far as it goes. Rhetorically, it is counter-metonymic: it represents a Greece that one might think comparable with the rest, or the more west, of Europe as instead a place apart, unique in itself.[16] Let it be granted: Greece is, in some respects, a place apart, unique in itself. But it is not, after all, unique in every respect, and certainly not so unique that it is simply what it is, and not like anything else. "Formalism," blithe and empty abstractness, may or may not be a bad Greek habit.[17] But an uncompromising particularism, even when deployed against scientistic reductions, is simply formalism's other side.[18] Both are strategic. Both have their effectiveness. But both often end up being nothing more than merely diversionary.

The most vituperative and elaborate indictments of the Greek present came, in the preceding century, from without. Perhaps in an effort to atone for them, contemporary Greece's most sympathetic external observers, its various ethnographers, have become the most uncompromising particularists of all. A few pastoralists remain among them. But most have abandoned pastoralism for the pursuit of nonconformity. Most find it: the evolution of the Greek family, of the Greek village, of Greek towns and metropolises, of Greek life itself does not always flow neatly within Marxian, or Durkheimian, or Weberian channels. The upshot: that Greece is, as no doubt it is, not simply a deviation, but a disproof of the notion that the channels of sociocultural evolution necessarily lead in any overriding direction at all. The Greek case shows us that urbanization is as consistent with familial extension as with nucleation;[19] that the normative universe of the village can sometimes at least be reinforced rather than disrupted by industrialization;[20] that personalism perdures in the face of and even against economic and political rationalization;[21] and so on.

Not all, but most of the ethnographers of the rest of Circum-Mediterranean Europe have gradually become just as sympathetic, and just as uncompromising particularists themselves. Theoretical functionalists arrived first. They discovered what, in retrospect, anyone could have predicted: a region of "imperfect" bureaucracies, "transitional" modes of governance, less than consummately "rational" domestic spheres and economics.[22] Schneider, Schneider, and Hansen's essay on "development" and "modernization"[23] inaugurates a certain withdrawal. Not yet antifunctionalist, it is considerably more hesitant in its conclusions than even a subtle functionalism would seem to demand. An ethnology of qualifications and counterexamples has supplanted it. Most ethnographers now confine themselves to noting the

Circum-Mediterranean's theoretical intransigence. So, for example, Kenny and Kertzer summarize the "most palpable contribution" of the essays collected in their 1983 *Urban Life in Mediterranean Europe*: "the empirical questioning of widely held assumptions about the traditional-modern, rural-urban polarity."[24]

In the thirty years since the publication of Campbell's *Honour, Family, and Patronage*, even in the ten years since the publication of Kenny and Kertzer's *Urban Life*, the ethnology of Circum-Mediterranean modernity has in some respects remained quite constant. It has remained an ethnology of the inchoate and the exceptional, of the "not quite" and the "other than." Its practitioners have largely confined themselves to registering "deviations." Not all have found cause to doubt the analytical utility of the developmental typologies that social theory has bequeathed to them. Skepticism, the "empirical questioning of widely held assumptions" about the content and form of the traditional and the modern, nevertheless now prevails. It may be laudable. But it accomplishes little in itself. If not merely a prelude to some concerted effort at reconceptualization, it runs the risk of degenerating into the very intellectual quietude that it is supposed to subvert.

Aerodhromio

It may well be that, sociologically at least, Circum-Mediterranean ethnology can do little more than end with skepticism; the structural and functional categories and concepts it has to use may simply be too shortsighted to allow of technical readjustment. Culturologically, however, it can do better. Or so I think: and to venture upon something of a demonstration, I return to Greece, and take up a rather singular incident: stumbled upon, not entirely explicable, rather ludicrous in its uncertain end, exemplary even so. It occurred, for no particularly special reason, on the evening of 19 June 1987. I was dining with a small group of guests at the home of a quite prominent social and political activist. Sometime after 10:00 P.M., my host received a telephone call from a journalistic colleague, informing him that Aerodhromio, a well-known discotheque located in Ghlifadha, about eight kilometers from central Athens and directly across from the eastern runways of the Ellinikon Airport, was the site of what in demotic would be called a *fasaria*: an imbroglio, a disturbance, a to-do. Guests and host agreed collectively that the affair was worth investigating.

Aerodhromio had apparently received a number of complaints that it had done little to answer. Ostensibly, its offenses lay in the volume of the music that it offered and in the volume of automobiles that it attracted. Like other voguish clubs, Aerodhromio did not open its doors before 10:00 P.M. and usually did not close them before 3:00 A.M. Ostensibly, neighbors were perturbed by the discotheque's constant disturbance of their nightly peace.

The club's owners were perhaps justified, if somewhat too literal, in dismissing the charges against them as they stood. Their business was in the immediate vicinity only of industrial warehouses, most of them windowless, all of them dark. It was served by a remarkably ample and virtually deserted avenue of approach. Shortly after the driver of the taxi in which I was a passenger turned onto it, however, he encountered a makeshift roadblock. I was consequently forced to walk. At first, the only distinct sound that I could hear was the periodic roar and rush of jet engines. If Aerodhromio's noise was under fire, the loudest noise it made was evidently symbolic.

Nearing the place, I did indeed begin to pick up brief fragments of music, but not the sort of music that I had been led to expect. In the near absence of a native "cutting edge," and no doubt in the interest of worldliness as well, Athenian discotheques collect their repertoires from abroad: particularly from America, but also from Great Britain, and now and again from France and Spain. What was being broadcast, however, was in Greek. The melodies and the instruments were vividly local, and unmistakably "traditional": the melodies and rhythms of country weddings and provincial Easter afternoons. One of my companions, whose fondness for folksongs was minimal at best, voiced consternation over the abandonment of a more usual program. But the discotheque, as it turned out, had retained its usual program. The music to which we had all initially been listening was being amplified over the speakers of several sleek, white vehicles, all stationed directly opposite Aerodhromio's frontage, each one facing, in a gesture of auditory defiance, the broad and lighted expanse of an outdoor dance floor and courtyard, furnished with two bars and a sparse scattering of tables and chairs. The courtyard was quite crowded with patrons, most of them carefully attired, most of them in apparent good humor, most of them affecting nothing more than enjoyment of the balmy atmosphere. Hurrying, quite uncomfortably, through a dense but rather desultory troop of police, I had time to read only one of several banners that were being displayed by the demonstrators. *Theloume Skholia, Okhi Dhiafthoria*, it said: "We Want Schools, Not Houses of Corruption."

The club, the exterior perimeter of which I entered through a low gate, was known to refuse, or at least to delay, admission. "But foreigners," I was told, "were always let in." So I was, without any request of identification. Beyond its courtyard, Aerodhromio's interior spaces, blocked out within the copious hollows of what had once served as a hangar, perhaps for two or three small planes, could not have been more fastidiously minimalist: a spare, stainless steel counter was fastened along the length of one wall; a pair of tortuous mechanical chairs, dentist's chairs, perhaps, stripped of their padding, sat atop low pedestals in an open area; the lighting was an understated mosaic of blue and red and green. Athens's discotheques tend not to charge a cover fee. They instead charge inflated prices for drinks, imbibing in one or two of which is mandatory. Imbibing at Aerodhromio was not mandatory, but the price for doing so very high: not less than 850 drachmas (about six dollars) apiece, steep even when compared with the prices charged at the two most popular discotheques in Kolonaki. Those drinking, a mixture of a few socialites, a few bohemian intellectuals, and a great many young urban professionals, tended in their stylistic diversity toward the "exoticism," the cosmopolitan deviations, of such notorious vacation spots as Mykonos and Corfu. Foreigners were of course also abundant. American soul was less popular with those who danced than more classic rock-and-roll.

Between the club and the demonstration, a variety of oppositions, aural and visual among others, were thus patently being enacted. That their fulcrum was not "civil peace," at least in the strict sense of the term, was evident enough. That their fulcrum was not political, again in the strict sense of the term, was perhaps less evident. Rumor had it that the protestors were Communist. Ghlifadha's mayor, who had reputedly encouraged and lent his aid to the protest, was Communist. One at least of the banners carried to the event in fact bore the initials KKE—for Kommounistiko Komma Elladhas (Communist Party of Greece). Rumor had it that the demonstration was at least conceived by the Communists; granted, others were involved in it as well. At the very least, however, the conflict could not have been entirely or even importantly "interparty." On the one hand, whatever the affiliation of Aerodhromio's owners—an undoubtedly signal consideration, but one that I was unable to explore—the affiliations of its patrons were by no means exclusively rightist; party commitments being, in Greece, as extraordinarily diverse as they are, there was no particularly plausible ground upon which to presume that the affiliations of its patrons were even predominantly to the right. On the other hand, the "communism" of the demonstration functioned at best as a catchall. Greece had, from 1968 and until 1987, two Communist parties: the *exoteriko* ("exteriorist"); and the *esoteriko* ("interiorist"). The platforms of the two had consistently and considerably diverged. The platform of the former had unflinchingly been pro-Soviet; of the latter, more lenient, and more allied with French and Italian than with Slavic principles and practices. The *exoteriko* faction had a largely blue-collar base; the *esoteriko* faction, which I strongly suspect to have been well represented inside Aerodhromio, appealed rather to the intelligentsia, to certain of the liberal professional sphere, and to various white-collar servants, both in the public and the private sector.[25] In 1987, it joined forces with several other minor parties to form a coalition known as the Nea Aristera—a "New" and by no means exclusively Communist "Left." The demonstration, whatever its party line, was tangibly recruited from strata well above the urban proletariat. Ghlifadha, after all, was altogether different from a proletarian suburb.

Still, the demonstration was unmistakably political in tone, even if what

it stood for was not. "We Want Schools": the discotheque evidently could
not but be taken as an icon of consumptive and fiscal priorities at odds with
the development of a viable, local socioeconomic infrastructure. Frivolous
spending in Greece as elsewhere runs counter to the logic of both invest-
ment and capital financing. Frivolous spending on imported luxuries—
consider the provenance of Aerodhromio's music—in Greece as in other
countries suffering from a chronic imbalance of payments diminishes the
possibilities and the standards of daily living. "Austerity" is, in Greece, accordingly a political byword. Its use is not specific to any party. Economic
and above all consumptuary isolation tends to be, however, a rather more
characteristically leftist exhortation. During my tenure in the field, the tenure as well of a socialist administration both metropolitan and national,
public buses typically had bumper stickers exclaiming that *ta lastika [tous
itan] ellinika!*: "[their] tires [were] Greek!" Rightists would not always care.

"Not Houses of Corruption": what the Greeks call *xenolatria*, "worship of
the foreign," or *xenomania*, "madness for the foreign," spreads well beyond
such posh and stereotypically "fashion-conscious" neighborhoods as Kolonaki. Contrary to native judgment, it is, if generally middling, not restricted
to the petty bourgeoisie. It is instead characteristic of members of the middle classes of whatever segment whose capital, material or symbolic, is
largely and immediately derived from external productive enterprises, material or symbolic. It is above all characteristic of the *nouveaux-venus*, whether
they belong to the world of commerce, or of management, or of the mind.
It is, however, common as well among subsectors of the petty bourgeoisie,
or of petty bourgeois kindreds, that have fortunes immediately reliant on
external subsidies. Its localist alternatives, on the other hand, have their
most fervent advocates among those whose fortunes are either derived from
or are more or less immediately reliant on locally generated income. But not
even economic biography, much less economic category, appears in Greece
or elsewhere to predict political or "ideological" bent; much less, even in
"the ultimate analysis," does it predict tastes.

Norbert Elias identifies various vertical processes that, beyond or in concert with economic placement, appear also to determine something at least
of both the content and the structuration of tastes: for example, "the development of courtly customs, their dissemination downward, their slight social deformation, [and] their devaluation as marks of distinction."[26] There is
no question that various analogous processes mark the specific Greek history of occidentalizing politics and sentiments; no question that they also
mark the history of their orientalizing and localizing counterpolitics. So,
too, do other processes, "vertical" in their way but not those upon which
Elias concentrates: in particular, imperialist interventions, in peacetime and
in war. Imperialism is in fact of especial consequence. It decisively affects
the content, but also the ordering of the universe of contemporary Greek

sympathies and antipathies. It decisively affects the ordering of personal, but above all of sectoral intentions and acts.

The antagonists at Aerodhromio brought their vertically determined tastes with them but gave them a horizontal twist. Greece's most distinguished sociocultural strata tend to judge all extremisms, xenolatric or localist, equally "vulgar." They consequently tend to shun them. Its middling sociocultural strata frequently embrace them: sometimes in battles with their "betters"; most often in battles among themselves. Greece's most distinguished strata no longer have much use for extremes. But that is no surprise: extremism is not "useful." It inspires too many enemies. It consequently is not an especially effective strategy, either for securing stable control or for securing stable profits. Among Greece's middling strata as among other relatively dominated strata, it is more than anything else a reaction to some threat, perceived or real. But to what threat? Not primarily the threat of losing out to "betters" to whom one has already lost. Not primarily the threat of being usurped by "inferiors," either, who have yet to establish themselves. The various fragments and fractions of Greece's middling strata most directly threaten one another. Among them, fortunes are most in flux.

Extremism is always more, or other, than merely pragmatic. But so are middling fortunes themselves. Not just material, they are sentimental as well. At Aerodhromio and elsewhere, middling antagonisms thus express themselves at once in a pragmatic and in a sentimental discord. Vehement nostalgias set themselves up against vehement rejections of nostalgia. Champions of a past-looking and traditionalist authenticity set themselves up against the champions of a future-looking and situational authenticity. Advocates of gemeinschaft set themselves up against the advocates of gesellschaft. Proponents of exclusion set themselves up against equally intolerant proponents of permissiveness and inclusion. The theses and antitheses encompass more than mere resources. They encompass agency and place. They encompass all the domains of existence. They encompass even the definition of the right to be. They tend not toward accord but tend rather to grow further and further apart. Bateson has a name for the syndrome: "symmetrical schizmogenesis." He has a prognosis of its potential: "if not restricted, [symmetrical schizmogenesis] can only lead to more and more extreme rivalry and the breakdown of the whole [interactive] system."[27]

"Not Houses of Corruption": *dhiafthoria* are, in demotic, euphemistic brothels, the dens of prostitutes. The patrons of Aerodhromio no doubt read the metaphor as one more instance of "conservative" or perhaps "reactionary" moralism—the sort of moralism to which both the extreme right and the extreme left, both of them in Greece numerically too limited to exert, in real terms, much more than the voice of principle, are particularly prone. In some measure, the reading was correct. It is likely, however, that the metaphor was intended less to condemn the patrons' rumored behavior—one can after all get away with a great deal in Greece so long as one is more or less scrupulously discreet—than the putative "spirit" of that behavior. Or rather, lack of spirit: the xenolatric is above all suspect for its superficiality. It is suspect for not flowing from anything, indeed anything at all, "within." It is suspect, with all its allegedly thoughtless mimicry, as a sort of consummate selling out. The "Occident" perhaps has the role, in such a moral tropology, less of a Mammon—very few in Greece are against the accumulation of material things per se—than of Faust's Mephistopheles. Or perhaps it has the role of both. In any case, the trope of prostitution does less material than ideal service: the seller of the body is more essentially a seller of his or her soul. Nor, of course, is the panderer's love real; nor are his promises anything more than promises.

"Not Houses of Corruption": *aerodhromio* is demotic for "airport." Its personification of transiency, of the antilocal, could as a consequence hardly have been more loud. If the demonstrators' charge was, in a more existential vocabulary, a charge of both the establishment's and its patrons' "inauthenticity," it was a charge grounded in and given substance through an adamantly localist construal of authenticity itself. The critique was not antitechnological; the sophistication of the demonstrators' own transportation made that clear enough. It was rather what, in America at least, would have to be construed as at once economically and culturally "minoritarian": a critique not simply of the forgetting but also of the betraying of rootedness and of roots. It was what, in Greece, might alternatively be construed as a critique of doing at home what one would only do "in Rome"; of preferring to be a tourist on one's own native and natal soil. In theory, the critique left itself open to a variety of responses and rebuttals. In theory, a Sartrean decisionism was available: a declaration of one sort or another of the self's radical ontological liberty. In theory, the way of the distinguished was also available—the symbolic or practical declaration of the imperative of substantive eclecticism over the imperative of substantive purism. In practice, neither carried the day (or night, as it happened to be).

The air inside the discotheque grew increasingly humid, and the courtyard outside increasingly inviting, as the night passed. As a result, the protest gradually came to face an impressive audience, the members of which remained, however, initially more attentive to one another than to anyone else. That posture of indifference nevertheless finally dissolved. It gave way to a gesture the meaning or meaningfulness of which was not entirely self-evident: a few trendsetters began acknowledging the pieces blared at them from across the way with outbursts of condescending applause. Their act was pregnant, and bore suddenly a more communal offspring: at the commencement of a lively and pointedly "laic" bouzouki instrumental, a large company formed a circle and set off on what to my admittedly untrained eye looked to be an entirely proper performance of the same choreography that I had witnessed at a Delphic festival earlier in the year. With its conclusion the bulk of the discotheque's patrons erupted into enthusiastic cheers, then into a chant, which turned, in a few moments, away from the dancers and toward the protesters. As it did, its tenor modulated as well: from an appreciative Bravo, Bravo, to a far more pungent *Dhiaolo, Dhiaolo* ("the Devil, the Devil; To Hell, To Hell"). It is difficult to say whether the protesters lost heart in the face of the taunt, or whether they were proceeding in accord with a schedule of their own devising. They did not linger. Instead, they simply silenced their equipment, collected their banners, and drove away. Some fifteen minutes later, at about 3:00 A.M., Aerodhromio terminated its own operations for another night. It would reopen on the next. The demonstration would, so I heard, be there again as well. In any event, very little had been resolved. Whatever else it had been, the evening's last dance had failed to be either an assertion of autonomy or an execution of synthesis. The silence with which both the demonstration and Aerodhromio's patrons disbanded was, as the dance had also been, merely anticlimactic: the mere reasseveration of an already unsubtly imposed impasse, a more quiet repetition of an already vocal and visual enough *Dhiaolo*—"The Devil," "Go to Hell," *tu quoque.*

Meaning and Modernity

A modern incident? Most everyone, native and foreign alike, presumes that the answer to such a query can come only by determining first and foremost the extent to which the incident was similar to one that might happen in the "Occident," and the extent to which the Greeks who were involved in it might themselves be like the French or the Americans, or perhaps the West Germans or the northern Italians or the Dutch or even the Swedes. The presumption is understandable, and even somewhat accurate; whatever social theory has tried to make of it, the concept of modernity is neither essentially general nor essentially generalizable. It is an essentially imbedded concept, and some piece of the "Occident" its substantive cement. To be sure, the "Occident" is a rather vague and ad hoc entity itself. But a priori, some piece of it at least has to be modern. One can always quibble about just what piece that might be: France rather than America, West Germany rather than northern Italy. Semantics alone cannot prevent infighting.

Semantics alone cannot prevent anyone from construing some piece of the Occident as "consummately modern," the imago in whose perfectly mature light the modernity of everywhere and everyone else must be judged. Semantics alone cannot, on the other hand, compel anyone to be a perfectionist. Social theory may be teleological; but modernity itself need not have any singular end. It need not have any end at all. Logically at least, it might not be one but instead concretely many things.

Not just possibly but in fact, that is precisely what it seems to be: variable in content, perhaps polythetic in form as well. But what, then, do all its various modalities have in common? What is it that makes them all "modern"? Not just diffusion, though it does play some part. One can always resort to a more structural checklist of "features." But not even featural checklists can, as Bendix[28] points out, "easily avoid . . . [implying] that change once initiated must run its course along the lines indicated by [some] 'Western model,' and that in the transition to modernity all aspects of the social structure change in some more or less integrated and simultaneous fashion." They do not often make sufficient room for the vagaries of "sequence and timing."[29] They do not often make sufficient room for themselves. They should: the definition, the conceptualization of what modernity is and of what it is to be modern is itself a social and cultural phenomenon, one aspect of modernization among many others.[30] Not just that: it is in part responsible for both the direction and the substance of modernization. It is in part responsible for the plurality of modernization's outcomes: as conceptualizations of modernity differ—and they do differ, and differ dramatically, not only in "the Occident" but elsewhere—so modernity itself differs as well.

Only Weber offers an analytical approach capable of coping with the resemblances among many distinct modernities. One can, at least, extract something like that approach from his thought, which itself often tends toward a sort of despairing "perfectionism" and which too often relies on a quite specific "Western model." One can extract two theses: not testable hypotheses, perhaps, but the provisional axioms from which a somewhat less presumptuous and somewhat more comprehensive anthropology might profitably proceed. The first: whatever else they may be, modernities in all their variety are responses to the same existential problematic. The second: whatever else they may be, modernities in all their variety are precisely those responses that leave the problematic in question intact, that formulate visions of life and practice neither beyond nor in denial of it but rather within it, even in deference to it. Other responses are possible: "traditionalizing" and "countermodern" responses among them. Other responses may even be more satisfying. So at least they seem to be, if not for most, still for many among us. The world is certainly not yet all modern. It is not likely ever to be.

In the essay, originally published in 1915, that we have in English as "Religious Rejections of the World and Their Directions," Weber finds the existential threshold of modernity in a certain deconstruction: of what he speaks of as the "ethical postulate that the world is a God-ordained, and hence somehow *meaningfully* and ethically oriented cosmos."[31] Take this reference out of context, add to it certain of the closing paragraphs of *The Protestant Ethic*,[32] and Weber perhaps sounds like just another theorist of secularization. Habermas[33] among others continues to read him precisely as a theorist of secularization, and to understand his analysis of the European passage to modernity as an analysis of those processes "of disenchantment which led . . . to the disintegration of religious world views [and the issuance of] secular culture." Weber himself, however, makes no such claim for his analyses at any juncture in his work whatsoever. Aware of secularization, he does not attribute decisiveness to it. He does not even assert that "modern European culture" is a "secular culture." He is perfectly aware, as he ought well to be, that both religious commitment and religious belief are still "modern." He is just as aware that the deconstruction of the ethically ordered cosmos does not result, either, in the passing of commitment to or belief in one or another ethically ordered cosmology. He asserts something quite different: that the deconstruction of the cosmos pushes such commitments and such beliefs "from the rational into the irrational realm."[34]

Here as at so many other junctures, Weber is focusing above all on a thematic of legitimation. What he asserts—what in any event might be extrapolated from his assertions—is that the threshold of modernity has its epiphany precisely as the legitimacy of the postulate of a divinely preordained and fated cosmos has its decline; that modernity emerges, that one or another modernity can emerge, only as the legitimacy of the postulated cosmos ceases to be taken for granted and beyond reproach. Countermoderns reject that reproach, believe in spite of it. Moderns may still believe, but only *non quod, sed quia absurdum,* "not what, but because it is absurd to believe."[35] For all of this, modern belief still has its legitimacy. But it has, in Weber's judgment, no other legitimacy and no more legitimacy than that of anything else chosen or adopted, no other and no more legitimacy than that conferred by the relativistic and calculative economy of subjective interests itself. Weber sees, in that modern existential economy, at once the birth of radical valuational conflict and the death of "the public sphere." He blames the gradual ascendance of the norm of calculability, whether bureaucratic, scientific, or capitalistic, for both.

Weber's specification of the threshold of modernity is, it seems to me, entirely on the mark, even if his construal of it is too theocentric: the "God-ordained" is surely only one type of "ethically oriented cosmos" among many others. It remains on the mark even if its sociopsychological underpinnings are somewhat outmoded. As we now know, neither the peasant nor the primitive is quite so unreflective and uncritical a believer as Weber presumed. The New Guineans, among many others, have certainly demonstrated that. On the other hand, the purely economic individual, free of any compulsions but the compulsions of good form and subjective interests, is also a fantasy, no less than the pure economy in which he is supposed to reside.[36] Even the most ardent of cultural cynics, New Guinean or Greek, remain tied inextricably to the events and the practices that have shaped them. Like the rest of us, they remain creatures of their traditions among other things. Like the rest of us, they can make occasional existential readjustments. Redefining and reshaping their traditions, they can redefine and reshape themselves. But the process can never be more than piecemeal. It always has its limits. The distance that can be wrought between the creatural and the re-created self has its limits as well. *Pace* Baudrillard (and a variety of other "postmodernists"), tradition in sum total can never be reduced, in Athens or anywhere else, to being "just another commodity" after all. Some traditions, some customs may be commodities for some persons all the time: especially the pasts and traditions of "others." But some are bound always to retain too much existential force and flavor to allow for brokerage.

Weber's specification of the threshold of modernity remains, however, on the mark precisely because it does not, in the end, refer either to "commodity fetishism" or to the "commodification of tradition." It does not, in other words, simply reiterate, in a rather less materialist phraseology, the Marxist problematic of alienation. It points to a quite distinct problematic, and a quite distinct moment: one in which traditions, however dearly cherished and however rigorously maintained, cease to be their own defense; one in which tradition itself ceases to serve as the ultimate court of ethical or existential appeal. To be sure, Weber does not identify "tradition itself" with the "ethically and meaningfully oriented cosmos." But the difference between the two can only be one of degree, not one of kind. Tradition itself, even if not God-ordained, is always more or less ethically and meaningfully oriented; the ethically and meaningfully oriented cosmos is always of necessity more or less traditional. The former may well be less rationalized, and in particular less "value-rational," than the latter. But the grounds of both are similarly transcendental: if not otherworldly, at least a priori rather than a posteriori. Weber's threshold of modernity is the threshold at which the grounds of both become suspect. Across the threshold, "traditionalists" are just as common as "cosmologists" and other transcendentalists. But they are one and all rhetoricians, no longer simple sages.

New Guineans, though famously skeptical of traditions, may or may not as yet be skeptical of the legitimacy of tradition itself. Greeks, though many cleave to their traditions, may be skeptics, and consequently be rhetoricians, of "tradition itself" in spite of themselves. That "the meaning of tradition itself" is far from certain or secure is telling enough. A review of the long and detailed history of the battles between a "conservative" Orthodox church and its "progressive" adversaries would be telling, in its way, as well. But some further consideration of the incident at Aerodhromio can, for the time being, suffice.

Metalepsis, Irony, Counter-Metalepsis

Whatever else it may have been, the incident at Aerodhromio was not mere sport. Those who participated in it may have been playing on their pasts. But the incident itself was not mere play, superficial—or, for that matter, "deep." It was not the acting out of a story, already composed, effectively eternal, that Greeks were once again ritually or quasi ritually telling themselves about themselves.[37] It was a reflection and a particular expression of ongoing and enduring contests: over the control of resources, over the maintenance of position, over the legitimacy of certain practices and the legitimacy of the standings with which those practices are always inextricably intertwined. It was, in its expression, undoubtedly more allegorical than literal. Literalism, with its relative nakedness, would not have been acceptable. The fate of a suburban discotheque was at the very least a less serious, a more comfortable matter of controversy than the fate of actual women and men. Still, art was on the verge throughout of slipping dangerously and too blatantly into life. If not the manifest controversy then at least the players were and could not help but be actual men and women. However displaced or disguised, the stakes over which they were struggling were quite high. However displaced or disguised, they were known to be quite high, and known as well to be very much up for grabs.

The incident at Aerodhromio might bear more pertinent comparison not with Balinese cockfights but with another of the key performances that Geertz has described for us: the lamentable and somewhat botched funeral that serves as the occasion of his "Ritual and Social Change: A Javanese Example."[38] Greece is rather distant, historically and sociostructurally, from Java, and a demonstration against the improprieties of a nightclub rather distant, conceptually and circumstantially, from an obligatory ceremony meant to facilitate a young boy's passage into the realm of the dead. The demonstration and the ceremony nevertheless have something more in common merely than their unpleasantness. Among other things, neither is a testament to unmitigated anomie. Aerodhromio's patrons and its detractors alike were willing to recognize a "common law." Both took considerable pains to be "civil"—not so civil as to seem sheepish, but civil enough that the troop of police who had assembled on the roadway came to seem merely a theatrical flourish. Vulgarisms were limited to those that were speakable.

Conflict was limited to posturing, and timetables, such as they were, remained inviolable on both sides. Patrons and detractors alike agreed, and agreed without much trouble, on how appropriately to disagree. Compare Geertz's observation on the classificatory calm of the funeral he witnessed: "there was no argument over whether the slametan pattern was the correct ritual, whether the neighbors were obligated to attend, or whether the supernatural concepts upon which the ritual is based were valid ones."[39]

Not quite anomie: but even here the similarities are inexact. The participants in the incident at Aerodhromio agreed upon the conceptual frame within which their disagreement ought to proceed. They perhaps shared a "culture of civility": not ancient, not sacred, but not taken lightly either. What they shared was not entirely without content; the rules they were following, the rules that they chose to transgress, were not empty rules. But they did more to constrain conduct and symbolism than positively to determine either one. They did nothing to determine the meaning of patronizing or indulging in the pleasures of a discotheque. The attendants at the funeral that Geertz has described were not in dispute over whether a ceremony ought to be conducted, and conducted in a quite specific manner. The definition of the situation was clear. The awkwardness of the proceedings, their delays, the untoward display of emotions they provoked: all these had a different source. They had their source, according to Geertz, in the gap between what those involved assumed and accepted about living and dying and how they actually lived and died; in the gap between a "form of integration" stipulated culturally and another form, stipulated socially and practically. The Javanese villagers who suffered through their painful and clumsy funeral had, Geertz suggests, no other culturally articulate choice but to be "folk"; but suffered through it quite so painfully because they had no other practically feasible choice but to behave as the urbanites that all of them had already become.[40]

The patrons and demonstrators at Aerodhromio suffered, in contrast, from an overabundance of choices. Culturally and practically, they may all have been urbanites. But there were many more than one way to be an urbanite, many more than one way to be a "Greek," more than one way to be a human being. The patrons had their ways, the demonstrators had their own, and neither had very much admiration for the ways of the other. Civilly framed, the discord between those on the one and those on the other side of the discotheque's fence was nevertheless virtually "total." It touched upon everything from economic imprudence to existential errancy, from the rights of privacy to the duties of social cooperation, from political wisdom to moral evil, from bad to good taste. Only the religious dimension seemed to be absent. The fit between the incident's more explicit dimensions was at best loose: another reason, perhaps, why literalism had to be supplemented by a more vast and more absorbing symbolism.

Could the incident have occurred in America? Similar incidents occur continually, but the symbols that guide them are usually quite different. Disputants in America are fond of appealing to "traditions": liberty, the pursuit of happiness, health, well-being, equality, justice, even God and country. At Aerodhromio, however, the key symbol, the key trope, was indeed "tradition" itself; the debate, a debate over just where it belonged in the larger picture, over just what it had to do with anything and everything else.

The demonstrators set themselves up against blind and conspicuous consumption, against the soullessness of imitations, against the great idol of the foreign. They set themselves up in favor of austerity, self-sufficiency, purity, interiority, and if not the *conscience collective*, at least the collectivist and communitarian conscience. They were localists. They were isolationists. Were they "traditionalists"? Not if one understands the "traditionalist" to be an opponent of all change, of all innovation, all technological or social "progress." The demonstrators at Aerodhromio were advocates of change: they wanted more schools, among other things. They were evidently advocates of at least some innovations, some technological refinements and advancements. They did not, after all, bother to hire a live band. They came with a convoy of the most up-to-date accoutrements to aid them. The vehicles must themselves have been imported: Greece may manufacture tires, but it does not manufacture automobiles. But that was all right. The equipment was there not to despoil "tradition," but rather to broadcast and to amplify it. It was acceptable because it could be used to further "tradition": a higher, the highest of ends.

The rhetoric was metaleptic, but the metalepsis one that Bloom would classify as "introjective." The demonstrators identified themselves with the past, sided with and proved the integrity of the past precisely by replacing an earlier with a later technology that, far from compromising "tradition," turned out only to serve it better. Call it "traditionalist"; call it more accurately "culturally classicist":[41] it is among the most familiar rhetorics to which Greeks have had resort in preserving the priority of the past even as they have "modernized." In the preceding century, its executors were in their majority either genteel or petty bourgeois.[42] In this century, they belong in their majority to the older middle classes and the literati.

The counterdemonstrators at Aerodhromio hardly intended to put themselves forward as proponents of "blind and conspicuous consumption" or "soulless imitations" or the "idolization of the foreign." Nor did they intend to put themselves forward as proponents of change and innovation for their own sake. They did not altogether reject their detractors' critique. They rejected instead the idea that they ought to be subject to it. Enemies of tradition? "Antitraditionalists"? Impetuous "modernizers"? They did not think so. But their retort was not simply a denial; it was a rebuttal of the

accusations that were being leveled at them. Tradition? That was fine, so far
as the most activist of Aerodhromio's patrons were concerned. But it was
not the *summum bonum*, not the totality that those on the other side of the
fence declaimed it to be. The activists among Aerodhromio's patrons demonstrated to everyone else that they, too, could "be traditional," that they,
too, could "do the traditional thing." They could dance in a collective and
popular circle with the most past-looking of their peers. But they could do
more: the alleged marionettes of the foreign were pulled by many puppe-
teers, owned by none.

The rhetoric was ironic, the tropology a tropology of negations. The discotheque was not what it seemed to be. Its patrons were not doing what
they seemed to be doing. The preservation of tradition was not the end of
all other ends. No enemies of tradition among the activists at Aerodhromio;
but no ardent enthusiasts of it either. No real "modernizers": ironies may
bring to light something other than, something "beyond" tradition, but not
necessarily anything at once connected and discontinuous enough to be
properly alternative to it. The rhetoric of ironies contracts the domain of
tradition but does not fill the void it leaves with any singular substitute. In
the past century, its executors were diverse; some at least belonged to the
grande bourgeoisie. In this century, they belong in their majority to a newer
middle class of more purely meritorious and meritocratic administrators
and provisioners.

Summum bonum or one good among others: with these two, tradition has
in Greece a third rendering, less common but in some respects more decisive. The demonstrators at Aerodhromio were eclectic in their means, but
only for the sake of fortifying a more puristic end. The counterdemonstrators were also eclectic, perhaps only for the sake of variety itself. Other
Greeks are eclectics, but treat the multiplicity of their local pasts together
with the multiplicity of more distant historical and cultural currents as the
thematic matter of a further synthesis. Whatever Athens may be, the interiors of Ersi Khatzimikhali's apartment are not a mere stockpile of disparate
artifacts. They are not arranged sheerly at random. The neo-Byzantine exteriors of her family estate are not a mere stylistic stockpile either. Zakhos,
their architect, ran the risk of pastiche. But he was convinced that the risk
was worth taking. He was convinced that it had to be taken: "believing contemporary Greece to be the descendant of the Byzantine, and believing the
vernacular architecture of the Turkish Domination to be itself Byzantine, he
thought that support would have to be found [in that vernacular] for a real
[*sosti*] Greek architecture."[43] The rhetoric is once again metaleptic, but the
metalepsis projective. For Zakhos as for other "historically constructive"
assimilationists, "tradition" is neither whole nor end, and the priority of the
past only "temporary." For Zakhos as for his projective fellows, tradition is
only a metaphor for the Greek, and the past a material that, when imposed

upon or reinserted into what has come later, might give rise to and become part of a "new present." For Zakhos, who reinserted the Roman and the Cycladic into later, "modernist" forms, the past itself was derivative, and derivative because it was partial. In his hands, it became part of a new, but also more "Greek" present. For other "historical constructivists"—so I intend henceforth to refer to them—the "Greek" has not always been either as important or as ultimate as the act of assimilating and amalgamating itself.

In the preceding as in this century, historical constructivists have in their majority come from the intelligentsia and the socioculturally dominant strata. Not all have been aesthetes. Some have been educators, others politicians. Aesthetically, socially, and politically, their impact has been quite out of proportion with their numbers. Because they are dominant, or because their project is somehow more adaptable, more "adequate" than either of its middling alternatives? Both, no doubt: but I leave a more detailed response for the chapters that follow. I must note here, though, that however adaptable and however "adequate," historically constructive assimilationism is still itself only one "alternative," and as incompatible with both of its middling counterparts as each of them is with the other. It may provide some Greeks with an existential direction, but it does not as yet provide Greece with any determinate or singular direction. It may offer some Greeks a sort of spiritual method for arriving at some sense or conception of the collective. But other Greeks still prefer other methods, and both the content and the form of the collective are consequently still publicly unresolved. It may rest upon one coherent rendering of the status of precedence. But there are other renderings nearly as coherent and more widely held. The transcendence of "tradition itself"? Certain of the rhetoricians we have met in the previous several pages might insist upon it, but many others would immediately protest. As a consequence, "tradition itself" cannot, in Greece, consistently fulfill its Manchesterian function. It cannot consistently serve to resolve conflicts; it can, in some cases at least, serve only to reveal and represent them. The legitimacy of "absolute values"? Certain of the rhetoricians we have met in these several pages might insist upon that as well. But what would be their argument? Only, as they surely realize, that certain others might support them. But what support they might gain would still fall short of consensus; it would, however unflinching, fall short of the sort of consensus that could keep the Weberian threshold of modernity consistently at bay.

4

SOVEREIGNTY AND ITS DISCONTENTS

WHAT HAS INDUCED tradition's demotion? What precisely
has brought Greeks, some of them at least, face-to-face with
modernity's threshold? One can no longer appeal to Weber:
however incisive, however serviceable his analysis of that threshold may
be, his diagnosis of the antecedents and precipitants of it has its limitations. The incident at Aerodhromio is far from atypical. On the contrary, it
is in many respects representative of the current metropolitan "scene," in
many respects simply symptomatic of a far more pervasive state of affairs.
No adequate diagnosis of that state of affairs can, however, depart from a
Protestant reformation. Greece has yet to have, or even to absorb one.
Herzfeld observes that hard work is proof in Greece as elsewhere of goodness of character.[1] But Greece has yet to be significantly affected by a religious ethic functionally equivalent to the Calvinist ethic, even if it has been
affected by its utilitarian successor. Whatever the effect of the latter, no
adequate diagnosis can depart from the onset of capitalist industrialization
either. A "disarticulate" and latter-day phenomenon, industrialism is—so
the available data suggest—still somewhat marginal, even in Athens itself.
In Greece, as Keith Legg and others have observed, a fortiori in Athens,
politics has always had infrastructural pride of place. Diagnostics must consequently depart from the "political sphere," even if that sphere must be
more broadly and generously construed than is usual. The Occident is a
vague and ad hoc entity, and in many respects Greece has as much claim to
belonging to it as any other country. But not for its politics: its prevailing
political struggles, its prevailing categories of political experience, the
norms and dispositions of its prevailing tactical practices are all notably
"elsewhere."

Sovereignty I: The International Setting

Not even they, however, are unique. Legg, for example, notes significant
historical parallels among a variety of countries whose parties had not yet by
the end of the 1960s advanced beyond being "cliques":

> The critical struggles of these countries were directed against colonial regimes
> or foreign domination. There was, in most cases, no indigenous monarchical or

aristocratic tradition. The elites that had . . . [guided the movement] to independence could occupy . . . parliamentary institutions, along with other seats of
power, without a struggle; these institutions became no more than another
arena for the usual bargaining for power.[2]

Legg has many of the newer nations of Latin America in mind. But he also
has Greece in mind, and rightly so. The most salient opponent of western
European and North American republicanists was an "internal" one:
the aristocracy. The great opponents of Greece's birth as a nation were not
socioeconomically privileged classes. They were not strata, either, long accustomed to thinking of themselves as communalistic unities. Its great
opponents were the Ottomans: categorically "foreign" imperialists. Greece
indeed had no indigenous monarchs, and even if a few of the Phanariotes
put themselves forward as descendants of the Byzantine nobility, it had no
indigenous aristocracy. From the revolution forward, from the revolution
nearly to the present, its elites have certainly fought among themselves for
control over parliamentary and other institutions and seats of power. But
from the revolution nearly to the present, they have fought for control, not
often for "parliamentary procedure" itself.

The Ottomans were of course forced to retreat. But neither colonial regimes nor foreign domination retreated with them. In order to carry out
their revolution, Greek nationalists were compelled to seek the support of
the Great Powers: Russia, France, and Great Britain. They were not disappointed. But after the revolution, they found that they had simply managed
to replace their former overlords with newer ones. Was there some misunderstanding? There were many. Greeks were striving first of all to free themselves from an arbitrary conqueror, to recover a sovereignty long lost. They
were not especially striving, and some of them not striving at all, to come
under the umbrella of the European sphere of influence. The leaders of the
Great Powers did not share the same priorities. Or rather, they held them in
reverse. The Greek revolutionaries appealed to various romantic ideologies
of nationhood in order to justify their claims of sovereignty. Some preferred
the French rhetoric of "civilization." Most preferred a more Germanic rhetoric of "race."[3] They did not expect to persuade the Ottomans of their righteousness. But they did expect to persuade the Europeans, from whom,
after all, they had imported the spirit, if not the letter, of their verbiage.
They met with some success: recall the hordes of philhellenes who came to
their defense.

Romantic ideologies of statehood, however, served quite different purposes in Europe than those to which the Greek nationalists tried to put
them. They were indeed ideologies of sovereignty. They were deployed in
order to justify territorial claims: but to more territory rather than less; not
to territory *tout court*. The leading European ideologies of civilization and

race alike flowed from territories that were, by the 1820s, already secure. They could begin to rethink and to entertain again the twin dreams of empire and hegemony. Dumont accordingly observes:

> The old ethnocentrism and sociocentrism which exalts *us* and disparages *others* did survive in the modern era, but in two different ways: the Germans saw themselves, and tried to impose themselves, as superior *qua* Germans, while the French consciously postulated only the superiority of [a] universalist culture, but identified with it so naively that they looked upon themselves as the educators of mankind.[4]

The Greek nationalists seem to have received both the French and the German romance of the nation as something of a sufficient justification, not only of the claim over a certain territory but also of the claim to self-determination. Most Europeans, and certainly the governors of the Great Powers, saw the matter differently. They may have thought that proof of "civility" or of "racial genius" was a necessary condition of the establishment of a legitimate sovereignty over some territory or other. But they all took for granted that a proof of self-sufficiency was necessary for the establishment of any right to self-determination. Greek nationalists may have seen the support they received as the fulfillment of a moral obligation, nothing more. The exchequers of the Great Powers, however, saw it as something else: an invitation to dominate, the foundation of a right to intervene.

Since the 1820s, western Europeans and North Americans have intermittently responded to threats to their sovereignty: some real, and some less real than anticipated. None of them, however, have had more than intermittently to cope with a sovereignty so merely pro forma as that of Greece. The Great Powers have passed. But Britain continued to dominate Greece until the conclusion of the Second World War. The United States took its place after 1950. It remains to be seen whether the current powers of the European Community will do more to correct than to reproduce the older pattern. Since the 1820s, western Europeans and North Americans alike have intermittently had to defend their sovereignty. But Greeks have had to confront far more regular encroachments. At the center of the Occident, national sovereignty itself has rarely been a pressing issue. Those at the center have usually had the luxury of indulging themselves in subtler concerns: over the relative weight to be accorded to individual liberty over collective cooperation and the maintenance of the "social whole," over the rationalization of differential material and social privileges.[5] Greeks have addressed the same concerns, in the past and in the present. But they have had to address them within the more general thematics of national viability. In "the Occident," the issue of national sovereignty has ceased to have an everyday character. It has ceased there, except in times of war, to have any exceptional saliency. Not in Greece.

Sovereignty II: International Issues and Intranational Tactics

Nor, in all probability, would sovereignty cease to be a salient issue in Greece even were the independence and inviolability of the nation somehow finally secured. For what, after all, is "sovereignty"? From the medieval age forward, political theorists have conceived of it as a sort of raw or unqualified power. The sovereign is supreme, obedient to nothing and no one else unless, of course, he (or she, or it) chooses to be. From the medieval period forward, the sovereign is the atom of an essential potency. Dumont[6] has traced the occidental course of that atom's shifting temporal designations. The original temporal sovereign was the church. It gradually gave way to the prince and the state. With the English contractarians, with Rousseau and with Hegel, the sovereign assumes what has come to be its final incarnation: the rational individual.[7] Through all its various incarnations, however, it has a quite constant contrary: the involuntary "subject," the slave.

All these conceptions of course reflect a bellicose past, a chronology of tensions and antagonisms: between church and state, between feudalists and republicans, between aristocrats and the bourgeoisie. Dumont has argued that from the turn of the nineteenth century onward, they have also become increasingly entangled in an almost frantic effort to justify "subjection" without resort to any metaphysics, either of law or of hierarchy.[8] They reveal the clumsiness of that effort. But what else? Among other things, that sovereigns can preserve their unqualified and essential potency only by remaining anarchic. It is not enough that their obedience be voluntary. Hobbes can be credited with the demonstration. His contractors willfully surrender to the Leviathan; but surrendering, they lose their sovereignty in the process. The Hobbesian contract is an extreme and limiting example. Virtually all political theorists afterward withdraw from it, in some measure at least.[9] All, however, have had to address its implication: that the moment that sovereigns agree to any structured limitation of their liberty, the moment that, however voluntarily, they cede their entitlement to renegotiate or even to reject any qualifications placed upon the exercise of their power, they stop being sovereigns.

Are there no true sovereigns? Perhaps, as Dumont would insist, there are no sovereign "individuals." But Hobbes's example would be far less provocative if there were no persons, individual or collective, sovereign at least in their standing to one another. It would be far less provocative if there were in fact no tactics of sovereignty distinguishable from the tactics of either hierarchical or regulative politics. It would be far less provocative if there was in fact nothing to distinguish the interactions between one sovereign and another from the interactions of other political types: "rational contractors," "bureaucrats," or "involuntary subjects." But there is: "occidentals" have celebrated sovereignty in theory, marginalized it in practice, but still know it and maintain it at their social margins. The tactics of sovereignty play themselves out in the interaction among imperial states, but also in the unroutinized interactions between other "enemies" and "friends." Sovereignty is not, however, egalitarian, either in theory or in practice. It permits and even encourages ranking, even if a ranking that can never be anything more than occasional. Sovereigns must perpetually reiterate their superiority over other sovereigns. They must perpetually renew their roles as *primi inter pares*, as "big men," as "patrons" of their "clients." Relegated to the back rooms of the Occident, too "personal" but above all too "unsystematic," the politics of sovereignty has yet to be relegated to the back rooms of Greece. It has, for that matter, yet to be relegated entirely to the back rooms of the rest of the Circum-Mediterranean.

Does Weber provide us with a sociology of sovereignty in his typification of "charisma"?[10] He nearly does, though he surely exaggerates charisma's removal from everyday life.[11] He makes, in his analysis, no clear distinction, either, between political action and its legitimation. But these are technical complaints. Sovereign actors have charisma as their usual and only precise defense, and much that is characteristic of sovereign tactics is also characteristic of charismatic authority. Both are personal, though nothing prevents sovereignty from being ascribed to a group, and nothing prevents charisma from being ascribed to a group either.[12] Both are indeed unroutinized. Neither sovereign tacticians nor charismatics know any "regulated 'career,' 'advancement,' 'salary,' or regulated and expert training."[13] Sovereigns must constantly reestablish themselves: "pure charisma does not know any 'legitimacy' other than that flowing from personal strength, that is, one which is constantly being proved."[14] Sovereigns are not yet hereditary monarchs; charismatic warlords become institutionalized kings "only at the stage when a following of royal professional warriors rules over the working or paying masses,"[15] and only when charisma itself is assigned no longer to a person but, instead, either to his office or to his "blood." Sovereign tactics are, if not always illegal, still "extralegal." The charismatic attitude stands in principle against any other authority than its own. Its motto: "'It is written, but I say unto you.'"[16]

The Circum-Mediterranean is not without its share of routinized institutions. Neither is Greece. The family, the church, the various apparatuses of the state and of governance, the civil administration: all these "great orders" display definite structural permanence, though a permanence perhaps more "patrimonial" in quality than (ideal-typically) "bureaucratic."[17] The relations among them, sometimes even within them are, however, another matter. Consider one example, not exhaustive but well studied: democratization.[18] The process has been a stormy one. Douglas Dakin is perhaps right to note that its storms have not been any more "violent than elsewhere—only more frequent."[19] But why so frequent? In part, because Greece's political atmosphere has so often had to absorb external agitations.[20] In part, however, because it has had relatively little internally to temper it: no enduring social consensus; no enduring popular regard for the ideal of the "rational contract."

The independence movement brought a power elite of patronal landowners and *grands bourgeois* into a temporary alliance.[21] After the war against the Ottomans was won, the alliance collapsed. There was nothing at all routine about Greece's first dozen years as a state. There were innumerable battles between one elite fraction and another. There were three constitutions, each of them quickly discarded. The period came to a close when the Great Powers installed Othon at the head of an absolute monarchy. Othon soon proved to be as sovereign a tactician as his supposed subjects. His charisma was, however, thin at best. After only a decade, on the heels of a military revolt and under foreign diplomatic pressure, he was compelled to install a republic. The constitution laid at his feet was patently an affront; it severely restricted his own discretionary domain. Was it "enlightened"? It recognized the principle of legal parity. It guaranteed the right of suffrage to all adult males. On the other hand, placing lower-level political appointments in the hands of small central committees, it did hardly anything either to discourage favoritism or to encourage federalism.

A second "democratic uprising" occurred some eighteen years later. It amounted to no more of a popular victory than the first. Its executors, too, were various local oligarchs, all of them seeking little more than to further their "absolutist inclinations" at the expense of Othon's own.[22] They succeeded: after an abortive coup, the king vacated his throne. The Great Powers, however, quickly intervened. The British managed, considerable local resistance notwithstanding, to see through the coronation of the Danish Prince Christian, locally Yioryios I. Another constitution was devised, the most enduring Greece has as yet known and a noticeable liberalization of its immediate predecessor. It further restricted royal privilege; it fixed the right to assembly. Its text, debated and cultivated in the contentious cafés of an Athens that had, since the 1837 opening of its university, become the home of an astonishingly diverse press and a fervent intellectual cadre,[23] stood for nearly a half century. The era saw the emergence of feminism, a literary florescence, and the abolition of the tithe. It also saw the vague foreshadowings of what might have become a dualistic party system.

But parties, organizationally sustained, national in scope, enduring beyond the careers of their founders,[24] did not emerge. Not even those leaders who tried were able to extract themselves from the rich personalism of the Greek *politique vécue*. Not all did try. The constitution did not remain a central preoccupation for long, either. Political leaders and their publics soon put their civic consciousness aside. They had other, more sovereign ambitions: to recover Constantinople and the territories of the lost Byzantium. The Turks did not cooperate. Greece lost its first irredentist war in 1897. Its governors and generals found that they had lost much of their charisma with it. The malaise of the war's aftermath had its denouement in yet another military insurrection, and yet another deposition. Yioryios I remained on the throne. But his heir apparent, Crown Prince Konstandinos, was forced to cede his own post as commander in chief. The state nearly dissolved. In 1910, however, Eleftherios Venizelos stepped in to save it.

Venizelos did save it, and did many other things in the course of the next two decades both to prove and to preserve his charismatic preeminence. A Cretan, he was responsible for carrying out the *enosi*, the "union" of the island with Greece. He was deemed responsible for those victories in the Balkan War that led to Greece's annexation of several other Aegean islands. Like all charismatics, he was at once a missionary and a servant. He served the "new" Greece; Konstandinos, who acceded to the throne in 1913, the "old."[25] Setting up a provisional government in Thessaloniki, splitting Greece in two, he may have perpetrated a near civil war. But the Split itself had unifying consequences. In its aftermath, neither the "old" oligarchs nor any of the "old" regional networks would ever again be able to exercise all their former pull. Venizelos may have been more an Anglophile than a consummate "liberal." But if anyone deserves credit for establishing the first of Greece's genuine parties, Venizelos surely does.

On the other hand, he was not beyond the politics of sovereignty. He did not invent, but he did continue to incite the radical irredentism that led to the Asia Minor Disaster. He could be, and often was, a majoritarian demagogue. He refused to cloud his reputation with appointments to any dictatorship. But his respect for constitutional democracy was qualified. The constitution ratified in 1864 with the ascension of Yioryios I underwent revision during his later tenure as prime minister. Nor did he do much to assuage the tensions brewing from even before the turn of the century among parliament, the monarchy, and the army. Perhaps the contrary. Mouzelis, among others, does not see Venizelos as a democratizer at all. He suggests that the political transformations Venizelos wrought amounted to little more than a shift from "a type of 'feudal domination' . . . to a type of 'patrimonial domination.'"[26] Venizelos himself, however, was not yet a patriarch; his domination was too unroutinized to be other than sovereign.[27]

Yioryios II was placed in the throne of his father, Konstandinos, in 1926, but was exiled himself not long after. His return, by the invitation of a rigged 1935 plebiscite, may have marked the commencement of what has been called a "parallel state": a consortium of what had become a profoundly reactionary army, the monarchy, and the police that persisted, often in whimsical disregard of either parliaments or constitutions, until the fall of the Papadhopoulos junta in 1974. Its initial figurehead was General Ioannis

Metaxas, that quasi fascist or at least somewhat uncertain fascist who with the new king's approval fashioned himself dictator over a "Third Greek Civilization."[28] He held his self-made seat into the early days of the Second World War. Less his uncertain than the German's far more determined fascism soon gave rise in occupied Greece to a resistance movement. In good Circum-Mediterranean fashion, many of the rebels took to the hills and provinces and, under the guidance of disciplined guerrilla bands, slowly managed to recapture a startlingly large portion of the homeland. Greek "peasants," for lack of a better term, were exposed to the quotidian workings of *topiki aftodhiikisi*, "local self-administration," at that time. They were, as Woodhouse and others have reported, deeply and rightly impressed with the administration's potential.[29] They were impressed as well with the training and the ideological stance of their tutors. Many, but not all the guerrillas were Communist. Some were fiercely anti-Communist. The collaborationist officials in Athens were also anti-Communist. So was Winston Churchill, who had bargained with Stalin to keep the Aegean under British sway. Campaigns of terror, determined to purge both countryside and cities of leftist sympathizers, arose shortly after the Germans fled. In 1946, the king, who had sagely removed himself to Cairo before the German advance, returned. In 1947, the Emfilios Polemos (Civil War) formally began. The Communists may well have won had the Soviet Union, apparently at Stalin's decree, not effectively abandoned them. As it was, they were defeated only through the intervention not merely of Great Britain but also of an America increasingly determined to contain any opportunity for Soviet expansion. The Civil War itself left eighty thousand Greeks dead. "Class struggle" had definitively inscribed itself into the political landscape.

The first stable postwar constitution was ratified in 1952. It endowed Greek women with the right of suffrage. On the other hand, it diminished the scope of the right of assembly and of the right to strike. It restricted the freedom of the press. It enlarged the purview of military courts. The "extraordinary measures" put into law with it—licensing among other things the requirement that any citizen, whether seeking employment in the civil service or in the majority of public and semipublic corporations, whether seeking university admission or even a passport, prove not only his own national loyalty but also that of his closest relatives—were not actually rescinded until 1974. The parallel state, for all its internal discord, grew even more entrenched. Concomitantly, however, the country saw the rise of the direct precursors of its contemporary political personalities: Konstandinos Karamanlis, whose conservative coalition governed from 1956 to 1963 and who still remains the grand old man of the republican right; and Yiorghos Papandreou, whose immediately subsequent cabinet included his son Andreas. The season was one of prosperity, but also of increasingly venomous resentments. It was indeed a season of secret plotting. Certain members of the elder Papandreou's Center Union, Andreas insinuated to be among them, allegedly conspired to disrupt the functioning, or more precisely the CIA's control of the functioning, of the Greek Army. A scandal erupted when, in May 1965, the conspiracy (never proved) was brought to light. In its wake, the government effectively collapsed. Elections were finally called for May 1967. The king was prepared, should the election's returns not have been to his liking, to support a generals' coup. His aims were, however, preempted by Papadhopoulos and a bevy of other colonels ill-disposed toward their superiors and somewhat ill-disposed to the king himself. Trained by the commanders of NATO, perhaps instructed as well by special American advisors, they imposed a battalion of tanks on Athens's thoroughfares on 21 April 1967.

Let us recall their policies. During the seven years of its rule, the junta professed itself a champion of a "healthy and disciplined" society.[30] It professed itself to be historically and religiously pious. It devoted itself to the betterment of a "Nation of Hellenic Christians." To a "nation," perhaps, but not to the people:[31] it prohibited dissent, and did not hesitate to silence dissent with both torture and guns. It was quite ready to sacrifice the rule of law to the preservation of order. It was unabashedly anti-intellectual, and adverse to the worldliness of the upper sociocultural strata. Not popular, it was populist, and declined in the name of absolute validity of its populism to safeguard any of the usual constitutional freedoms. It promulgated a "constitution"; several scholars since have refused even to acknowledge it.[32] Compared with Perón or Marcos, the colonels were perhaps only "slightly evil." On the other hand, evil does not readily admit of degrees. Were the colonels would-be sovereigns? Undoubtedly they were. Were they sovereigns without charisma? Not at first: many Greeks fled them, but many others remained literally to applaud them in the capital's streets. Not even yet: whatever they may admit or confess to other Greeks, some Greeks are still prepared to confess to presumptively sympathetic strangers—this one among others—their conviction that "the junta was the best government that the country has ever had."

But whether the best or, as most would agree, the worst, the junta took form within a structural matrix that has largely collapsed. The parallel state disappeared with the 1975 abolition of the monarchy. The army has, for the time being at least, lost virtually all its political or logistical self-determination. Since Karamanlis's return to power in 1975, republicanism has ceased to be in any clear or present danger. The force of clientelism has, in some measure, come to rest in more informal spheres. The media have secured and, with the recent advent of "free radio,"[33] even expanded their freedoms. The rights to assembly and dissent have ceased to be questioned. The courts—an occasional rumor to the contrary notwithstanding—have secured the inviolability of their labors. Elections have ceased to be uniformly suspected of fraudulence.

But neither sovereign tactics nor charismatic authority has been alto-gether deprived of its former spontaneity. Democracy in Greece has not as yet entirely taken on the obsessively routine and regulative complexion that it now has in most of western Europe and North America. Not that the contrast should be overdrawn: Thatcher's Britain had something of its own sovereign pretensions. But even in Britain, as recent events have shown, political tactics lose their legitimacy the more blatantly sovereign they be-come. In Greece, recent events have not obviousy shown the same. Andreas Papandreou, prime minister from 1981 until the autumn of 1989, remains perhaps only slightly less charismatic than any politician in this century besides Venizelos himself. The sources of his stature are diverse: they are in part constituted of his descent, in part of his academic achievements, in part of his extraordinary envisioning of a neutralist and mediative nationhood intimately bound to prevailing Greek conceptions of society and self. They were sufficient, in 1985, to see Karamanlis ousted from the presidency he had held continuously from 1981, after his own prime ministership came to an end. Papandreou replaced Karamanlis, and was obliged practically to re-place him, with another minority luminary. The man he chose, subse-quently elected to the presidency outright, staunchly conservative, was a distinguished jurist. What he lacked was Karamanlis's own charisma. Ka-ramanlis went into retirement. Since my return to America, he has come out of it again. His party, Nea Dhimokratia, has continued to make strides. Pa-pandreou, as chief and founder of the Panhellenic Socialist Movement, suc-ceeded during his mandate in insulating his administration somewhat at least from the consequences of unpopularity. He succeeded specifically in revising the constitutionally governed accountancy of electoral returns to-ward a proportionalism that, given the demographics of partisanship, would provide protection against even outright defeats at the polls. In spite of his revisions, Papandreou indeed lost his steerage of the Greek government in 1989, not least because he had been accused of what, in the United States, might now be considered "typical" politicians' crimes. Whether or not he was actually guilty (he insisted that he was not), he has recently been acquit-ted. His trial was broadcast daily on Greek television, apparently to huge audiences. PASOK may well be shortly due to rise again.

Sovereignty III: Some Ethnological Remarks on a Political Ethos

Sovereign tacticians can be found virtually the world over. They can be found in southern European capitals; but they can, as several ethnographic accounts at least hint,[34] be found in virtually every other Circum-Mediterra-nean locale as well. The sea, however, is no special magnet. There are sovereigns in the New Guinea highlands, sovereigns in North American corporations and academies. There are sovereigns, as a rule, wherever decision making, the "allocation of resources,"[35] or domination itself is not yet routine. There are likely always to be sovereigns wherever decision making or the allocation of resources or domination itself cannot be made routine.[36]

Sovereigns are "persons," though sometimes particular, sometimes corporate. Are they, as a good many observers would have it, also "individualists," antagonistic to any social, any conventional or collective fettering of their "wills to power"? So they may conceive themselves, and so they may put themselves forward. Compare Weber's more complete description of the (ideal-typical) charismatic attitude: it is "revolutionary and transvalues everything; it makes a sovereign break with all traditional or rational norms."[37] The Nietzschean "beast," utterly unconcerned with what others may think of him, is nevertheless a sociological radical, a political being endowed with authority only in its own eyes. Legitimate sovereigns, genuine charismatics, always require an audience. Weber emphasizes that they require more: a "following,"[38] a chorus of approval. Radical sovereigns may be agents of sheer anarchy. Legitimate sovereigns may be agents of fragmentation, but a fragmentation that can never be categorically antisocial. Radical sovereignty may only be "for itself." Legitimate sovereignty is always for others. Legitimate sovereigns must always "prove" themselves against standards that they do not set alone. They may think themselves obedient to no one; but they must always play their part within a drama that can never be entirely of their own devising. The chorus must approve.

Attitudinal individualists, sovereign tacticians can be blithe deceivers; but they expose themselves as less than sovereign the moment they are discovered. Attitudinal subversives, sovereign tacticians may claim to be revolutionary; but they legitimately pursue their revolutions no further than their chorus is prepared to pursue them. Sovereign tacticians may sometimes be revolutionaries. But they may be nothing more than performers in an agonistic theater of prestige in whose script they have no autonomous hand at all.

Throughout the "traditional" Circum-Mediterranean, in the "Greece" described by most ethnographers from Campbell forward, that is just what they seem to be: performers, only within strict limits authors in their own right. In all of these sociocultural settings, sovereign tacticians enact a political script more than they write it. The script concerns individualism less than it concerns the definition of the tolerable forms of individuality. It is about egalitarianism far less than it is about the grounds of a legitimate inequality. Its theme is perhaps "honor." But honor is a moral catchall.[39] In some settings, there is more honor in being a determined egoist than in being a determined loyalist. In other settings, the contrary. In most settings, there is honor in being some relatively idiosyncratic mixture of both. There is shame in failing to find the balance. But the morality of honor and shame is not exclusively the morality of sovereigns and charismatics. It is the morality of all personalists, sovereign and patrimonial alike. Only the politics of regulation breaks with it. Regulators, economic or bureaucratic, have no obsession with honor. They need only concern themselves with a far more impersonal morality of respect.

Sovereignty IV: Toward a Postscriptural Modernity

In "traditional" settings—in the archetypical "village," for example—sovereign politics simply provides the underpinnings of a busy homeostasis. Sovereign tacticians contribute to its dynamics; the collectivity enforces its equilibrium. Even in more fluctuating settings—in pastoral hinterlands, for example—the same politics provides the underpinnings for what is often, in effect at least, a macrostructural equilibrium, even between distinct communities, though an equilibrium perhaps less agonistic than frankly antagonistic. Throughout, there are broad connective threads. Throughout, "honor" and "shame" are the bywords of virtue. Throughout, social interactions are predominantly personal. Social life is personal. It relies on "gossip." It inspires, often quite reasonably inspires, "paranoia."[40] It revolves around "friends," patronal or fraternal. It revolves around favors, not around strict adherence to legal maxims or to administrative rules. It is a guarded life: sovereigns everywhere know how to protect themselves against covetousness and know that they must. But sovereign protection is the protection of the daring. Sovereigns, male or for that matter female, rely not so much upon their material weapons as upon bluff and intimidation.

In the most permeable of settings, however, in urban settings above all, sovereign theater often disbands. But it can disband with quite different results. Even at the center of the Occident, it has not vanished. But it has been displaced by a political theater of far more regimented tactics and a far more abstract, far less intimate and circumstantial apologetics. At the center of the Occident, political theater is, to borrow a phrase from Foucault, "governmentalistic": a theater of regulation, of means and "standard deviations," a theater not of persons but of populations and their "welfare."[41] But the two great occidental catalysts of govermentalism—the Protestant routinization of personal conduct and the industrial automation of production—have had, to reiterate, relatively little impact on Greece. The Orthodox church has been able to rebuff any Protestant challenge. Industry emerged in Athens around the turn of the century. It nevertheless failed then, and still fails, to attract an especially large body of laborers. In 1928, only some 18.5 percent of economically active men and 15.7 percent of economically active women worked in one or another industrial enterprise.[42]

The percentages have increased only slightly since.[43] Most industrial enterprises are quite small; most are in fact family businesses. In 1938, some 93 percent of Greece's industrial laborers worked in intimate establishments that employed no more than five persons.[44] Vermeulen reports[45] that in 1963, "the figure was still as high as 88 percent." Many of the country's larger establishments, most of which inaugurated their operations only after 1960, are foreign-managed and foreign-controlled.[46] The native managerial cadre remains minuscule.

The economy of Athens is an epitome. In 1987, unemployment approached 10 percent, and the standard of living was slipping with the value of the drachma. But the capital was still no Mexico City, no Ankara, certainly no Calcutta. It had no real slums, either. It had seen shanty towns crop up around its outskirts at various earlier periods; but by the late 1970s, they had virtually all disappeared.[47] Greece has the second lowest per capita gross national product in the European Community. But between 1950 and 1980, it rose in world rank from forty-fifth to twenty-eighth, a rate of increase surpassed only by Kuwait, Saudi Arabia, and Libya.[48] By 1970 and until 1980, only some 2 to 3 percent of Athenians were officially unemployed. Family incomes approached an average of about $25,000. They were, on the average, probably far higher: official figures make allowance neither for the "hidden" monies earned from second or third jobs nor for the monies retained through tax evasion.[49] Violent crime has remained extraordinarily rare by American standards. Residents of Athens can still walk their avenues and streets well into the night, even alone, without fear of assault.

Even if relatively deprived, Athens thus has its felicitous side, of which Peter Allen offers an important, if partial, analysis. He points above all to the contribution of ambitious provincials. Greeks who have immigrated to the capital have generally been more skilled and better educated than those who have chosen to voyage beyond Greece's borders. Many of them have come to jobs that kinspeople have arranged for them. Many have come to houses or apartments that they already own. Provincials frequently invest their savings in "urban residential real estate."[50] Provincial families more and more frequently include some portion of Athenian real estate in their daughters' dowries. Daughters so endowed are better able to find Athenian husbands, and to establish metropolitan connections for their brothers.[51] All to the metropolis's benefit, of course: it has both thrived and long depended upon the economy and society of small-town boys and girls with big-town hopes and dreams.

But small-towners have invested and settled in Athens not to hope and dream but, symbolically and materially, to reap profits. They have frequently managed to do just that. For the most part, however, they have been neither inclined nor compelled to join the ranks of the urban proletariat. Greater Athens encompasses "fifty percent of Greece's total manufacturing capacity and industrial labor potential."[52] Its secondary economic sector is still minuscule. Its tertiary sector of private and public services is enormous. The imbalance is not unusual: many capitals produce far less than they consume. Many are less "autocephalous" than "hydrocephalous."[53] But the hydrocephaly of Athens is extreme. Greece as a whole produces far less than the metropolis alone consumes. Konstandinos Tsoukalas has drawn the obvious conclusion: the capital is sustained by foreign sources of income.[54] Tourists—whether from America, Europe, or Asia—are perhaps the most indulgent of Athens's patrons, but they are neither the most generous nor, in the age of terrorism, the most reliable.[55] Both the metropolis and the nation have been able more consistently to count on the gifts—given their obligatory character, they are better called "prestations"—not of immigrants but of emigrants. What the local infrastructure has not been able to supply, the infrastructures of western Europe and America and Australia usually have; and the Greek underclasses especially have long been willing to go to them. Even in 1971, a prosperous year, some 5 in every 1,000 Athenians migrated abroad; 135 in every 1,000 of the residents of the Epirote city of Thesprotia, and 116 of every 1,000 residents of the Macedonian city of Dhrama, emigrated as well. Overall, about a third more Greeks left the country than returned to it.[56] The pattern has been in place since the middle of the preceding century.[57] Tsoukalas among others suggests that emigration has consistently acted as a Greek safety valve, letting off the potentially subversive steam of a population many of whose members might otherwise have been idle.[58] It was surely among the most determinant sources of "full employment" in Greece through the 1970s. It has also proved to be a source of substantial foreign currency. Migrants have rarely left Greece intending never to return. They have rarely left it with the intention of breaking their family ties. On the contrary: the Greek underclasses especially are fiercely familistic, and the migrants among them have regularly sent their extra earnings back to their families even when they could not come back with them.[59]

Athens's own most dependable, and certainly its largest employer has since the 1830s been *to kratos*, "the state": the enduring apparatuses of control (*to kratos* proper), of legislation and regulation (*i kivernisi*), and of administration (*i dhiikisi*). From its inception, the state, thus broadly construed, has been notable for the number of its functionaries. Around 1800, "the number of civil servants per 10,000 of the population was approximately seven times higher in Greece than in the United Kingdom."[60] The proportions have not significantly changed since. Nor have aspirations: as in Dostoevsky's Russia, state service is in Greece still something of a vocational terminus ad quem. More than in Dostoevsky's Russia, it is in Greece still something of a post of command. From its inception, the state has been notable as well for its relative autonomy from the local forces of material production. Rarely their pawn, it has more often been their overseer. But it has been able to exert an inordinate influence over them in large part because it has never been able significantly to support itself with their bounty. From the late 1830s forward, it has itself had to rely instead upon the often manipulative grants and loans of various foreign benefactors. Until the Second World War, the United Kingdom was its most forthcoming source of funds. After the war and until recently, the United States paid it hundreds of millions of dollars annually for the rental and maintenance of four military bases. In 1990, two of the bases were closed, though less because of their local unpopularity than because of the end of the cold war. Some decade before, Greece had formally become a member of the European Community.[61] Leftists, especially pro-Soviet leftists, objected. Their complaints now seem moot. But if the advocates of confederation were, in some respects, choosing the West over the Rest, they were also rejecting America for what many of them believed would be more amicable, more brotherly influences.

The sovereigntist has accordingly faced more than his or her share of assaults. So have sovereignty's many Greek auditioners; socialized into relatively straightforward tactics, they have had to adapt to an increasingly ambiguous and elusive script. Even in "traditional" Greece, the criteria of legitimate sovereignty, of genuinely charismatic authority, are diverse. In urban Greece, they are even more diverse. They are also less mutually consistent, and the audiences and followings who would confirm them much less reliable, especially in advance. The politics of sovereignty may have given way in the Occident to a more routine and more abstract politics of regulation. It has given way in Greece not precisely to something else but to something more "awkward."

Though an urban phenomenon, the "awkwardness" of the contemporary political scene cannot simply be ascribed to "urbanization." There was, after all, nothing especially clumsy about the political scene of the "ancient city," however thoroughly urbanized it may have been. Political discontent must, in Greece and so in Athens, be derived as well, perhaps more fundamentally, from the local dynamics of permeability and dependency themselves. Not that the dynamics has been unchecked, of course: but Greeks have, for better or worse, more often felt the influence of the "world system" than they have exercised influence over it. They have resisted. If not always in the short run, the prevailing Greek condition has in the long run nevertheless been one not of lesser but of greater receptivity: to conceptions of community, to conceptions of society and of self, to scripts by no means their own. In the short run, Greeks have been ardent enthusiasts of homogenization. But as we have seen, neither linguistic nor ethnic nor religious homogeneity has spelled an end to significative multiplicity. No need to speak here of victims: neither Greeks as a whole nor Athenians more particularly have simply suffered through the various invasions that they have had to endure. Most have tolerated them; many have actively promoted them.

I cannot cite the precise second at which Athens itself first became not less but more "receptive." I can, however, cite a few pivotal events. The first, and the earliest, would be the return, to the new Greek nation, of the Phanariotes. They were thoroughly "Frankish" in their manners, in their tastes, and in their visions. So, too, were many of those who returned to the new Greek state from one or another diaspora community in Italy or France. Both the Phanariotes and the usually wealthy, repatriated scions of the "occidental" diaspora were successful, not simply in shaping and assuming control over the early organs of Greek government and education but also in enforcing the local validity, the high distinction, of their syncretic and relatively exotic styles of life in the face of what was then at best an only inchoate, or unprepared, opposition. Nationalist Greece needed a "high culture." The diaspora above all originally provided it with one.

The collapse of the Greek imperialist project, presaged by Greece's defeat in the 1897 war with Turkey but made final with the Asia Minor Disaster, saw various purgations: religious, cultural, and linguistic. It had its own reactionary and neotraditionalist aftermath. The ideological void it left, however, was gradually filled with a far more multifarious imagery of both community and personal identity than had preceded it. The self-consciousness of class that emerged more or less concomitantly with that void compelled, or in any event went hand in hand with, comprehensive reassessments: most broadly, of the lineaments of the ethnos; most narrowly, of the weight of family ties themselves. Consensus was not forthcoming. The 1949 Civil War confirmed the absence of consensus, and confirmed its absence with horrifying clarity. The 1967 junta, at least to the extent that it was an internal affair, perhaps served more than anything else to reiterate the same absence, indeed as much in the eyes of those who supported it and thought it necessary as in the eyes of those who condemned it from the outset. Its effect, however, has been quite broad. It has led to a certain political restraint. More remarkably, and perhaps more fundamentally, it has led as well to a questioning of "character," national and personal, that has by no means been restricted to the academy alone. Admonishments have been answered with defensiveness, of course, all the more as they have been repeated by various "external observers." But they have also inspired an openness, or in any event the opening of a sociocultural space of indefinition, within which both a virtually Zolan journalism and a politics, in part renewed, in part unprecedented, of identity formation have come to thrive.

Positive, auspicious events? Perhaps: but they have also been critical, and the crises they have provoked have not gone unnoticed. On the contrary. Consider the remarks of one native diagnostician: "if there exists a stable element that might strictly characterize the political development of Greece, that would be a virtually yearly *crisis of legitimacy*."[62] Compare the remarks of another: "anyone could say, without risk of exaggeration, that the crisis of identity constitutes the central problem of neo-Hellenic society, the fundamental element of contemporary Hellenism, and the axis around which our modern [*neoteri*] history revolves."[63] Somewhere in the previous century and a half, some Greeks at least found themselves at the problematical threshold of modernity. Some still find themselves there. But most have crossed it—or been pushed over its edge. And must one not conclude that they have, if only in bits and pieces, taken their metropolis along with them?

5

"EVERYTHING IS POSSIBLE":

NOTES ON THE GREEK MODERN

W HERE HAVE those Greeks who have crossed or found themselves pushed over the threshold of modernity consequently been placed? Once again, one can no longer appeal confidently to Weber. If his analysis of the antecedents and precipitants of modernity's threshold is not entirely persuasive, his analysis of the consequences of crossing or being pushed over the threshold is less persuasive still. It does not do complete justice either to modernization or to modernity in the "Occident." It does not do passable justice to either modernization or to modernity in Greece. Between modernity in the one place and modernity in the other there are, to be sure (and there must be), certain points in common. It is just as accurate, for example, to say that modern occidentals as to say that modern Greeks live in a more secular world than the world of the "traditional" past. And just as inaccurate: what Robert Bellah notes of "us" can also be noted of Greeks. Our mutual drift has not been away from belief but rather "beyond" it, toward "belief" recognized and defended as such.[1] For "occidentals" and for modern Greeks alike, both the ethically ordered cosmos and tradition itself may have lost their rational transparency; but among both, cosmologists and traditionalists are still a legion. The "occidental" and the modern Greek world is not faithless. Is it, as Weber would have it, rather "disenchanted"?

Modern and Disenchanted Ends:
An Occidental Genealogy

Weber borrows the term *Entzauberung* from Schiller:[2] "disenchantment," but more accurately in English, "demagification." Habermas, in his grand rewriting of Weber's diagnostics,[3] primarily restricts his attention[4] to the disenchanting process that Weber describes as "the conscious sublimation of man's relation to the various spheres of value, external and internal, as well as religious and secular."[5] For Habermas, as for an uncharacteristically evolutionistic Weber, the refinement of self-situation presses "towards making conscious *the internal and lawful autonomy* of the individual spheres."[6] Habermas finds in that valuational differentiation the *locus clas-*

sicus for his own learning theoretic and cognitivist rendering of cultural modernization.[7] Weber, whose "spheres of value" only vaguely resemble Habermas's, finds in it instead the beginning of an irresolute conflict, a drifting "into those [perspectival] tensions which remain hidden to the originally naive relation to the external world."[8] He finds in it moreover only one of the processual motors of our disenchanted, modernized, rationalized condition. There are other motors, perhaps more important.

In the emergence of science as in the codification of law and of the religious life, Weber notes a certain movement toward epistemic formalization: "Plato's passionate enthusiasm in *The Republic* must, in the last analysis, be explained by the fact for the first time the *concept*, one of the great tools of all scientific knowledge, had been consciously discovered."[9] Science as we know it, however, would come into its own only with the Renaissance, only with Leonardo and Galileo and Bacon and the other practitioners and theoreticians who would finally succeed in devising the "rational experiment": "a means," as Weber puts it, "of reliably controlling experience."[10] The achievement motivates, or is in any case emblematic of a profound, and profoundly modern, transformation of the West's positing of the world. It is emblematic, if not of the end, at least of the debasement, of any ontological mysticism: "one need no longer have recourse to magical means in order to master or implore the spirits, as did the savage, for whom such mysterious powers existed. Technical means and calculations perform the service."[11] Thus the crux of "demagification."

The antimysticism of modern "physics" has moreover its existential and practical analogues or affinates. In the fourth chapter of *The Protestant Ethic*, Weber notes that Catholicism had not carried "the rationalization of the world, the elimination of magic as a means to salvation," nearly so far as Puritanism had itself.[12] He characterizes the Catholic priest as a "magician who performed the miracle of transubstantiation, and who held the key to eternal salvation in his hand."[13] The Catholic believer could atone for his or her sins through repentances and please God through good works. "The God of Calvinism," in contrast, "demanded of his believers not single good works, but a life of good works combined with a unified system."[14] Weber continues:

> The moral conduct of the average man was thus deprived of its planless . . .
> character and subjected to a consistent method for conduct as a whole. It is no
> accident that the name of Methodists stuck to the participants in the last great
> revival of Puritan ideas in the eighteenth century just as the term Precisians . . .
> was applied to their spiritual ancestors in the seventeenth century.

Christian or, for that matter, Hindu asceticism had of course already embodied, even relatively early on, an ethos of rigorous control and self-discipline. The same or a very similar ethos had, as both Weber[15] and Foucault[16] have shown, long imbued militarism and military organization as well. What Calvin in any event "added," at least to monastic *principia*, was "the idea of the necessity of proving one's faith in worldly activity."[17] He thus provided "broader groups of religiously inclined people a positive incentive to asceticism."[18] What devolved from Calvin's contribution was not, however, simply the ecumenicalization of an already rationalized devotion. The Renaissance savants had managed to fashion, in theory and in practice, the conventions of an experimental proceduralism through which physical nature could be induced to reveal its invisible matrices. Calvin managed to fashion the doctrinal guidelines for a life itself lived as an argument or experiment, a life instrumentalized to generate the only graspable evidence, the only certainty it could have of its own salvation.

What the Puritans "taught" their more "utilitarian" successors was thus not simply the advantageousness of those specialized vocations upon which the "modern division of labor" would depend.[19] Nor was it simply the effectiveness of that sober and depersonalized habitus, "*sine ira ac studio*," upon which bureaucracy would come to rest.[20]

Puritanism brought about more, in the long run, than a rationalization of the habitus, or even of the habitus's involvement in "worldly affairs." It also offered the thoroughly disenchanted promise and the thoroughly secular revelation of the calculability of those very affairs. It thus brought about not simply a rationalization of "the moral conduct of the average man" but also a rationalization of ends. However loose, however fragmented his oeuvre may be, Weber chooses many years after the publication of *The Protestant Ethic* to define the type of action he took to be dominant, or in any case most called for, in the modern Occident with what must have been the Puritans' utilitarian successors above all in mind. *Zweckrational* or "purposively rational" action is determined, he says, by the actor's assessment of the objective chance of obtaining one of his or her own "rationally pursued and calculated ends."[21] Elsewhere in *Economy and Society*, commenting on the bureaucratic discharge of business, he comments that "the peculiarity of modern culture, and specifically of its technical and economic basis, demands . . . [the] 'calculability' of results."[22]

Weber sees in all the central institutions of modern occidental order, in science and in capitalism as well as in bureaucracy, a terrible stability. All of the modern Occident's central institutions enforce, by their very functioning, an overriding norm of "calculability." Each is thus opposed, by its very functioning, to personalism, to the play of passions, above all, in Weber's eyes, to the lofty indeterminacy of transcendent values, of ultimate ends. Each, in its own way, undermines the authority and the legitimacy of transcendent, of ultimate commitments, and does so all the more as its stability increases. The natural sciences, rigorously disenchanted, scrupulously objective, "are apt to make the belief that there is such a thing as the 'meaning' of the universe die out at its very roots";[23] religious sentiment, if it can speak against the sciences at all, is forced to speak against them from a self-consciously irrationalist stance. The "more the world of modern capitalist economy follows its own immanent laws, the less accessible it is," Weber says, "to any imaginable relation with a religious ethic of brotherliness."[24] Bureaucracy "develops the more perfectly the more [it] is 'dehumanized,' the more completely it succeeds in eliminating from official business love, hatred, and all purely personal, irrational, and emotional elements which escape calculation."[25] It has no need of followers:

> Modern loyalty is devoted to impersonal and functional purposes. Behind the functional purposes, of course, "ideas of culture-value" usually stand. These are *ersatz* for the earthly or supra-mundane personal master: ideas such as "state," "church," "community," "party," or "enterprise" are thought of as being realized in a community; they provide an ideological halo for the master.[26]

Puritanism was still genuinely informed by its transcendent, its ultimate values, which did, in their own way, remain personal. Its "ascetic educational influence" consequently could generally be felt "only after the peak of purely religious enthusiasm was past." Then "the isolated economic man who carries on missionary activities on the side takes the place of the lonely spiritual search of the Kingdom of Heaven of Bunyan's pilgrim, hurrying through the marketplace of Vanity."[27]

The tone of despair belies what might be dismissed as spiritualist nostalgia; it belies at least a haunted awareness of the spiritual privations that self-maintaining modern "systems," which have little respect for abiding passions, for inclinations toward the ultimate, or for "religious needs,"[28] can effect. "Modern culture" is not, for Weber, one in which all religious ponderings are exhausted. It is not one in which either the Dostoevskian or the Tolstoyan queries are without relevancy. Modernity is rather a state, a "lot," in which such queries take on a particularly tragic undertone, in part because the answers that might be adequate to them seem indeed to be allotted less and less conceptual and practical space. "It is not accidental," Weber writes in one of his wisest and most luminary asides, "that our greatest art is intimate and not monumental, nor is it accidental that today only within the smallest and [most] intimate circles, in personal human situations, in *pianissimo*, that something is pulsating that corresponds to the prophetic *pneuma*, which in former times swept through the great communities like a firebrand, welding them together." He goes on:

> If we attempt to force and to "invent" a monumental style in art, such miserable monstrosities are produced as the many monuments of the last twenty years. If one tries intellectually to construe new religions without a new and

genuine prophecy, something similar will result, but with still worse effects. And academic prophecy, finally, will create only fanatical sects but never a genuine community.[29]

The compartmentalization, the lessening of the conceptual and practical space of substantive engagements is, however, not the only process upon which Weber's prediction stands. There are other processes at issue, perhaps even more "tragic." Modernity's particular horror lies, for Weber, not only in the compartmentalization, the "splitting apart" of formerly integrated "spheres of value." It also lies in the ineluctable irrationalization of those values, and of all passions, of all inclinations toward the ultimate, of all religious needs as well. It lies not in a purposive rationality "without roots" but in a purposive rationality finally capable of severing its roots and of making a mockery of whatever surrogate roots happen, for whatever reason, to be grafted onto it.

Reaching the Threshold: Greece and the Occident Compared

One can disagree with a great many of Weber's finer points. But virtually all analysts do agree that modernity was, in the Occident, an "emergent" state of affairs, that it emerged in the course of an extremely complex interplay among various "theories" and various practices, and that if the capitalist organization of free labor was not its first, it was its central infrastructural force. Modernity, in Greece, has perhaps not been altogether "invasive" in contrast. But the capitalist organization of labor gave rise to a "world system" that did not emanate from Greece but instead absorbed it, peripheralizing it in the process. Greeks were consequently brought to the threshold of modernity not through any purely internal conversion, either of religious doctrine, or of tactics, or even of economic practices. They were brought to it instead as their locally prevailing human orders were gradually put into an ever more inescapable competition with imported ones. They were brought to it as their traditional scripts were gradually eroded by others that had increasingly to be taken into account. Sovereign tacticians entertain no real compromise and charismatics insist upon the "absolute validity" of their contentions and claims.[30] But what can they do in the face of other charismatics, insisting upon the absolute validity of contentions and claims increasingly more inconsistent with their own? Struggle with them to the death, perhaps, or strive at least to shame them into submission.

But whose side is a poor audience to take? Sovereign tactics are discursively absolutist, as any brief review of the past 150 years of Greece's "official ideologies" clearly reveals.[31] Sovereigns can be agents of "perfect" stability only so long as they remain unchallenged. Sovereign contests for domination can, however, unfold upon a macrostructurally stable stage so long as they are not contests over the institutionalization of inconsistent absolutes; so long, in other words, as all the contestants share the same "transcendent values," the same "finalities." But in Greece, contestants have not always shared the same finalities, and they share them now less than ever before. Even though sovereign tactics are discursively absolutist, sovereign contests in Greece have, in the long run at least, turned out to be relativist in effect. For every one "transcendent value," there has in Greece turned out in the long run to be some equally plausible, equally dubious other. Sovereignty's unfolding, through a long sequence of scriptural restructurations and dissolutions, has managed to bring forth what a gradually ascendant formal rationalism managed to bring forth variously in Germany, in France, in Great Britain, and, to be sure, in the United States: the subversion of social consensus; the subversion not simply of the transparency of tradition but also of the transparency of the Good itself. In the Occident, rationalization has at least left modernity with a "functional habitus," however small, and petty, and calculating it may be. In Greece, as the diagnosticians of the crisis of identity surely attest, the dissolution of tactical scripts has left modernity not even with that. Practice has lost much of its former sociality. Has a disenchanted world come in its wake? In Athens, at least, it has, even if a few natives might still hope for an occasional bit of magic.

After the Threshold: From Otherworldly to Worldly Valuations

But how bad is it, really? Is modernity, in "the Occident" or in Athens, actually as bereft of substantive consensus as Weber would believe? Habermas, for one, thinks that, in "the Occident" at least, it is not. He regards Weber's diagnostics as far too extreme:

> [Weber's] underlying assumption is that the disenchantment of religious-metaphysical worldviews robs rationality, along with the contents of tradition, of all substantive connotations and thereby strips it of its power to have a structure-forming influence on the lifeworld beyond the purposive-rational organization of means.[32]

If Habermas means that Weber could not, in theory, make any distinction between "irrational" and "rational" ends, then he is quite mistaken. Weber's distinction between "transcendent values" and "purposes" is just that. If, however, Habermas means that Weber defined the "formal rationality" of any substantive end only as its "calculability," if he means that Weber had no means of distinguishing between the relative "rationality" of two equally calculable ends, then he is quite right. Weber regarded one calculable end as being just as rational or irrational as any other. He regarded them all as having no other ultimate ground but "subjective interest." Habermas rejects Weber's contention that modernity's dominant rationality is merely "formal," and rejects it with some justification, regardless of whether "communicative reason" is even normatively as dominant as he claims. He also rejects Weber's substantive subjectivism. Modernity is not for Habermas a state or lot in which the intersubjective "lifeworld" has been utterly destroyed. It is a state in which formalistic "systems" have taken on their own independence; but however "uncoupled" from systems it may be, the lifeworld still survives.

I cannot follow Habermas so far. Neither in "the Occident" nor, so far as I can see, in Athens does an intersubjectively valid *congregatio corporum* or *universitas rerum*, a "culture," still inform daily life. But against Weber, perhaps against such contemporary Weberians as Niklas Luhmann, Habermas nevertheless has his point. Even if there are, in "the Occident" or in Athens, no longer any "immanent" cultures, even if there are no longer any indubitable designs for living or indubitable "values," there are still socially and culturally enduring substances out of which designs for living and values both might be made. They may not be "objective"; but they are not, whether in their apperception or in their actual consequences, entirely or merely "subjective" substances either. Not even in "the Occident" do moderns, *qua* moderns, come to their ends and values simply by heeding some indeterminable and inscrutable inner voice. Nor in Athens.

With the disintegration of the ethically ordered cosmos, moderns perhaps have no other "rational" ground for their particular values than the actual world itself. But the world is not as bereft as Weber sometimes took it to be. Moderns everywhere continue to have available and continue to be swayed by a common substantive repertoire. The well-being of the body, its security, its physical and political vigor: all these belong to the repertoire, and without them neither the motivations nor the regulative ideals of the welfare state can even begin to be understood.[33] On the other hand, neither the technologies of "discipline" nor the aesthetics of Nazism can, without appeal to the morality of the body, begin to be understood either. Weber, for his part, recognized clearly enough the disciplinary exploitation of the moral body;[34] what he saw was simply another facet of formal rationalization. He did not live to see the rise of Nazism; but there is no cause to believe that he would have been any more an enthusiast of the Nazi heroization of the body than of its later "biotechnical" regulation.

The environment—nature as we perceive it, as it touches us—has rather recently come to belong to the modern repertoire of substances of valuation. Even in its brief tenure, it has, however, shown itself eminently susceptible to the body's own posttraditional transformation. It has shown itself susceptible to being rationalized into nothing more than another puzzle for the ethos of world mastery; susceptible, on the other hand, to being reified into a countermodern weapon against even the most circumspect proponents of "progress."

History, Temporality, and Valuation in "The Occident"

History, the concrete matter of past and present, is a third substance of intersubjective valuation, though no more than the body is it an exclusively modern substance. The simple distinction between past and present, between present and future is, as Kant pointed out, constitutive of human experience itself, not a "cultural" so much as a "precultural" universal. The same distinctions appear, however, universally to be put to at least some cultural use, everywhere to be imbedded in and to serve as an organizational framework for some at least of the practices of everyday life.[35] There may be peoples without archives. But there are none, of course, genuinely without history, and none altogether inattentive to history.

Not all designs for living are, however, temporalizing. Not all grant ultimate "truth," epistemological or existential, to the passage of time. Not all attribute any ultimate epistemological or existential importance to that passage. Lévi-Strauss famously declares the "savage" the archetypically ahistorical metaphysician.[36] Geertz finds a similarly ahistorical and cosmic metaphysics in Bali; Sahlins finds one in the kingdoms of precolonial Polynesia.[37] All mythological metaphysics are ultimately ahistorical. Even classical metaphysics, though "post-mythological,"[38] does not reject the mythological regard of history itself. Plato's forms are eternal. Aristotle's universals are not. But even for Aristotle, wisdom derives not from experience but from the revelation of the constancies of experience. Even for Aristotle, the cosmos is still all that is and all that could possibly be. History simply brings it to earth.

Reinhart Koselleck finds the same attitude toward history dominant until about the end of the eighteenth century. Until then, history does not in the Occident stand on its own. Until then, it is still dominantly comprehended as the expression or manifestation of some preordained cycle or sequence. Until then, history was "intranatural." But not afterward. Koselleck notes "the decisive registration of the discovery of a specific historical temporality":

> This involves what might be called a temporalization of history, which has . . .
> detached itself from a naturally formed chronology. Up until the eighteenth
> century, the course and calculation of historical events was underwritten by two
> natural categories of time: the cycle of the stars and planets, and the natural
> succession of rulers and dynasties. Kant, in refusing to interpret history in terms

of astronomical data and rejecting as nonrational the course of succession, did away with established chronology on the grounds that it provided a guideline that was both annalistic and theologically colored, "as if chronology were not derivative of history, but rather that history must arrange itself according to chronology."[39]

He adds that, once the naturalistic basis of time disappeared, "progress became the prime category in which a transnatural, historically immanent definition of time first found expression."[40]

The historical hermeneutics of progress would not, in the Occident, immediately lose the "perfectionism" of the hermeneutics that preceded it. It would not immediately cease to be metaphysical. Nor has metaphysical history ever entirely disappeared. But after Kant, even metaphysicians would try to understand the world in and through history, and not history in and through some already created world. Even Hegel was a metaphysician in and through history more than a metaphysician of it. Kant's declaration of the impossibility of a purely a priori physics was the beginning of the end of a purely a priori hermeneutics of history as well. It was the beginning of a temporal consciousness that would focus far more on the epistemic and existential particularities of situation than upon the goal either of contemplating the cosmos or of realizing some transcendent fate. It was the beginning of an ethical and moral consciousness that put more store in the human capacity to alter reality[41] than in man's subjection to it. It was the beginning of a temporal and a moral consciousness that had its theme not in any millenarian resolution but rather in a potentially limitless process of surpassing. Hans Blumenberg writes accordingly of the "infinitalization" of the idea of progress:

> It was certainly a result of the quick disappointment of early expectations of definitive total results that the idea of progress underwent expansion into that of "infinite progress." Descartes still seriously thought of the attainment during his lifetime of the final theoretical and practical goals of his program of method, that is, the completion of physics, medicine and . . . ethics. Thus, the introduction of infinity here was . . . initially a form of resignation. The danger of this hyperbolizing of the idea of progress is the necessary disappointment of each individual in the context of history, doing work in his particular situation for a future whose enjoyment he cannot inherit. Nevertheless the idea of infinite progress also has a safeguarding function for the actual individual and for each actual generation in history. If there were an immanent final goal in history, then those who believe they know it and claim to promote its attainment would be legitimized in using all the others who do not know it and cannot promote it as mere means. Infinite progress does make each present relative to its future, but at the same time it renders every absolute claim untenable.[42]

Koselleck attributes the emergence of this new temporality to the experience of the French Revolution.[43] Blumenberg attributes it not simply to the disappointments of the scientific methodists but originally to the failure of the medieval effort "to save the cosmos of Scholasticism."

Let us grant at least that the temporal and moral consciousness that has its theme in an infinitalized progress appeared first in "the Occident." History, however, has not fared very well there. The "historical temporality" that Koselleck identifies has always had to compete with others: the momentary temporality of lyricism and latter-day mysticism; above all, the "reclassicizing" temporality of "laws-and-causes" science. States and governments—not only in "the Occident," of course—enforce antihistorical and absolute policies when they can, whether under the essentializing rubric of "nationhood" or under the epochalizing rubric of "manifest destiny." Bureaucracies also neutralize history. Bureaucrats have at least to try to neutralize it; they cannot but comprehend any irresolute hiatus between past and present, between present and future, as an irrational bother, to be coped with as best it can. They treat time as something to be "managed."[44] Moral proceduralists must try to neutralize history as well, at least so long as they have to insist upon the moral equivalence of one spatiotemporally particular situation to the next.[45]

Nothing precisely premodern about the withdrawal from an ultimately historical hermeneutics, then: but the modern withdrawal differs from both the "savage" and the classical. Modern atemporalists, whether epistemic or moral, must face the challenge of historical hermeneutics outright, and unlike classical atemporalism at least, they must face it continually. Classicism is, virtually by definition, the overcoming of history.

Modern atemporalism cannot dare to be otherworldly either. If it does, it is vulnerable to the empirical and nominalist mockery of the "good historian" at every turn. It must settle for being inductive, for extrapolating its constancies through some convincing argument from a field of contingencies. Or it must settle for being artifactual, for imposing itself "rationally" as both bureaucratic and ethical proceduralisms do upon the undisciplined and always too "political" succession of particulars themselves.

Historical hermeneutics retains in the Occident a certain prestige, whatever its actual empowerment may be. It is, particularly when wedded to the principle of an infinite progress, Croce's (or Vico's) great "countermethod," a singularly effective rhetoric against the absolutist pride of states and bureaucracies alike.[46] At its best, it can indeed be productive. At its worst, however, it can lead to the sort of aristocratic cynicism embodied in Horkheimer and Adorno's "negative dialectics." Against the "irrationality" of historical hermeneutics, against its threat of cynicism as well, the mainstreams of the occidental literati and intelligentsia both have made a concerted effort to defend one or another more systematic alternative. Bureaucrats have, in practice, tended to encourage them. Later capitalists have not been quite so encouraging: the more particularizing a historical hermeneutics can be, the more it promises to proliferate desires; the more it promises to proliferate desires, the more it promises to expand the markets that cater to them. But the late capitalist market has its restraint: too much in the way of historical particularization, desires and sentiments turn out to be too idiosyncratic efficiently and profitably to be served. For late capitalism, not history but the body is a far more manageable material of need and of value. The environment may, in the end, prove to be equally manageable.

What, in the Occident, does a historical hermeneutics continue to inform? A "countermethod," perhaps. Some broad situation of identity. But occidental modernity has no real need of the substance of history; or needs it only to articulate its break with it. In the Occident, a historical hermeneutics still informs the projects of a trivialized poetry that virtually no one any longer reads. It informs a trivialized production of fashions in which virtually no one can any longer afford to partake. Does it continue to inform the occidental production of the person, a modern occidental existentialism, as well? In some measure, it does. But the recovery of moral proceduralism—in the United States, with Rawls; on the continent, with Habermas—belies less an enthusiasm for than an aversion to the irreducibly particular substance of history. Procedures may be unfulfilling; but they are at least "ruly."

History, Temporality, and Valuation in Greece: Historical Constructivism as the Greek Modern

What, in Greece, does a historical hermeneutics inform? Simply put, it informs not any countermethod but "method" itself. Greeks have sometimes reacted to the existential threshold of modernity with hostility, sometimes amicably. But until very recently, neither the body nor the environment has provided nearly so much substance for either its countermodern or its modern valuations as history has itself. One cannot be surprised that Greeks have so often been dismissive, often plainly suspicious, of the rationalism that "occidentals" find so attractive. Sovereign tactics and charismatic modes of legitimation are both personal. They are both at odds, at least in practice, with the normative impersonality of any proceduralism, epistemic or moral. But that is not all. Proceduralism, epistemic but especially moral, has like most other formally rationalist dogmata come into Greece, not come from it. It has come into it, in the guise of parliamentary procedure or some other very serious game, less as an instrument of truce than as a weapon of sovereign advantage. Greeks have often deployed it against one another and, just as often, had to cope with others deploying it against them all. The result: proceduralism tends in Greece to look like just another technology of domination, with not much more to recommend it than its rigorous politesse. Politesse is something; but not everything.

After the cosmos there are procedures, but after purportedly universal procedures reveal themselves to be just another technology of domination, what to do? One can always reavow the "eternal verity" of precedent: a turn as typical of the new fundamentalists of America as of the abiding "traditionalists" and "cultural classicists" of Greece. But fundamentalism and cultural classicism share with proceduralism a common weakness: all are forced to treat every novelty as a provocation. All are, in the face of change, constantly under siege. One can always be eclectic for the sake of variety itself. But critics of the pursuit of variety are no doubt right to complain of its lack of direction, of its "decadence." The pursuit of variety is not yet ethical; at best, it is exploratory. After the exhaustion of the meaningfully oriented cosmos, after the exhaustion of universal procedures, one can also turn to contextualism, to "relational" moralities and "situational" ethics for which neither the good nor the right is definable in advance, or even definable at all. Not precisely aimless, not "decadent," relational moralities and situational ethics are instead "topical." Whether conservative or, as they more familiarly are in America, self-consciously "progressive," they share an emphasis on the irreducible contingency of decisions and choices, but especially upon the irreducible moral and ethical immediacy of the here and now. That is perhaps their strength, but it is a strength with a weakness; relational moralists and situational ethicists are always in danger of becoming victims of immediacy whenever the here and now begin to pass into the there and then. Consider the fortunes of the American "Generation of Love."

Americans have, however, long known an ethical practice, a practice of self-formation, still situational in its premises but less topical and less occasional in its goals. It has given rise, among other things, to what Harold Bloom has called "the American difference" in poetry, but it has given rise to an American character and style in other domains as well. It is a practice not just in poetry but of *poiēsis*, of the "making" of everything from a poem, through the self and its spaces, to society. It is at once transcendentalist and thisworldly. Call it the project of an "American modernity," or simply "the American modern."

Like Harold Bloom, Bellah and his associates see Whitman as among the first to undertake the practice, and Whitman's song of self as among the first and most clear of its articulations. Whitman is among the first of America's "expressive individualists."[47] The "successful life" was for him "a life rich in experience, open to all kinds of people, luxuriating in the sensual as well as the intellectual, above all a life of strong feeling."[48] Freedom was, for him, "above all the freedom to express oneself, against all constraints and conventions."[49] Whitman's self is blatantly bodily. But it is not realized through the body merely. Whitman's distinctively American and modern self is realized rather through its identification "with other people, with places, with nature, ultimately with the universe."[50] Whitman strives to be everyone and everything that is, and will be.

The Greek practice that I would like to speak of as "historical constructivism" is comparable with Whitman's—it, too, is at once transcendentalist and thisworldly—though not quite the same. Searching for one of its earliest executors, one might—so I suggested in my Introduction—arrive at Adhamandios Korais: the acknowledged "father" of that "grave linguistic error," katharevousa.[51] His example is not without controversy. Surely the father of an archaizing and puristic language, a language literally "ideal," must have been a "cultural classicist." The fathers of that language surely were cultural classicists. They were men who "subscribed to the view that the Greek language had been debased in proportion as the nation had been enslaved," and that the revival of ancient Attic was the only, or at least one of the best means by which the nation could once again become worthy of its past glory.[52] They were rhetorical metalepticians, but their tropology once again introjective, their aim the aim of updating an ancient language in order to reestablish or reveal again the incorruptible ancient essence of a metaphorical Hellenic ethnos. Korais, however, was not one of those men. As Michael Jeffreys points out, he was well aware that "languages change, that the clock cannot be put back, that the arbiters of [any] . . . language are those who speak it."[53] He was a linguistic democrat, though opposed to leaving Greek's "shaping and creation to the vulgar imagination of the mob."[54] He thought well of purifying demotic of "foreign words and constructions."[55] But he wanted above all to style a language that would synthesize the speech of the past with the speech of the present, and so serve as a pedagogical bridge between what Greece once was and what it had come to be.[56] He, too, was a metaleptician, but his tropology projective. The ideal he sought not to reveal again but rather to construct anew was not the language of Plato and Aristotle, suitably updated. It was rather the language of his contemporaries, "archaized" and "purified" enough to enable its speakers to regain control of the past, to recover it without having to surrender to it.

Korais's katharevousa may thus be one of the first artifacts of historically constructivist *poiēsis*. Might there nevertheless be earlier prototypes? Perhaps not: but Greek literary scholars have with some good reason come generally to agree that the "neo-Hellenic" canon has its beginnings in the tenth-century epic of the *Dhiyenis Akritis*, "Two-Blooded Borderer," a prince combining in his blood and in his acts the heritage of an "Arab" mother and a "Greek" father and dwelling on the *akres*, the "borders," between East and West.[57] There is no current term in demotic for "historical constructivism."[58] There is no current term, either, for the "prime category" or regulative idea that appears to guide it. Certainly, demotic has a term for "progress," and contemporary Greece its share of progressivists, especially in politics and in journalism. But just as many Greeks today are scornful of "the myth of progress," and many give more allegiance to precisely the sort of "resolution" that the *Akritis* represents: an "accommodating synthesis" of traditions living and dead, endogenous and exogenous, into a unified "historical personality" that surpasses, but does not necessarily "better," them all.

As the canonization of the *Akritis* would suggest, the "Greek difference" in poetry and in prose has, from Solomos to Kazantzakis and forward, resided in a striving toward a synthetic unification of past and present "influences." It has resided in a striving for a "completion" that is nevertheless not essentialist. This "Greek difference," this "Greek modern," is not Baudelaire's. It is not the capturing of "the eternal in the fleeting moment."[59] Like progress, syntheses of tradition are never more than momentarily complete. The former is vulnerable to every intuition that things "might be better." The latter are as vulnerable to every "discovery" or "rediscovery" of the past as they are to the inevitable brevity of what is not yet past. Like progressivists, historical constructivists strive toward a totalization that they know they can never achieve.[60] The Greek modern is not Baudelaire's; it is not, precisely at this juncture, Whitman's. Historical constructivists do not strive to be everything that is or will be. They strive instead to be as much as they can of what the world has left them to be.

As with selves, so with their spaces: I have already noted the historically constructive character of Ersi Khatzimikhali's apartment. It is no exception, but rather one substantive modality of the rule. The Athenian home of the late impresario Alexander Iolas is another. Like the Khatzimikhalis estate, it has also been ceded to the state: a guarantee, among other things, of both the preservation and the canonization of the collection that it holds. No accident that it has already been featured in a recent photographic documentary on "Greek style."[61] The home has its quirks: Iolas, who spent much of his time in New York, was painted by Warhol, and made one of his Athenian sitting rooms into a gallery of Warhol's portraits of him. Self-conscious? Quite: but so is every other "modern." Ersi Khatzimikhali gives stress in her apartment to the "primitive" and the "rustic." Iolas gave stress to other, less laic elements. He furnished his master bedroom with Hellenistic statuary and bone-white spreads. The beds there are, however, single: a tradition inspired, or at least rationalized, by summer heat. The floors of the room are marble. The rug that covers them is colorful and hand-woven, perhaps Thessalain or Macedonian. A Venetian chandelier hangs from the ceiling. There are two large chairs, both of ornately carved wood, both upholstered in worn, green velvet. One may date from the Byzantine Renaissance; both reflect the tastes of the European baroque. One of the occasional tables is English; various others, geometric and spare, once again of marble, are late modernist. A small brass figurine, a carved alabaster box, and *komboloi*, a string of Greek worry-beads, sit on the table nearest to the central bed.

The room "works": but what else would one expect? Iolas was a connoisseur, and historically constructivist *poiēsis* is largely the project of connoisseurs who have both the materials and the leisure not simply to pursue it but to become virtuosi at it. Not that it is restricted to the intellectually and culturally and socially most endowed. It is not. In theory at least, anyone in Greece might be a historical constructivist, and many Greeks, especially those who belong to the new and endemically mimetic middle classes, try to be. But the Greek intelligentsia is better equipped intellectually to command it. Greece's sociocultural upper strata are more "blessed" with the leisure but also with the confidence that experimentation requires. An elite project, yes: but that is, in part, what has given it its primacy.

Why History? From Culture to the Regime of Signification

Much of Athens's exterior architecture is historically constructive, whether neoclassical, neo-Byzantine, or modernist. The neoclassical incorporates such "Mediterranean" elements as full-length shutters and balconies. It incorporates "Anatolian" grace notes of wrought iron and wood. The neo-Byzantine may be a more masterful synthesis of vernacular planes, Roman arches, and Gothic proportion. But even "modernism" in Athens is less a "purification" than an historical synthesis. Even modernism cannot escape—could not, even if modernists wished—from the dominant historicities of both Ionic and Cycladic forms. Even its grandest and most uncompromising Athenian expressions—the Hilton Hotel, a vast, bent rectangle of white stone, the main entry of which is crowned with hieroglyphic entablatures—are thus inevitably "postmodernist"[62] in their way. Even the Acropolis is perhaps in its present state best described as postmodernist—well before its time, of course.

But why historical? Because the Acropolis could not be torn down? Because "Greek culture" is more sensitive, more devoted to the substance of time than most others? Neither: history invaded Greece as much as "modernity" did itself. The Acropolis might have been torn down. Greeks would originally have objected less strongly than their philhellenist supporters. But the Greek intelligentsia, singularly capable of the intellectual task, had to take up history; the past provided the only ground upon which the new nation could establish its raison d'être to a Europe that had already concluded that Greece had little other reason rightly to be.[63] A "specifically historical temporality" would invade Greece as well. Traditionalists, cultural classicists, would reject it. Historical constructivists would embrace it, and transform it in the process into the temporality of a far more provisional and far less presumptuous ethic of self-formation than Europeans further west yet know. "Greek culture" would be transformed as a consequence: no longer simply given, it would itself become an object, one ground or medium among many others of synthetic recombination.

After "culture," what more internal, more habitual, compulsion is left? Among other things, the historically constructive enterprise itself is left, along with the revisionary "methodology" that accompanies it. Is it, too, merely "decadent"? The judgment is far too harsh. If meaning is destroyed by some revisionary acts or events, it gets started in others. Harold Bloom identifies three:

> Meaning gets started by a catastrophe that is also a ruining or breaking creation—originally a Gnostic formulation. Or else meaning gets started by a transference of a purely fictive earlier authority to a later representative—originally a Hebraic formulation. Or else meaning gets started by an act of violence, textual or physical, in a family grouping—originally what Vico called a Gentile formulation, both Asiatic and Greek.[64]

Once it gets started, there is nothing but further revisionary events, analogous to tropes or actual tropes, to keep it going. Weber saw revision in every charismatic rupture with authority: "It is written, but I say unto you." Bloom similarly sees it as an inevitable "usurpation of authority."[65] Cultural anthropologists know revision, or some aspects of it, as "ideologization,"[66] though not all revision is "ideological," even in Geertz's expanded sense of the term. Not all revision is "modern" either. But none of us would ever have reached, much less crossed over, the threshold of modernity without it.

If revision always goes against some authority, it always depends for its legitimacy on some other. Even the charismatic needs a following, and if revisionary prophecy is sometimes haphazard, its reception is not. Foucault notices that "each society has its regime of truth, its 'general politics' of truth":

> the kinds of discourse which it accepts and renders operative as true; the mechanisms and the circumstances which permit the distinction between true and false statements, and the way in which the former and the latter are sanctioned; the techniques and the procedures which are valuable for securing truth; the status of those who have the responsibility of saying what is or is not true.[67]

More carefully put, the legitimation, the reception, the production, and the reproduction of "truth" are all inherently social, hence at least somewhat "regimental." Not just "truth" either: Foucault's regime is only a part of something broader, a "regime of signification" or "general politics" of the legitimation, reception, production, and reproduction not merely of truth but also of opinion, also of fiction. Not everyone is a charismatic; not every would-be prophet is accepted as a prophet. Everyone may have his or her own opinions, but not everyone is in a position to proffer them or see them taken seriously or put into effect. Not all fictionalists are equally "good" or "talented," not all fictions equally valid.

If no longer a culture, there are still several regimes of signification operative within and across the boundaries of contemporary Greece, some restricted to one or another technical practice, others far more encompassing. There are several regimes even of existential signification in Greece, but there is still an elite that dominates the production and reproduction of existential determinations almost as much as it dominates the validation of them. In the long run, it is practically identical with the sociocultural elite, with those who have their credentials in some collection of birthrights and diplomas. In the short run, not necessarily: common producers can gain at least probationary entry into the elite of existential signification if their products meet with the approval of those already established. In theory, the system is democratic. Common producers, however, rarely garner the approval of the establishment unless they show themselves to be masters of what has become the established Greek modern practice of revisionary existentialism: historically constructivist *poiēsis* itself. Common producers rarely have either the intellectual or the material leisure to master it. Members of the sociocultural elite remain the practice's most adept and polished virtuosi. They may speak neither of "historical constructivism" nor of "accommodating syntheses" nor of "unified historical personalities." But they have a few favorite phrases that acknowledge them all.

"Athens is chaos": so this ethnographer was often told. "In Greece, everything is disorganized. Anything is possible." Such comments are not always comments "of" or "in crisis." But they are nevertheless "critical" in two respects. On the one hand, they express a sage suspicion of the security of any order, human or superhuman. On the other, they announce an existential situation as poorly informed by the patterns of the past as by the sheer indefinition of an "open future." Running thoroughly counter to the "fatalism" that is supposedly so fundamental to the Mediterranean cast of mind,[68] they cannot yet be said to disclose that confidence in the self-creative capabilities of the human will that Blumenberg among others has deemed the point of departure for any positively modern metaphysics of being in time.[69] But some of Greece's elite have another favorite phrase, in which that confidence is more apparent. "Here," some of them sometimes declare, "*everything* is possible."

Nihilist? On the contrary, I would submit that the declaration is not just metaphysical but plainly religious.[70] At a time when America's most radical cultural classicists have begun to generate bestsellers, at a time when historical relativism is in greater danger than ever of being conflated with a sort of militant subjectivism, Greece's constructivists surely provide a salutary counterexample. A historically sensitive habitus tempered in the crucible of continual "invasions" and instabilities need not reject either truth or validity. It need reject only untested and untestable absolutes. Dedicated to contingency, it has little affinity for either millenarian cosmodicies or for the philosophies of history that have succeeded them. Disposed to favor the "situational" over the "context-free," it perhaps has little affinity even for those decidedly modern, or modernist, proceduralisms that Rawls and Habermas have championed. But if not "rule-governed," historical constructivism is still ruly enough. If not an emanation of "communicative reason," it still has its inherent norms, its by-no-means entirely subjective "raw materials," and its by-no-means purely formal "good sense."

Unstable itself? Often enough it is. But historical constructivism is also stabilizing in its way. If it permits, if it indeed encourages conflict, it also encourages the institutionalization of those social checks and balances that, in the long run at least, constrain the tyranny of any absolutism; if it encourages an agonism of meanings, if it is consequently productive of among the most resilient modernities in all of Europe, it also imposes upon the revision of meanings the ordering constraints of a historicizing pragmatics whose tolerance of revolution is always somewhat reserved. "Meaning" consequently lends "order" to Greek as to other Circum-Mediterranean "societies" and "cultures";[71] lends it, however, less through its constancy than through its always limited, and always systematically limited change from one critical moment to the next. Or so, in the final chapters of this essay, I try to show.

PART III

AFTER THE COLONELS: PROJECTS OF
SELF-DEFINITION AND SELF-FORMATION
SINCE 1974

6

THE SELF MADE: DEVELOPING A
POSTNATIONAL CHARACTER

... consciousness of a tumultuously realized social transition is
one of the fundamental characteristics of our epoch and there
is no doubt that this consciousness inevitably leads as well to
people becoming ever more aware of their relation to history.
(Vassilis Filias) [1]

L OGICS OFFER a means of characterizing the conditions under
which, in the argumentative movement from premises to conclusions, truth is preserved. Rhetorics offer a device for treating
the perlocutionary force of statements and other acts. They offer a device
for refining a symbolic analysis, for distinguishing between tropes of one
sort and tropes of another. But they also offer a means for characterizing the
conditions under which, in the revisionary movement from literalisms to
tropes or from one trope to another, sense can be preserved even in the
absence of truth or reference. They consequently offer a means, as yet
hardly noted by analysts of "culture change" or "symbolic action," of characterizing the constraints that revisionists of everything from society to the
self must respect if they are to "make sense" rather than to lose it as they
proceed. No more than logics are rhetorics determinative of what must
come next. But they nevertheless give definition to the very ancient intuition that reformers, in making sense rather than losing it, have only certain
moves available to them. Rhetorics give structure to significative strategies.
They give definition to the very ancient intuition that, in the short-run at
least, not just every reformation, not just every revision, not just everything
is in fact possible.

Constraints on Modern Self-Formation

Nor is the practical obligation to make sense rather than lose it the only
constraint under which revisionists must labor. Consider the revision, or
simply the "realization," of the self: as "popular" a project in Athens as it is

in "the Occident." If not a pure text, the self is surely textual, and its motifs, its compositional themes, its conceptualizations vary considerably from place to place and from time to time, as much of ethnography attests. They vary dramatically in their details, always an important source of the anthropological exotic. But they do not, as Marcel Mauss perhaps originally saw, vary nearly so dramatically in their "provisional axiomatics," which are far less subject to limitless differentiation than the more ardent of cultural relativists often presume. Granted, the matter does not resolve neatly into some Great Divide between, say, "traditional" and "modern" selfhood. There is no more of a Great Divide between traditional and modern selves than between traditional and modern "cultures." The lack of a Great Divide notwithstanding, there are nevertheless broad and systematic differences between those characterologies that uphold the integrity of the "ethically ordered cosmos" and those that put the integrity of that cosmos in doubt, or in brackets. The former are paradigmatically "primitive" or "traditional"; but they are also classical, also medieval, also "countermodern." The latter are perhaps paradigmatically "modern," but also "countermythological" and "counterclassical," sometimes only inchoately modern or "protomodern."[2]

Criticism of the ethically integral cosmos is itself quite ancient. Hecataeus, who wrote or professed in Ionia in the sixth century B.C., is among the first critics on record to attack it—apparently in the name of the truth of history, of the contingency of process. Neither Hecataeus nor the sophists who follow him in the fifth century B.C. confine themselves to an ethical skepticism alone. The doubts they raise are doubts not simply of the world's ethical ordering, its moral predestination. They also challenge the world's ontological ordering, the axiom of being's predestination. Their challenge undergoes suppression with the reinstatement of classicism. It remains suppressed, in the philosophical Occident, at least until Kant, who for his part still insists that the idea of an ordered and unitary "nature," if devoid of empirical content, nevertheless cannot be abandoned.[3] Late nineteenth- and twentieth-century Europe and America have their share of far more radical ontological relativists, from Nietzsche to Jean-Paul Sartre and Nelson Goodman. But Kant articulated the principle that contemporary ontological relativism itself takes largely for granted: the principle of an agency exercised before or prior to nature; the principle of an agency capable, in its most extreme and most historicizing formulations, of "mastering and altering reality," of making or remaking both the self that it inhabits and the world in which it lives.[4]

Though always an antithetical gesture, the casting aside of existential preordination, of the idea that any individual's telos or fate is given in advance, is of course not always negative. Transmuted into the idea of infinite progress, it is constitutive of the cast of both "constructive" occidental criticism and "pragmatic" occidental hope. Transmuted into the principle of responsibility and self-determinacy, into the principle of a self that is no longer an instrument of the cosmos but instead an end in itself, it is constitutive of the most prevalent of occidental ethics, and legalisms, and existentialisms as well. A gesture made, however, against the presumption that *telē*, "purposes," inhere and are given in the cosmos—the casting aside of the idea of immanent destiny—is still problematic. The problem it inevitably provokes is precisely the problem of devising meanings to give, if not to the cosmos, at least to the individual life itself.

The problem resembles those that Geertz, closely following Weber, deems the inspiration of all religious ideation: "bafflement, suffering, . . . a sense of intractable ethical paradox."[5] It perhaps reinstates those problems, which modern existentialisms classify under the general rubric of the "Absurd." The great world religions have responded and continue to respond to the Absurd by denying its ultimate reality, even while affirming its proximate and secular truth.[6] They thus recover the cosmos, though only through resort to a "metaphysics of meaning." The problem provoked by the casting aside of the cosmos permits of no such solution. Once the absurd is itself elevated to the status of an "ultimate reality," once it is accepted or enforced as an ultimate reality, it spoils the possibility not of religiosity, which certainly still survives. It spoils instead the possibility, or at least the plausibility, of soteriologies other than those that place the task and the power of salvation in the hands of human beings themselves. It spoils the plausibility of cosmodicies whose existential *telē* are anything other than "man-made," whose *telē* are at the very least anything other than the products of "human nature."

Hence a cardinal restriction on the moves available to any project of self-revision or self-realization that would be modern: the admission of the Absurd limits the materials out of which meaning can legitimately be made to the body, to the environment, to history, or to other "innerworldly" concreta. The postcosmic problem of meaning, however, is not simply, and perhaps not fundamentally, the problem of dwelling within a more constrictive universe of potential sensibility. In Greece and elsewhere it is also, and more fundamentally, the problem of making do with, and making something of, what materials of sensibility still remain. It can lead to nihilism, whether resigned or simply exhausted. But it more often leads elsewhere, and is more often resolved into a quest for what Paul Rabinow has recently called[7] the "norms and forms," not simply of such materials of sensibility as still remain, but also of the disciplines capable of analyzing those materials, and of synthesizing them into meaningful wholes.

The ethically ordered cosmos is, by definition, seamless. Cosmologists who take its existence as given proceed from the axiom that particulars are instantiations or embodiments of universals, that processes are determined by specifiable ends, that individuals have only to decide against or decide in favor of their fates. The search for the norms and forms of possible sensibilities shares with its "fatalist" counterparts a preoccupation with individualities, with totalities, and with the relations between them.[8] But that search is constrained by a "facticity" with which its fatalist counterparts are not forced to cope. Constrained by that facticity, by that innerworldliness, the search for norms and forms almost never achieves either individualization, or totalization, much less the establishment of connections at once immediate and perfectly generalizable between the individualized and the totalized. Its failures would be more devastating if the purposes for which it is usually deployed were either revelatory or predictive. But modern strategies of individualization and totalization, especially those outside or beyond the sphere of the exact and natural sciences, are more often executed with quite different purposes in mind: not to reveal but rather to regulate; not to predict but rather to manage and to control. The terrible bestiary of normality and deviance that Foucault explores in *Discipline and Punish*,[9] if neither consummately individualizing nor consummately totalizing, if neither revelatory nor predictive, serves the purposes of regulation and management well enough. It could, with its plausibility still intact, hardly do more. Even as it stands, so modern a "science" of character is not entirely without paradox. On the one hand, it imposes upon character as it imposes upon all other innerworldly entities the limiting concept of a determinate and lawful naturalism. On the other hand, it treats the person as it treats no other innerworldly entity under the limiting concept of a will free, if not to thwart nature's laws, at least to be a law sui generis.[10] But whether or not it is a matter of fact, the will's freedom is itself a matter of obligation. Whether or not modern persons are, by nature, condemned to be responsible for devising their own fates, they are asked, with the passing of the cosmos, to behave as if they are.

The Typical Greek?

As Marcus and Fischer note,[11] the anthropological address of the self "is not strictly new." They suggest that recent ethnography "has a much firmer grasp" of the cultural variability of conceptions of the self, but I am not certain that they are correct. Such American culturologists as Kluckhohn and Leighton,[12] or for that matter Bateson and Mead and Benedict, seem to have grasped that variability quite clearly. It is true, as Marcus and Fischer claim,[13] that latter-day psychologistic or "psychodynamic" ethnographies of personality, among them those by Crapanzano[14] and Obeysekere,[15] show more theoretical and critical sophistication than many of their predecessors. It is also true that many latter-day ethnographic analysts of emotion and sentiment, among them, for example, Levy,[16] or Rosaldo,[17] or Lila Abu-Lughod,[18] have found newer and somewhat more effective methods, particularly methods of presentation, than their predecessors had available. But not even these contemporary ethnographers diverge from the position that Bateson, following Ruth Benedict, put forward more than fifty years ago: that "cultures," rather than any of the loose array of metacultural and metahistorical constraints and guidelines that I have elicited in the preceding chapters, are effective, if not fully in determining the personality, at least in "standardizing" it.[19]

If the Batesonian position merely pointed to the inevitable formative influence of the various *rites de passage* and practices of socialization through which people everywhere pass, it would be largely unexceptionable. In contemporary Greece, for example, virtually everyone continues to be formed and influenced by the church in which he or she is christened, in which he or she acquires godparents, and under the auspices of which he or she is married and buried. Everyone is formed and influenced by the formal educational system, which establishes collective and individual markers for the transition from infancy to childhood, and from childhood to youth and young adulthood. Everyone continues to be formed and influenced by the domestic environment in which he or she is raised and by the patterning of parental and other socializing roles with which he or she comes constantly into contact. So far, so good: but the Batesonian position is typically far stronger, and much less plausible. It typically rests on the presumption that something like a *Geist*—or a "lifeworld," or a "structure"—surrounds and encloses the self in an ideational and valuational shell outside of which it can neither feel nor see nor believe anything at all. Such mentalistic insularism is surely as much of a conceit as its geographical analogue. Supplemented with some dynamic theory of "structuration," it can perhaps cope with certain aspects of "cultural change." But it cannot cope with the objectification of "culture" that one encounters in such places (or processes) as Athens. It cannot cope, either, with the revisionary self-consciousness—historical or, it might be added, anthropological—that the objectification of culture always implies.

In Athens, the self among many other significative artifacts has undergone elaborate objectification, and is often subject to historical and culturological analyses of precisely the sort that I might propose. Athenians of all cadres are in fact quite avid historians and quite avid anthropologists of personality and personhood, whatever their formal education may be. They are of course constantly exposed to foreigners, whether sojourners or tourists. They are, almost as constantly, exposed to the rhetoric of ethnic identity and difference, and even the least-schooled of them can be adept enough with that rhetoric to deploy it not only for analytical but for critical purposes as well. Waiting for a bus one morning, I overheard an exemplary conversation between two evident "commoners":

A: Look at the garbage in the street. It's disgusting.

B: Yes, you're right. The municipality does nothing.

A: But is the municipality to blame? I see the collectors come every day. Two hours pass. The streets are full of garbage again.

B: Of course. It isn't the municipality. It's the Greek in the Greek [o ellinas]. Foreigners, you see them, they have a piece of garbage, they put it in the trashbin. But the Greek, he always throws his garbage into the street.

A: Indeed.

Neither of these conversants doubted for a moment that personality allowed of culturological generalization. On the other hand, the force of their critique would be negligible if it did not also rest upon the presumption that the general Greek character was a contingent character, liable to change, to improvement, to bettering. Fatalist stereotypes notwithstanding, "progress" is certainly alive and well in Greece, especially for the man and woman on the street; so, too, the distillation of progress into an ethical norm of self-betterment.[20] Both conceptions presuppose that the will, for all its definitions and determinations, is still autonomous. Both suppose that it is still free, in the ultimate analysis, to define and determine itself.

The norm of "betterment" may in fact be the most "common"—at once popular and widespread—of the norms that govern Greek projects of self-realization. But there are other norms, as "common," that govern those projects as well. Among them, *ilikrinia,* "honesty," has a peculiar prominence. It is far more frequently declared and sought in the personal advertisements that can be found in Athens's various newspapers and magazines than any other characterological virtue: a testament, perhaps, that deception, whether to put forward or to save face, is still a very familiar practice. Greece's historical constructivists, however, are more likely to grant priority to another virtue, compatible with the deception of others, but not with deception of self: *gnisiotita* or *afthendikotita,* "authenticity." Not "progressivist," not quite the same as those of honesty, nor are the standards of authenticity quite the same as those of a more purely aesthetic originality, at least in the abstract. The authentic self can be a mannerist self, so long as its manners are self-willed. It can reflect precedent, it can even repeat precedent, so long as its repetitions are not passive, so long as they are chosen at will.

The historicization, the temporal particularization of personhood, tends, however, to erase in practice the abstract distinction between the authentic and the original self. The historically authentic self, true to the particularities of its own life course, cannot but be unique. The self obliged to realize itself in its historical authenticity is obliged, de facto, to be unique. "National character" tends to fall apart, tends to disintegrate, in the solvent of that obligation. The stability of personhood and personality tends to disintegrate as well.[21]

So much for "cultures." Against the "philosophical anarchy" of historicizing projects of self-realization, however, the prerequisite of making sense imposes some, the prerequisite of making it "constructively" many other civilizing strictures. There would be no "Greek modern" without them. The point is not quite Bourdieusian, not quite Batesonian, but is still functionalist and interactionalist: self-realization is autodestructive, it reduces to something equivalent to madness, if pursued without regard for a reasonably well developed and collectively sanctioned "picture" of personhood and personality, if pursued without regard for an always somewhat generalizing, somewhat totalizing picture of what, or who, persons intelligibly and legitimately might be. If there is no "typical American," if there is no "typical Greek," that is in part because various regimes of signification continue, in both territories, to be at odds with one another, and at odds with one another over the portraiture of legitimate self-realization among many other things. There is no "typical American," there is no "typical Greek," not just for that, but also because the projects of self-realization dominant in both territories still come with only a minimum of civilizing strictures, leaving to individuals the burden, or privilege, of making more concrete determinations on their own.

Thus historical constructivism: like other modern projects of legitimate self-realization, it is normative but less revelatory or predictive than simply regulative. Its structure is loose. It offers rules of thumb, not absolute or inviolable prescriptions. It offers guidelines for the devising of substantive *telē*, not those *telē* themselves. It is not, to be sure, entirely without a substance of its own. But individuals bring to it more particular and, from one instance to the next, more idiosyncratic concreta, derived among other things from the idiosyncrasies of generational and familial standing, of the experience of critical events and the experience of everyday life, of acquired horizons and inherent temperament. They bring to it the necessarily idiosyncratic vantages derived from or consequent of a unique course through life, a unique personal history.

Does a historically constructivist *poiēsis*, as a *poiēsis* of the Greek modern person, demand of those who enact it a manifestly historicizing consciousness? Does it, in other words, actually demand that recognition be paid, that some enduring "truth" or "sense" be granted to the self's idiosyncratic historicity, to the inevitable singularity of its temporal path? It does, though perhaps only indirectly. At the very least, it presupposes the contingency of the self, and thus presupposes that the self belongs to the same realm to which all historical beings belong. But not all Greeks, and not even all of them who take the project of a historically constructive realization of self as their own, are historians, much less conscious historicists. Not all of them attend, with any special devotion, to "the past." The sensible difference between the Early and the Late may be the constructivist's ultimate imagistic springboard, just as projective metalepsis may be his or her ultimate trope. But not all constructivists have as yet arrived at their rhetorical end. Many of them are as yet on their way. Many of those who came of age during the Papadhopoulos junta, many of those who consequently experienced the junta as their first great creative catastrophe, have as yet quite a long rhetorical way to go. They are often well aware that they remain "unfinished." They are often well aware that they must someday come to terms with pasts of much greater depth than those that can be traced back no further than to 1967. The generation of the junta nevertheless remains less caught up in the depths of the past than in a temporally much more shallow, though still extended, present. It has not, as yet, been able to put the junta entirely behind it. No surprise, then, that the self-situating tropology it tends to favor is frequently less temporalizing than spatializing, even if not strictly timeless and synchronic.

"Maro": Typifying the Atypical Greek

The woman whom I call Maro is a member of the generation of the junta; but Maro, *stricto sensu*, does not exist. She is rather a composite of five different people, with each of whom I became more than merely incidentally acquainted during the course of my fieldwork. Maro's "originals" do not all know one another but still belong to a dense network; if not all friends, they are all friends of one another's friends. Only three of them are actually women; but all are roughly of the same age, and all belong to a sociocultural elite for whom differences of gender are, if of course still relevant, less pronounced and in many respects less consequential than Greece's lower sociocultural cadres continue to find them. None of Maro's originals personally provided me with anything quite so complete as a "life history." On the other hand, each was more forthcoming about his or her "friends," and each has consequently left me more information about his or her friends than I perhaps "should" have. But Maro violates no secrets. She is literally no one. She is a "fiction" in some rather strong sense of that term.

Many other anthropologists have constructed "composite" and "fictional" persons, or so I have been told. Only a very few of them, so far as I know, have admitted to it in print.[22] Why? All anthropology, all interpretive anthropology, may be *fictio*, as Geertz says,[23] something that, rather like the Greek self, is less found than made. But many of even the most avidly interpretive of anthropologists seem to be uncomfortable with the tasks of *fictio* even as they pursue them. An anthropology less found than made seems to be too "humanistic," not "informational," not "scientific" enough. One can confess to practicing it privately, among one's inner circle; but one cannot publicize practicing it too far. Hypocritical, yes: but the attitude is also confused. Anthropological *fictio* can be "fiction" in a rather strong sense of the term and still be "informative," even "testable," in its way.

I create Maro, however, not to take a slap at anthropology, nor to exercise my would-be authoriality for its own sake. I create her instead to protect and to disguise what I have been expected to disguise: the particular identities, the individualities out of which she is made. I understand the obligation to require more than the usual ethnographic device, more than the mere invention of a false name. My fieldwork was itself a public affair, and my "informants" widely known as well. Merely to call them by a name other than their own—a device that has, after all, always fallen short— would hardly be to respect their privacy or to ensure their anonymity in anything else but name. Why, on the other hand, fear publicity? Not all of my "informants" did in fact fear publicity; a few actively sought it. The majority nevertheless resisted divulging anything too intimate—if not always about their "friends," at least about themselves. I was, to be sure, not just a stranger but an "occidental" foreigner, and Greeks have good cause to be suspicious of the labels that "occidental" foreigners to whom they have spoken too much might finally pin on them. They have some cause to be suspicious of one another as well. Greece, I would reiterate, is "sovereign territory." Within it, social potency rests with reputation, the politics of reputation infuses everyday life, and among its chief weapons are intimate details. Paranoia is not pathological; it is rather a mark of political maturity.

Maro is not a composite of intimate details, to which I rarely had secure access, even at a remove. As a "fictional individual," she is accordingly rather pale. She is not, in what individuality she still has, anyone whom I happen to know. She has, however, much in common with several individuals whom I do in fact know, and not simply with her more particular models. She could, for all I know, actually exist; her resemblance to a variety of individuals who do actually exist is not merely coincidental. Maro is, if not an ideal-typification, still an intelligible typification of a self delimited and defined by the same axes along which virtually all Greeks, as Greeks, are defined: by her age, by her status, by her familial background, by her education, by her occupation, by her "style." She is an intelligible typification as well of someone disposed, by her background and by her education among other things, to press her personality beyond its merely axial definition. There are no "typical Greeks." But Maro is typical in pressing her personality toward a historically constructive realization, though of necessity an atypical realization of her own devising. Not all Greeks embrace the project of the "Greek modern," not even in the pursuit of self-realization. Maro does. My claim for her is that Greeks would know her, and know her to be Greek, if they met her. That is her "test."

Maro is the child—somewhat unusually, the only child—of a now diminished but still prominent Athenian family. Secure in the distinction of her heritage, she never feels compelled to boast of it. She would never characterize herself as among the "upper classes," nor even as being from them. At most, she might occasionally let slip a suggestive anecdote: of a celebrated statesman whom she calls *thie*, "uncle"; of an evening party attended only by the metropolis's socially "registered." "Upper class? But I am a *worker*": a self-consciously populist remark that exploits the "traditional," indeed ancient Greek association between the elite and leisure. Her acquaintances, however, point out that her patronymic is still capable of opening the weightiest of Athenian doors. Her ancestors were, in the preceding century, residents of Asia Minor: "*Ellino-Tourki*," Greco-Turkish, she would emphasize. The current rancor between Greece and Turkey exasperates her; it obscures a more fundamental communion. Her father, if not himself a Phanariote, was well versed in typically Phanariotic skills: entrepreneurialism and administration. Her mother belonged to the Anatolian gentry. Her parents immigrated to Greece well before the Asia Minor Disaster, bringing a modest but still substantial fortune to Athens along with them.

They settled in Keramikos, after the Plaka Athens's second oldest district and before the Second World War its most elegant. Maro describes her early neighborhood as a "*vrai quartier*: you could really live there." She still strolls sometimes through its streets and lanes, many of them now nearly deserted. "Yes, I am a little nostalgic": but what is past, for Maro, is past. She remembers playing in the vacant, shadowy lots near the ancient Keramikos cemetery. She finds them appropriately ghostly, especially after twilight. But she approves of what has become of the environs: thinks the few brothels that do business there "colorful," thinks the emptiness "serene." She would not mind seeing most of the district absorbed into the archaeological park that Parliament and city councils have been planning for years.

She was a "happy" and must have been a very clever little girl. Unlike many of the children of the grandest Athenian families, she was not educated primarily by tutors, but did attend a private school. Would her education have been neglected had a brother been in the house? Almost certainly not: she would have been expected to cultivate certain feminine graces that a brother could of course have ignored; but she would have been no less expected than he to learn her letters and languages. She has learned both very well.

Maro would like a house of her own someday. For now, however, she lives in a spacious and sunny apartment, three kilometers or so from Keramikos, several stories above one of Athens's more congested thoroughfares. The traffic perturbs her. But she is close to her work, and within walking distance of most of her other daily necessities as well. After she completed her university training, she lived for a few years in Thessaloniki, a city for whose Romanesque and neo-Byzantine architecture and for whose contemporary liveliness she still has praise. She visits it every several months, whether to see friends or to present lectures or seminars. But she returned to Athens when she was able. She loves Athens, all its contemporary strains notwithstanding. She loves the alleyways and roving musicians of the Plaka, loves the cafés and early morning throngs of Omonia Square, loves the city's activity, its confusions, its pace. She has lived outside Greece. But she no longer thinks that she could live anywhere else but Athens.

Maro's father is now dead. Her mother no longer lives in Keramikos but still lives in Athens. I would have liked to learn more of this *"mana"*—the term is affectionate and colloquial—whose marvelous Christmas sweets I once sampled but whom I never actually met. I would like to learn more about the relations between daughters and their mothers in Greece. The ethnographic record, though by no means silent about them, is not yet as complete as it might be.[24] We know, or know more vividly, of the intense loyalty and almost tearful affection of "good Greek sons." Maro's apparent feelings for her own *mana* were more complex. She spoke at times as if the relationship was largely one of duty. She "had to take *mana* out to dinner"; she "had to telephone *mana* at least once a week." But she spoke of her duties, such as they were, with enough self-conscious amusement to indicate that she bore them lightly. *Mana* was a "fine cook." She was "dear." She may even have been something of a confidante. She was also the source of some rather vague sadness, revealed less in what Maro said than in what she did not. Because *mana* was alone? Perhaps; but also, I might venture, because Maro saw in her mother's solitary old age a discomfiting presentiment or phantasm of her own.

VOCATION

Maro was nearing the end of her "youth"—a stage of life that extends in Greece to about the age of thirty—when the junta came to power. She was enrolled at the University of Athens when the colonels executed their street blockade. "Have you ever, James, run for your life?" Maro left Greece immediately. She went to study in Paris. She received a doctorate, in psychology and aesthetics, from the Sorbonne about eight years later, now nearly twenty years ago. She spent more than a year in New York after she completed her Sorbonne degree. She was "curious," she says, about America, and wanted to see firsthand the New York art world as well. She is fluent in

French and in English, proficient in German and Italian. Like many Greeks of her stratum, she is "multiprofessional." She practices psychology at an office in central Athens. She is also a member of the editorial board of a prestigious and successful journal, a journal largely devoted to the analysis and criticism of the fine and plastic arts. She is uncertain whether there is such a thing as the "Greek modern" in the arts, and even less certain what its particular themes and particular variations might be. She has given thought to the issue. She would like to resolve it. She has solicited opinions on it from several of Greece's most celebrated artists. The responses she has received have, however, not been especially convincing. She is not altogether surprised. "We're submerged in what we do," she says; "we have a hard time breaking the surface."

She is committed to Greece's artists, particularly to its artistic avant-garde. Raised in a highly cultivated, "Phanariotic" home, she is confident of her taste. But she does not consider herself an artist, and certainly not an artist by profession. She is an analyst and a critic, both psychological and aesthetic. In 1987, she was still in the process of translating her dissertation from the French into demotic. She had not sought to publish it in Paris. But she has published shorter essays, in French and in Greek, on a wide range of topics, both psychological and aesthetic. She is an occasional lecturer, in Athens, in Thessaloniki, in other European cities as well. She is not a didact; she is modest about her erudition, judicious in her evaluations, rarely moralistic in her reviews.

Maro has her strength—a quality widely, if not always glowingly, remarked by her "friends." She has opinions of her own. On Greek academics, for example: "I could never be one. They work. Simply that." On the current Greek arts: "I shouldn't say it, but they're not in very good shape." In spite of them, Maro sees herself, and sees herself above all, less a judge than an educator. She is a practicing psychotherapist—still a rather uncommon profession in Greece, though one in which women appear to be no less frequently involved than men. She also teaches clinical psychology, and in fact devotes less time to her practice than to her teaching. She sees her role as an editor as a teacherly role as well: one of putting into circulation the ideas and perspectives of the artistic community; one of posing hypotheses, exploring methodologies, orchestrating discussions and debates. Maro "serves," and serves her contemporaries in accord with the humanitarian and collectivistic *arkhi* of service that the gentry from which she is descended long upheld. Maro's father was a minor midcentury statesman. Greece still has very little room for women in its public political arena.[25] Maro has pursued vocational avenues that are not strictly feminine but far more open to women than politics itself.

Why aesthetics? Why psychology? Maro is concerned with "transition." She is especially concerned with the transitions that her compatriots must, in the face of an invasive "modernity," often suffer rather than command.

She would like to see them in greater command: as artists; simply as human beings. But then, "artists" and "simple human beings" are not quite so separate in Greece as they are in America. The aestheticization of the self, the predominantly aesthetic tenor especially of the project of a historically constructed and historically constructivist selfhood, draws them in fact very close together. Maro's dual interests have a broad, if socioculturally specific, motivation. They have, however, a more strictly biographical motivation as well. After a largely "traditional," though privileged, marriage, Maro's mother has in her later years professionally pursued what had formerly only been a hobby. She is a painter, though by no means a member of the avant-garde. Maro does not undertake to be a special advocate of the women among Greece's artistic avant-garde. She does, however, dedicate much of her psychotherapeutic practice and her psychological teaching to "women in transition," in whom she often "confronts herself," sometimes "embracing," sometimes "discarding" what she finds.

POLITICS

Maro was affected by the junta, as many others of her generation were, lastingly, and intractably. Her comments about it tend toward abstraction, though not toward banality. I do not know what particular impact the coup d'état had upon her family. Her father was rightist. But he was also a republican. I do not know if he actually left the country. But Maro's own move to Paris must have had more than a little to do with her father's opposition to the colonels. It must have had something to do with the colonels' suspicions of him as well. The junta naturally brought an end to his political career. But the colonels did not simply seek to drive out or neutralize the republicans, whether rightist or leftist, in their midst. Their authoritarianism was not exclusively political, and their policies of neutralization not directed toward exclusively political ends. They were less severe with the conservative and pro-American right than with any of the left. They allowed all of Greece's rightist dailies to continue publishing, for example, but forced all its leftist dailies out of business. The editors of the respected rightist newspaper, *Kathimerini*, nevertheless suspended their own operations voluntarily. The suspension was a protest against censorship. It was also a protest against an anti-intellectualism that had with the colonels' usurpation become a literal state affair. The colonels were famous demagogues. They were also demagoguishly petty bourgeois, and famous as well for their resentment of virtually all cadres of the sociocultural elite, from poets to the royal family itself.[26] They reinstalled the Greek king, at least as a figurehead. But they were surely not sorry to see others of the elite, rightist or leftist, exile themselves of their own accord.

Nor were they the only Greeks who were pleased. Initially at least, the colonels had substantial local support, especially from others of their own stratum. But the youth who directly or indirectly witnessed the 1967 coup have not tended to dwell at length upon its domestic wellsprings. They have not denied those wellsprings, or at least not denied them as vigorously as a variety of foreign commentators insinuate. In my experience, in fact, the opposite is true: they have been quite prepared to admit that the junta, initially at least, had its popularity, and quite prepared to admit that it had a number of entirely domestic precipitants as well. They have even been prepared to take straightforward responsibility, if not for all those precipitants, at least for permitting the colonels to retain their power for quite so long as they did. Several scholars—Mouzelis and Tsoukalas prominent among them[27]—have followed suit.

The junta is an awkward topic in Greece, and particularly awkward when raised by an American. But it is not, for all its awkwardness, a topic either suppressed or repressed. Very few Greeks would deny that the junta had its domestic predictability. Many of them regard the acts of exclusion and torture perpetrated by its agents as entirely unconscionable. But very few of them would deny that acts just as unconscionable have been perpetrated by Greeks upon other Greeks before. Very few would deny that the Greek past, more or less ancient, has had its share of dictators, some not any more benign than the colonels themselves. Viewed domestically, the junta was perhaps only another moment, if for many Greeks a particularly ugly moment, in the chronicles of a politics of sovereignty that had always permitted men, when they could manage it, to be laws unto themselves.

The junta has, in its "ugliness," perhaps done its part to disturb the legitimacy of sovereign tactics, at least in the short run. But if it continues to be regarded, by many, perhaps by a majority of Greeks as having been caused "from without," that is not simply because it very likely was caused from without, and quite certainly maintained from without, particularly through American aid. Nor is it because the colonels signed themselves over to an America that was not already Greece's overseer. Greece had been a client state since its inception, and the client of a decidedly patronal America since the end of its Civil War. The trauma externalized in an emphatic externalization of the junta's causes was the trauma of a patron's betrayal, not simply of its clients but of its own apparent political principles as well. The junta was a renewed proof, especially for Greece's younger generations, of vulnerability. It was proof, especially for those same generations, that not even patrons could be trusted; proof as well that some patrons at least could not even be effectively impugned. The colonels were all imprisoned. America has simply been reviled: ceremonially, in annual demonstrations; tactically, in a socialist politics of neutrality.

Maro does not participate in the anti-American marches of Polytechnic Day. She thinks them escapist. Like more than a few of the younger descendants of the patronal gentry, she is, however, committedly leftist. In 1986, she belonged to Greece's "interior" Communist party. In 1987, as I have already mentioned, the party took steps to ally itself and, in effect, to merge with a somewhat broader coalition, a "New Left," predominantly intellectual and white-collar in its constituency and predominantly neutralist in its platform. She approved of the merger—now somewhat beside the point—which left the "exterior" and pro-Soviet Communist party somewhat more isolated than it had been previously. In spite of her affiliations, Maro had rarely voted for Communist candidates, most of whom were quite unlikely to win the seats for which they vied. She had more often voted for the socialist candidates of Papandreou's PASOK. She thought that Papandreou's party "had its problems." But she thought that it had done Greece a great deal of good as well.

She is not sweepingly anti-American. She enjoyed New York, was impressed with its vitality, and with its size. But she attributes nothing extraordinary to it. "Europe has everything that America has," she says. "It's just that in America, everything is bigger. Americans like big things." She holds Greeks responsible for the junta; "we were all responsible," she says. But she holds America responsible for causing it, and thinks it capable of installing other juntas, future juntas as well. She would like to see Greece relieved of all of the American military bases it houses. She would like to see it relieved of the CIA, whose vast, "secret" headquarters in central Athens she enjoys pointing out, hoping to be "overheard" in the process. She would like to see Greece relieved of most other American influences as well. She does not restrict her contempt to the American government alone. She is somewhat contemptuous of Americans generally, whom she regards, a good European in this respect, rather naïve, and rather daft as well. They too often betray the "shallowness" of a country that has abandoned the past, a country that has instead dedicated itself only to the future, and only to "results." The past, history itself, is for Maro the primer of self-formation and self-understanding. If it has lost its status as a *magistra vitae* in "the Occident,"[28] it retains that status for Maro. The wisdom it offers her is a vaguely tragic wisdom. It teaches her less that all similar events unfold in similar ways than that human beings are usually entangled in events that they cannot fully see, or comprehend.

A Woman's Worlds: Gender, Urbanity, and Class

Like her mother, Maro lives alone. But unlike her mother, Maro has never been married: not the "normal condition," as she puts it, of women her age. But what is the "normal condition" of women her age? Jill Dubisch rightly observes[29] that "sexual segregation and gender roles play a large part as organizing principles in Greek society, both on the ideological plane and in the ongoing activities of daily life." Both sexual segregation and gender roles have received considerable ethnographic attention. Both are variable from one site and region and class to the next. One can nevertheless extract a few general trends from the ethnographic records so far compiled. The segregation of the sexes appears, for example, to be far more extreme in the more isolated of rural villages than in towns and cities, and more extreme among the lower than among the higher socioeconomic classes. Women may command considerable domestic and spiritual authority—all the more when the conjugal residence pattern is not virilocal, and all the more as they grow older—but rarely find themselves in positions of authority in political or other public arenas. Female domains tend, in rural Greece, to be private and interior domains; male domains the opposite.[30]

Women in Athens, however, hesitate very little, and certainly far less than village women, to venture out of their homes. Women of Athens's middle and upper classes hesitate least of all. They may, without apparent reproof, take solitary walks in one or another park or along the city's streets. They frequently take their children or their pets to neighborhood squares: still "public," but in Athens no longer exclusively male places.[31] They do most of the daily shopping: those of sufficient means may have a housekeeper or maid to do it for them. They appear to involve themselves in the making of larger purchases more regularly than they did even in the recent past.[32] They regularly visit the department stores and boutiques in Kolonaki and on Hermes Avenue.

The rural *kafenio*, "coffee shop," and the *taverna* receive women only on the rarest and most particular of occasions.[33] In Athens, however, I knew during my stay only one *kafenio* patronized exclusively by men, and it was located in a working-class district, the population of which was largely made up of provincial immigrants: its attractions were not especially sought out by tourists. I was told of many others, though all were located in similarly "undistinguished" districts and patronized by similarly "undistinguished" clienteles. Women perhaps hesitate to enter *kafenia*, and certainly hesitate to enter bars, on their own. In neither Kolonaki nor the university district, however, do they any longer appear to hesitate to enter the latter in the company of other women or men. The young women (and men) of Athens's middle and upper classes may now "date" without risking too much reproof.[34]

It is difficult to assess the degree to which the relatively more "liberated" manners of foreign vacationers have lent legitimacy to native commingling. Foreigners will notoriously "do anything" and are usually humored; but they are—to reiterate—not always considered worthy of emulation. Still, Athens's middle classes are great mimics, and its upper classes great importers, and there can be no doubt that their imitations and importations have, especially since the junta's fall, brought about marked transformations of an earlier urban style. Economic expansion has brought about transformations as well. Many Athenian women work, and no longer merely in the family

businesses to which they were formally confined. The city's kiosks are predominantly, though not exclusively, run by men. All its janitors are, if native, women. Far fewer women than men hold managerial and professional
posts. Far fewer women than men have active and independent political
careers. In most of Athens's shops and stores and boutiques and offices,
however, women can be found as frequently as men and, if not in charge of
men, at least working alongside them.[35]

A few older Athenian women, and especially older widows, continue to
dress in the "dark, shapeless" woolens demanded by rural *pudeur*. Most,
however, dress themselves more fashionably. Many Athenian women,
though not so many as their more "occidental" counterparts, wear makeup,
costume jewelry, and carefully coiffed hair. Virtually all have abandoned the
rigorously antierotic vestments of the traditional "virgin" or "matron." They
can, however, go too far. Makeup worn too thickly, clothes too revealing or
worn too tightly, hair dyed blonde: all of these are looked upon as "cheap"
and are likely to be taken as signs of prurience or sexual pandering. Athenian
women can thus indict themselves. But they are rarely indicted simply for
being women. One man once spontaneously declared to me that women
"made him crazy," that he could "neither live with them nor live without
them." He was rather astonished when I asked him what, more precisely, he
might mean. Whatever his meaning, I doubt that he was altogether alone in
his sentiments. Women remain psychoerotic objects. But Athenian women
no longer seem particularly burdened by the ethical and ontological stereotypes that rural ethnographers continue to report.[36] Neither Maro nor any of
the other Athenian women with whom I was acquainted believed or portrayed themselves as being ethically inferior to men. Not one of them regarded herself as pollutive. Not a single one of them showed the slightest
embarrassment in speaking about childbirth or menstruation, and none assumed that I would be embarrassed or perturbed by what she said. Rural
women can, apparently, be quite as frank; at times, quite bawdy.[37] A few of
the women in my circle were very much in the same league; one or two, with
spectacularly foul mouths, perhaps in a league all their own.

Athenian women may still make some men "crazy." They may, for all I
know, still occasionally be seen at once as the "agents of the Devil" and
"Mothers of God" that they have, in several rural villages, long been portrayed to be.[38] The portrayal no doubt persists, as do the structural conditions that nourish it. But in Athens, it has lost whatever rural currency it
may still have. At the very least, it has gone underground. No one, or in any
event virtually no one concerned with being genuinely "urban" and "up-to-
date," dares admit to approving it.

Tourism, imitations and importations, the blindness of the market, the
prestige of social democratization: these are among the impetuses of the
Greek passing of sexual dimorphism. Particularly, though not solely, in the
preceding ten years, feminism has been an impetus as well. At its inception,

some hundred years ago, feminism in Greece was the prerogative of socially elite women. Its leaders still belong to the elite: Margaret Papandreou was at once undertaking a divorce from her husband, Andreas, and leading the country's largest feminist coalition during the course of my fieldwork. Since the junta's fall, however, feminism has come to have a wider appeal, particularly for women of the urban, and newer, middle classes. As in America, however, feminism in Greece remains less a revolutionary than a reformist movement. It encourages women to engage themselves politically: at the "Green Line" in Cyprus, for example; or in "Mothers for Peace." It seeks to open to women various roles and statuses, especially occupational roles and statuses, traditionally monopolized by men. But its efforts to carry out a thoroughgoing revaluation of the manly as well as the womanly, of masculinity as well as femininity, are in effect as yet quite limited. It is not clear whether they would, even if seriously pursued, have as yet any real chance of succeeding at all.

As in most of America, so too in Athens, women are now more free to set foot in traditionally male domains but not nearly so free to rid themselves of traditionally female duties and obligations. Whatever their professional achievements, women in Athens are still expected to be competent and proficient *nikokires*: the term designates "ladies of the house," domestic cooks and bottle-washers and manageresses. Perhaps working women in Athens are not criticized as harshly as women in the provinces for neglecting on occasion the chores of domestic management; perhaps they are praised more generously for tending assiduously to them. The virtuous Athenian woman tends to her chores in any case. She cooks: men prepare food regularly only in Athens's restaurants and other public kitchens. She mothers. Maro recognized that, in remaining single, she could hardly be considered "normal." Women of all Athenian classes except the highest are strongly urged to marry and nurture families. Dubisch has noted[39] among the women of Tinos "a certain ambivalence . . . regarding children." I can report something of the same ambivalence among women of the Athenian bourgeoisie. Whatever ambivalence they may feel, though, they are still expected to be loving and devoted parents, even permissive parents, indulging especially the whims and wills of their sons. They are expected to be loving and devoted wives: all the more so as matrimony has become a matter not of arrangement but of choice and romance. For all the lifting of the strictures of traditional *pudeur*, some Athenian women still feel the force of what strictures remain. One high-bourgeois matron repeated to me the same maxim that many rural ethnographers already know. Greek women, she said, should never be flirtatious, should never be sexually receptive, should never be the seductresses of men; but should always be flirtatious, should always be sexually receptive, should always be the seductresses of their husbands. The paradox, which might be characterized as a clash between an "official" and a more "muted" female model of comportment, is more pointed in demotic than in English. The demotic term for a "man" and the term for a "husband" are the same: *andras*.

Maro has had her share of suitors and has had her share of affairs as well. Most of her involvements have, however, been brief, and most have also been disappointing. She thinks that men, Greek men at least, generally expect too much, and on the other hand too little, of the women whom they choose to pursue, and certainly of the women whom they choose to marry. She doubts that they expect, or for the most part even desire, genuine friendship: "They turn," she says, "to other men for that."[40] She doubts that they are, for the most part, even capable of coping with a woman who might be their equal. They are comfortable only with intellectual subordinates: women who are, or who are prepared to appear to be, less intelligent, less clever, less successful than they are themselves. On the other hand, they are comfortable only with "a parent," only with a woman who will nurture them as their mothers did, who will prepare their meals, who will keep their houses clean and in order, who will "manage." Maro agrees that Greek women are in something of a double bind: forced still to be vassals and executives, eternal maidens and eternal Circes, children and mothers and sirens at the same time.

She thinks that she sometimes frightens men: with her skills and talents and gifts; simply with her unpredictability. She is an accomplished cook. She cares about the disposition of her home. She would like to have a child, and would very much like to be married, happily and well. She admits that she is often lonely and often troubled by her solitude. She is not a cynic. She may fear, but she does not consciously think that she is condemned to be by herself for the rest of her life. She would, however, rather be by herself than live "for someone else." She thinks that she is herself sometimes frightened by the men with whom she involves herself, that she sometimes resists them for fear that she might be submerged by them, that she might turn, in her involvement, into someone whom she does not really want to be. She thinks sometimes that she is not yet capable herself of giving and receiving love "generously, authentically," without qualms. Before she can, she says, she must learn how to live "for herself." She says that she does not yet know how to do that. But she is trying. She thinks that everyone must try: that, she says, is what it means, to her, to be modern.

ACCOUTREMENTS

There are a few matters at least over which she does have command, a few domains in which she is "herself." She is an attractive woman, and she dresses with considerable self-attention. She is always stylish. But her attire is not cautious, not conservative, not understated. It is purposefully the contrary. She eschews the "uniforms" that "fashionable" Athenian women tend to adopt from one season to the next. In 1986 and 1987, those women were wearing angular shifts in black or olive or gold, padded shoulders, leather coats, and high heels. Maro could have afforded them; but she chose to wear leotards, snug jerseys, flowing skirts, and embroidered slippers. She preferred intricate patterns and intense colors. Her palette was consistent but vaguely "folkish." She intended the effect. Like many other descendants of Greece's gentry, particularly of its Anatolian gentry, this daughter of her mother tends, and tends self-consciously, toward both political and stylistic populism. She reviles the "bourgeoisie"—a term she deploys with the indiscriminateness of most of the more "dominated members of the dominating strata"[41]—for their artificial urbanity, for their vulgar materialism, for being interested only in "making money." She praises "the people" for their social "tolerance." She praises them for being Greece's "real cosmopolitans." She says that it is the bourgeoisie that has driven from Athens much of its former diversity. She pities "the people" for their plight: for their poverty, and for their diminished chances. She admires them for their remarkable resilience. She feels some bond, some rather genteel community with them, though she is willing to admit that her sentiment is "abstract." She stops short of claiming that she is "of the people." She stops well short of "dressing like a peasant." Her costumes incorporate a variety of other *topoi* as well: Parisian and Berliner above all.

Her apartment's spaces are also elaborately personalized spaces, and in them she passes much of her spare and private time. She vacations each summer on one or another of the Greek islands. She sees films, attends exhibits, eats out regularly with one or another of her friends, most of them "cultural workers"[42] like herself. She is not and does not want to be an academic—recall her estimation of the profession in Greece. But she has a study of her own, crowded with books and appointed with a vast desk at which she spends many of her evenings and weekends attending to the two or three projects that she usually has simultaneously before her. In 1986 she was, while translating her dissertation, also rereading Nietzsche, and Dumont, and Foucault. She was interested, she said, in "subjectivity": its emergence, its forms, its aesthetic expressions.

Her living room is less cluttered than her study, and more relaxed. It is lined with tall plants, most of them placed in front of the French doors that open onto her balcony. She is not interested in "views," though she has a view of Mount Likavittos. She does not use her balcony—a standard feature of Athenian apartments—at all. There is too much noise, too much smog, too many eyes. She prefers to be inside. Her furniture, perhaps heirloom, is dark, ornately carved, and periodistic. It evokes nineteenth-century Turkey and—a convergence with Iolas here—Byzantium's Paleologean Renais-

sance. Her end tables are piled with still more books, and with current journals, in French, in English, and in Greek. Her floor is covered with a Turkish
carpet. She lines a capacious banquette with handsewn pillows, Turkish in
origin. She displays an opulent silver tea service, also Turkish. She has several paintings: an icon, apparently from the eighteenth century; a couple of
romantic landscapes; a variety of expressionist and minimalist tableaux,
many but not all of them Greek. She has a large collection of music: American jazz; Kurt Weill; German and Italian opera; Greek *rembetika* and
mournful *amanedhes*, those "songs of despair" that make for a local version
of the blues.

THE MATERIALS OF LIFE, THE MAKING OF LIFE

Maro is confident enough of the coherence of her quarters, of the consistency of its juxtapositions and its tonalities. She is aware that they incorporate, if not a bit of everything, at least a bit of a wide variety of things, of
elements taken from widely different places and distinctly different times.
She is aware of the syncretism of the whole. She is in fact a devoted syn-
cretist and devoted to Greece for allowing her to be the "collector" that she
desires to be. She speaks of France as relentlessly "systematized" and speaks
of America as "all organization." She thinks of both places as already finished, already resolved. Greece, she says, is still very much "in transition":
one of the phrases to which Greece's historical constructivists have very
frequent appeal. Greece, for Maro as for many of her compatriots, is a "disorderly," a "chaotic" country. She thinks as ardently of any of the rest of her
compatriots also do that Greece is a place in which "anything" and "everything" is still possible. For Maro, the condition is liberating precisely in
being unformed. Greece is its potential. But for Maro, Greece's potential is
perhaps only a figuration of the self's potential, and for her it is a potential
that has more than merely to be recognized. It has also to be used, to be
made into something actual, into something *gnisio*: "authentic," or "real."

Familiar images: but Maro, for all her historical sensibilities, tends not to
characterize the task of actualizing the self's potential as one of metaleptic
projection, of substituting the "early" for the "late" in order to fashion the
new present of a "unified historical personality." She tends to be concerned
with a more preliminary task: overcoming or surpassing the limitations that
have been placed upon the self "from without." Recall Bloom's identification of "inside-outside dichotomies" as the imagistic stuff of metaphor, and
his identification of metaphor as a trope that tends to "curtail meaning"
rather than to "re-present" it,[43] a trope of "limitation." Bloom is often obscure, but he is also correct: the overcoming or surpassing of limitations, the
denial of definitions that have been placed upon the self "from without"

may be liberating; it is, however, not yet a "construction." It is merely a deconstruction that perhaps restores potential, but leaves it entirely undetermined. It does not, as a consequence, restore or recreate a "self." The "live possibility" that it discloses has no "meaning," no specific identity. It is not yet a "person."

Maro in fact displays all the symptoms of being precisely in as much transition as she says Greece is itself. However confident she may be of her taste, she is not especially confident of the coherence, the identity of the person that she is making of herself, and by no means confident that the person that she has made of herself thus far has the coherent identity that she would like it to have. She is uneasy with herself. She vacillates, in her mannerisms, between the quite intentional vulgarity of an *épateur de la bourgeoisie* and the trained gentility of an aristocratic ascetic. She vacillates between "Romaic" and "Hellenic" tastes. She vacillates between emphasizing and downplaying her own "orienticity" and the "orienticity" of Greece. She drinks boiled and frothy "Greek coffee" or "Turkish coffee," never café au lait and never the Nescafé that has become so common in Greek *kafeteries*, "coffee shops." She drinks it with the traditional glass of water. She orders it *metrio*, with "measured sugar," as most other Greeks do. But she also dabbles in vegetarianism: a very untraditional culinary habit and a very untraditional diet. On the other hand, she only dabbles in it. In the name of health? That would not be quite Greek enough; real, *gnisii* Greeks still find their values less in the body than in the substance of time, and the substance of time provides diet with no consistent directions. The ancient Greeks were careful dieticians but enthusiasts of meat. Contemporary Europeans and contemporary Americans provide the alternative. Maro can see their point, but cannot fully embrace it. She cares about "life," she cares about her health, but she does not care about it above all else. She knows the dangers of smoking. She is not a habitual smoker. But she still smokes on occasion: "for the taste." She means the justification literally, though not altogether so.

Maro sometimes labels herself a "Greek," sometimes a "Greek European," sometimes simply a "European." Her ambivalences are less pronounced when the drift of conversation or the precision of a context dilutes them. She is "Greek," she speaks "as a Greek," for example, when she contrasts her predilections or her view of the world with those of the "French" or the "British." She speaks "as a Greek" when she speaks analytically of an "aggressiveness" that she shares with her compatriots, or when contrasting analytically the rich textures of local emotionality with French "pomposity" or British "reserve." She is a "Greek European" when she defends the centrality of the continental arts against the American challenge, or when she contrasts Europe's historical sensitivity or its experiential traumata with

America's "blindness." She is a rather homeless "European," or an even more homeless "internationalist," when she attacks Greeks for their philistinism or for their greed.

Maro's present identity, or rather her present self-identifications, are not, however, merely situational. She is not part "Greek," not part a "Greek European," not part a "European," one or the other as the moment seems to demand. Her tropology of self is not really metonymic, in part because the various reference groups to which she has appeal themselves lack identities coherent or stable enough for the metonyms to work. Maro's situational self-partitioning may be largely strategic. But beneath it, a more comprehensive uncertainty remains.

One native scholar claims that Greeks have been in the habit of putting forward self-identifications less "for themselves" than "against [external] others" at least since late Byzantium.[44] Bloom's distinction between tropes of limitation and tropes of representation suggests that the habit is more closely entangled with existential uncertainty, if not a full-blown "crisis of identity," than it might initially seem. But Bloom also suggests that metaphor, though a trope of limitation, is not at a great dialectical distance from metaleptic representation (or re-presentation); that it is, on the contrary, just one dialectical step away. "The limitations of metaphor are restituted," he writes, "in a final . . . metalepsis or transumption," which he characterizes not simply as "the revisionist trope proper" but also as "the ultimate poetic resource of belatedness."[45] Instead of poetry, I would prefer to speak of *poiēsis*; instead of "belatedness," simply of a directly or indirectly historicizing consciousness. Maro, then, is perhaps on the verge of a metaleptic and projective *poiēsis*. Her more immediate concern with the "inner" and the "outer" is not, however, just a "step away" from culmination. As for many others of her generation, it is also a step back from, and so a step against, the junta itself. Maro occasionally asserts that the junta was "caused from without." But she cannot be accused of what some Greek journalists are fond of calling *efthinofovia*, "fear of taking responsibility."[46] Maro's position must rather be interpreted as an act, rhetorical among other things, of resistance against the colonels' own introjective metalepsis, against a cultural classicism that was as much in favor of technological "modernization" as it was staunchly opposed to all cosmopolitan "spiritual pollutions." Maro's concern with the "inner" and the "outer" reveal an incorrigible conviction that the junta's preliminary internalizations and externalizations were "all wrong."

But Maro is, like many others of her generation, not as yet certain what might be more right. Maro sees "tradition," she sees an authentic continuity between her own cultural past and her own cultural present, not in the habits of Greece's economic middle and upper classes, not in the habits of the "bourgeoisie" that she disdains, but rather in the habits of "the folk." She speaks, for example, of island fishermen who continue as the ancients did to pour libations of wine before beginning their meals. "There," she says, "you have a living past. There you have something really Greek." But she knows, and knows perfectly well, that the practice has lost the significance it once had. An ancient pagan offering to the sun, it has been reduced to an item of provincial etiquette. She has read most of the pertinent monographs. She knows, and knows perfectly well, that "the folk" is itself a construction, and a thoroughly academic construction, of the preceding 150 years. She knows, in addition, that even if she is for "the folk," she is certainly not of it, that she is virtually as distant from it as from the nouveaux riches.

She speaks, on the other hand, of not realizing how "Greek" she was until she lived, and lived for quite so long as she did, in France. She knows that she is not quite so "occidental" as "the French" are themselves. But she also knows, and knows perfectly well, that such credentials and such experiences as she acquired in Paris have distanced her from "the Greeks," and even from the Greek she was before she took up residence in Paris. She knows that she has internalized something at least of her "occidental" acquisitions. She knows at the very least that she deploys them, and defines or redefines herself as a consequence. Maro's Greekness, her "Hellenicity," is something "old," something at least acquired from the local past. But it is also something from which her cultivation has removed her. It is something whose substance she consequently cannot any longer take for granted, something whose substance is—as she knows, and knows perfectly well—left for her to decide. Her "occidenticity" is rather newer, and much of it acquired "elsewhere." It is an adornment. But it is an adornment that has come to be definitive of her "potential" because it has come to be definitive of her occupation, of her specialties, of many of her acts. It has come to force an "inherent" Hellenicity out. It has itself "come inside," infiltrating the habitus at the expense of its legacy. Maro's person—indeed, her person among many others—hangs in the balance.

But the balance is elusive: for Maro, and for many others like her as well. Maro is Greek, and she is not. She is European, and she is not. The paradoxes would be more genuine if the attributions were not all of them metaphorical, and so literally false.[47] But whether or not they are genuinely paradoxical, the attributes are still indicative of a fragmentation of the self, a fragmentation of personal identity and personality alike. Maro admits all of this. She is aware that her sense of self is far from consistent, and far from complete. She is as yet more concerned, however, with casting off what has been put upon her than with putting all the cast-off pieces back together again. She in fact identifies that concern as "Greek," though "Greek" in the second order. I once told her that I had myself, while in Greece, come existentially somewhat "apart at the seams." She understood the English idiom. "Ah," she said, "then you, too, must be becoming Greek." Or rather, a Greek modern. But neither of us was quite yet there.

Postscript: The Psychoanalytic and the Historically Syncretic Self

Psychoanalysis has as yet made few inroads in Greece,[48] and fewest of all as the rhetoric or methodology of self-realization that it has become, especially in America. Maro, who has undergone psychoanalysis, does not find much local application for it and does not teach it. "We already have those myths," she says. I presume her to imply more than that Greeks have heard of the lives of Oedipus and Electra already. The psychoanalyst would no doubt take her pronouncement as a denial—if not of the subconscious per se, at least of its "secrecy." But Maro's dismissal of psychoanalysis is not itself just another defense. It conveys a distrust—not unique—of the scientization of the self, perhaps of scientism generally. It conveys a distrust as well of confession, an institution whose legitimacy has never been quite as assured among the Orthodox as among their directly or indirectly Catholic counterparts. The politics of sovereignty has perhaps added even more motivational fuel to the fires of a Greek quest for spiritual independence, whether the Orthodox quest for a personal gnosis or the secular quest for "autonomy." The project of an historically constructivist *poiēsis* of the self allows of both religious and secular construal. Whether religiously or secularly construed, it differs importantly from the project of personhood derived from the Catholic tradition. It differs as well from the Judaeo-Catholic project that Freudian secularism itself pursues. Freudian psychoanalysis still confirms the Augustinean and Spinozan presumption that the self is, and not simply metaphorically, its prior determinations, and that its freedom consists in recognizing such determinations as it has. Greece's Gnostic fathers, Hellenistic and early Christian, are the ultimate precursors of a less deterministic and far more agonistic vision of the self's project: a vision for which the self's determinations are only its degradations, but degradations that might nevertheless be discarded and transumed: through *theosis*; through union with God, which in Orthodox theology has always meant union with the *gnisio*, with the "authentic" or really "real."

7

THE WORKS OF MARGHARITA KARAPANOU:
LITERATURE AS A TECHNOLOGY
OF SELF-FORMATION

Je suis la plaie et le couteau!
Je suis le soufflet et la joue!
Je suis les membres et la roue,
Et la victime et le bourreau![1]
(Charles Baudelaire)

IN 1987, Margharita Karapanou was writing her third novel. Her first, *I Kassandhra ke o Likos*, or *Cassandra and the Wolf*, was first published in 1976. It had appeared in English and French before it appeared in Greek; it had reached its fifth Greek edition in 1986. Her second novel, *O Ipnovatis*, or *The Sleepwalker*, was first published in 1985. It appeared in French translation in the autumn of 1987.

Karapanou was born in Athens in 1946, after the Second World War but before the official beginning of the Greek Civil War. Her childhood and youth were spent in something of a constant shuffle between Athens and Paris. Her mastery of demotic is evident in her prose. Her French is by all accounts standard Parisian. It was in Paris that she pursued her postsecondary studies. She speaks impeccable English. Imported governesses, who appear to inspire several of the more humorous episodes of the *Cassandra*, introduced her to the language. With time and considerable travel she has developed a strikingly American idiom as well.

In many respects, Karapanou could have been among Maro's five "originals." In fact, she is not: her resemblances to Maro are, strictly speaking, "unintended," though by no means arbitrary. Karapanou's social background and social standing are both very "high." Her ancestors, however, belonged not to the gentry but to the *grande bourgeoisie*. Her father was a poet: "not a very good poet," she told me, and not a canonized poet. Like Maro's father, he was a statesman, but one of Greece's most prominent and most respected statesmen, the scion of a family that had for some considerable time before been intimately involved with both politics and statecraft. She never mentioned his political career to me. It was he, however, to whom many other of my Greek acquaintances referred, and referred without fail, in assigning Karapanou herself to Greece's social elite. I doubt that she would, if pressed, resist the classification. She did, however, once tell me of her exasperation with anyone too concerned, indeed concerned at all, with issues of "status." Such matters, she said, were of no real interest to her at all. Nor did I suspect her remarks of any real insincerity. She did not, among other things, appear to restrict her friendships to those who would be regarded as her social "peers." She was, on the other hand, somewhat aloof. But a psychic delicacy, hinted at in some of the *Cassandra*'s more disturbing vignettes, apparent more than anything else in a nervous stutter, has left her somewhat withdrawn.

She has not, whatever her remove, disowned or denied her privileges. Her marriage was reportedly among Athens's premier social events. By 1986, she had separated from her husband. She had, presumably by choice, been employed, at least before her marriage's end. The back jacket of the *Cassandra* reports, for example, that she had worked as a kindergarten teacher, or supervisor. By 1986, she had devoted herself exclusively to her writing. She has spent past summers at the villa that her family maintains on the island of Hydra. She not infrequently spends time with friends in Paris. For most of 1986, however, she remained at her Athenian home: a demure, modest, and elegant Kolonaki apartment, whose windows look out on Mount Himettos.

Writing I: Some Sociological Notes on the Greek Literary Scene

Social anthropologists have not paid much attention to "literature," perhaps because so few of them have actually met up with it in the field. Cultural anthropologists, sociolinguists, and folklorists have paid more attention to it; more attention, at least, to something like it: "oral poetry," "traditional narrative," and so on. Not all their efforts have been confined simply to the description of performative contexts, to transcription, to genre and formula analysis, to the parsing of the relation between form and message. Anthropologists of "traditional literature" often undertake to be aestheticians as well: a reasonable enough enterprise, but an enterprise that always runs the risk of evaluating texts in the light of standards quite irrelevant to those who produce them. At its worst, it devolves into condescending mockery. Or, not much better, it devolves into some liberal appreciation of the virtues of "earthiness" and "naïveté." Or, not much better than that, it devolves into an apologetics, a defense of the "primitives'" or the "traditionals'" capacity to feel as finely and create as beautifully as anyone else.

The aesthetic capacities of "primitives" and "traditionals" need no defense. The taking up of "literature" as a categorically distinct, and distinctly aesthetic, phenomenon; the taking up of "imaginative poetry" and "imaginative prose" as distinct, and distinctly aesthetic, discursive forms: these deserve to be treated not just as aesthetic but as the more broadly cultural and social events that they are.[2] They cannot be abstracted from the emergence of "subjectivity," or from the gradual methodization of the pursuit of "objective truth," or from the gradual articulation of the difference between disciplines of "fact" and disciplines of "fiction." They cannot be abstracted from the ascendance of the "assertive" self. They cannot be abstracted from the pursuit of distinction.

The sociology of "modern" Greek literature has yet to be done. I can offer only a few crude impressions. The first: that "imaginative literature," literature "as such," was the original preserve in independent Greece of the sociocultural upper strata. In the early nineteenth century, few other Greeks than those of the sociocultural upper strata could read; even fewer could write. In Great Britain and in North America, the producers of literature "as such" have belonged in their majority to the socioeconomic middle classes, though usually to those segments of the middle classes more rather than less culturally endowed.[3] In Greece, the production of literature has, with the institutionalization of free and public schooling, drifted downward; Greece now has a few middling writers, most of them employed, however, as journalists.[4] The great majority of urban Greeks are now literate.[5] Only a few of them, however, do much reading. In 1984, for example, even newspapers sold at a rate of only about one for every ten Greek citizens per day.[6] A 1982 survey, conducted by the editors of the journal *Dhiavazo* ("I Read"), indicated that some three-quarters of the populace of greater Athens never read books at all, and that of those members of the populace who did, only some one-fifth of 1 percent read more than one book a month.[7] Of those who did read, almost 80 percent preferred prose; only about 7.5 percent preferred poetry. A plurality preferred to read in bed.

The authors of a 1985 survey on cultural policy in Greece note, especially after the junta's fall, "an unprecedented increase in publishing and an increase of the reading public, especially among the young."[8] The same authors report government subsidization of both Greek and Cypriot literary societies, with funds in 1984 amounting to some 2,700,000 drachmas (about $20,000). The government also awards ten literary prizes annually, and provides pensions for well-known authors and their families—some twenty-two of them, again in 1984.[9] So there is, perhaps, some recent money to be had in writing; at least, in succeeding at it. But unless one happens to be Odysseus Elytis, a recent winner of the Nobel Prize, or the late Yiannis Ritsos, or some one of the minuscule number of subsidized laureates, there is not very much money to be had. Greece has three major literary presses: Hermes, Estias, and Exandas. It has myriad minor ones, most of which barely cover their own expenses. There are far too few Greek readers and not nearly enough money to be had in writing to explain why so many Greeks do, in fact, write.

How many? I can offer no comprehensive statistics and have, by personal acquaintance, only a very biased sample with which to work. Nor could very many even among that sample be classified primarily as "writers." Of the near dozen Athenians with whom I had the most regular and least superficial meetings and conversations, only one, only Karapanou, was a "writer" *simpliciter*. Three others were known as "writers"—essayists or poets—among other things. All, to be sure, were published; but a third were academics, and another third were "intellectual professionals" for whom writing, usually essayistic or expository, was something of a quotidian duty. Of the wider network of Athenians with whom I came into contact (between 150 and 200, not all of them properly labeled "elite"), perhaps two-thirds had seen something of their own in print. For Greece's sociocultural elite generally, the fraction is likely greater.

Statistics alone, however, cannot in any case account for what might, in Greece, be called the "heroization of the Word," the extraordinary and widespread prestige accorded both to writing and to those who write.[10] The heroization of the Word is perhaps linked, indirectly but securely, to the heroization of education; or so the matters that I discuss in the section that follow tend to suggest. It is, however, linked more directly to the politics of sovereignty itself. Some Greek politicians are writers; certainly not all. But the nondiscursive tactics of sovereignty have a clear discursive counterpart, their "functional equivalent," in revisionary writing, in the writing that announces its author's self-assertion, if not of material then of significative autonomy: "It is written; but I say unto you." One can question whether the ancient Greeks actually advanced any norm of discursive "originality" at all. Greek writers from the middle of the nineteenth century forward surely imported it. But they have had to do very little adapting. The norm of originality fits into Greece's political scheme of things very well, even if it has done its part to undermine the stability of the scheme itself.

Greece's politicians may even fare worse than its writers. Practical power in Greece is usually checked by the world system. Writerly authority is often enhanced by it. No wonder, really, that the Greek state has provided its more famous writers with financial support. The critical success—local but especially international—of Greek literature, and especially of Greek poetry, is no doubt due to the talent of various Greek prosodists and poets. It is also due, however, to a peculiar, and peculiarly modern, twist in the standards by which imaginative literature has, in the "Occident" quite pervasively, come to be assessed. What might be called the Greek advantage in literature[11] is the advantage of a presumptive historical "authenticity" to which other national literary traditions, those at least that are also expected to trace their origins to Homer, can at best aspire. "Classical" references are, in all occidental literatures but the Greek, always a partial contrivance. The same references in Greek literature are never more than partially contrived. Poetic forms and poetic diction are, in all occidental literatures but the Greek, essentially borrowed. The same forms and the same diction are, in contemporary Greek literature, necessarily "adulterated" and necessarily derivative, but still derived through a historically continuous path of "authentic" linguistic evolution. An occidental literature that has come to be governed by the originary precedents of ancient Greece, an occidental literature that has come to be governed by the historicizing presumption of its origin in Greece, is in many respects made for Greeks, or made for those at least who are prepared literarily to be vocal and vivid about their own "national" roots and origins. Hegemony comes, for once, full circle: dominant categorizations tend for once toward an empowering of the dominated. Governments would be foolish not to capitalize on a cultural distinction that has fallen into their hands.

Talent, Refinement, and Literary Distinction

Write in Greek, and you might still be read and reviewed first elsewhere; there are, after all, translators and critics in France, in Great Britain, and in the United States who are fluent in demotic. Write as a Greek, write for Greeks, and you might still be read and reviewed first elsewhere; but not necessarily as the Greek you strive literarily to be. Write as a Greek and for Greeks, and you might still appeal to "occidentals" on their own literary terms; what has come to be "Greek literature" is by no means so distant from the "Occident," either in its forms or in its themes, that it can be appreciated and deciphered by ethnographers alone. Write as a Greek and for Greeks, however, and your task is somewhat different from the task of writing as an "occidental" or for "the Occident" alone.

The dominant Greek regime of signification is as formally democratic as any of its occidental counterparts. In principle, it treats talent as a "free-floating" variable, independent of class or status or background, independent of anything but the self. In principle, it rewards talent wherever and in whomever it might find it. In principle, anyone in Greece might be a discursive sovereign, an intellectual or artistic "hero." But the talented writer, even if willful or determined enough to succeed, has no guarantee of being published and, even if "serious," has no guarantee of being taken seriously. "Talent"—not just a free-floating but also a highly elusive and ineffable variable—may or may not be a prerequisite of the garnering of literary distinction. But there are other prerequisites, more definite and in practice rather more difficult to come by.

Herbert Phillips rightly notes that "the ordering of literary priorities" differs from one social place and time to another.[12] Contemporary Greece's most prominent literary priorities are comparable with "the Occidents'": technical linguistic flair, vividness, wit, poignancy, but originality above all.[13] The preeminence of originality is distinctly modern, emerging in "the Occident" explicitly no earlier than Lessing's *Laokoon*.[14] Among other things, the norm of originality imposes upon any artwork an essentially historical being; nothing can be original except in relation to a past, a corpus of relevant precedents. Originality is normatively "countermimetic." Thus Bourdieu: "an art which ever increasingly contains reference"—one might better say, is expected to contain reference—"to its own history demands to be perceived historically; it asks to be referred not to an external referent, the represented or designated 'reality,' but to the universe of past and present works of art."[15] Normative originality demands of the artist and of the connoisseur alike something other than talent. It demands of both a sensibility refined through a historical and civilizational education.

The more that art is closed off from other intellectual domains, the more an exclusively "artistic" education will suffice: at least for the artist. Art, especially literary art, is not, however, quite so closed off in Greece as in "the Occident." Even if it were, the practice of historical constructivism would still place upon the serious Greek artist the task of knowing much more merely than the history of art. No accident, then, that Greece's historical constructivists from Korais forward have consistently been among the most educated of their compatriots. No accident, either, that the sociocultural elite has long had not just a political but also the artistic upper hand.

The better the artist, as a rule, the better his or her education. The better his or her education, the more likely that he or she descends from the sociocultural elite. Education is even more formally democratic in Greece than in the United States. It is and has long been a state responsibility, free to both boys and girls, women and men. It is and has long been greatly valued, as a means of both mobility and distinction. It has in fact served as a means of both. But it is in practice still productive and reproductive of ascribed hierarchies. Education is, if not precisely better, at least more distinguished in Athens, to the inevitable disadvantage of provincials. Schooling may be free; but living in Athens, whether as a student or in any other occupation, is not. Education is better in Athens's private and foreign schools than in its public and native ones. Postsecondary education is, by general elite consensus, not as good in Greece, even in Athens, as it is in Berlin, or Paris, or, in spite of everything else, in the United States. It is of course less costly to live in Athens than in Paris, or Berlin, or the United States. But Greeks who receive their educations at the University of Athens typically acquire less social and cultural capital with their degrees than those who receive their educations even at relatively undistinguished universities abroad. Greece's economic underclasses have proved willing to make considerable material sacrifices for the education of their sons especially. Its economic upper classes have nevertheless been able to convert their resources to the greater educational advantage of their sons and daughters, at least when they have been so inclined.

Educations acquired solely in schools, even the best of schools, even abroad, are not, however, socially as convincing as those acquired at one's mother's, or father's already cultivated knee. Neither wealth nor diplomas nor simple worldliness is socially as convincing as the "aristocratic asceticism" that one might absorb in an already cultivated, an already polyhistorical, polylingual, and polycultural home.[16] The scions of Greece's economic upper classes have had to try harder to distinguish themselves than the scions of its great estates: its gentry and its administrative officialdom. Not all of them have cared to try.[17] Some have: a few, in order to secure for their families a status that money itself could not buy; many, in order to assert their resistance to a style of life they could not for one reason or another follow or could not for one reason or another entirely condone. The scions of Greece's great estates were among the country's first literati: some secular; others of the church. The scions of the *grande bourgeoisie*, those at least who found or felt themselves alienated both from their class and from the statuses to which the literati were natural heirs, were among its first intelligentsia. Only from the turn of this century would the scions of what had become a displaced gentry and a diminished mandarin cadre come in significant numbers to join them.

The Greek intelligentsia now includes a few petty bourgeois and a few urban proletarians. Most of them are university students and most will remain of the intelligentsia no longer than they remain in university itself. The intelligentsia, whether intellectual or artistic, is still a necessarily educated and necessarily cultivated cadre. It is, as it is most everywhere else, a cadre of "marginals." Its most enduring members in Greece are, however, its most consistently and most securely "daring"; and its most consistently and most securely daring come almost to a man (or woman) from the established sociocultural elite. The penchant for daring, to which the penchant for "originality" closely corresponds, is perhaps common to all sovereign structurations of the political personality. In Greece, it is not just a "political" but also an expressive penchant. Consider again Ersi Khatzimikali's mother, Angeliki, and her solitary ethnographic adventures among the Sarakatsani. So "unwomanly" an enterprise was not undertaken without risk of censure. On the other hand, it was not undertaken, and perhaps could not have been undertaken, without a certain confidence that the risks were not too great, that what censure the enterprise would inspire could not be too damning, that it was in fact far more likely to have its outcome in a heightening of status rather than in a lessening of it. "Daring," whether Greek or not, has never been prudent under any other circumstances.

"Daring," in Greece as elsewhere, has occasionally been manifest as a call for revolution. But it has, in Greece at least, rarely been as effectively critical as when it has been manifest as a call for reformation. It has rarely been as effectively critical as when its voices have been those of a higher sociocultural provenance. Not all of the upper echelons are of course "critical." Not all members of the upper echelons who, for one reason or another, find themselves at some remove from the orthodoxies of their distinction gravitate toward the intelligentsia. But "privileged marginals"—distinguished women, distinguished "homosexuals," distinguished "provincials"—belong to the Greek intelligentsia, and especially its aesthetic intelligentsia, with at least as much consistency and regularity as they do in France, or Great Britain, or the United States. In fact, their prominence—as privileged, if not as marginal—is even greater in Greece than in Greece's less ambiguously "occidental" counterparts. Many of them must be counted among the masters of historical constructivism.

Writing II: The Signature and the Self

Karapanou's novels bear all the traits of what has come, in the twentieth-century "Occident" and in twentieth-century Greece, to be regarded as the most serious of serious fiction. Both are, among other things, formal experiments. Both are quite brief. The *Cassandra* is a bare 130 pages, many of them unfilled. *The Sleepwalker* is 50 pages longer. Neither is quite surrealist. Neither is quite an antinarrative; both are, however loosely, at least chronologies. Both are broken narratives, concatenations of vignettes that parodize rather than respect the conventions of narrativity itself. Karapanou's stylistic mentors are undoubtedly the French *nouveaux romanciers*, though her forms are not as "structuralist" as those of Robbe-Grillet. Both the *Cassandra* and *The Sleepwalker* are, like those of their French predecessors, still cinematic, less continuous than fragmentary and framelike. Karapanou in fact studied cinema, and studied it in Paris.

Both novels display considerable linguistic craft. Both are written in a sparse vernacular, colorful and concrete but refined of all its flourishes. Both are not simply formally but also linguistically worldly; both incorporate brief titillations of English and French. Neither is "academic." But both are replete with rhetorical allusions to the literary and quasi-literary past, allusions highly self-conscious and undoubtedly by design. Both works are unmistakably "novel." Neither is explicitly political in tone or theme. Both, however, undertake an implicitly political "reviewing" of the world, a historically constructive but critical reviewing that could never be the work of a literatus. As a novelist at least, Karapanou fits squarely into the center, the inevitably marginal center, of the neo-Hellenic literary intelligentsia.

But why should she write? To display a social distinction she already has? To display a marginality that she could display in myriad other, less taxing ways? Both perhaps. In addition, perhaps, because a critical and antithetical literature allows sovereignty—certainly not an exclusively male preserve— an outlet that it might not otherwise have. In addition to that, perhaps, because language in Greece remains the least costly and by far the most salient medium of intersubjective expression. But there are surely other reasons as well, which must be seen not just in a Greek but in the general light of the marker, or operator, that has come to epitomize and to govern the modern relation at once between those who produce texts or works and their products and between texts or works and those who receive them: the marker, or operator, designated by the signature itself.

Conceived simply as the sign of an attachment between creator and work, conceived simply as the sign of a spatiotemporal localization or relativization of a thing created, a thing made, the signature has nothing exclusively writerly or even distinctively modern about it. Myths, at least in their Lévi-Straussian rendering, are by definition "unsigned." Their detachment from circumstance, and in particular from the circumstances of their production, is a correlate of their "transcendence": a correlate of their presumptive objectivity; a correlate of the presumptive timelessness of the cosmogonic and cosmological truths that they enunciate.[18] But other oral and "traditional" works do bear signatures of sorts. Traditional oratory, for example, typically bears the signature of the orator, an individual whose "name" is thus given to his pronouncements. Modern political oratory is of course attached to its orators in much the same way, all the more inevitably as their pronouncements are put into print.

The modernization of the signature does not, however, necessarily have anything to do with the ascendance of the printed word per se. The modern signature is not remarkable for being actually inscribed or written down. It is remarkable rather for its presumptive ubiquity: a byline, a localizing and relativizing "stamp" presumptively affixed not simply to certain pronouncements but rather to ideation as such. It is not in itself a stamp of falsehood, or error, or blindness. It does not in itself constitute a challenge to the universality of truth, of rightness or goodness, of beauty or originality or any other standard against which ideas might be judged. It constitutes instead, in its negative moment at least, a reminder of the limits, the spatial and temporal constraints, the particularity of the conditions under which ideas are produced. Whether it thus constitutes a reminder of the fallibility of all thought (I doubt that it does), it certainly constitutes a reminder of the historicity of thought, a historicity that has its most extreme notation in the first-person singular: "I think."[19]

The signature, conceived as a mark of the spatiotemporal relativization of the production of ideas, does not itself necessarily designate the pure particularity, the pure subjectivity, that the first-person singular does, at least not in all cases. Communities, among them scientific communities, are capable of producing, and thus "signing," ideas in common. The results, for example, of a physical experiment, once replicated, may well retain the signatures of those individuals who have arrived at them. But they also bear another signature, not in the first-person singular but in the first-person plural. The signature indicates in general not the pure subjectification of thought but rather the refusal to detach ideas from the persons, singular or collective, who think them. That refusal informs a variety of characteristically "hot," and in that respect characteristically modern, discursive praxes, from the praxis of liberal theology to the praxis of liberal ethics. It informs, for that matter, the praxis of both the sociology and the anthropology of knowledge, at least to the extent that both are devoted to discerning the "existential constraints" upon or "circumstantiality" of claims of fact, or worth, or world disclosure. It informs "ideological" or "mythological" criticism from Marx to Barthes. Without presuming the presence of the signature, the ideological or mythological critic has no guideline at all to follow in exposing ideologies as "mere" ideologies or myths as "mere" myths.

The same refusal to detach creators from their ideational creations informs both the production and the consumption of "authentic" art as well.[20] Foucault saw, or momentarily believed that he saw,[21] an escape from the tyranny of an enforced authenticity in the poststructuralist distinction between "works" and more free-floating "texts."[22] If he hoped for a freedom from the signature as well, even in the poststructuralist "discovery" of the "text," if he did indeed hope for the death of what, roughly following Blanchot and Barthes,[23] he called "the author," his hope was surely in vain. In retrospect, his essay on authorship can perhaps most usefully be read as an admonition not against the attachment of creature to creator but against that sort of reductive, and largely destructive, hermeneutics that would reveal, particularly in philosophical and literary works, nothing more nor less than the "case" of the life responsible for them. The relation marked by the signature has, to be sure, allowed for that hermeneutics. But it also leaves room for other hermeneutics, in fact even for contrary hermeneutics, that would reveal in a work or in a text not, or not merely, its author's self-projections but also his, or her, exercises of self-formation.

Writing III: Fiction, Self-Validation, and Self-Formation

Why write? Karapanou spoke to me of the vexations of writing, of what hard and exhausting work it was for her. She mentioned that *The Sleepwalker* had gone through thousands of emendations, minor and major, before its submission for publication. She told me that she had been advised, in fact ordered, to write. I asked her if her "occupational therapy" had actually made her more at ease with her world. "No," she said, quite definitively. "But it has helped me in other ways." She did not elucidate the comment any further. I can, however, offer some estimate of what she might mean.

Thanks to the signature, writing factitious or fictive, critical or poetic can be among the most multifunctional technologies of self-determination, of the determination of the self in and through its works of any we have.

Thanks to the signature, it can be even more: a medium of self-validation, of the validation of the self in the work but also of the self behind it. Everything depends upon whether what is written is well received, upon whether it becomes "canonical."

The signing, the subjectification of a work, collective or singular, is not incompatible with its canonization. But subjectification and canonization are countervailing processes. In theory—though the matter is often different in fact—the canonization of a work is not a popularity contest and has nothing "personal" about it.[24] In theory, a work, factitious or fictive, crosses the threshold of goodness or greatness only by passing certain acid tests, only by measuring up to such putatively universal standards as truth or beauty or to such more distinctively modern standards as novelty, or originality, or "world disclosure." In theory, canonization is a process legitimately conducted only by a cadre of "experts," either trained to judge or deemed by those so trained to have judgments or intuitions worth heeding.[25] It is, in that respect, always specifically "antipopulist."

The canonized work, for its part, typically acquires not simply a "suprapopular" but also a "supralocal," transhistorical dignity, even when judged in the light of explicitly historicizing standards. A scientific treatise or a poem is genuinely novel or original or world disclosive only in a specific spatiotemporal context. But its originality is itself effectively timeless, and its precedent one against which the originality of any subsequent treatise or poem, even if produced quite independently, is likely to be assessed. The canonized work differs, however, from the Lévi-Straussian myth precisely in retaining, or in being supposed to retain,[26] the signature that the myth lacks. It differs from the sacral work[27] precisely in its attachment to that "subjectivity," that "point of view," to which the signature always points.

Still, the transitivity of the relation that the signature marks usually confers not just upon the work but also upon the subjectivity in and behind it a certain heightening, a partial freedom from the limitations of place and time. The canonized work "stands the test of time." The subjectivity in and behind it "sees through" or "sees beyond" his or her place and time, whether to truth, or beauty, or the future itself. The canonized work is a work of "talent," of "genius," of "mastery"; the subjectivity in and behind it transitively a genius, a talent, a master. Publication is the process through which writers gain entry as writers into regimes of signification, but canonization is the process through which they gain entry into a significative elite of "major figures." No writer can take the canonization of his or her work for granted. The canonized work, however, confers upon the self in and behind it something at least of its own esteem. That writing, and particularly the sort of writing that is most intimately self-concerned and self-centered, is so prominent a vocation—not simply in Greece but in other national tradi-

tions troubled like Greece with sempiternal crises of identity—is as a consequence perhaps not as sheerly coincidental as it seems.

Karapanou writes, among other reasons, for literary validation, for the
canonization of her vision. I once asked her if she were pleased that both her
novels had sold so crisply. Some sixteen to twenty thousand copies of the
Cassandra are circulating in Greece today,[28] an astonishing number in a
country of only ten million. Of course she was pleased. But she was also
perturbed that the local "critical establishment" had largely ignored her. For
good enough reason: the local establishment has long favored male over
female writers; notoriously conservative, perhaps simply insecure, it has long
been slow to approve of works as "daring" as Karapanou's own. During one
of our conversations, I suggested to her that she might have to wait another
generation to be recognized. "I'll be dead by then," she said: quintessen-
tially the remark of a writer who writes not only for her time but for her life
as well. But she may not be dead. She may well live to see her laurels.

The dominant Greek regime of signification, in spite of its linguistic isolation, is not closed entirely. It is particularly susceptible to judgments "from
the center." Karapanou's novels have in fact been quite well received "at the
center." Her Greek publisher, though no doubt less interested in Karapanou's own validation than in both the canonization and the distribution
of her work, chose to print, on the back cover of the Cassandra's fifth edition, two "central" responses to its earlier English translation. The first was
a fragment from a letter of praise that Karapanou herself had received from
John Updike. The second was a fragment from an equally praiseworthy review, written by Jerome Charyn for the New York Times. For the original
novelist, the praise could hardly be higher: "No analysis of Cassandra and
the Wolf can explain the charm and the mystery of the book. Margharita
Karapanou's first novel, Cassandra and the Wolf, is one of those rare creations that is born mysteriously, without any precedent. The book is a prototype, terrifying and complete."

Self-validation, yes: but if Karapanou's novels have not "cured" her, if
they have not helped her to live more easily in the world, they have beyond
any self-validation helped her to give form to her uneasiness. Giving form to
it, she has perhaps been able to resist it. Perhaps not: I cannot say. But she
has at least been able to indict it. Her novels are not strictly "autobiographical"; but they are filled with autobiographical details. Her uneasiness is
personal; but as her readership indicates, not exclusively personal. Why,
then, should Greece's most influential contemporary critics continue, for
the most part, to ignore her?

In part, because she is a woman. But more important, because she is
among the first voices of the generation made in the crucible of the junta
and in the creative catastrophe of its fall. Greece's critical establishment is

not necessarily "reactionary"; but it is older and has itself been made in the crucible of older catastrophes: the Asia Minor Disaster; the Second World War; the Civil War. Karapanou's *Cassandra* alludes to the Civil War, but is set in its aftermath. It is set before the junta, but draws terrible and critical parallels between the cultural classicism that preceded and the cultural classicism enforced by the junta itself. Neither the *Cassandra* nor *The Sleepwalker* could have been published during the junta's tenure. They would have been censored: too "scandalous," too "obscene." Greece's critical establishment, tutored on former catastrophes, has yet to appreciate Karapanou's critique of classicism, which at once condemns obscenity and celebrates it. The majority of her readers, however, who must surely be no older than she, are experientially better prepared.

Karapanou's Rhetoric: Some Notes on Tradition and the Individual Talent

The mythic Cassandra, daughter of the Trojan king Priam, was a prophetess whom no one heeded. She spoke truths that everyone dismissed. She revealed fate, but it was her own tragic fate to be deemed a madwoman. Karapanou's Cassandra alludes to the tragic sibyl, makes use of her, revivifies her. Similar devices are standard in Greek poetry (and in Greek prose) since the middle of the previous century:

> Whether it is Palamas contrasting the "people of relics"—who reign among the temples and olive groves of the Attic landscape—with the modern crowd crawling along sluggishly, like a caterpillar over a white flower . . . ; or Cavafy evoking—perhaps ironically, perhaps erotically—some scene out of his poetic world of ancient Alexandria; or Sikelianos endeavoring to resurrect the whole pantheon of the ancient gods and to be a hierophant to their mysteries; or Seferis searching for the archaic king of Asine—a substantial man who fought with heroes—and finding only the unsubstantial void of contemporary existence; whichever it is, the ancient world in all its aspects preoccupies the imagination of these poets constantly.[29]

The master imagery of early and late, the master trope of metalepsis, could hardly be more prominent. But the metaleptic ends of Greece's literary lumieres have not always been "projective." The Greek canon has almost as many cultural classicists as historical constructivists. Palamas[30] and Sikelianos[31] must often be ranked among the former. Cavafy can, like Kazantzakis after him, usually be ranked among the latter. Seferis, a nostalgist who nevertheless discounts the possibility of a return to the past, often wavers between the two.

Karapanou? At first sight, her Cassandra appears to be a "modernization" of the ancient sibyl, an "update" that identifies with the past by proving its perfect transferability into the present. At first and indeed at second sight it betrays a certain nostalgia for a more mantic and oracular revelation than the present allows.[32] But Karapanou is not, in fact, a classicist and the *Cassandra* itself not a classicist tract. Karapanou shares with such introjective metalepticians as Sikelianos a variety of literary penchants. She imports and experiments with form. She fashions very much her own linguistic dialect: "a crucial factor," as Peter Bien points out, of any contemporary Greek's literary "individuality."[33] She makes use of ancient figures. But unlike Sikelianos, unlike most of her other immediate predecessors, she has no reverence toward antiquity. Not even Kazantzakis can match her impiety. Nor does Karapanou aim at the same revelation that her predecessors pursued. Solomos, Kazantzakis, Palamas, Cavafy, Elytis, each in his way seeks, in the presence of the past or in an epiphany of the relation between the present and the past, a distillation—if not always of the self of Greece at least of the Greekness of the self.[34] Whether introjective or projective, the result has the same form for all: an existential unity, perhaps present, perhaps forever past.

Karapanou's "swerve," her rhetorical distance both from her literary predecessors and from her cultural surroundings, appears first of all as irony, and in particular as an ironization of the present's degradation of the past. Karapanou is a poet of both impurity and decadence. Unlike her predecessors, however, and unlike the majority of her cultural contemporaries, she rejects neither. If anything, the contrary: but her inverted moralism is based on an altogether principled understanding of self. She is not a poet of Hellenicity. When I asked her what Greece was, what it meant to her, she simply said that it was "the smell of the sea, and the thyme." She loved Greece, she said. But she did not think of herself as Greek. Or not Greek. What difference did it make?

A subterfuge? Something of one, perhaps. Karapanou was, however, pointing out not only her distance from the quest for Hellenicity but also her claim to other traditions, other "cultures" beside the Greek.[35] Her cosmopolitanism—or assimilationism—is quite self-conscious. Whether in her works or behind them, it is elaborately and meticulously "cultivated." Does it pose a particular analytical problem? It poses a problem, at least, for any approach that would presume either the literary work or the self behind it to be a "reflection" of some "culture." It poses a problem even for an approach that would presume the work or the self to be a "refraction" of some culture. In an age of wandering assimilationists and avid reformers, there simply are not any more "cultures" either to reflect or to refract. There are practices, some more determinative than others. There are "situations," in Sartre's sense. There are even "traditions," but no longer so subliminal or so

In *The Anxiety of Influence,* he is quite adamant that his theory is a causal theory. In *A Map of Misreading,* however, he has this to say:

> The theory, deliberately an attempt at de-idealizing, has encountered considerable resistance during my presentation of it in a number of lectures at various universities, but whether the theory is correct or not may be irrelevant to its usefulness for practical criticism. . . . One of the functions of criticism, as I understand it, is to make the good poet's work even more difficult for him to perform, since only the overcoming of genuine difficulties can result in poems wholly adequate to an age consciously as late as our own. All that a critic, as critic, can give poets is the deadly encouragement that never ceases to remind them of how heavy their inheritance is.[38]

One does not always have to have read a work in order to have encountered or to have been influenced by its "vision." Bloom's hermeneutics of revisionism is, moreover, as much a hermeneutics of the historically sensitive reader's comprehension of the texts that he or she reads as of the practice of "original" *poiēsis.* But in what follows, I sidestep these complexities. I treat Karapanou as revising—though not consciously revising—only what she has actually read.

The *Cassandra*: Imagination Is Perversion

The *Cassandra* opens with a chapter only two sentences long, entitled "The First Day."[39] "I was born in July," it reads, "at twilight, under the sign of Cancer." The second sentence is virtually impossible to translate. This is one alternative, perhaps the more likely: "When they brought me for her to see, she turned toward the wall." This is the other: "When they brought me for him to see, he turned toward the wall." English requires pronouns where Greek does not. The third party could be anyone. The gesture is more important: one of shame, perhaps, or disgust; one of rejection more certainly. The child born to rejection is born at twilight: the term in Greek is *likofos,* "the light of the wolf." The wolf himself occupies the *Cassandra*'s second chapter:

> "Come on. Let's look at the book with the pictures."
> I would hurry to his room with the book underneath my arm and would give it to him with tenderness.
> The first picture had a wolf opening his mouth and gulping down seven juicy little pigs.
> Usually, I felt sorry for the wolf. How will he gulp down so many little pigs all at once? I would always say it to him and ask him. He would put his hairy hand in my white panties then and touch me. I didn't feel anything but a kind of

warmth. His finger moved back and forth and I would look at the wolf. He would pant and sweat. It didn't bother me much.

Now when they fondle me, I always think of the wolf and feel sorry for him. (6)

The identity of the third party is again obscure, but the metaphor is not. The man who beckons the child to the picture book, the man who molests the child, is confused with the wolf. He is a wolf.

The metaphor recurs, even though the wolf, by name, does not. The *Cassandra* is in fact filled with figures of gluttony, of violation, of insatiety. There is Petros, a servant, who is likely the second chapter's unidentified man-wolf but who comes later on more explicitly into his own:

> "My little sweet pea, I kiss your little feet piously . . . I look at them and cry, white and clean on the carpet, I melt, I become wax, I will tear you to pieces."
>
> . . . Petros trembles, from his hair to the soles of his feet, with his eyes closed he sings a prayer to himself, he rocks slowly like a steamship in a storm, his mouth softens and slackens, his face falls down, nothing holds him together anymore, on my back something hard like the thrust of a knife, now Petros opens up and blossoms, he screams like a toothless baby, he chokes and suddenly withers upon my back, slides and rolls himself into a coil down on the rug. (21)

But there is also Uncle Kharilaos, who wants to "swallow the whole sea" (13). There are other relatives, in fact a whole family, endowed with a fortune they did not earn, endowed with a bygone gentility, occupied with little more than the time on their hands, with trips to Paris and trivial "good works," with clever conversations and elaborate Sunday dinners prepared only to be consumed.

The wolf, however, is not a simple figuration of decadence, and the *Cassandra* is in no simple sense an exposé of the decadence, whether of a particular class or of a particular time. The young Cassandra—the child is named for her mother, the elder Cassandra of the novel—is not victimized by decadence alone. She is also victimized by righteousness. Leaving Sunday School one morning, she wants to "kiss the little boot" of her attendant English governess, to tell her "that she is ready to love her":

> "Miss Benbridge —."
>
> I take her by the hand, I shove my nose underneath her skirt. I squeeze her little feet in my embrace, I bite her thighs—they are like a sponge. I worship her.
>
> "Wretched child," she screams. "I can't take you anymore—and we just came out of the Church! I know you, my God, I know what you are. You filthy little brat!"
>
> She takes me by the hair, trembling. She doesn't know what she's doing—let me forgive her. Her little boot kicks me in the mouth, I fall backwards in the

snow. With my hand I secretly wipe the blood from my cheek. She doesn't know what she's doing—let me forgive her. I straighten my hair and my skirt, smiling. (116)

The child is victimized by convention, by order. Her elementary school entry examinations are disastrous:

> They gave us some white and fibrous sheets of paper and told us to paint a tree.
> I chewed on the end of my pencil with a slight uncertainty: I didn't remember what colors I had seen on the trees and all around. I took the red and I made an all-red tree on a little blue mountain. All around a sky black and thick. All the children passed except me. (132)

Even in her victimization, however, at whatever hands, the young Cassandra is never indignant, and never herself righteous. Her prevailing reaction is rather one of pity: for the wolf, as we have seen, for her uncle and others of her family, for Petros, occasionally even for Miss Benbridge, in the face of whose scorn she calls upon herself to be both God the Father and Jesus the Son. "She doesn't know what she's doing," our little heroine reflects. "Let me forgive her." Such superhuman mercy is, however, sometimes squandered on inappropriate objects. In other circumstances, it is blunted by ignorance:

> I thought . . . of Uncle Kharilaos's ear, which was hairy and had something like yellow spots inside.
> "He killed himself," Grandmother told me, crying.
> "He killed himself," the ladies and gentlemen who had come to the house wearing black and who were eating something like sugared beans cried out all together.
> "This must be some new game," I thought, quite delighted. (43)

Karapanou sounds here not unlike Axioti, whose *Difficult Nights* opens with a suicide, and whose child is just as nonplussed:

> One day I heard my parents say secretly and with fear that the officer [who tutored me] killed himself. When I showed myself they signaled one another to cut off the conversation. But I felt at peace! Khrrap Khrrap his spurs and that fear of mine of [his military braids] tangled on the door-knob. (26)[40]

Peace, however, is for Axioti's child short-lived. The officer's death is for her only the prelude to another, far more devastating loss:

> . . . I wanted my mother. No one had told me yet that mothers can go away. (31)

The young Cassandra's mother as well is, if not lost, still often "away." In *Difficult Nights*, the mother's absence is a figure of the child's condemnation to maturity, a figure soon made literal; Axioti's child is sent off, "locked away" in a school in order to "become a person," to become an adult (38). The young Cassandra is perhaps maimed by her own mother's absence. But she knows how to turn everything, even maiming, into a game. By playing at and playing out the parts of all the external forces that affect her, our young synthesizer becomes them, taking them in and taking them on at once. She masters them by absorbing them. Her mother is among the first to fall prey to her imaginative cannibalism:

> One day, my mama, Cassandra, brought me a pretty doll for a gift. It was big and its hair was made out of yellow strings.
> I put it to bed in its box, after first cutting off its feet and its hands so that it would fit.
> Later I cut off its head so that it wouldn't be heavy. Now I love it very much. (11)

Capable of being the mother whose name she shares, capable of being a "grown up," the young Cassandra is accordingly capable, for all her ignorance, of quite intentional, of quite inner wickedness:

> At Iraklis's party they had a large table, all covered with cakes with cream. And some strawberries, red as cherries. I had to go pee-pee. I couldn't hold it in. It came out of me from everywhere. I go near the strawberries and pee on the glossy parquet.
> I call Zakoulis, who was passing by. I stop him over the pond.
> "Zakouli, if you budge from here I'll slaughter you and skin you alive," I said.
> When the party ended, Zakoulis was still crying from the beating he got. Inside myself, I felt a great joy and was stuffed with the sweets [that I had eaten]. My eyes were sparkling. (16)

She is capable of deriving pleasure, whatever the wickedness. God and Jesus prove to be a little devil, too.

What sets young Cassandra apart from her elders is thus not her innocence. What sets her apart is rather her encompassing, her comprehension of a perversity that her elders are not quite able to comprehend themselves. That hyperbolic perversity has its most sublime figuration in the child's capacity to dream, her capacity for vision:

> It was the time that I was sick, and would see butterflies and swallows before my eyes. I would also see crabs and spiders and crocodiles and poppies. (76)

With this imagery, Karapanou's rhetoric nearly arrives at its "revisionist trope proper." The mad and persecuted prophetess of the ancient myths, the original Cassandra, takes her final and fuller form as the "sick child" of contemporary Greece's postwar dusk. The end has, however, a twist. The first Cassandra was merely the metonymic mouthpiece, the voice of a truth fated but unheeded. Karapanou's metaleptic Cassandra is the vessel only of her own imagination, "perverse" in the precise sense that it "turns" from any normativity, whether the normativity of decadence, of righteousness, even of "truth." Thus the final note of the *Cassandra*'s final chapter, "First Day of School":

> I think . . . of Grandfather, by himself down in the cellar, and I yell out:
> —"Two and two make two and two, and not four. Join two Grandfathers with two other Grandfathers, they make two and two Grandfathers, and not four. Or, rather no, they make one, two, three, four. If you stir them together in a casserole, and boil them, then yes, the one two three four Grandfathers will become one round and juicy Grandfather, maybe even younger."
> Fanny waits for me at the door.
> —"How did school go?"
> —"Very well, I learned to speak, to answer, and to think with syllables."
> —"Then why are you crying?"
> —"It's the syllables. I hurt, when I cut the words in the middle."
> —"You'll get used to it," Fanny says to me. "You'll get used to it." (137)

But she won't get used to it, of course. She will not be imposed upon by even the most essential of laws and orders. That juicy Grandfather of whom she dreams brings us back to the juicy little pigs with which our story began. He brings us back to the wolf, who seemed to disappear but has been present all along in the person of our voracious heroine. She may be little, but she is every bit as "bad." Do her injury and sooner or later she will gobble you up, too.

The Generation of 1930 and the Generation of 1974

So limited, so "literary" a reading of the *Cassandra* would perhaps be inappropriate if literary and other rhetorical acts were more independent. It would perhaps be inappropriate if literary statements had no political resonance. But in Greece at least, they have long had a political resonance, often of the most blatant sort. Consider the writers—with some of whom, as we shall see, Karapanou has a great deal in common—who have come to be identified as the *yenia tou trianda*, the "Generation of 1930." Most of them began to write in the immediate aftermath of the Asia Minor Disaster, but also found their first voices in their efforts to come to terms with that disaster.[41] Greece's defeat in Anatolia provided the experiential substance for themes that dominated literature and culture alike for another quarter-century: disorientation, displacement, disappointment, debasement, disintegration, but also the theme of will, especially the will to survive. The Second World War and the Civil War renewed many of those themes, which were circulating in any case long before 1924. Traditional song and oral verse had treated them for centuries, from the fall of Constantinople onward. The Asia Minor Disaster, however, endowed them with a finality that they had never really had before. The demise of the Great Idea, of the irredentist dream of a recovered Greek empire, was perhaps presaged in Greece's failure in the 1897 war against Turkey. But the Greek "Generation of '97" acknowledged the omen only in part.[42] It admitted in the defeat a delay; but it did not abandon the dream of empire itself. By 1920, its often missionary, often romantic syncretism had largely ossified into a rhetoric of the ethnos, a rhetoric that subordinated any earlier countenance of spatiotemporal diversity to the master trope of singular nationhood. It had become classicist.

The Asia Minor Disaster robbed that master trope of most of its literary and political substance, and for a time at least, of much of its practical point. It accordingly provided a rhetorical aperture, a clearing of symbolic ground, which the Generation of 1930 soon claimed as its own. Earlier Greek writers had struggled with their country's civilizational confluences. The writers of the Generation of 1930 did not simply reembrace those confluences but also enlarged them. They were ardent, though selective, importers. Among other things, they brought to Greece the modernist poetics of Pound and Eliot and the surrealist aesthetics of Breton. They were experimenters, often in the name of experimentation itself. In the end, they succeeded, though not only through their own devices, in casting off the stigmata of the "avant-garde" for those of a new literary establishment, still largely secure. The generation had Seferis, who was awarded Greece's first Nobel Prize in literature in 1963. It also included Odysseus Elytis and Yiannis Ritsos. It included a number of novelists less broad, but as distinguished as Ritsos himself: Stratis Mirivilis, Ilias Venezis, and Angellos Terzakis. It included several women, among them Dhidho Sotiriou, Elli Alexiou, and Melpo Axioti, whose *Difficult Nights* won the Women Novelists' Prize in Greece in 1938.

The generation had its anticlassical manifesto, however, in Yiorghos Theotokas's *To Elefthero Pnevma*, or *The Free Spirit*. Theotokas, a ponderously educated, well-traveled, high bourgeois, was also profoundly influenced by the Nietzsche of the *Zarathustra*. *The Free Spirit*, a collection of critical essays, is nevertheless not as Nietzschean as it is simply projective in its call for both Greek poets and Greek critics to "recover their wits":

> Hellenic minds [*enkefali*] do not yet have the power to spread themselves out free in the world of ideas, and with each step they seek absolute Truth, that is to say, a prison. This madness for the absolute, for the determinate, for the pure, that reveals itself in all Hellenic discussions, makes quite apparent the level of our spiritual development. It is a pitiable sight that Hellenic criticism presents today, or rather this thing that we typically call criticism in Greece, which resembles genuine criticism as much as the Bavarian barracks of Syntagma Square resemble the Parthenon.[43]

Theotokas renders the same position allegorically in his most acclaimed novel, *To Dhemonio*, or *The Daimon*. But *The Daimon*, written in 1938, betrays a certain exhaustion, a beleaguredness that the exuberant scorn of *The Free Spirit* does not. One recent reviewer summarizes it, tellingly enough, as the story "of the family of Khistoforos Khristofis and its ultimate misfortune":

> The daughter, Iphigenia, a young woman of great imagination and sure of her genius, does not fit in—any more than her brothers, Romulos and Thomas— with other people. They live, they fly better in other worlds—certainly they do not tread on the earth; they dream, but their successes are only in their dreams; life leaves them with nothing.[44]

By 1938, for Theotokas at least, the imaginative spaces that had opened after the Asia Minor Disaster had perhaps already begun to close again. They had already begun to close for others of the Generation of 1930, most of whom would return sooner or later to a more essentialist and more "nativist" conception, not simply of Greece's literary project but also of the self behind that project.

Nor were they alone in their retraction. From about 1940 onward, political rhetoric as well became increasingly nationalistic and increasingly puristic, the rhetoric of a Greece not simply "for the Greeks" but of them as well. Whether literary or political, the return to a classicist and purgative revivalism was by no means independent of Greece's invasion by foreign militarists and industrialists. Whether literary or political, that return, though not total, was a response to the foreign presence, and a response in particular to the dependencies and the "occidentalizations" that it inevitably imposed. Particularly after the Second World War, Greece's literary practitioners began to rid their works of the most tangible at least of "extraneous influences." "Purity" and "impurity," "innerness" and "outerness" gradually reemerged as the most dominant and most productive of literary dichotomies. A "pure" and "inner" Hellenicity gradually reemerged as the guiding literary thematic of both situation and self. Still in 1984, Elytis for example praised the photographer John Veltri for capturing in his work those "three components which, with all their sequences and correspondences, constitute the invisible yet all-inclusive continuity of Greece in [its] second but true being: . . . the light, the sea, and poverty."[45]

The junta, however, disrupted at least the complacency of these Hellenizing poetics. Its effects were not as dramatic as those of the Asia Minor Disaster. But they were, and have remained, real enough. Whatever else the colonels did or did not do, they did indeed manage to send a substantial number of Greece's postwar artists and intellectuals into exile. Still others left of their own accord. Not all who left chose to repatriate after the colonels were ousted. Those who did choose to repatriate, however, frequently brought ideational souvenirs back along with them. The souvenirs proved, in some cases at least, to have more impact than they might well have had before the colonels came to power. The junta did not itself encourage "openness." Quite the contrary. The colonels were—in their rhetoric—cultural classicists, purists, and pure Hellenists, to a man. But the "purity" of the "nation" of "Hellenic Christians" in whose name they worked turned out with the most terrible irony to be a byword of repression, of torture, of literal purge. The "innerness" they sought to restore turned out to be a byword of intolerance: whether of "free-spiritedness," or of "perversion," or of political dissent. Rhetoricians of a pure and inner Greece have yet to regain all the confidence undermined by the colonels' bad example. Theotokas wrote *The Free Spirit* in an epoch whose people had been forced to confront the shattering of a nationalist dream, and had little else to do but pick up, and reformulate, the pieces. Karapanou published the *Cassandra* in an epoch similarly, if not so brutally, shattered, and similarly, if perhaps not so broadly, open. She wrote it, no doubt, for herself. But its enthusiasm for difference, for otherness, its defense of the boundless imagination, has proved to have more than a merely "subjective" meaning. So, too, the "rhetorical question" with which it implicitly ends.

The little Cassandra is Karapanou's self in the work, a portrait of the revisionary artist as a young girl. Who is Fanny, the speaker of the novel's final words? Like Petros, she is a house servant, the family's cook and maid. Fanny is, at the novel's end, the voice of experience. She is speaking for herself, someone who has herself "gotten used to it." The reader has met her several times before. Near the novel's opening, Cassandra asks her to say something about "the war"—surely the Civil War. Fanny, evidently, was a Communist sympathizer working in a rightist home:

> "AFTERWARDS," she roars, "when we were left to ourselves and our songs had swollen the stones and the sky, the poet and asshole-minister and would-be terminator Mr. Aris dove under the table screaming 'Historic moment!' And your grandfather said to your grandmother: 'Sappho, time for me to die.' We came down into the streets, we sucked in air like madpeople, like we couldn't get enough. But you had all shrunk. You were like beans."
>
> Fanny smells blood and comes near me.
>
> "You ruined us again. You ate us. Gutless moneygrubbers . . ." (9)

Fanny had her brief taste of sovereign freedom, her own brief moment of gluttonous indulgence. But order was restored. Was it fate? Hardly: just plain human brutality. Fanny tells the little Cassandra that she, too, will become inured to the orders brutally imposed upon her. Perhaps, an underling in her own way, she will. But the question remains: why should she? Why should anyone?

After 1974, Greece saw the publication of myriad political indictments, some scholarly, others literary, of the colonels and of the Greeks who helped or let the colonels remain in power. Only with Karapanou's *Cassandra*, however, has the generation of the junta, the "Generation of 1974," been provided with its own spiritual manifesto: a historically constructive indictment not simply of the colonels but of all would-be champions of "purity" and "order"; of all who presume to know the absolute and presume their right to enforce it. Does Karapanou know what she has written? I am not certain that she does. But some of her audience does. I met one man, imprisoned during the junta, who told me that the *Cassandra* was *ena apo ta pio dhinata mithistorimata*, "one of the most powerful novels," that he had ever read. His remark suggests that Karapanou's self-determinations are on the brink of entering even the local canon. It suggests that we do, indeed, have a talent on our hands: an opportunist who has seized her own historical moment in order to work for and upon herself, who has worked with and revised "tradition" in the process, and whose achievement turns out to "make sense" for many others as well.

The Sleepwalker: Literary Constructivism as Political and Cultural Deconstruction

Karapanou's second novel continues, in its historically constructivist way, the critique to which the *Cassandra* gave a first expression. It is, in its way, even more brutal, and considerably more pointed. It mocks the colonels, though allegorically, at virtually every turn. It makes of the *Ellas Ellinon Khristianon*, the "Greek Christians' Greece" of which they appointed themselves "protectors," its primary target. The colonels were not in fact above figuring themselves "missionaries of God." *The Sleepwalker* is thus provided with its anterior trope. It opens, however, with God himself—not the one the colonels might have conceived, but one worthy of their evangelism:

> God was tired.
> He had spread out on a rock high in the sky and had turned his back to the earth. For the first time he felt sadness and a great boredom. He saw people small, laughable—whom in his own tongue he would name beings—and a terrible anger seized him, because he had created them with so much love. But that had happened so long ago that he could remember nothing. And now he was old. His love seemed to him itself ancient, and he was seized with nostalgia for the emotion he had had when he dreamed up the Cosmos. (9)[46]

The God of *The Sleepwalker* is not precisely the *deus absconditus*. He has not fled the world; he has simply turned his back to it. He even suspects himself of responsibility for its flaws:

> He thought that he might have made it in a moment of lapsed judgment [*pa-ranomias*], that for that reason it bore the stigmata of error. There were moments when He felt Himself unlawful to Himself, moments of unspeakable, forbidden pleasure. He feared that the earth might be a child of that moment, a child of pleasure and not of the Law [*tou Nomou*]. (9)

But no matter. He feels that the earth, His child, should repay Him for the life and the passion with which He had graced it. But people have harassed Him. The earth has betrayed Him instead. So He decides "to send to the earth a new God," whom people "would recognize and worship from the beginning, a God in His own image and likeness, a God who would be worthy of them" (10).

The new God is not the Christ, and the Second Coming not the return of the Christ, but the arrival instead of an ironized counter-Christ, "who would make enemies, not believers." He would have to be an Adonis, have to be beautiful, since people had come to worship beauty alone. He would need "narrow hips," but need also to be "man and woman," since people "no longer respected the Law" (10). He would be unfettered with the true Christ's self-consciousness. He would "walk in his sleep," like all the others around him. He would be endowed not with the self-sacrificing spirit of the Demiurge's love of humanity but rather with the spirit of His disgust:

> [God] stuck His hands in His middle, bent over the earth, and puked. And the skies opened, and great thunder was heard.
>
>   Manolis was sleeping on the mountain. He put his hands in front of his face to protect it from the thick-flowing and foul liquid that was striking the shrubs and the stalks of grain. But once he opened his eyes, he understood that it was only a dream and that the vomit was rain. (10)

The new Emmanuel lives on a lovely little Greek island. After his anointing, he comes down from his mountain to the village where he makes his home. Carnival is in progress, a parade of clowns and transvestites. But it is not a mere ritual of inversion. The island itself is "inverted," topsy-turvy, "against the Law." It is, of course, occupied and preoccupied with foreigners, as most lovely little Greek islands are these days. From the native's point of view:

> "The Greek, even if he's a bugger, has principles. Sick ones maybe, but even so he's a family man in his way. Only a foreigner could be a bit of everything. You see, they've learned to be. I've heard that in Sweden they take their bath, and other things, too, everybody naked together, parents with their children. Eh, how can the wretches not be messed up later on?" (142)

It is infiltrated by the foreign:

It is infiltrated by the foreign:

From the bar . . . you could hear a fragment of Steely Dan:

> Learn to work the saxophone,
> I play just what I feel,
> Drink Scotch whisky
> All night long,
> And die behind the wheel. (77)

It is a place of all sorts of illicit penetrations, of seductions, of perversions. It is a place of tensions that Carnival only brings to the surface. The parade collapses into a confrontation between a pederast and a vengeful "schoolgirl"—actually the costumed father of a pretty son:

"... he's going to his first year of elementary school, and over and above that I'm paying for violin lessons, my son takes violin lessons and you, you dared lay your hands on him. I raise him doing construction work, I spit blood, bastard, so my son can do the violin, and you, you fondled his curls and bewitched him. . . . All you foreigners go get buggered in London or in Australia, but our kids, you leave them alone, you hear me?"

Mark was shaking all over, no one could tell whether he was crying or laughing, and when the schoolgirl saw it, she wiped the rouge from her mouth, spit in Mark's face, and raised her knife. (49)

The assault is, however, aborted "from above":

Someone grabbed her from behind . . . and took the knife.

"Who is it?" she cried.

"I am the organ of order."

She turned and saw the uniform. The face of Manolis was smiling at her, but squeezing her hand hard.

"A pity that it rained. It ruined your Carnival." (49)

The ruined Carnival is, however, only the first of many ruinations, the aborted assault only the harbinger of later, more finished crimes:

The same evening, they found the corpse of Alex Kopesky. He had fallen near the sea from a great height. His back was nailed to a rock; the rock almost passed through his chest. The Authorities deduced that it was murder, ruling out that he could have fallen with such precision on that particular rock-tip. The old woman who discovered him said over and over that what made an impression on her was that the corpse was smiling, looking at the sky. (51)

The junta's colonels were famous champions of both law and order. They proved themselves willing to license both torture and execution in the name of their cause.[47] Karapanou's Manolis is not simply a figuration of their fleshly aspect; *The Sleepwalker* is not simply a "political novel." But it is no police deputy, responsible for the investigation of Kopesky's "fall." It is no literary accident, either, that the murderer is destined never to be revealed; that the murderer, though Manolis suspects it least of all, is Manolis himself.

Other murders follow, not all at Manolis's hands. The new Emmanuel is only a catalyst. He inspires, he sets into motion a process that, in its last stages, is literally inhuman, executed only by the forces of a vengeful nature. There is no reprieve, not even for the faithful. The devotees of the Virgin are crushed by stampeding mules when delivering Her icon to the sea:

> First the icon flipped over and disappeared. Then, everyone was lost under the black bellies that were passing over them. Cries were heard, the howls of children who were covered by the terrible trampling. The bodies exploded, were dismembered, human parts were flung into the air. (162–63)

The pandemonium, at once an allegorical reminiscence of the junta's last years and a hyperbolization of the biblical apocalypse, is utterly unrestrained. Its crossbred, sterile mounts have no riders. They are driven to the sea only by a relentless Greek sun, a sun that rises one day over the island and fails afterward to set. The sun provokes thirst. It burns. It is no longer the ground for an aesthetic, no longer what it has been for so many of Karapanou's literary precursors: an illumination of Greek life. It is, in *The Sleepwalker*'s closing scene, instead the terrible principle of a counteraesthetic,[48] of the grotesque and fruitless purity of death:

> The island had never been so beautiful. The sun revealed it [to apokalipte]. Silence became sound.
>
> It was a perfect [telia] day. . . . At the market, the fruit crates were laid out on the benches, the baskets piled in the back of the shops, the scales were hanging empty and ready. Further in, the police station and the hospital looked, with their doors wide open, like hotels. At Bill's the patio, with its canisters all in a row, with its umbrellas open, with its white lacquered tables, waited for customers. Up the seashore, the cinema advertised the evening show. In the photographs, a woman was exchanging kisses with three different men, taking care not to mess her hair.
>
> It was a perfect summer day, and in the sky the sun was shining motionless. (185–86)

Life, Time, and Art

Once purity is exposed as death, the ineluctable mongrelism of the synthetic historical personality seems singularly vital. But *The Sleepwalker* liberates the telos of constructivism from the junta's dungeons only hypothetically. Its voice is more concretely and more forcefully a voice of disen-

integral that they can simply "saturate" either literary works or the selves who compose them. In an age of assimilationism and reformation, "traditions" must, in part, also be chosen. They inevitably change in the process. Karapanou has as much claim to be "Greek" as anyone else. Her works are as "Greek" as any others. But "the Greek"—a rhetorical figure itself, after all—was something ever so slightly different before she came along.

It was Karapanou who first announced to me that Greece was a "chaos" and that in it not just anything but "everything" was possible. The claim is less true of Greece than of Karapanou, at least the Karapanou in the *Cassandra* and *The Sleepwalker*. As a theorist or allegorist of chaos, Karapanou's originary precursor is neither Gnostic nor classical but instead the pre-Socratic Anaxagoras, whose own allegories similarly have less plausibility as allegories of the world than as allegories of the self. Karapanou shares certain stylistic predilections with Garcia Marquez, whom she has read, and with the Russian "fantastic realist" Bulgakov, whom she indicated that she had not read. But the most important of her more proximate literary precursors is another Greek writer, Melpo Axioti, like Karapanou a woman, and in part because a woman admitted rather late, and even then somewhat uncertainly, into Greece's upper literary echelons. Karapanou told me that she had read Axioti's works but that she did not recall them clearly. A "defensive" remark, perhaps: Axioti's novel, *Dhiskoles Nikhtes*, or *Difficult Nights*, contains the "anterior trope" that the *Cassandra* injects with an even earlier past and projects into a newer literary present. The central character of *Difficult Nights* is a little girl. The central character of the *Cassandra* is also a little girl, called "Cassandra" herself. Axioti's little girl is the vessel of a stark vision of being and becoming. So, too, the little Cassandra: but Axioti's little girl is an apparent innocent; Karapanou's is morally indefinite. Axioti's little girl is the victim of what she sees. The little Cassandra, the first figuration of a perverse creativity or creative perversity that has its more adult fruition and more considered apologia in *The Sleepwalker*, is at once victim and victimizer. She uses her vision to resist, even to conquer her own oppressors—the past among them.

Is Karapanou's "revision" of Axioti self-conscious? Very unlikely. Is it in some sense willed? Bloom writes of revisionism first in *The Anxiety of Influence*.[36] The term refers there to the poet's perhaps unconscious rebellion against the canon that precedes her, a rebellion carried out in an imaginative "misreading" of that canon, a "misreading" that amounts to a "clearing of imaginative space." To study processes of revision is, Bloom insists in a later work, to study "poetic influences": not, he says, "the passing on of images and ideas from earlier to later poets" but "a critical act, a misreading or misprision, that one poet performs upon another, and that does not differ in kind from the necessary critical acts performed by every strong reader upon every text he encounters."[37]

chantment, and not merely of disenchantment with the junta alone. Karapanou is, as her occasional reflections on being and not being "Greek" also suggest, less simply disinterested than disenchanted with Hellenicity itself. She once tellingly mentioned that her third novel "had Greeks in it," but was not set only in Greece. She mentioned that she was even considering writing it in French.

The rhetoric of *The Sleepwalker* is hardly the product of the imagination of anyone who could be described as either religiously or ethnically devout. But it is not the product, either, of someone able to disengage herself entirely, either from her Hellenicity or from Hellenicity's precedent canonizations. Every heresy betrays anxiety over the influence of some orthodoxy; like the transcendentalist plot of Theotokas's *Daimon*, the sociopolitical critique of *The Sleepwalker* betrays a somewhat beleaguered, somewhat resigned self-critique. Among the novel's characters is a certain Louka, a writer whose first work was, like *Cassandra and the Wolf*, published in America. Louka's second work is stalled. She sits at her desk each day, the white paper before her "like a mirror." She drinks down the ink she cannot use. Her veins flow with its colors. Louka immediately recognizes that Manolis, that "purest" and most "purgative" of Greeks, is in fact the new Emmanuel. She finds him as irresistible as his God made him. She is seduced. Once seduced, she ceases to drink her inks; the white paper before her begins to fill with words. She in fact completes a book. But she completes it only to bury it, like a stillborn fetus, in her back garden.

Between Louka and Karapanou, there is certainly a difference. Louka's second novel is the result of being seduced by a monstrous purity; Karapanou's is the result of resisting it. Louka buries her novel; Karapanou has not buried hers. But if *The Sleepwalker* is thus the artifact of a certain overcoming, it still bears all the stigmata of what it has overcome. Its "terrible disclosure," the revelation that genuine creation at once requires pollution and is tantamount to it, is one that "every modern artist must face": so Karapanou responded when I asked her about the novel's lessons. But she is quite aware that, however "placeless" its lessons, *The Sleepwalker* is still unmistakably "Greek"—not least, in its reliance upon the religious legacy that it so thoroughly "desecrates." It is thus "authentic" virtually in spite of itself.[49]

So, too, Karapanou herself, who was accordingly somewhat surprised when I once suggested to her that *The Sleepwalker* was "about" the contemporary problematics of Hellenicity. She clearly had a more intimate conception of the work, a conception the validity of which I of course do not deny. To be sure, there are other interpretations, other valid interpretations of what is after all a rather obscure novel, whether those of the writer or those of less "ethnographic" readers than I am myself. Do the *Cassandra* and *The Sleepwalker* nevertheless corroborate Geertz's assertion that "to study an art form is to explore a sensibility, that such a sensibility is essentially a collective formation, and that the foundations of such a formation are as wide as social existence and as deep"?[50] What can be said of "art" and "culture" can be said of "art" and "collectivities" as well. It is surely a mistake to treat art generally—and especially such art forms as "modern" and "revisionary" literature—simply as expressions, or reflections, or even articulate refinements or refractions, of the "sensibility" of "collectivities." It is at the very least dangerous to presume that art forms—particularly "modern" art forms—attach to "collectivities" at all. Modern art is a self-assertive and so a historicized art. Whenever governed by the standard of originality, the producers of a modern art are always asked, as modern artists, to leave the "collectivity" somewhat behind. All artistic production is constrained by its social and cultural environment. It is, as Karapanou's works surely are, determined in part by that environment. But it is not in general utterly determined by it. Modern artists are asked not simply to reflect but to "think for themselves." They are asked to be "different," to be "novel." That they are expected to be "individuals," that they are expected to have individual visions or voices, is itself a "social fact." But it is a fact that accounts in some measure at least not simply for modern art's frequent social distance but also for its exclusion from the "core" of what is in fact left of collective modern life.

8

MEN ARE NOT ALWAYS WHAT THEY SEEM:

FROM SEXUAL MODERNIZATION TOWARD

SEXUAL MODERNITY

IN LATE JANUARY and early February 1987, the front pages of Athens's more progressive and sensational dailies intermittently bore photographs of a gaunt and emaciated young man, Khristos Roussos, also known as "The Angel." He lay in a bed at Piraeas's Tzanio Hospital, under constant police guard. He wore a beard: hirsute symbol since the junta of antiauthoritarian protest. He was being fed intravenously. He had been refusing to eat, had not been eating for some three and a half months. On 26 January, a journalist wondered in Athens's most popular daily, *Ta Nea* ("The news"), whether Roussos would at last be granted mercy. On that day, the president of Greece planned to decide on Roussos's appeal for mercy, an appeal to which some thirty-seven European parliamentarians, "from all countries and political groups,"[1] had lent their support. Roussos was a prisoner and had, before his hospitalization, been incarcerated in the notorious state penitentiary on Corfu. Thirty years old, Roussos had been a prisoner for more than a decade.

In the first few months of 1976, he was still free, and fulfilling a compulsory term of service in the Greek Navy. On 6 April 1976, however, he committed murder, stabbing to death his twenty-two-year-old lover, Anestis Papadhopoulos, in the studio apartment that the two maintained together in the Athens suburb of Kallithea. From another edition of *Ta Nea*:

> The cause of the murder: the pressure that the victim was exerting on "The Angel" in order [to make him] wear dresses and walk the streets. On the fourteenth of October of the same year, the Military Court sentenced Roussos to "life imprisonment without possibility of parole" [*isovia kathirxi khoris elafrindika*: literally, life imprisonment "without extenuating circumstances"]. The case was also judged by the Military Court of Review, but once again, no extenuating circumstances [*elafrindika*] were acknowledged. The first petition for mercy . . . was received by the Council of Pardons on 11 October 1982. [President] Karamanlis rejected the petition. Second appeal in March 1984. Mr. Karamanlis rejected it once again.[2]

Karamanlis, or so I have been told, would very likely have commuted Roussos's sentence in 1986. But he resigned from his post late in 1985. Roussos entered a third appeal to Karamanlis's successor, Khristos Sartzetakis, on 24 February 1986. Sartzetakis had impeccable jurisprudential credentials. A former Supreme Court justice, he was famous for his harsh prosecution of the junta's henchmen. A strict social conservative, however, he was equally harsh with Roussos. Several months after he rejected the third, Sartzetakis was presented with a fourth appeal. Like the others, it asked that the prisoner's sentence be reduced from life to twenty years. On 27 January 1987, Sartzetakis promulgated with the full support of the Council of Pardons what *Ta Nea* would call a *"tetarto 'okhi,'"* a "fourth 'no.'"

Roussos was not immediately informed. The papers reported that his mother and father had no idea what to say to him. His physicians at the Tzanio Hospital were uncertain whether he would survive being told. A variety of public figures offered their comments on the turn of events. From the European representative of the Greek Communist party, Kostas Filinis: "The denial of Khristos Roussos's petition indicts our humanity as Hellenic citizens and compromises our country internationally."[3] From the celebrated composer, Mikis Theodorakis: "I remain astonished and speechless. What's going on here, what country are we?"[4] From one of Greece's most respected novelists, a "surprised" Costas Taktsis: "This decision was taken by someone who has known what prison means."[5] As the day proceeded, other objections and other protests came to light. A hunger strike in sympathy with Roussos's own was staged at the foregate of the University of Athens. Later on, a crowd of demonstrators set out from the stadium for the Royal Palace. Roussos's father was among them but appeared only to call for restraint: "Let us be good people. . . . They do not want us here. . . . We ourselves should force them, then, to applaud us for our behavior, and not curse us. . . . Let us leave."[6] But the crowd did not disband. It lingered through the night, demanding the president's audience. Sartzetakis did not humor them. For the most part they remained peaceful. Roussos's mother, however, was struck with a baton when she tried to press through a police barrier. A young student suffered injuries during another minor clash.

Roussos himself could not be kept in ignorance for long. *Ta Nea* reported that from the morning of 28 January, "he had insistently been requesting papers from his father." It continued:

> When his father understood that he could not elude him [any longer], he said to him:
> "Khristos, you're a brave young man [*pallikari*], so accept this too [*dhexou ke afto*]. . . ." Crying, Khristos looked at him and said: "All right, Father, I understand."[7]

Afterward, he was virtually silent. His despair lingered until week's end.

On Friday, 31 January, however, the Tripartite Criminal Court of Piraeas offered a gesture of reconciliation. Katarina Iatropoulou, a well-known activist and attorney, had submitted a request that Roussos's punishment be suspended until his health improved. The court granted it, ruling that the prisoner should remain, though still under guard, at the Tzanio Hospital a further month. Roussos's spirits were uplifted. The media reported that, for the first time in seventy-five days, he took a bit of milk. He wanted to make a statement. He wanted other Greeks to know that his actions were "pure": "When in prison language we want to say about someone that he is right on [sostos], we say that he 'cuts clean as a sword' [ine spathenios]. So, then, this strike was a strike that 'cut clean as a sword.'"[8]

His supporters reacted to the court's reprieve with mixed sentiments. Glad that the hunger strike was done, they were nevertheless exasperated at the magistrates' lack of any real charity. One of them announced that, like Roussos, they too would go on struggling, and that, like Roussos's, their own struggle "had broader implications about the right to be different" and would be wrought "against racism and in order to close the Dachau of Corfu." On 3 February, members of a group calling itself the Epitropi Simparastasis, the Committee of Co-Support, Katarina Iatropoulou among them, gathered at the Tzanio to publicize their strategies. They voiced their intention to make Roussos's case known not only in Athens but also in Greece's other major cities: Thessaloniki, Patras, Ioannina, Iraklio. They told the press that they had been in contact with a Dutch representative of the Green party, who had assured them that an international cohort of elected officials would undertake to bring the case before a session of the European Community's Parliament in Brussels.

Disclosures

The events of January and February 1987 were in many respects without precedent. Greeks had, many times before, stood up en masse in defense of political prisoners. But never had so many been willing publicly to identify themselves with the defense of such a prisoner as Khristos Roussos. Roussos himself, however, was already accustomed to the public spotlight, and certainly well aware of that spotlight's power. Athens's newspapers had breathed virtually no word of his crime when he committed it. They had breathed virtually no word of his original sentencing. From 1981 onward, however, Roussos began to send letters to various ministries, complaining of abuses at the Halikarnassos and Corfu penitentiaries, between which he was periodically being shuffled. Even before that, he had come to the attention of one of Greece's most respected cinematic directors, Yiorghos Katakouzinos. Katakouzinos composed a film loosely, though pointedly, based on Roussos's life: *O Angelos*, or *The Angel*. The film's title gave to Roussos the epithet by which he has since been known. The film itself won first prize at the 1982 Thessaloniki Festival. The actor who portrayed Roussos, Mikhalis Maniatis, was also honored. Maniatis was a leading spokesman during the January demonstrations, and a leading member of the Committee of Co-Support.

Roussos, though of an underprivileged background, is a painter. In 1983, his works were given a private showing at a gallery in Thessaloniki. Soon after, he was interviewed on state radio. Pursuing a reduction of his sentence, he has also maintained his writerly efforts to expose the horrors of the Greek penitentiaries. In January 1987, a small Athenian publisher distributed Roussos's *Filakes Alikarnassou, Filakes Kerkiras, Vasanismi Kratoumenon* (Prisons of Halikarnassos, Prisons of Corfu, Tortures of those held). A brief, autobiographical report, it opens with these remarks:

> I do not have talent as a writer, do not know the rules of composition and the writerly measures that construct, that decorate a text, a story. I don't know such things, but I want to write and so I write, or rather record the events of my imprisoned life.

Roussos continues:

> These [events] do not need [*dhen khriazonde*] adornments and rules to become beautiful. They must be dry, they must be written without premeditation, but with the primitivism of the spontaneity that leaves their truth intact and unadorned, because it's a question of real events and they must be recorded as they happened, plainly, without literary tricks.[9]

He regards it "his duty" to "denounce the torture chambers [*vasanistiria*]" in which he has been held, because he is "not either in Turkish prisons, or in the prisons of Guatemala, or of the South Africa of apartheid, or of Chile." On the contrary:

> I live in a country with a democratic form of government that was the first in the world to enact and to vote in its Parliament on a special law against torture chambers. In this country there must not, there cannot be torture chambers!

Roussos ends his preface with his signature, and a brief self-description: "homosexual sentenced to life imprisonment for the murder of a friend, [a murder committed] under extenuating circumstances [*ek peristaseon*]."[10]

Gender Old and New

"Homosexual" translates the demotic *omofilofilos*, lover (*filos*) of the same (*omo*) sex (*filon*). The term is good Greek but unmistakably a neologism. It is unknown in the classical language. Nor was it originally a Greek invention. Its invention can rather be traced to a German sexologist, who resorted in

1869 to the Greek and the Latin to devise a more scientific and more neutral appellation for a "condition" that could only be spoken of disparagingly in his native tongue.[11] Thus, *Homophilität* and *Homosexualität*: in English, "homosexuality," and in demotic, *omofilofilia*. Until about a decade ago, *omofilofilia* had no demotic currency whatever. Until about a decade ago, it seems to have had no actual referent, either.

Foucault remarks in *The Use of Pleasure* that "one would have a difficult time finding among the Greeks . . . anything resembling the notion of 'sexuality' or 'flesh'":

> [It is] a notion that refers to a single entity and allows diverse phenomena to be grouped together, despite the apparently loose connections between them, as if they were of the same nature, derived from the same origin, or brought the same type of causal mechanisms into play: behaviors, but also sensations, images, desires, instincts, passions.[12]

He is of course writing of the Greeks of antiquity. But his observations have at least some measure of contemporary validity as well. To be sure, Greeks today can talk about "sexuality." But the theme remains no less novel and exotic, and its novelty and exoticism even more terminologically transparent, than *omofilofilia* itself. "Sexuality" in demotic is *sexoualikotita*, a blatant barbarism. Demotic offers another term, derived from the same sources: *sexoualismos*. Literally "sexualism," *sexoualismos* is in fact a partial synonym for the more archaic, feminine singular, *i afrodhisia*. Both *sexoualismos* and *i afrodhisia* designate "sexual instincts," "carnal attraction," or "genital arousal." *Ta afrodhisia*, the neuter plural, has come to have a rather special sense of its own. It is now preferred as a designation of "venereal disease."

That pleasure and sickness should thus be conjoined indicates itself something of a shift from a more ancient regard of the body. Indeed, there have been shifts. The church, disapproving for centuries of all sexual relationships outside marriage and at best ambivalent toward the seeking or taking of sexual pleasure even within it, has had its particular impact. Enlightenment moralisms have had their impact as well. The pederastic erotics in which Foucault, following Henri Marrou and Kenneth Dover,[13] finds the essence of ancient pedagogy is now an illicit erotics, frequently sidestepped by native classicists and explicitly prohibited by Greece's contemporary Penal Code. The erotics of sexual relations between men, and between women, of similar ages is of a rather more complex status. But the embarrassment now provoked by ancestral pedophilia has its aesthetic moment as well. The male physique, and especially the male nude, is now a considerably more marginal subject than it was in the age of Praxiteles. The female nude is still popular with both sculptors and painters, and apparently far less likely to be regarded as risqué or obscene.

There have been shifts: but there are in spite of them still tangible traces of an ancient comprehension in the contemporary address of sexual mores and sexual practices. Foucault quite plausibly suggests that "moral conceptions in Greece and Greco-Roman antiquity were much more oriented toward practices of the self and the question of *askēsis* [exercise, training] than toward codifications of conduct and the strict definition of what is permitted and what is forbidden."[14] The orientation endures, though of course not without exception and not without rival. Its rapport with the sovereign ethos, and particularly with the personalism of the sovereign ethos, should not be overlooked. Perhaps more than all others, sexual acts and sexual relations are, in Greece, traditionally personal acts and relations, exclusively private affairs. The Orthodox church has long been and remains remarkably circumspect in its dealings with them. State law remains circumspect in its dealings with them as well. Informal sanctions against sexual "deviations" are, among all but the most self-consciously cosmopolitan of social circles, still severe. Nor are they simply enforced from without. Guilt as well as shame have their effect not simply upon sexual conduct but also upon the determination of self-worth.

The archaic can survive merely by accident, or because "it is so fundamental that any transformation . . . has been neither possible nor necessary."[15] The archaic orientation toward the practices of the sexual self rather than the codes of sexual conduct survives in Greece today, however, more because it still has its strategic function. However "inauthentic" or "insecure" its deployment may be, it continues to serve as an ideational weapon: against latter-day legalisms, but against the psychopolitics of *sexoualikotita* as well. The archaic calculus of being grants no priority to the politics of sexual over the politics of masculine and feminine comportment. It enforces a uniform evaluative taxonomy: some acts, whether sexual or nonsexual, are honorable; others not dishonorable; others shameful or degrading. It enforces a uniform dualism: between the "active" and the "passive"; between the dominant and the submissive. Both the taxonomy and the dualism allow for their contextual variations. But both still generally govern the traditional assignation of sexually indexed roles and of sexually indexed prestige.[16] Both still generally govern the traditional assessment of what it is, and what it is not, to prove oneself an *andras*, a "man."

To Be or Not to Be a Man: Traditional Themes and Contemporary Variations

If the Athenian women are still expected to remain "women," some of them at least have greater liberty than ever to "be themselves." Athenian men do not as yet have quite the same measure of liberty. They are still expected to act like *andres*, "real men," who for all their urbanity have much in common with their rural prototypes. Women may or may not any longer manage the home, but *andres* should still provide for it. Barring monastic retreat, they should still marry, still become fathers: stern but intimate with their sons; doting with their daughters. The asymmetry that colors most contemporary sexual reform colors contemporary Greek reform as well: women are now more free to indulge in traditionally masculine pursuits; but men still run a considerable risk of censure for indulging in traditionally feminine ones. Herzfeld[17] writes that the archetypically virile Cretan mountaineer, or at least the mountaineer who is "'good at being a man,' must know how to wield a knife; dance the acrobatic steps of the leader (*brostaris*) of the line . . . ; respond in elegant, assonant verse to a singer's mockery; eat meat conspicuously whenever he gets the chance; keep his word but get some profit from it at the same time; and stand up to anyone who dares to insult him." Further:

> He must protect his family from sexual and verbal threats, and keep his household at a level that befits a "master of the house [*nikokiris*]." He must dispense hospitality at every possible opportunity, deprecating the poverty of his table while plying his guests with meat and wine. And in all these . . . domains, his every action must proclaim itself a further proof of his manhood. An action that fails to point up its own excellence is like the proverbial tree falling in an empty forest.

The knife, as Elias might have predicted, has become vulgar in middle- and upper-class Athens. Improvisational dance and improvisational versifying have largely died out. "Culture" has once again given way to diverse practices. But diversity here has its limits. The Athenian "good at being a man" should still be a capable orator and a formidable wit. If he has intellectual gifts, he should not keep them in reserve. If he has physical charms, he should not keep those in reserve. Blatantly revealing attire is "low-brow." But middle- and upper-class Athenian men are quite concerned with their outward appearance, and often quite meticulous about it. They are often more "fashion conscious" than their female peers, and masculine self-expression often intentionally more provocative than its feminine counterpart. The once standard moustache has lost its popularity. A well-placed acquaintance of mine, who had formerly sported one, told me that he had grown tired of being photographed by the Germans and the Japanese. Like women, however, bourgeois Athenian men had in 1986 and 1987 their standard uniform. In Kolonaki especially, they were wearing slick, black leather jackets, pleated slacks, and loafers. But the themes were no more important than the variations. Woolens competed with jeans. Hair was longer or shorter. Shoes differed in style and color.

Manners at the bourgeois Athenian table, though lapsing on more festive occasions, have become considerably more "civilized" than they are at the

Cretan. But at table as elsewhere, the urban *andras* should display his lar-
gesse. He should "treat," and be willing if necessary to do battle for the
privilege. He should be chivalrous, able to commandeer cabs and places in
line for himself and for his friends. Masculinity in Athens is still staged, and
the stage upon which it is enacted still one of agonistic spectacle. The Athenian *andras* is still an "egoist," though perhaps less "on behalf of a collectivity"[18] than simply "for the benefit" of others. The masculine is a principle of
eneryia, "energy"; it is a principle of domination. But the masculine will is
not, even in bourgeois Athens, so shorn of its collectivism as to be reduced
to nothing more than an atomistic will to power. It remains sovereign: a will
to impress, to acquire, to reign.

Eneryitikos, "energetic" or "active" as a social force, the *andras* should
also be *eneryitikos* as a sexual force. If it is true that "a man's sexual life," so
long as it does not interfere with his familial and professional duties, is very
much "his own business,"[19] it is also true that, even in the conduct of "his
own business," he should always *pidhai*, "jump," rather than *pidhiete*, "be
jumped." He should always *khtipai*, "strike" rather than *kathete*, "sit." If he
reigns over nothing else, he should at least reign over the inviolable territory
of his own body.

Women, still the enduring "subjects" of the Greek sexual regime, are
properly "penetrable." But men should always penetrate, should never allow
themselves to be penetrated. The traditional hermeneutics of masculinity
and femininity, in Greece as apparently throughout the Circum-Mediterranean, is unflinching in its respect for that dichotomy. Not even the object
is important. The "active homosexual," the man who sexually "takes" from
another man, is, as one recent analyst has asserted and as many of my acquaintances corroborated, still entirely and unambiguously "a man." "He
transgresses only the religious prohibition and does not place into doubt his
masculine role."[20] The religious prohibition, against *arrenokitia*, "a man
lying with another," is quite strict. But not even it generates the distinction
between what the modern "Occident" calls the "heterosexual" and the "homosexual."

The traditional categories of sexual being in Greece are performative categories, not categories of desire or cathexis. The traditional dimorphism of
sexual being is a contrary, not a contradictory dimorphism, and consequently allows for an "unmarked" and indeterminate middle ground. A
whole gestural catalog occupies that ground, in principle and, in some measure at least, in practice. Male friends in Greece, male friends in Athens, are
to the American eye at least remarkably physically demonstrative with one
another, and their associations remarkably "cozy." They kiss, though now
usually upon the cheek. They walk arm in arm. One may even walk with his
arm around another's shoulder or waist. Men in Athens do not hold one
another's hand. But I have seen men strolling, one with his hand in the back

pocket of the other. They drink together, shop for clothes together, "treat" one another at tavernas and cafés. I have no idea whether men today, as they did in Athens's ancient past and as they still allegedly do in the Arab world, demonstrate their friendships sexually. If they do, they are little inclined to speak of it. They might, or at least traditionally could without calling their manhood into question. Some sexual performances are, if perhaps "sinful," still politically neutral.[21]

Sexual liaisons between women, traditionally by all accounts quite difficult to classify as anything but politically neutral, have for their part been less "sinful" than virtually incomprehensible. The church, lacking any explicit biblical condemnation, formally overlooks them. The Greek Penal Code overlooks them as well. They remain "licit," as one juridical commentator has put it, "because of the difficulty of proving and the difficulty of defining the terms of criminal practice."[22] Delicate phrasing: but its implications are sufficiently clear. The manly woman, the "man-woman" or the "male woman," of aggressive temperament and perhaps talented at one or another unfeminine task or skill, has a place in traditional Greek society.[23] But not even she has the phallic endowments that would allow her to transform her social role into a sexual reality. Women are, by traditional definition, phallicly inactive, or at least phallicly "nonactive." Women may perhaps "play" with one another. But they are without the single, crucial implement that could lend to their sexual play genuine political import. Of no political consequence, sexual liaisons between women are traditionally not of any particular categorical consequence either. At least one contemporary Greek "lesbian" has found in the law's silent permissiveness "an unconscious denial" of her existence.[24] The law's silence at least indicates indifference. Sappho's fame notwithstanding, the "homosexual woman" receives little more traditional attention than the "'active' homosexual man." Her predilections may be suspect. But her acts remain politically "normal." She is not equipped—again, by traditional definition—to act in any other way.

Figurations of Anomaly

The manly woman is something of a curiosity, but not traditionally a Greek pariah. Herzfeld among others reports that she may even be accorded considerable admiration and respect.[25] The effeminate man is judged far more harshly. Why a double standard? In Greece as elsewhere, the sexual division of labor belies an asymmetrical distribution of prestige.[26] There is perhaps as much prestige, as much "social honor," in being a good mother as in being a good father, as much honor in being a good "mistress of the house" as in being a good master of it. But the traditionally female domestic sphere offers fewer, and lesser, prizes than the traditionally male public one. The woman who proves capable, whether as a versifier or in business, of garnering public prizes, the woman who is assertive and quick-witted enough to beat men at their own public games, steps beyond her traditional bounds. She reaches for more than a "mere woman" would be due. But so long at least as she does not abandon her womanly tasks in the process, she poses no significant threat to the principles of the traditional sexual economy. She does not challenge or question the value of the prizes she seeks and the games she plays. She instead confirms the value of both.

The man who comports himself like a woman, the man who seems to prefer the woman's world and the woman's roles, poses a quite urgent threat to the sexual economy. Born for the more honorable, he gravitates toward the less. Even worse: made to aspire to the more honorable, he instead rejects it for the less. The effeminate man in Greece, traditionally and still today, is among the most scorned of social subversives. He is not always, and of course should not be, confused with the "homosexual." The "active homosexual," so long as he is a competent husband and householder, so long as he is manly and keeps his dalliances private, may be a sinner. But Greek men are not expected to be overly pious, and the "actively homosexual" but otherwise "proper" man can accordingly hardly be deemed subversive at all. With the passing of arranged and the ascendance of romantic marriages, however, he is likely to be more troublesome now than he once was. The bachelor has always been somewhat troublesome, though less because of any alleged sexual perversion than because of his allegedly unrequited sexual appetite. The "homosexual couple," the male *dhesmos* or "tie," is still virtually unknown in Greece, or rather known primarily as a "foreignism." It nevertheless exists. Often "passing" for friendship, it may simply go unnoticed. Most cultivated, bourgeois Athenians resist disapproving of it, in principle at least. But even the most cosmopolitan Athenian, especially a man, is more likely than not to voice unease or even disgust at what the "tie" may imply: that one of the partners regularly submits himself sexually to the other. Behavioral effeminacy has its specifically sexual counterpart in the "passive" homosexual posture. The visibly effeminate man is perhaps a greater subversive than the man who "is jumped," if only because he is less able to hide. But the visibly effeminate man who is also a "passive homosexual," the man who advertises with his effeminacy or through transvestism his willingness to "be jumped," is the greatest subversive of all. Like most other subversives, he is widely believed to be not merely immoral, but mentally deficient as well.

What the Greek Penal Code calls *i metaxi arrenon para fisin aselyia*, "licentiousness against nature between males," is not technically a crime, at least so long as its perpetrators do not prostitute themselves and so long as both are "consenting adults." "Passive anal sodomy" is not technically criminal. But the passive anal sodomite is nevertheless reprehensible, now and indeed in antiquity as well. Though ancient Attic does not allow for reference to the "homosexual," it does have a term for the boy or man who behaves effeminately and who "gives" himself to other boys and men. The term survives as rather stilted demotic: *kinedhos*, most accurately a "catamite." Another demotic term is more common: *poustis*. Male friends, especially young friends, charge one another often enough with being a *poustis*, though remain friends only if they do not mean exactly what they say. They have other favorite curses, also sexually malignant. The most blithe, and by far the mildest, is *malakas*: literally, a "masturbator." The verb *malakizome*, "to masturbate," provides a rather more denigrating, and passive, participle: *malakismenos*, "having been masturbated." Still more denigrating, ethnographically better known but rather rare, is the *keratas*, the "cuckold." No term is more of an insult, however, than *poustis* itself.

Used in jest, all these sobriquets roughly have the force of the French *conard* or the English "jerk." All highlight failures of social or intellectual finesse. The *malakas* is clumsy, gawkish, perhaps vaguely infantile. He is liable to utter *malakies*: "stupidities," "nonsense." He is liable to be gullible. The *malakismenos* and the *keratas* are, if not immoral, still without existential fiber. They are without wit, and not uncommonly the dupes of others more witty or cunning. The *poustis* is irremediable. He is a hopeless clown, a buffoon. Others always get the better of him. Not simply that: he is also likely to let them.

The *malakas*, the *malakismenos*, the *keratas*, the *poustis*: as literal and as figurative characters, all are a rather shameful company. All fail of full manly prowess. All fall, literally and figuratively, well short of the performative sine qua non of fully manly prowess: the exercise of sexual sovereignty, the sexual overpowering of another. The *malakas* is least pitiable.[27] He is, if not utterly and supremely manly, nevertheless still a man. He remains a man not in spite but because of his politicoerotic solitude. If not dominating, he is at least not himself dominated. But what Brandes asserts of the cuckold in both Andalusia and in Greece[28] is true of the *malakismenos* and the *poustis* as well: all are unmistakably feminized. Each is the "patient" of another's maneuvering. Each is the victim, unwitting or willing, of a more "energetic" and more sovereign sexual executor. The *keratas* in Greece is the victim of a stereotypically but not exclusively feminine craft: *poniria*, "guile" or "deception."[29] The *malakismenos* is "manipulated." The *poustis* allows himself to be had. He surrenders without a fight. He unmans himself.

The *poustis* is altogether a disgrace: to himself, to his name. A man seriously accused of being one may well turn on his detractors with considerable violence. Nothing less than his social being is at stake. The actual *poustis* has, however, no authentic means of self-defense. But even traditionally, he may have some excuse, some partial pardon. Consider du Boulay's observations on the hermeneutics of gender operative in the village of Ambeli:

The people of Ambeli do not argue that gender characteristics are inherent in the biology of the sexes; they argue from the gender characteristics themselves, with both men and women being understood to possess a "nature" and a "destiny" as a direct inheritance from their society. What I [call] "destiny" is an ideal pattern that is prescribed *a priori*, while what I [call] "nature" consists of the observed deviations from this destiny that answer to the pattern of temptation in daily life. The villagers themselves, however, do not use the terms "nature" or "destiny" but embody these concepts in images—on the one hand, of Adam and Eve, and on the other hand, of Christ and the Mother of God.[30]

The Ambeliote comprehension of gender does not in all respects survive in Athens. The rhetoric of "nature" has among other things become far more explicit. But it continues to be deployed for its traditional and apologetic purposes. It continues, though with a rather more secular and "enlightened" imagery, to be of singularly effective service in the moral neutralization of sexual deviations of all kinds. The comprehension of gender in Athens remains strikingly idealistic as well. Among Athens's higher classes, such ideals as remain have lost much of their traditional loftiness. They have been brought closer to earth. They have, in part at least, been "normalized." But the hiatus that persists between contemporary standards and the facts of sexual and erotic life is still more Platonic than merely statistical. No one is sexually or erotically perfect; everyone deviates a little less or a little more. The hiatus—characteristically "formalist," perhaps, but also characteristic of any morality oriented less toward codes than toward practices—makes the assessment of sexual personhood always somewhat holistic, and always somewhat imprecise. But it is not, either in Ambeli or in Athens, the only source of indeterminacy. The erotic accountant must, as best he or she can, weigh the actual against the actually possible, the elected against the involuntary, the quality of the public posture above all against the quality of more private positions. The limits of the ordinary are inevitably vague. The interpretive passage from deviation to deviancy is inherently vague as well. It is, as the events of the preceding decade have shown, inherently liable to rerouting.

Revelations

The sovereign is a territorialist.[31] The *poustis*, the man who willingly relinquishes his sovereignty, relinquishes with it not only his masculine social being but also his claim to any social place of his own. He is a creature not of the day but of the anonymous "antistructure" of night. He occupies the night's deserted parks and squares. The National Garden still attracts him. But he habituates other Athenian gardens: in Kolonaki; in Exarkhia and Keramikos. "Homosexuals" linger in the early morning precincts of Omonia. Prostitutes, male and female, stroll the sidewalks surrounding it. Transvestite prostitutes are, however, not particularly welcome there. Archetypical deviants, they have been confined for many years to another sector: a labyrinth of back streets and alleyways not at the center but at the industrial outskirts of Athens, devoid after sunset of anything at all resembling "ordinary life."

Not all transvestites—now *transvesti* but earlier called *karnavalia*, after the celebrants of the religious holiday—are "homosexuals." Not all homosexual transvestites are prostitutes, and not all of those costume themselves consistently or find their costumes especially pleasing. Transvestism is a technology of display: Roussos, "forced" to adopt it, can hardly be considered a willing or "psychologically genuine" transvestite at all. The same might be said of many other "homosexuals," who cross-dress not for the erotic excitement or for the psychological satisfaction of it but rather in order to disguise themselves, to hide if not necessarily to save "face." One man accordingly confessed to an interested Athenian journalist that he regularly "became a Carnivalite" because he "could not bear the idea of being recognized" in the course of his sexual pursuits by some one of his more ordinary "acquaintances or friends."[32] Transvestism has a linguistic analogue: a secret argot of double entendre called *kalliardha*.[33] A perquisite of initiation into the sexual underworld, it is still virtually unknown and virtually incomprehensible to the world above and outside.

The segregation of sexual deviants has endured with more vigor in Athens than the segregation of ordinary women and men. In the past decade, however, particularly under the pressures of a humanist politics of civil desert and civil rights, it has shown some signs of giving way. The determinations of sexual deviance have shown some small signs of giving way as well: less, however, because the traditional hermeneutics of gender has come under wholesale attack than because certain of its substantive axioms have, in the hands of one or another capable rhetorician, proved to be far less determinative and far vaguer than had long been supposed. In April 1977, a group of "transvestites and homosexuals" congregated publicly at Athens's Louzitania Theater "to speak about their problems."[34] The journalist Fotis Sioubouras describes the event in a 1980 monograph as *enas sismos yia ta ellinika dhedhomena*, "an earthquake for Hellenic givens," for what Greeks had previously taken for granted. He notes first of all its terminological effects. Before the assembly, "the press but most other people as well made use only of the words *kinedhos*, *dhiestrammenos* [perverted], *anithikos* [amoral, immoral], and so on."[35] After the assembly, both the press and the public began instead to refer to the homosexual, the transvestite, to *ekdhidhomenes yinekes* (prostituted women), *engkhirismenes* (those having been operated upon, transsexuals). By 1987, the "homosexual" had become a rather common figure in the discourses of Greek public affairs, all the more so as the AIDS epidemic itself begin to infiltrate the daily news.[36] It had not, either as a figure of speech or as a figure of thought, been introduced into the discourses of public affairs only by the press. It did, however, gain something of its acceptability and much of its currency through the press and through the agents of Greece's other public media.

Journalists in Greece often incline toward sensationalism. But their role within the local regime of signification often demands sensationalism. Not simply purveyors of the "odd," of the unusual and the anomalous, they are more than any other contemporary professionals of signification responsible for broaching with the mass public and offering for the mass public's consideration issues previously inarticulate and unspoken. They are, in Greece as elsewhere, primary publicists not simply of the uncommon but also of the morally and semantically untoward. Journalists of "homosexuality" as of other "scandalous" issues have run and continue to run the risk of censure, and even of censorship. But they have, and have evidently taught Khristos Roussos among others, a ready riposte. Sioubouras, for example, the cover of whose monograph is emblazoned with a banner announcing *erevna sok*, "shocking research," and *apokaliptikes fotoghrafies*, "revelatory photographs," declares explicitly that his aim is only "to present daily reality in Greece and particularly in Athens."[37] The author of a 1987 exposé in the popular periodical *Ena* introduces her interests as the interests of merely one, ordinary, realistic Greek among others:[38]

> In the Middle Ages, they were burned alongside witches. The Nazis stuck a pink triangle on their lapels and sent them to concentration camps. Men and women confronted them always with guardedness and with overt animosity. And they chose the path of guilty silence or—contrarily—of provocative behavior. They are homosexuals! Greek society at last begins to view with honesty the problem, of which it used hypocritically to be dismissive [or to disbelieve: *amfisvitouse*]. It accepts the existence of the "third sex" realistically, and investigates the causes that formed it.

Realism, honesty and forthrightness, a commitment to the truth: whether or not they are "Greek" virtues, they are every Greek journalist's moral stock in trade.

Sexual Acts and Sexual Figures Reconsidered

Not all Greeks think of homosexuals as a "third sex." Not all Greeks have, even after a decade of journalistic and other exposés, any particularly cogent "theory" of the homosexual at all. But revisions of the traditional categories of gender are in the air, even so. On the other hand, sociologist Nikki Patsalidhou could still remark at a 1982 Cyprus conference on "homosexuality" that "old opinions . . . continue even today and with the same obstinacy to present the homosexual man as the person who wants to play the role of the woman and the homosexual woman as she who identifies with the role of the man."³⁹ Older opinions still persist, though not with the same intellectual confidence, even among the educated elite of Athens. One very well schooled woman, for example, conveyed to me that she was rather uncertain whether the "active homosexual" man was "really a 'homosexual' at all. "He is," she said, "still an *andras*." Patsalidhou, however, reported at the Cyprus conference on an attitudinal survey taken among a group of Cypriot men willing to identify or at least to define themselves as "homosexual." The survey is not nearly so out of date, and not nearly so unrepresentative of the attitudes of Athens's self-identifying "homosexuals" as one might at first presume.

Patsalidhou's respondents were semantically far more sure of themselves than the population at large:

> [With] the impression that the [male] homosexual is the passive member of a sexual relation and wants to play the role of the woman, ninety-nine percent of the sample responded categorically that they did not agree. . . . More than half, fifty-seven percent, responded that they express themselves both passively and actively, sixteen percent only actively, and fourteen percent only passively.⁴⁰

My homosexual acquaintances in Athens, not all of whom were from the sociocultural elite—stigma makes for odd bedfellows—were equally adamant. None of them agreed that the homosexual man was only sexually passive. None of them agreed that the "homosexual" was necessarily effeminate, either. One young man told me that he had at first been extremely reluctant to inform his parents of his preferences. "But," he said, "people had begun, in the past ten years or so, to see that you could be homosexual and still be 'manly' [*andrikos*] and 'serious' [*sovaros*]." He had finally found the courage to reveal himself. His parents were upset. But they had, he said, finally come to accept him "as he was."

He was, however, exceptional in his openness. Patsalidhou reported that some 70 percent of her respondents made every effort "to conceal their homosexuality from those around them [*apo to perivallon*]."⁴¹ A policeman told her that were his fellow officers to learn of his habits, "they would kill him right where he worked."⁴² Another man told her that "he suspected that his parents must understand, but that he could not himself accept their understanding, because he was sure that they would no longer view him as their child."⁴³ I confronted fears as poignant, and as bleak, during a conversation that I had with a young Athenian politician, rising in the ranks of the republican right. From my field notes:

> "I asked my parents once whether they thought it was worse to be a homosexual or a murderer." "A homosexual," they said. . . . He does not practice "safe sex."

"Why should I?" he said. "I can do that by myself." He lives with his parents. "They don't want to live by themselves. They give me anything I want. If I need twenty thousand drachmas, I ask. They give them to me. They gave me my car. Everyone has his price. I have my price." He also said that should his party come to power, the few bars patronized primarily by homosexuals would close. (Not true, another acquaintance insisted.) "And without Alexander's [the most famous of those bars], I wouldn't know what to do with my life." None of his political cohort, or of his soccer team, knows that he prefers men. "If they did, they would banish me." He lives an entirely duplicitous life. He will move away from home when he marries. He will, he says, marry. I asked him whether he were able to have sex with a woman. "Oh, surely," he said, showing how: with his hands covering his eyes. He will have children. "I will be a husband," he said "until two in the morning." He was not overly concerned about the emptiness of matrimony. He told me that relationships between men and women in Greece were usually empty.

Patsalidhou reported that some 60 percent of her respondents conceived of their homosexuality as an "inborn predisposition." "Along with it," she added, "they nevertheless cite as contributing causes [*paraghondes*] homo-sexual experience in childhood, twenty-one percent of them, and a domi-nating mother or father, twelve percent."[44] A great majority of my "homo-sexual" acquaintances in Athens insisted that their "homosexuality" was the result of an "inborn predisposition." I have no clear sense of how many believed or would insist that their preferences were neither "sinful" nor "perverted." Most, however, were quite adamant that homosexual "passiv-ity" deserved no more disapproval in and of itself than its "active" antithesis. Many of them pointed out to me that "family men" were, if homosexually inclined at all, as inclined to "give" as to "take." I should add that none of my "homosexual" acquaintances were recognizably or overtly "deviant." None, so far as I know, was even an occasional transvestite. Not all, but still an overwhelming majority of them insisted that what merited disapproval was not "homosexuality," "active" or "passive," but rather *thiloprepia*, the effeminate presentation of self. Athens's "masculine homosexuals" in fact often shun transvestites. In 1987, Athens had seven of what a weekly enter-tainment guide, *Athinorama*, had begun to list, in English, as "gay bars." The management of most of them regularly prohibited transvestites from entering.[45] "They have their own bars," one man told me. "Why should they come to ours?" Overtly effeminate men were not excluded, but were often disparaged. Again from my field notes:

> "Yiorgos" said that he often had sex with "those kinds" (tone of condescension) because "it didn't matter. With someone who's strong, someone whom you can respect, more is at stake." "Dionysos" stated to me that he "could not under-stand" why some people—people evidently repulsive to him—wanted "to be like women" and "pretend that they didn't have penises."

Tradition is malleable. In part because of its malleability, its elaborate checks and balances, it is evidently far from dead. The "homosexual" man finds himself, if not entirely within it, still often in accord with it. It stigmatizes him for his deviations. But it continues to offer him the excuse of factors beyond his control, natural or social. Developmental psychology, for all its lack of traditional precedent, serves him particularly well. The "homosexual" can and often does have recourse to the rhetoric of political humanism when struggling against the oppression he suffers. But he can and often does have recourse to a less "enlightened" rhetoric of sexual politics when struggling to define his own legitimacy. Perhaps he is compelled to protest too much against the traditional weighing of sexual "give" and "take." But the *andrikos* and *sovaros* homosexual man can still participate in the traditional denigration of the "feminine" and can still claim the dignity of the masculine public posture as his own. He can still traditionally claim to be an *andras*.

The "homosexual," the category itself, is nevertheless at odds with the traditional calculus of sexual being in at least one quite important respect. The "homosexual" is a being semantically determined solely by the sex of the objects he or she selects. The "homosexual" is a "lover of the same." The traditional calculus of sexual being is perhaps not entirely incognizant of the objects of intercourse. It grants priority not, however, to the objects of sexual or, for that matter, social intercourse, but rather to intercourse's mood. As a figure, as a trope, the "homosexual" was in 1986 and 1987 among the general Greek public still predominantly nothing more than a trope of limitation, an ironic negation of traditional sexual meanings. Among "homosexuals," however, it had already been resolved into a representational synecdoche, a whole to which the *poustis* as much as his "improbable" female counterpart, to which the masculine male lover of other men as much as the feminine female lover of other women, all elementally belonged. The amalgamation of what previously was at most a vaguely related miscellany of proclivities and personae has not been without its discursive "surprise." And it has proved not to be without its social consequences. But neither its discursive nor its practical repercussions could entirely have been predicted in advance.

Nor are its present discursive and practical fortunes guaranteed to carry through to the future. One might imagine, for example, that the homosexual man in contemporary Greece would just as likely be identified with the *poustis* as with his masculine "taker." Semantics themselves do not preclude that outcome. But homosexual men have in the preceding decade fought, and fought with considerable success, against it. What success they have had has in part been due to their conservatism. They have sought to effect and to enforce a separation between the visible mood of comportment and the insinuated mood of private sexual "self-expression." But they have for the most part been at pains to leave scrupulously intact the ideal of the comportmentally masculine man, the ideal of social masculinity itself. They have for the most part been at pains to leave the *poustis* himself to his own devices, to leave him as far as possible behind. The agents of the media, of the "progressive" media, have so far supported them. They have so far acted in what they evidently believe to be "good faith."

The Angel: Seduction and the Sovereign Will

The Angel was neither written nor directed by a "homosexual," and though Roussos himself has apparently given his approval to it, it has not been especially well received by other "homosexuals," either in Greece or abroad. It appropriates, or in any event makes use of, the tropology of the "homosexual" mainstream. But whatever Katakouzinos's intentions may in fact have been, it can hardly be read as "prohomosexual." It is, strictly speaking, exploitative of the "homosexual." The deviating underworld is simply its symbological substratum, a substratum oppressed but also evocative of weakness, of social pathology and existential folly. Its force is allegorical, even apological: whatever its author's intentions, it is above all a politicohistorical cautionary tale. Often at the expense of the "homosexual," the story it tells is the story of an oppressive seduction, but also of the character capable in the end of striking back against, of overcoming its bondage. Humanist by design, it is morally localist in effect. It does very little to advocate any abstract "right to be different." It is instead a very traditional, and traditionally Greek, tract: on the assertion of an honorable manhood, on the triumph of the sovereign will. But it is also altogether timely. It would be virtually without meaning, perhaps without sense, had the junta not risen, and fallen, before it.

The Angel opens in the National Garden, at night. The year is perhaps 1974 or 1975. Its images are startling, a *sok* as the Greeks say: men, one anally sodomizing another. The scene is interrupted by a police raid. Officers chase down the offenders, load them into vans, cart them off to jail. Khristos is strolling the garden that night, but he escapes the police. A sailor, a massive, burly man, instructs him where to hide. Later on, the two meet in a café. The sailor is solicitous, flattering; he gives Khristos money for a cab. He arranges a meeting: at an amusement park by the sea. Khristos heads home. He enters to find his parents, aged and ugly, having sex. He flees to his bedroom. His sister waits there: severely palsied, she needs his caress and his gentle kiss to fall asleep. He alone can feed her; she starves without him.

Khristos has a job. He is a jeweler. We meet him at work engraving a bracelet that he will later be given and wear on his own wrist. The lettering is apparent: *Angelos*, "Angel." We see Khristos at Monastiraki Square, arranging a meeting with the man who will bestow the gift. The man professes his love. Khristos accepts the bracelet. But the sailor has already won him. The two meet at the amusement park. Under the boardwalk of a pier nearby, they make love for the first time. The sun sets over them.

Not long after, Khristos decides to leave his family. The sailor and he find an apartment to share. His mother and father are perturbed but do not stop him. There is no doubt that he is the "passive" party in the relationship. He serves the sailor food. In bed, he places his head on the sailor's chest. He continues to visit his sister. But he is free of the territory of his childhood.

Still, not altogether free: Khristos receives a present from his newfound lover—a box of women's underwear. He is greatly disturbed. He refuses it. But the same evening, the sailor and he attend an underground party. "Men" are present. But several transvestites are present as well. Khristos witnesses his lover—among the paragons of a dominating Greek virility— grow excited at the flirtations of one of the "girls." He fears losing the man unless he, too, adopts the same role. He allows himself to be led off to a bedroom. He allows his face to be painted. The company around him insists that there is nothing at all wrong with what has been done.

The sailor is not just a fetishist. He is a pimp, and soon cajoles Khristos into joining the other prostitutes who work the back streets of Athens's industrial south end. We meet them in all their colorful and egregious finery. The soundtrack accompanies their antics with the oom-pah-pah of a carousel pipe organ. Khristos is at first horrified at what is demanded of him but gradually inures himself to his new vocation. Angelic of demeanor and angelic in his solicitude, he is popular with his customers. He is terrified of being exposed: all the more because, after a compulsory conscription, he is forced to spend his days training for the armed services. It is not long, however, before he is exposed. Engaged with one of his customers in a dark garage, he is attacked by a group of police thugs, beaten severely, and hauled off to a precinct station. The officer in charge sends him home to his parents. We find him at dinner with his mother and father and sister. His father, visibly drunk, begins to mutter under his breath: "*poustis . . . a poustis*; my son is a *poustis*." His rage increases. Ranting, rampaging through the apartment, before his family's eyes, he grabs a pair of scissors and stabs himself repeatedly in the chest and gut. A fictional episode: the actual father Roussos is still alive and well. Not the film's, though: he is rushed to a hospital but cannot be saved. Khristos is present when the attendant orderlies prepare the naked corpse for delivery to a funeral parlor. The mise-en-scène is a masterpiece of hyperbole, of the grotesque aspect of the poetic sublime.

Though he tries, Khristos still cannot break away from the sailor. He is soon out on the sidewalks again. One evening, he is approached by the driver of a large truck. He is reluctant to go with the man, but the sailor, on a motorcycle nearby, nods him ahead. The truck pulls off. The sailor follows it briefly, but loses interest and returns to his friends. Next morning, we find

Khristos lying, bruised and unconscious, at the edge of a garbage dump. He wakes, pulls himself up, walks in his tattered wig, his soiled dress and broken heels past a company of bemused laborers. Sometime later, he arrives back at his own apartment. The sailor is waiting. Khristos screams at him: "You made me do it! You made me do it!" He pummels him with his fists. But the man is much more powerful, and pressing his "angel" onto a bed, proceeds to rape him with cold efficiency. Later, we find the two lying together, both asleep. Khristos opens his eyes, moves his hand as if to caress the sailor's chest, but catches himself. Still in his smeared make-up, he instead brings himself to his feet, staggers into the kitchen, and retrieves a large knife. He raises it over the sailor, brings it down. The sailor gasps, tries to escape. But Khristos grabs him from behind, and cuts his throat. He leaves us with the knife still in his hand, dazed and blood-spattered, crumpled in a corner, his discarded dress pulled over his bare groin.

The Angel had a revival during Roussos's hunger strike, and played to tittering audiences at a downtown theater for several weeks. Only a few of my "homosexual" acquaintances in Athens had seen it when it was initially released, and most, exasperated by what they had heard of its analytical crudity and its melodramatic excesses, were determined to boycott it. I can sympathize with their indignation. Were the film nothing more than a treatment of "homosexuality," it would merely be distorted. No doubt its titillations have won it some of its public appeal, and its neorealist grittiness some of its critical acclaim. But I suspect that it has its attraction not for its "forthrightness" or for its "honesty" but rather for its catharsis. Greek audiences have for the most part apparently failed to recognize its symbolism as a symbolism. Its subliminal message is nevertheless far from obscure. The Angel's brutish pimp—what a useful coincidence that the actual model upon whom he is based was named Papadhopoulos—can only be a figuration of the junta; Khristos himself, spiritually sublime but physically frail, seduced and sullied, at once a latter-day hero and a Greek Everyman. His final act has all the trappings of classical tragedy: a recovery of will, a moral vindication, a sacrificial setting of the world aright again.

The Junta and the "Homosexual": On the Emergence of AKOE

The junta has in its aftermath fostered the burgeoning of a variety of creations that it most certainly would itself have opposed and that would likely have been opposed even in the era that preceded it. Political "liberalism" has of late enjoyed a resurgence, but authoritarianism has, if not disappeared entirely, at least been pressed into retirement. *The Angel* could not, practically speaking, have come before the junta's rise and fall. The Apeleftherotiko Kinima Omofilofilon Elladhas (the Greek Homosexual Liberation Movement), known acronymically as AKOE, could not, practically speaking, have emerged any earlier than it did, either.

The junta's Ipouryio Dhimosias Taxeos (Ministry of Public Order) in its later years under the supervision of the now infamous Yannis Ladhas, had among other things the task of protecting and preserving Greek "propriety." It regularly authorized punitive and purgative "operations" in order to achieve that end. "Purism" once again: and the impure, those guilty of "licentiousness against nature," were among its most consistent targets. Many of them, fearing persecution or having suffered from it, fled Greece for one or another country in western Europe, and in particular for Italy and France. Those who stayed behind, by choice or by necessity, did so at great risk. The police raids and paramilitary muggings depicted in *The Angel* were quite common. Transvestite "homosexual" prostitutes, at once the most visible and most disparaged of "deviants," were also among the most frequently victimized.

The junta was distinctively racist and distinctively fascist in its conflation of social with moral and moral with political rectitude. It must, precisely for its conflations, be held historically responsible in part for the transformation of "sexual deviance" from a once largely sociocultural to an explicitly sociopolitical matter. Feminists in Greece had succeeded in politicizing gender long before: in the last decade of the nineteenth century. But only in the junta's aftermath would a new group of activists succeed in politicizing sexual acts and sexual relations themselves. The colonels' willingness to intervene, paternalistically or hygienically, in spheres long considered "one's own business" has been answered since 1974 with a privatistic backlash that still shows no signs of waning. Their policies of exclusion were answered in the 1975 Constitution with the guarantee of every citizen's specific right to "develop his or her personality [*prosopikotita*] and to participate in the social, economic and political life of the country."[46] The guarantee has given the "homosexual personality" one of its most potent political and juridical weapons. Inviting the integration of sexual politics with a humanist politics of being, it has allowed Khristos Roussos among others to cast his case and his interests as something other than merely "special." Humanist laissez-faire has become the cause of all who were the junta's enemies. No accident that the chief of the Communist party was so prominent a spokesman during the events of January 1987. Not that leftists have been Roussos's only defenders. Moderate rightists have, in the name of social tolerance, also come to his support. Only the most sociopolitically extreme, leftist and rightist, have been inclined to approve, or at least not to disapprove, of his having been persecuted so severely simply for being the "passive homosexual" that he was.

For all that ceased with the colonels, the raiding of the National Garden

did not cease, at least not immediately. The raids could not be constitutionally warranted. But they were justified by appeal to two minor legal statutes,
both of which the colonels themselves had enthusiastically enforced. The
first, which still exists, prohibits public obscenity. The second gave half-
paternalistic, half-hygienic license to interventive policies *ex afrodhision
noson prostasias*, "of protection from venereal diseases." The statute was
venerable. It dated from 1933, one of the last years of Venizelos's "liberal"
heyday.

AKOE arose formally in 1977, some few months after the assembly at the
Louzitania Theater. Its literal pretext came a year before that:

> A documentary monograph [*vivlio-dokoumendo*] that had homosexuality as its
> theme and referred to the dark period of the Colonels' dictatorship. . . . It con-
> cerned the recounting of one of the notorious instances of "Operation Virtue"
> with which the existence of the Greek Ministry of Public Order, at that time in
> the "clean hands" of Yannis Ladhas, had been tied.[47]

The author of the pamphlet, Loukas Theodhorakopoulos, had already established himself among the more socially conscious of a literary new wave.
Both his education and his experiences were solidly international. He was
not AKOE's founder. But the movement's actual founders conformed as
precisely as he to the pattern of the Greek "modernizer," in the precise
sense that Schneider, Schneider, and Hansen would lead us to give to the
term.[48] They were "students who had studied abroad, . . . who were familiar
with the action of foreign homosexual movements,"[49] and who brought
what strategies and technologies they had acquired back home with them
after the junta's demise. Their first step was the promulgating of a "Declaration," which "was passed from hand to hand . . . in the center of Athens,
provoking the curiosity and the interest of the press."[50] Theodhorakopoulos
joined forces with AKOE shortly after the Declaration appeared. For several
years, he served as the movement's principal spokesman, its principal rhetorician, and the editor of its official journal, *Amfi*.

From its outset and still today, AKOE resists ready political-theoretic
classification. In some respects, it has much in common with what Claus
Offe calls "new sociocultural movements."[51] Its space of action is, for example, predominantly the space of "noninstitutional politics." Though a coalition of individuals from different classes and of different statuses,[52] it is not
a definitive party. Like other "new sociocultural movements," it has had and
continues to have resort only to "legitimate political means": the exercise of
the right to assembly, the exercise of freedom of speech, and so on. Like
other "new sociocultural movements," it has not for the most part sought to
make its "ends and values" binding on the civil community at large.[53]

On the other hand, and rather more like what Offe calls "new sociopolitical movements," it has periodically sought to enforce certain interpreta-

tions—of the human and the inhumane, of the sexually acceptable, or the sexually "natural," or the sexually "healthy"—that would, especially if legally institutionalized, inevitably have their effect on the civil estimation of the legitimacy of both the manners and the substance of its pursuits. AKOE's interpretative politics has sometimes assumed the form of a "politics of identity." But not always: especially in recent years, its politics has left behind the inevitable generality of a politics of identity for a more particularistic and more strictly nominalist politics of *prosopikotita* and *idhieterotita*, "idiosyncrasy." It has taken its political turns with the contingencies of the moment. But like other Greek movements, it has owed its prevailing directions above all to the agenda and the sensibilities of its chiefs of significative staff.

AKOE's earliest preoccupations centered understandably enough upon the "hygienics" of the postjunta police force. It gave priority to the overturning of the statute on "venereal diseases." I am uncertain whether the colonels or their republican successors presumed homosexual conduct to be indicative, or simply to be likely to further the spread of such diseases. But whatever its medical rationale, the statute itself had become unpalatably intrusive. It had become "backward." AKOE's members undertook to "mobilize Greek public opinion"[54] against it. They collected "thousands of signatures." They sought and frequently obtained the advocacy of Athens's community of foreign diplomats. They took their cause even further abroad. In their behalf, homosexual activists organized marches on Greece's embassies and consulates throughout Europe and America. Not simply Sartre and de Beauvoir but also Foucault, Jules Dassin, Costa Gavra, and Julia Kristeva added their names to the protests.[55] The campaign was ultimately victorious. In January 1979, Spiros Dhoxiadhis, then Greek minister of public services, publicly conveyed that neither he nor the administration under which he worked "had any intention of policing the sexual lives of any individual whatever."[56] In March 1980, the Greek Parliament replaced the 1933 statute with a noticeably more "progressive" alternative.

Even at its outset, however, AKOE did not restrict itself to the pursuit of legal reforms alone. According to Theodhorakopoulos:

> One of the most basic of the ambitions of AKOE and of *Amfi* is the informing of the social body on the theme of homosexuality and of sexuality generally— themes that remained taboo in our country [even] a few years ago, in contrast with the countries of Europe, with America and virtually the entire world.[57]

He continues:

> On the theme of homosexuality specifically, which is but one of the manifestations of [a] multifaceted human sexuality, it is time moreover that we become conscious and accept that things are not as the conventional, patriarchal, and

reproductive ethic tells us they are: homosexuality is not a perversion and anomaly, but a natural possibility for all people, independently of whether it is realized or not.

He reiterated much the same position when, as AKOE's representative, he spoke at the Cyprus conference:

> Beyond whatever reasons may make homosexuality necessary in nature, . . . the fact remains: heterosexual and homosexual practice constitute two of the basic facets of ungoverned [*anarkhis*] sexuality. The human being [*o anthropos*], as a living being, carries within him, by nature, both of these facets of sexuality.[58]

Throughout his tenure at AKOE, Theodhorakopoulos was always an ardent social critic, an ardent humanist, and an ardent "naturalist." Against a tradition that had proved itself all too liable to confuse the *anomalos* with the *paranomos*, the "anomalous" with the "illegal," his position no doubt provided a salutary, liberalizing counterpoint.

Perhaps it still provides that counterpoint. But it has its perils as well. The naturalization of homosexual pleasures and homosexual acts can itself be merely "negative," less a move toward than a move away from representation, less a claim of meaning than a claim of mere "nonmeaning," of simple insignificance. It is perhaps nothing more than "negative," so long as it remains strictly nominalist. But Theodhorakopoulos is not strictly or consistently a nominalist. He is not strictly a theorist only of particular sexual pleasures and particular sexual acts, but also of "sexuality in general." As a concept, "sexuality" partakes rhetorically of the objectivity inherent in any other "purely empirical induction." There is nothing necessarily innocent, however, in the tactical field that it circumscribes, a field in which individuals are "led to focus their attention on themselves, to decipher, recognize, and acknowledge themselves as subjects of desire, bringing into play between themselves and themselves a certain relationship that allows them to discover, in desire, the truth of their being."[59] Occidentals should be aware by now of the "monsters" that such a dynamics can yield. They at least should be aware by now that its newer compartments are not necessarily more liberating than the older ones it replaced.[60]

AKOE Today: Notes on a Present Leader

If not Theodhorakopoulos himself, AKOE has gradually retreated from a rhetoric of sexualities. The retreat is reflected in a revision of the subtitle of *Amfi*. Originally, the journal was dedicated to the *apeleftherosi ton omofilofilon*, "the liberation of homosexuals." Beginning with its second volume, however, it was rededicated. No longer for the liberation of "homosexuals," it would instead struggle *yia tin apeleftherosi tis omofilofilis epithimias*, "for the liberation of homosexual desire." Still concerned with the "subject of desire," it would nevertheless seek to speak to a broader constituency, to "homosexuals" but also to "all those who have homosexual desires in parallel with their heterosexual identity." It would oppose any "hierarchy, [which] restricts like the police [*astinomeftika*] the possibility of freedom of choice in the realm of pleasure, and is the essence of the misery that we must overcome."[61] It would argue for an egalitarianism of desire.

Amfi translates as "bi-" or "dual," but the journal's present editor, Ghrighoris Vallianatos, emphasized that the allusion was not to *amfisexoualikotita*, "bisexuality," but indeed to *amfisvitisi*. The journal is one of "questioning," of methodical "doubt." *Amfi* first appeared under Vallianatos's editorship in May 1987. The issue retains the subtitle of its immediate predecessors. It remains dedicated "to the liberation of homosexual desire." Vallianatos, to whom I introduced myself at an AIDS benefit held at Alexander's, prefers the later subtitle to the earlier one. But he would like to distance the journal from any concern with the "homosexual" at all. He regards the notion of "homosexuality" only as "provisional," of worth only to "raise consciousness," to "make people sensitive" to something that they had previously tried to ignore. He uses it himself, he says, only to "denounce" it. He thinks another notion, another term, far more ideal: the English "gay."

Vallianatos is, by self-designation in part, a marginal. But like Karapanou, like so many other members of the reformist and revisionary sectors of the Greek elite of signification, he is of exceptional privilege as well. His surname suggests Cephalonian ancestry, but he was raised in Psikhiko, not the most monied but among the most cultivated of Athens's grand *faubourgs*. His father was prominent in both business and government. He remains close to his family. He remains attached to Greece: at least to "his" Greece. His love of country is a love of heritage, a delight in the wealth of the cultural past and a delight in the promise of the cultural future. It is a love of Greece's cultural resources, but a love in which there is more than a hint of resistance, as much against philhellenism as against its Romaic antithesis. Vallianatos thinks the Acropolis "a fine thing." He admires the achievements of the classical era. But when he points to what is really "Greek" about Greece, to what is still living, still worth preserving and using, he points neither to classicism nor to the "traditional" village. Shortly before I returned to America, he conveyed an irritation with his fellow natives. "They do not allow foreigners to see this place, this culture, for what it really has to offer," he said. "Ten years ago, that was perhaps understandable. Today it is not." I acknowledged that I had frequently encountered the problem myself. He obligingly directed me to three books. Two concerned the church. One of those was an essay on the theology of the New Orthodoxy: a contemporary and self-consciously Greek gnosticism that has reinterpreted the ascetic quest for *theosis* as a quest not for communion with the perfection of God but for a reflexive communion, each human being with the immanent perfection of his, or her, worldly self.

This historical constructivist has returned to Greece: in the most literal of senses among others. Vallianatos took his university schooling abroad: in Paris, in London, and rather more briefly in the United States. He is polylingual, and his English accent so polished that one could easily mistake him for a born Cantabrigian. He suggested to me once, I cannot say how sincerely, that he might never have repatriated. But some four or five years ago, he was offered a post in the Papandreou administration's Ministry of Youth. He was a competitive gymnast. He was invited to supervise the arranging of nationally sponsored sporting events and oversee the management of summer athletic camps that would bring Greek children together with children from other states of the European Community. He accepted. Soon after he settled into his job, he became involved with AKOE. Soon after that, he began to serve, virtually alone, as AKOE's "representative" before the press. "You didn't have to be very smart," he said, "to notice that the Vallianatos in the ministry was the same as the Vallianatos who was speaking for AKOE." Someone noticed. A minor scandal ensued. But in the progressive atmosphere of postjunta politics, it dissolved quite rapidly.

In 1987, Vallianatos took the formal oath of civil service; "the dream," as he sardonically put it, "of every young Greek man." The oath brought with it considerable professional security, and some measure at least of insulation from the slings and arrows of partisan head-hunting. Vallianatos was for his part no more easily politically classifiable than the movement he had recently come to guide. He was neither "leftist" nor "rightist." It would even be inaccurate to label him "libertarian," a party that has not yet made its way to Greece. For all his ambiguities, though, he was still straightforwardly a "political type." He had the sovereign tactician's interest in the acquisition of power, and the sovereign tactician's disinclination to share what power he has acquired. Like all revisionists, like all of them at least who gain an audience, he was charismatic. Like others of the privileged strata, he had little actually to lose and like many of the rest of them, he enjoyed the gambles of political investments. An aunt once asked him, he said, why he would, after achieving what he had already achieved, persist in jeopardizing himself; why he should not simply rest on the laurels he already had. I asked him the same question myself. "Because," he said, "it would be boring."

Vallianatos was not the only "homosexual" publicist in Greece, and *Amfi* not the only "homosexual" publication. A transvestite activist, whose autobiography Sioubouras prints in his own monograph and who calls himself "Paola," irregularly distributed a newspaper of his own: *Kraximo*, "Bird's Call," literally, but perhaps also "Screech" or "Scream." Its subtitle: *Periodhiko epanastatikis omofilofilis ekfrasis*, "A periodical of revolutionary homosexual expression." Its supertitle: *kathe erghasia me skopo to kerdhos einai pornia*, "every occupation with profit as its aim is prostitution." The newspaper was, like *Amfi*, part social critique and part erotica, but Paola could not, and perhaps did not want, to command the respect accorded to Vallianatos himself. He belonged, by background and by vocation, to the urban proletariat. He had no movement of his own. Vallianatos was left to speak to the mainstream. He was, in fact, AKOE's only contemporary spokesperson. He understood that the organization's other members might justifiably fear the public eye. But he still complained about a lack of commitment. There were plenty of people, he said, who were glad for what AKOE does; but very few who were willing to join it.

Vallianatos was among those most abidingly involved with the case of Khristos Roussos. He was in 1986 and 1987 a member of the Committee of Co-Support. He was also instrumental in bringing Roussos's plight before the European Parliament's first session on the treatment of "homosexual men" and "lesbian women." Roussos contributed a long letter to the May 1987 issue of *Amfi*. With it, Vallianatos published a translation of the European Parliament's *communiqué*. The *communiqué* made mention of oppression in Ireland, and even in Turkey. But it reserved its most specific condemnations, as Vallianatos had hoped, for the president of Greece.

With the Greek press at least, Vallianatos had chosen to make of Roussos's case the humanist affair that Roussos himself had chosen to make of it. Questioned at the Tzanio Hospital with others of the Committee of Co-Support, the "representative of AKOE" stated:

> From the moment that the Roussos affair went beyond the Homosexual Movement—as it had to, in any case—and thousands of people named and anonymous aligned themselves [*takhtikan*] with the struggle for the reduction of his sentence, and the whole issue took on a humanistic character, we ourselves took a step back and are [now] proceeding with all of these people together, aiding and upholding [a] just struggle.[62]

The rhetoric of equity, of human rights, of justice is among the characteristic tools of Offe's "new movements," sociocultural and sociopolitical. Vallianatos made use of it again during a later interview, broadcast without precedent on Greece's state radio to mark the eighteenth anniversary of the Stonewall riots: "gay pride day."

But he was not always so legalistic. In the May 1987 *Amfi* he offered a reverie of sorts on the *omofilofilos dhesmos*, the "homosexual couple." His thoughts were self-consciously "nonoccidental," or in any event not too far western:

> A study by McWhirter and Mattisson on the "couple" is characterized by the transatlantic psychology of the *American realm*. The stages of common life are presented descriptively, almost sociologically. The comprehension of the phe-

nomena in their sum remains behavioral, objective, let us say realistic. Structured by [an] analytical practice, our own "clinical" approach is entirely different. The real questions are, we believe: *What is a pair [zevgari]? What compels
two people to create a particular, lasting relationship? What of the idiosyncratic
does the homosexual pair have? . . . What relationship is there between desire,
physical love [erota], and affection [aghapis]?*

He cited Plato, among others, in articulating his replies.

When I asked Vallianatos what meaning he gave to "being gay," however,
he did not appeal to classical exemplars. He stated on the contrary that the
classical morality of practices had lost its heuristic relevance: for him at
least; but also for other "Greeks." "We are not," he said to me, "those people." He evoked, by way of heuristic example, the scenes depicted in the
frescoes recovered from the ruins of Santorini. The frescoes are prearchaic,
perhaps some thirty-five hundred years old. The civilizations from which
they derive, Cycladic and Minoan, date from well before even the first glim-
merings of the Homeric and classical civilizations that would eventually take
root on the Greek mainland. Martin Bernal has recently claimed that the
Cycladics and Minoans both take their character from a more purely African
and oriental genealogy than either their Homeric or classical successors.[63]
Whether or not he is correct, both have long been recognized as Greece's
true indigenes. Referring to the frescoes, referring to those who designed
them, Vallianatos spoke of a quality of "gayness" that "Greeks," as "Mediter-
raneans," could understand.

Like the high Orthodox, the Cycladic and the Minoan are "third" Greek
terms. They allude to a pre-Christian paganism, but not to the paganism of
the ancient Hellenes. They allude to civilizations humbler, perhaps, than
the Hellenic or Hellenistic, but neither so humble, nor nearly so "adulterated," as the Romaic. It is of course a very long way from the Santorini
frescoes to what it means to be "gay." But the terrain between them has its
interest. It is for one thing little traveled, and its paths certainly far less worn
than the paths of philhellenism. It allows for more maneuvering, if only
because it is so much obscurer. Particularly for a Greek, the terrain is surely
more felicitous as well. It offers as plausible a ground of authenticity as its
Hellenic and Romaic counterparts. But it is not nearly so imposing as the
Hellenic, not least because it is not nearly so much a preoccupation of occidental genealogists themselves. It is less burdened than the Romaic with the
brand, either of "impurity" or of "devolution."

Fine and well: but the way from the Santorini frescoes to "gayness" is
considerably longer than one might suppose. When Vallianatos alluded to
the frescoes, I presumed that he was alluding to some I didn't know. Those
I did know are housed in Athens's National Archaeological Museum, and
frequently reproduced in photographic guidebooks. They are all brightly

colored and, though their technical quality varies, all are evidently products of some specialized artistic cadre. One depicts a troupe of monkeys cavorting over rocks. Another, the "Spring Fresco with Lilies," depicts swallows courting over a meadow of red flowers. Another depicts a field of papyrus plants; another a pair of oryx. The "Ship Fresco" apparently portrays some sort of marine pageant; the "Boxing Boys," an initiation ceremony; "The Ladies," a procession of island beauties delivering gifts to some shrine. "The Fishermen" is also religious in theme. Its figures are nude, and "Minoan males are never shown in the nude unless in the act of adoration; the god had to see you in all your purity."[64] They are offering their catches to a deity.

A few other frescoes were recovered from Santorini, but none of them explicitly homoerotic, none of them "gay" except in the most literal sense of that term. Vallianatos gave me no exegesis. He wanted me to "look at the frescoes again." Not a literalist, he was rather more of a "metaphysical poet," as his essay on the "homosexual tie" made clear. In that essay, he wrote that the genuine lover must be able "to give without seeking" anything in return. Is the link between the fishermen and "gayness" forged there?

Perhaps. Still, resort to the frescoes has the look and the feel of artifice. But all projects, whether of the formation of the individual or of the formation of the collective self, do not simply involve artifice. They would be nothing without it. The enterprise that Vallianatos set for himself, beyond "doubt" the metaleptic, the Greek modern enterprise at once of bridging and of maintaining the distance between a civilization now dead and a praxis as yet barely alive, requires more than a little artifice, and more than a little sheer rhetorical inventiveness as well. It is not yet done. The materials that Vallianatos was striving to incorporate, the materials that he incorporated, the materials of history, but also of the here, the elsewhere, and the now; his procedures; his style: we have nevertheless encountered all of these already. They are all the structural bits and pieces of the Greek modern, a modernity that shares, with other historicizing and revisionary modernities at least, the same ultimate ends: to bring the extraneous within; to make the old less an image than a feeble imitation of the new.

EPILOGUE

AFTER THE PRESENT

*A*MFI—not for *amfisexoualikotita* but rather for *amfisvitisi*: objecting, questioning, doubt. I suspect that the clarification, the reading that Vallianatos offered of his journal's title was largely his own. But like Maro's troubled dismantling of self, like Karapanou's *Cassandra* and her *Sleepwalker*, its resonance was not merely personal. Like the younger Papandreou's praise for the "critical perspective" brought to Greece by its various outsiders, its force was imperatival. Vallianatos and the younger Papandreou in fact turned out to be friends. "He is someone," said Vallianatos of the latter, "to whom I can talk." They have not their "sexuality" but many other things in common. Both have been educated and have lived at length abroad. Papandreou is perhaps more the progressivist. Vallianatos, more decisively a Greek modern, perhaps has the "purer" origins. Papandreou's mother, called Margarita in Greece, is not of Greek heritage. She is American, born Margaret Chant, a native of Illinois. But no matter: like Maro and like Karapanou, both Vallianatos and Yiorghos Papandreou have been formed as much by the extra-Hellenic as by the Hellenic itself. For both, the antithetical dichotomies that have become intrinsic to them serve as tropological provocations not simply of *amfisvitisi* but also of its constructive, or constructivist, resolution, from one case to the next. So it seems that we have come full circle.

A circle, however, suggests closure. Drawing it, I can bring a monograph that might, after all, go on indefinitely to a summary, if somewhat contrived, end. But here the monograph and its subject must diverge. The Greek modern is by no means closed. Sensitive to temporal change, stimulated by that change, duty-bound to be engaged with that change, it would seem liable to come to an end only with the cessation of history itself. History has, however, certainly not ceased in Athens, to which I returned during the summer of 1992. I stayed for the most part in the Exarkhia district, a less touristed and less westernized district than Kolonaki. I noted there several *kafenia* still catering to an exclusively male, but mostly elderly, clientele. Not too far away, however, "postmodernist" malls and office complexes had cropped up on a major thoroughfare (Plate 27). Computer stores were in vogue. In a controversial break with its former policies, the National Gallery was putting on a vast exhibition of twentieth-century art and sculpture called "Metamorphoses of the Modern: The Greek Experience" (Plate 28). The gasworks was being transformed into a cultural center.

Nationalist fervor had been brought to a peak with the declaration of an

PLATE 27. Postmodernism, left; neo-neoclassicism, center; modernism in the background.

PLATE 28. Exhibiting modernity at the National Gallery in the summer of 1992.

independent Slavic "Macedonia." Billboards and placards dispersed ubiqui-
tously in the capital, even T-shirts for sale to tourists in the Plaka pro-
claimed that "Macedonia was Greek!" But internationalism was also more
evident than before. Athens was noticeably more "plural." Immigrants from
the Philippines, most employed as domestics, were rumored to number
nearly two hundred thousand. The breakup of the Eastern bloc had sent
many other migrants and refugees to Greece as well. The November Seventeenth organization made an attempt to assassinate the minister of the
economy. It accidentally killed a bystander in his stead. But the general
diminution of terrorism worldwide was bringing an unprecedented number
of tourists into the country as well. One Athenian newspaper reported that
some ten million were expected to visit by year's end. On 1 August, the
Greek Parliament approved the Maastricht Treaty, and so gave its go-ahead
for the finalization of European unification. "Foreign restaurants" were
flourishing.

I could not reach Margharita Karapanou, but heard much about her. In
1988, the French government had awarded her the Foreign Novelist's Prize
for *The Sleepwalker*, or rather for *Le Somnambule*. Her husband had committed suicide. Stories varied as to why, and none were subject to convincing verification. In 1991, Karapanou's third novel appeared. Titled (in
French) *Rien ne va plus*, it was probably not quite the same "third novel"
about which she had previously told me. Its title notwithstanding, it is set
predominantly in Greece. It tells two versions of a broken marriage. In the
first, a homosexual husband abuses and victimizes his wife, leaves her, and
kills himself. In the second, a selfish and domineering wife drives her kind
and devoted husband away from her—but not to his own death. *Cassandra
and the Wolf* had increased in critical stature. *Rien ne va plus* was popular
but had not been critically lauded.

In late June, during "Gay Pride Week," I saw Ghrighoris Vallianatos's face
emblazoned on the cover of *Lipon*, a popular magazine. He subsequently
corroborated for me most of what *Lipon* had claimed about him. He was still
the country's best known "homosexual." He was still the leader of AKOE.
Unlike Paola's *Kraximo*, which had become quite glossy and was widely
available at the kiosks on Omonia Square, *Amfi* was published only irregularly. Konstandinos Karamanlis had reassumed the Greek presidency after
control of Parliament passed from PASOK to his own New Democracy
party. Karamanlis pardoned Khristos Roussos, who was living out of the
limelight. "The Movement," Vallianatos told me, "was quiet." But not Vallianatos himself. He had left the Ministry of Youth, and left the civil service.
For a time, he had been a member of the Greek Olympic Committee, whose
failure to bring the 1996 Centennial Games to Athens he had, he said, fore-
seen from the outset. He had become a promoter and an entertainer. He

was the host of what another of my acquaintances described to me as one of the "hottest" programs airing on local television. Its subjects: sex and love.

No stopping change, then; nor should we expect the cessation of those fundamental transferences or passages or acts of violence that have so far kept both history and meaning getting started, over and over again. The Greek modern has, moreover, become at least partially liberated from its exogenous stimuli. It may borrow creative and reformative energy from such assaults and irritants as the junta. But it is not altogether in need of them. A *poiēsis* of normative originality, of normative individuation, Greek modern *poiēsis* shares with its more strictly aesthetic counterparts farther west an inherent compulsion toward continuous rupture. It consequently makes history endogenously in the process of making sense. Greek moderns, for their part, are not so naïve as to think that history is anything else but what they make it; not so naïve as to think that they must always wait patiently for some provocative transference or catastrophe or act of violence to occur before they can proceed. They are wise enough to have realized that crisis, too, is always something of a *fictio*, and something that, in the absence of other sources, they are quite capable of fashioning for themselves.

If not imperiled by the cessation of history, constructivist *poiēsis* is perhaps more greatly imperiled by the antihistoricist *poiēsis* of that technical rationalism that Weber was the first to identify, and the first to condemn, at the Occident's core. It may be all the more imperiled as the unification of the European Community comes ever nearer to completion. Its prospects are in any event unclear. They rest—so it seems to me—on whether the unification of Europe also leads to its infrastructural, or more precisely to its politicoeconomic, homogenization. Should unification result in all the Continent becoming, with Great Britain and Ireland, a single "core area," should it result in the diffusion of the technocratic ethos of late capitalism from Europe's current "great powers" into all its semiperipheral states, the Greek modern might still survive. But it is likely to survive only as Whitman's modernity survives in America: in a minor and decidedly distorted key. Weber might have predicted such an outcome, though perhaps only at the cost of underestimating both the tenacity of sovereigntist politics and the role of charisma in everyday life. Wallerstein's analytics of the world system has more ambiguous implications, has indeed no determinate implications whatever. Everything hangs on what particular moves are to whose particular advantage at any particular time.

Whatever might turn out, perhaps it would in any event be better simply to bid the Greek modern a fond, if even a fond, farewell. Did it not, after all, emerge as symptom and sign of both political and cultural dependency? So I have argued. I have argued further, however, that it has since come into its own, come to be an alternative modernity, an alternative disposition to the threshold of modernity, capable at once of creating a meaningful way of life and of resisting, even of exploiting, the encroachments of its more technocratic counterparts. But even as an alternative, has it not tended to reinforce and reproduce dependency? Has its distaste for the technocrat's favorite themes—"progress," but even more "efficiency" and "organization" and "systematization"—not itself contributed to Greece's long-standing exclusion from the politicoeconomic and the cultural centers of the world system? Has historical sensitivity not become self-defeating? If not self-defeating, then collectively compromising? Is the Greek modern not, moreover, an essentially elitist alternative, its broad ideational breast merely a disguise for the maintenance of privilege and the perpetuation of dominance, however dominated such dominance might itself be?

Whether it would be better to preserve or to bid farewell to the Greek modern is a question that only Greeks are rightfully in a position to answer. I am certainly in no position to answer it for them. I am in no position, either, to say that freedom from technocracy is adequate compensation for that sort of dependency—that "cultural colonization"—that historical constructivism probably does promote; to say that elitism is of little consequence, so long as the elite are responsible to their station. Throughout *Modern Greek Lessons*, I have sought to keep constant a tone of sympathy, if not always a tone of unqualified approval. I do, in fact, have a great deal of sympathy for my Athenian circle, all of whom have had to endure a great many slings and arrows of outrageous fortune, the slings and arrows of the fortunes of dependency paramount among them. I cannot, however, pretend to have perfect empathy, even with those of them whose "condition" was most like my own. My most pressing problems were not theirs, their most pressing problems not mine. Our worlds and our views were always somewhat different worlds and different views as a consequence. Nor should I pretend to have left Greece with affection for everyone or everything that I had met there. My fieldwork often bordered on the unendurable. I was the loser of innumerable language games. If I was not admonished for "daring," as one of my acquaintances put it, "to speak *his* demotic," I was cowed into submission by a deluge of idioms over which I had no command. My good humor—which isn't all that good even in the cheeriest of circumstances—often wore very thin. Though I was involved in many arguments, some of them quite fierce, I never mastered the finer points of the local rules of the *agon*. I might have resisted cultivating them lest I come off as yet another "ugly American." More likely, I simply could not overcome the more passive style of aggression into which I had myself been socialized. I never regretted having chosen an urban setting for my research; nor has my conviction in the importance of studying up (as well as down) flagged. I did, however, often find myself wondering where the legendary warmth of "simple Greek villagers" had gone. I constantly had to remind myself that I would probably have been as much of a trial for a foreign ethnographer of my little American circle as some of my Athenian circle were for me.

But for all my difficulties, for all my discomfiture, I did manage to come away from Greece with many lessons, and hope that *Modern Greek Lessons* has succeeded in conveying at least a few of them. I was in fact witness not simply to an alternative but to a still viable modernity, whose virtues have since seemed to me in many respects to outweigh the virtues, or at least not to promote so many of the vices, of the technocratic modernity to which I am a socioculturally more direct heir. I was, it is true, witness to an alternative that, if not in principle, was for all practical purposes still in the hands of a hereditary—however weakly hereditary—elite. A further democratization of educational opportunity could perhaps expand the population who would be fluent in its maneuvers. But it could do nothing toward altering the stratified structure of the situation: those who have been raised with the Greek modern would always have an advantage over those who have merely been introduced to and instructed in it. It has become fashionable to despise not simply elitism, of which I am no fan, but also elites. After Bourdieu, in the wake of his rigorous, and rigorously functionalist, reductionism, the elites look to be nothing more than agents, if often self-deceiving agents, of dominance and oppression. Let us grant Bourdieu his point. Let us also entertain the idea that the *illusio*, the "false value," that Bourdieu presumes to govern all stratifying practices may not in all cases be quite such an illusion as, to either the militant petty bourgeois or the radical democrat, it seems. If they are to pass as values, even illusions must—at least in the long run—prove themselves able coherently to orient action, not in any possible world but in the world at hand. In an essay that I wrote soon after returning from Greece, an essay that reflected in both its abstraction and its disjointedness my failure yet to have come to terms with the difficulties and the discomfitures of my fieldwork, I put forward what I thought to be a somewhat strained conclusion. Among the lessons that I thought I had learned then was "that the task of being and becoming modern, however it might differ from place to place, is likely to be arduous everywhere." I concluded:

> A decidedly unsettling ethnographic (and of course ethnocentric) condescension has on several occasions resulted from making far too little of that arduousness. The issue is not, however, whether we can all be free of bias. We cannot be. We can, on the other hand, at least remind ourselves that a self-serving reverence of modernity is bound to do no more anthropological good than the orientalizing romanticization of the primitive has already done. The issue is whether and to what extent it might be plausible that the "modern alternative" is particularly suited, perhaps not to what the world once was but to what, in all

its unisolated, frantic, and relentlessly weird splendor, it is now; and that in its suitability—which is something else besides either its effortlessness or its adaptability—not simply its anthropological but its moral weight in fact lies.

With the Greek modern alternative particularly in mind, I would reiterate the same conclusion now. Only that its strain has disappeared.

NOTES

PREFACE
TERMS AND DEFINITIONS

1. See Sahlins 1985, R. Rosaldo 1980, and Price 1983.
2. See Lévi-Strauss 1966: esp. chap. 7.
3. See R. Rosaldo 1980. I discuss Rosaldo's objection in Chapter 5.
4. Eisenstadt 1987: 5.
5. Bourdieu 1977.
6. See Bourdieu 1977: 72–95.
7. Cf. Lévi-Strauss 1973: 380.
8. Cf. Aristotle, *Nicomachean Ethics* 2.2.
9. See Geertz 1973: e.g., 13–18.
10. Cf. Bourdieu 1977: 38–43.
11. So Bourdieu has, on occasion, characterized his analytical exercises.
12. See Bourdieu 1980: 66–67.
13. Cf. Kuhn 1970.
14. Cf. Weber 1975: 173.
15. Thus the fundamental hallmark of the "Protestant ethic."
16. See my discussion in Chapter 3.
17. See Chapter 3.
18. Geertz 1973: 241–44.
19. See, for example, Herzfeld 1987 and 1992.
20. Herzfeld 1987.
21. See Lévi-Strauss 1966: esp. chap. 1.
22. Bloom 1975: 3.
23. See Bloom 1973. Bloom prefers a psychological to a sociological idiom, and so does not speak, as I do, of either originality or individuation as "normative."
24. See Bloom 1975: esp. 4.
25. See Bloom 1975: 83–105. Cf. Bloom 1973.

INTRODUCTION
FOR THE TIME BEING: SOME NOTES ON
THE MANNERS OF MODERN LIVES

1. See Bloch, 1975b.
2. Geertz 1973: 100.
3. Geertz 1973: 101.
4. Cf. Comaroff 1975: 150–51.
5. Devlin 1977: 57–61.
6. Such a juncture does not appear to be specifically modern. See, for example, Bloch 1975a.
7. I allude here to Robert Bellah's essay on "religious evolution." See Bellah 1970.
8. Bellah 1970: 40.

9. See Lerner 1958.
10. See Bellah 1985.
11. See Bendix 1967.
12. So I have argued in "Possible Modernities." See Faubion 1988.
13. See Weber's remarks in the introduction to Parsons's translation of *The Protestant Ethic* (Weber 1958b: 13).
14. In that respect at least, the social structure of Greece allows comparison with the social structure of Japan. See Bellah 1985: esp. 14–15.
15. Cf. Herzfeld 1992: esp. 47.
16. See Weber 1958b: 18.
17. For an excellent discussion of the "paradox" of nationalist and ethnic movements in an increasingly rationalized era, see Tambiah 1989; for one example of the nationalist exploitation of rationalized technologies, see Urla 1988.
18. See Rabinow 1989.
19. See Herzfeld 1987.
20. See, for example, Price 1983; and Sahlins 1985.
21. See Herzfeld 1982.
22. Blumenberg 1983: 223–32.
23. Blumenberg 1983: 138.
24. Cf. Blumenberg 1983: 35.
25. Blumenberg 1983: 139.
26. Cf. Weber 1946e: 140.
27. Blumenberg 1983: 215.
28. Cf. Koselleck 1985: 17.
29. Cf. Stewart 1991: 7.
30. Cf. Herzfeld's discussion of Greece's image as "Oriental vassal" (1987: 19ff.).

CHAPTER ONE
MODEL IMPROBABILITIES: ATHENS AT FIRST SIGHT

1. Calvino 1974: 69.
2. My references are to the Doubleday edition (1956).
3. See de Ste. Croix 1981, Finley 1983, and Ober 1989 for such contemporary viewpoints.
4. See Dumont 1970 and 1977.
5. See Fustel de Coulanges 1956: 81. Cf. Weber 1958b.
6. Fustel de Coulanges 1956: 125–27.
7. See Panofsky 1957: 31.
8. Kerofilas registers the population of Athens at five thousand still in 1833. See Kerofilas 1985: 135.
9. See Allen 1986: 187. The figure is based on records existing in 1980, and is no doubt lower than the figure that would be accurate at present.
10. Braudel 1972: 258.
11. A review of such research is provided in Vermeulen 1983.
12. The illegal development of land is quite common throughout Greece, and the strategies of developers often remarkably clever. For an excellent survey, see Patton and Sophoulis 1983: 260–63. Cf. also Herzfeld 1991.
13. On the neoclassical champions of Greek "rhythm," see Filippidhis 1982: 28.

14. On the deterioration of the Acropolis, see the report of the Working Group on the Preservation of the Acropolis Monuments 1978.

15. See Pollitt 1972: 71–98. On the history and details of the plateau's several remaining ruins, see Boardman 1985; and Meletzes and Papadakis 1967.

16. Cf. Baudrillard 1976: esp. 194–96.

17. Cf. Herzfeld 1992: 66.

18. Cf. Jenkyns 1980: 4–13.

19. Clogg 1983: 19.

20. See Clogg 1983: 8; and cf. Bernal 1987: 289–336.

21. Cited in Clogg 1983: 24.

22. See Allen 1986: 189. Allen reports that some 500,000 private automobiles were registered in Athens in 1980. My figure is an estimate based upon the rate at which automobile ownership has increased in the intervening decade.

23. The ratio may no longer be accurate. Skiotis and Gagaoudaki (1977: 24) list Athens as having 2,395 vehicles per square mile in 1975. They list Los Angeles as having 1,670. But their data reflect the Los Angeles of 1960. Athens has grown much more rapidly than Los Angeles in the intervening years. Vehicle ownership has skyrocketed, especially in and around Athens; and the Athenian metropolis has a total of only 167 square miles. The Los Angeles metropolis in contrast has a total area of some 1,600 square miles.

24. Von Klenze's design for the Greek capital is in fact only an adaptation of blueprints that had been drawn by others; see the following chapter for further details.

25. Athens Center of Ekistics 1980: 237ff.

26. Athens Center of Ekistics 1980: 283.

27. On ancient Athens's festivals, see Parke 1977, and Pickard-Cambridge 1988; on elite participation, see Ober 1989: esp. 199.

28. See, for example, Hirschon and Gold 1982; Dubisch 1983, 1990; Hirschon 1983b; Herzfeld 1990; Hart 1991; and Stewart 1991.

29. So, in any event, says the *Blue Guide* (Rossiter 1981: 79).

30. I offer a more complete discussion of the status of Orthodoxy in the Ottoman era in "Absent *Ikonostasia*" (Faubion 1991). See Herzfeld (1992: 88) on the dissolution of the last Greek remnants of the *millet* system during the Papandreou administration.

31. Cf. Herzfeld 1992: 88.

32. The statistics are reported in the *Europa World Yearbook* 1991. Cf. also Stewart 1991 and Herzfeld 1992.

33. Cf. Stewart 1991: 131ff. Stewart suggests that the "new age mysticism" that O Pirinos Kosmos serves is indicative of the contemporary religiosity of Greece's urban "elite." It is indicative in its individualism, perhaps; but in my experience, not the trend that Stewart implies it to be.

34. See Herzfeld 1991: 75.

35. On what is known and on what is likely never to be known about the junta, see among others Papacosma 1977: 183–87; Tsoukalas 1981: 190–92; Veremis 1986: 140–45; and Yanoulopoulos 1977: 86–90. The still unrepentant Papadhopoulos continues to be confined to a Greek prison. No particularly informative account of the coup d'état can be expected without his cooperation.

36. See Luhmann 1982: 332–35.

37. Guy Burgel notes a correlation between the entrenchment of greenhouse agriculture and the repopulation of formerly declining Cretan villages (1986: 71).

38. See Fekete 1966: 72–73.

39. See, for example, Danforth 1982.

40. See Baudrillard 1976: esp. 149–91.

41. Bigot 1886: 41.

42. Bourdieu 1984: 6.

43. See Allen 1986: 187; and cf. Lagopoulos 1971: 382ff. Athens's growth patently violates the predictions of the "rank-size rule," on which, see Lagopoulos 1971: 380–82, and Petsemeris 1986: 54–56.

44. On *topiki aftodhiikisi*, see Manesis 1986.

45. See Gottmann 1983: 88.

46. Gottmann 1983: 88.

47. See Andrews 1967: 17.

48. See Augustinos 1977: 57ff.

49. See Tsoukalas 1982: 43.

50. See Frazee 1977: 133. Frazee provides a review of the complex course of church and state sovereignty from independence forward. On the "cooperativism" of the current arrangement, see Frazee 1977: 149.

51. See Fletcher 1977: 165–66. Paparighopoulos had a considerable impact on the folklorist Nikolaos Politis (cf. Herzfeld 1982: esp. 97–122), for whom proof of the continuity of ancient and modern Greek culture was the first principle of the legitimation of the existence of the Greek state. He has been joined by many others, native and foreign, not all quite such self-conscious ideologues. For a review, see Danforth 1984: 53–85.

52. Ritsos 1985: 44 (my translation).

53. The author in question is Dhimosthenis Aghrafiotis. See his *Politistikes Anadhiplosis* (1983: 25–47).

54. Cf. Herzfeld 1987: esp. 144–17.

55. Fallmerayer was one of the earliest. See Herzfeld 1982: 75–76.

56. Mouzelis 1978: 8.

57. See Tsoukalas 1982: 39.

58. Tsoukalas 1982: 39.

59. Phanariote "culture" was much admired by the usually scornful Edmond About. Epanimondas Stasinopoulos refers in his *Istoria ton Athinon* to the "amusing" About, who "wrote with spirit, bile, and bias against us" (1973: 403). About's *La Grèce contemporaine* appeared in 1854, and was translated into English several years later. It derives from its author's tenure as a fellow at the Ecole française d'Athènes and is in its way remarkably ethnographically thorough. About's successor at the Ecole, Charles Bigot, gave the monograph the following review (1886: 126–27): "Lorsqu'au retour d'Athènes, autrefois, j'ai habité le Midi une couple d'années, ce qui m'a frappé, c'est la prodigieuse grec [*sic*]. C'est la même vivacité, c'est la même gaité; c'est la même facilité aussi à se montrer tour à tour et à se calmer soudain. . . . Quel dommage qu'Alphonse Daudet n'ait pas passé par notre Ecole d'Athènes. Certainement sa *Grèce contemporaine* n'eut pas eté tout à fait la *Grèce contemporaine* d'Edmond About, mais elle aurait bien aussi son prix, et je crois qu'elle serait plus vraie."

60. Gellner 1983: 35ff.

61. Gellner 1983: 95–97.
62. Tsoukalas 1982: 304.
63. I have recently been told that ambitious Athenians have begun to enroll the names even of their unborn children on the waiting list of the *Amerikaniko Kolleyio* (Samuel Danon, personal communication). On the importance attached to education, see also Friedl 1976: 363–87; and 1959: 30–38.
64. Cf. Bourdieu 1984: 18. The father's occupation is, in Bourdieu's France, among the more independent of the variables determinative of social class.
65. See, for example, Campbell 1964; du Boulay 1984; and cf. Herzfeld 1987. For a broad review, see Davis 1977.
66. I am, I might add, fictionalizing rather liberally to protect the identity of the source.
67. See Friedl 1968.
68. Petsemeris offers a telling datum: a demographic survey undertaken in the 1960s revealed that some 60 percent of Athens's residents had been born elsewhere (1986: 58).
69. Cf. Stewart's discussion of "style" in *Demons and the Devil* (1991).

CHAPTER TWO
REMEMBERING AND REMODELING: THE METALEPTIC METROPOLIS

1. Seferis 1981: 55.
2. De Certeau 1984: 95.
3. De Certeau 1984: 94.
4. De Certeau 1984: 94.
5. De Certeau 1984: 91
6. Jill Dubisch has noted such a rule, or such an inclination, in her work on the shrine of the Virgin on the island of Tinos (Dubisch, personal communication).
7. On the historical and architectural details of Monastiraki and Kapnikarea, see Sicilianos 1960: 234–235. On the details of the proposal, ratified by the Greek National Assembly in 1863, to move Kapnikarea to a less trafficked location, see Stasinopoulos 1973: 421.
8. On the architectural reinvention of Athens, see Filippidhis 1982 and 1983; see also Stasinopoulos 1973: 366–67. Kleanthis was, for his part, the most distinguished native architect of his day. Several of his buildings survive. The group of Othonic architects responsible for the current homes of many of Athens's grander institutions was, however, composed largely of foreigners. With von Klenze (see subsequent discussion), it included Christian and Theophilus Hansen. The former designed the university; the latter, with Lissandros Kaftanzoghlou, the National Library. See also Fletcher 1977: 159.
9. See Filippidhis 1982.
10. Hitchcock 1977: 51. On von Klenze's career, see Hitchcock 1977: 45–54.
11. The Regency ratified von Klenze's blueprints on 18 September 1834.
12. Filippidhis 1982: 26.
13. Filippidhis characterizes Athens's urbanization as "colonial in type." On some of her more southerly sisters, see Fuller 1988, Rabinow 1989: 277–316, and cf. Abu-Lughod 1980.
14. Hitchcock 1977: 69.

15. Filippidhis 1982: 30.

16. Filippidhis reviews the most notable of later efforts in 1982: 27–30.

17. See, for example, Smith 1984: 159.

18. According to Kevin Andrews, there were no "ethnic" restaurants in Athens in the years immediately preceding the junta. He was overlooking the British-style pub in the Hotel Grande Bretagne; and may have overlooked a single Chinese restaurant as well. See Andrews 1967.

19. Considerable scholarly research has been undertaken on Greek migration, indeed on migration in all its facets. My central source here is Tsoukalas 1982: 97–123 and 147–59. But see also, for example, Condominas 1968: 215–34; Dimitras 1968: 235–43; Friedl 1976: 363–87; and Giner and Salcedo 1978: 94–123.

20. More carefully, with few whose separate presence is noticeable today. In the past, Greece absorbed thousands of Russians who were fleeing from the Bolshevik Revolution. During my stay, it was taking in a rather small number of Iranians who fled after the fall of the Shah.

21. For an excellent discussion of the Split, see Mavrogordatos 1983a: 69–80.

22. On the details of these exiles and returns, see Dakin 1977: 59–63 and Yanoulopoulos 1977: 64–69. On the Asia Minor Disaster's effects on Athens, see Stasinopoulos 1973: 480–88 and Kerofilas 1984: esp. 10–17. The best account of the exchange of populations is still that of Pentzopoulos (1962).

23. The figure is an estimate. Beyond Pentzopoulos, see Dakin 1977: 62.

24. See, for example, Dakin 1977: 62. Cf. Stasinopoulos 1973: 485–86.

25. Yanoulopoulos 1977: 71.

26. Yanoulopoulos 1977: 71.

27. For an excellent analysis of the Nazi appropriation of Greek prototypes, and of their aesthetics generally, see Ioannidhis 1984.

28. The curators of Athens's new Jewish Museum are beginning to correct the situation.

29. Stavroulakis 1986: 8.

30. The *Europa World Year Book* reports that some five thousand Jews were, in 1988, living in Greece as a whole. See *Europa World Year Book* 1991: 1214.

31. See Woodhouse 1977: 99–100.

32. See Mavrogordatos 1983a: 75.

33. Mavrogordatos 1983a: 75.

34. Du Boulay 1984: 550–51.

35. See Dumont 1986: 175.

36. Tziovas argues for the translation of *o ethnismos* as "nationism," a term which would refer specifically to "a process of exclusion, which determines the differences of the national group from other groups and establishes its 'otherness'" (1985: 253–54).

37. See Herzfeld 1987: esp. 43–46.

38. Herzfeld has devoted attention to such issues for more than a decade. See especially Herzfeld 1982.

39. New York's Astoria is perhaps the best known of contemporary outposts. There are, however, many others. Mousourou reports that some four to five million "Greeks" live beyond the national boundaries (1983: 173). With expatriate ghettoization, a tendency toward dispersal should nevertheless be noted. In America

itself, Greeks have consistently been the geographically most dispersed of immigrants. See Tsoukalas 1982: 52; citing Vlakhos 1968: 76.

40. Stewart 1991: 7.

41. See Rossiter 1981: 48.

42. See Hitchcock 1977: 69. On the "neo-Grec" movement, see Rabinow 1989: 53ff.

43. Filippidhis 1983: 218.

44. Filippidhis 1983: 218.

45. Filippidhis 1983: 218.

46. See Filippidhis 1982: 29.

47. Herzfeld provides documentation on this issue in his study of Rethemnos. See Herzfeld 1991: esp. 230–31.

48. Cf. Rossiter 1981: 323.

49. Cited in Andrews 1979: 323.

50. See Andrews 1967: 16.

51. See Mouzelis 1978: 129.

52. Herzfeld 1987: 19.

53. See Barth's introduction to *Ethnic Groups and Boundaries* (Barth, 1969). See also Bourdieu 1977: 3–4.

54. See the concluding chapters of White's *Metahistory* (1973). See also his *Tropics of Discourse* (1978: esp. chaps. 2–5).

55. Support for such a position can be found in, or extrapolated from, Ricoeur's discussion of the rhetorical basis of temporal experience. See his *Time and Narrative* (1984–88). For a discussion of ethnographic "realism," see Marcus and Cushman 1982.

56. Bacon 1967: 219–21. For a recent examination of Brasilia, see Holston 1989. On Chandigarh, see for example Evenson 1966.

57. See the fourth appendix of *A Grammar of Motives* (Burke 1945).

58. Bacon 1967: 205.

59. Bacon 1967: 206.

60. See Bloomer and Moore 1977: esp. 99–100.

61. Bloom 1975: 95.

62. See again Burke's fourth appendix to *A Grammar of Motives* (1945).

63. See Bloom 1975: 86–95.

64. See Bloom 1975: 102.

65. Cf. Bourdieu 1968: 599.

66. Bloom 1975: 103.

67. Though I cannot agree even here; see Chapter 7.

68. The characterization would seem justified by Çelik's recent study. See Çelik 1986.

69. See the *Blue Guide* (Rossiter 1981: 108). Kerofilas 1985: 21–26 and Stasinopoulos 1973: 447–51 provide more colorful accounts of the renovation of the stadium and of the 1896 Olympics.

70. Rossiter 1981: 135.

71. Rangavis's *Takhidhromos* should not be confused with a popular periodical of the same name published in Greece today. Katharevousa was developed by Adhamandios Korais most famously. Since the last years of the nineteenth century, the "lan-

guage question" has been widely discussed and debated. For the motives of Korais and other "katharevousists," see, for example, Herzfeld 1982: 17–18. Anna Franghoudhaki analyzes some of the problems of katharevousist pedagogy in her *Ekpedheftiki Metarrithmisi* (1986).

72. On such "revisionism," see Herzfeld 1982: 60ff.

73. See, for example, Dakin 1977: 27.

74. The term is Martin Bernal's. See Bernal on philhellenism (1987: 289–292). The more extensive study, still the most detailed, is St. Clair's. See St. Clair 1972. On British Hellenists and philhellenes, see Jenkyns 1980.

75. Fairweather 1901: 250–51.

76. Yanoulopoulos 1977: 91: "On 8 December 1974 a plebescite was held and on that day the Greek people decided by an overwhelming majority (69.2% to 30.8%) to abolish the monarchy. For the first time since 1924 no one contested the validity of the result." Couloumbis and Yannis regard the abolition of the monarchy as one of the most important early steps taken by the Karamanlis government to "restore the legitimacy and guarantee the longevity of democratic institutions" (1983: 360–61).

77. Cavounidis reports that women especially often take on industrial piecework in their homes (1983: 333–34).

78. Rossiter 1981: 105–6.

79. Cf. Luhmann 1980: 33 (cited in Habermas 1987: 358). Gregory argues that the process of urbanization in Seville has brought about a "pluralization of lifeworlds" (1983: 253–76). It is difficult to say whether urbanization in Athens has brought about "pluralization" or "decomposition." The answer, perhaps: some of both.

80. Khatzimikhali 1986: 53.

81. Cf. Lipset 1987: 62, for a comparison with Canada.

CHAPTER THREE
CROSSING THE THRESHOLD:
NOTES ON CONFLICT AT A CERTAIN GREEK AIRPORT

1. Butor 1986: 34–36.

2. Legg 1977: 289.

3. Parsons 1960: 10ff.

4. Cf. Parsons 1960: 138–68.

5. See Geertz 1973: esp. 144–45.

6. Cf. Habermas 1987: 316.

7. Compare Paul Rabinow's discussion of such a "socio-technical" museum in *French Modern* (1989: 351–57).

8. The term, so far as I know, was coined by Dhimosthenis Aghrafiotis, an artist, essayist, and sociologist at the Athens School of Public Health. See Aghrafiotis 1987: esp. 35. See also Aghrafiotis 1989: 13 for a fuller linguistic catalog of the semantic field of "modernity" than I am providing here. Ghrighoris Gizelis and his colleagues adopt Aghrafiotis's term in their study of the Greek family (cf. Gizelis et al. 1984); but few sociologists have followed them.

9. See, for example, Legg 1969: esp. 23. Legg, however, is very cautious about the ascription, and far more cautious than many of the foreign *philosophes* whom I met during my fieldwork.

10. See Tsoukalas 1969 and 1981. See also Mouzelis 1978 and Svoronos 1987: 283–309; and cf. Mavrogordatos 1983b.

11. For example, Tsoukalas 1982 and Franghoudhaki 1986.

12. Cf. Andrews 1967: 14: "How can we—fat with civilization and equality of opportunity, with a balanced diet and general education, with national responsibility and a knowledge of our phobias, know anything about another people's national inferiority complex? It has to be faced even if it makes us want to scream: one can run off the tracks here if one forgets how every local institution or native growth or product of the land and an imagination still communicating it has been steadily, progressively devalued ever since Greece turned her back on geography and history and, proclaiming the resurrection of Antiquity, said, I can be Occidental too!" On the complex of "fallenness," cf. Herzfeld 1987: 30–36.

13. Herzfeld 1985: xvi.

14. Cf. Herzfeld 1987: 58–59.

15. Tsoukalas 1983: 38.

16. George Prevelakis has recently reaffirmed such a position quite forcibly (1990).

17. Greeks have been diagnosing themselves as formalists for quite some time. Ion Dhraghoumis, an essayist and polemicist writing at the turn of the century, suggested for example that Greece's sheer cultural age had made it a "highly refined nation where form counted for everything" (cited in Augustinos 1977: 100). Nikos Mouzelis, however, gives to formalism its contemporary rendering. He regards it as a sort of escapism, especially from the "hard realities" of class conflict. For a critique of Mouzelis, see Tsoukalas 1991.

18. Mouzelis indeed notes that particularism can be and often is its other side (1978: 134–48). The question, however, is whether there is anything specifically "Greek" about it. The answer: not really.

19. On this issue as on others concerning the "relativity" or "adaptability" of tradition in urban contexts, see Hirschon 1983a: 299–323. For a more detailed analysis, see Hirschon 1976. Cf. also Safilios-Rothschild 1976: 410–18.

20. See, for example, Lambiri 1968: 261–68.

21. Cf. Vermeulen 1983: 109–32; cf. also Gutenschwager 1971.

22. See Banfield 1958. Cf. Boissevain 1979: 81–93, Gellner 1977: 1–6, Gilmore 1977: 446–58, and even J. Schneider 1971: 1–24. Davis is perhaps the least "orientalizing" of the functionalists in his approach (1977).

23. See Schneider, Schneider, and Hansen 1972.

24. Kenny and Kertzer 1983: 13.

25. Cf. Manesis 1986: 36–37.

26. Elias 1978: 101.

27. Bateson 1972: 68. On the schizmogenetic tendencies of Greece's middle class in particular, cf. Mouzelis 1978: 123.

28. Bendix 1967: 311.

29. Bendix 1967: esp. 311.

30. See Bendix's review of the occidental conceptualization of "the modern" (1967: 294–313), which begins with Schnelling and Adam Smith and ends with Daniel Lerner.

31. Weber 1946d: 351.

32. Weber 1958b: 180.

33. Cf. Habermas 1987: 1.

34. Weber 1946d: 351.

35. This patristic aphorism is Weber's enduring slogan for the modern response to the "threshold"—his enduring slogan as well for the modern spiritual condition.

36. Cf. Dumont 1986: 104–7.

37. The allusion is of course to Geertz's "Deep Play: Notes on the Balinese Cockfight" (1973: 412–53).

38. See Geertz 1973: 142–69. It is worth nothing that the position Geertz takes in this essay, all the "dynamism" of its functionalism notwithstanding, is still integrationalist, and consequently Parsonsian, in its guiding assumptions about both social and cultural change. Stasis, or in any event accord, is still theoretically normative. The position appears to be one from which Geertz drifts away in much of his later work.

39. Geertz 1973: 164.

40. Cf. Geertz 1973: 164–69.

41. Cf. Tsaousis 1983: 19. For a definition of "cultural classicism," Tsaousis resorts to von Grunebaum 1954.

42. Owners of property, large and small, were in any case the nineteenth-century's most rigorous opponents of "liberal bourgeoisification." They had an important ally in the church. See Mouzelis 1978: 12–13 for a summary analysis. The junta's colonels were, in their way, fierce "cultural classicists" as well. No accident that they were all scions of the "old" petty bourgeois strata.

43. Filippidhis 1983: 219.

CHAPTER FOUR
SOVEREIGNTY AND ITS DISCONTENTS

1. Herzfeld 1992: 134 and 166.

2. Legg 1969: 17.

3. A conception of race, in other words, that confused cultural, geographical, and physiognomic lineaments of identity, and that was by no means restricted to the Germans alone.

4. Dumont 1986: 131.

5. The rationalization of differential social and material privileges is a project of ethical philosophy at least since Locke. It is one of the central projects of contemporary theorists of justice, especially in America. For the two great opposing statements, see Rawls 1971 and Nozick 1974.

6. Dumont 1986: 65–103.

7. Cf. Dumont 1986: 81.

8. Cf. Dumont 1986: 72ff.

9. Robert Paul Wolff is perhaps the least compromising of contemporary "philosophical anarchists." See Wolff 1970. For a more tempered position, compare John Simmons's *Moral Principles and Political Obligations* (1979).

10. Charisma is a central concept in most political-scientific discussions of Greece. For a review, see Mavrogordatos 1983b: 16ff. Mavrogordatos also offers an

insightful analysis into the relationship between charisma and clientelism, and between both of those and sociopolitical cleavage. Anthropologists tend to focus rather more vaguely on the intensity and saliency of politics in Greece, sometimes at the risk of reification (see Loizos 1975). Mouzelis attributes the "Greek gift" for politics not to "culture" but instead to circumstance. He points, for example, to "the early dependence of the village community on the State, which makes involvement with patronage politics and the securing of a political protector a vital necessity for survival and advancement" (1978: 101). One must point further, beyond the very real hinging of Greek fortunes upon political maneuvers both near and far away, to the social and cultural profits of political activities and political careers themselves. In a country in which the state is not and has never been merely an organ of the economically dominant classes (see Tsoukalas 1982: 225; Mouzelis 1978: 17), in a country moreover in which the state organization provides by far the most stable mechanism of heritable authority, politics can hardly help but be supreme. A heritage of statesmanship—let us grant its "archaic" eminence as well—and especially of elected statesmanship in fact remains among the most decisive and the most salient determinants of a scion's sociocultural superiority.

11. Weber 1946g: 245.

12. Weber 1946g: 247.

13. Weber 1946g: 246.

14. Weber 1946g: 248.

15. Weber 1946g: 252.

16. Weber 1946g: 250.

17. Cf. Mouzelis 1986: 155. Legg classifies the Greek political system as part "consociational" and part "bureaucratic." He does not, however, follow Weber's definition of bureaucracy, but rather David Apter's. Apter stresses bureaucratic authority's relatively high public accountability and relatively dispersed assignation of privileges and powers of decision. But he neglects two features of bureaucratic administration that Weber thought crucial: impersonalism, and intercoordination. The Greek political system is "bureaucratic" in neither of those respects.

18. In the survey that follows, I rely on several essays and monographs by both native and foreign scholars. Among them, above all: Manesis 1986: 15–59; Svoronos 1984: 21–38; 1987: esp. 275–309; Tsoukalas 1981; 1982: 561–94; 1986b: esp. 316ff.; Mouzelis 1978; 1986: 149–62; Yanoulopoulos 1977: 64–91; Clogg 1986; Couloumbis, Petropoulos, and Psomiades 1976; Dakin 1977: 21–63; Holden 1972; Legg 1969; 1977: 283–96; and Woodhouse 1977.

19. Dakin 1977: 21.

20. See especially Couloumbis, Petropoulos, and Psomiades 1976 for a review of "foreign interference." See also Legg 1969: 62ff.

21. Cf. Mouzelis 1978: 11–12.

22. Cf. Mouzelis 1978: 16.

23. On the emergence of the press, see Dimakis 1977: 210–15.

24. This rather stringent definition of the "party" is used in Legg's *Politics in Modern Greece* (1969: 17).

25. On the distinction between the "old" and the "new" Greece, see Mavrogordatos 1983b: esp. 274–76.

26. Mouzelis 1986: 155.

27. It might be added, though, that Venizelos's own charisma has undergone some routinization. There is still a Venizelos prominent in Greece's contemporary liberal right.

28. The "first civilization" in Metaxas's mind was the Hellenistic; the second, the Byzantine.

29. Cf. Woodhouse 1948: 166–67. Cf. also Yanoulopoulos 1977: 73.

30. See Mouzelis 1978: 129. "Discipline" and "health" were to be maintained by the army, of course; also to be determined by it.

31. On the postwar distinction betweeen *ethnos* and *laos*, see Alizivatos 1983.

32. For example, Aristovoulos Manesis. Cf. Manesis 1986.

33. Among the causes célèbres of Andreas Papandreou's son, Yiorghos, radio at last became "free" of state control in June 1987.

34. See, for example, Pitt-Rivers 1966: esp. 24, Caro Baroja 1966: 98ff., and J. Schneider 1971: 2–3.

35. Cf. J. Schneider 1971: esp. 6.

36. Hansen and Parrish make something of the same point in their essay on elites (1983: 257ff.)

37. Weber 1946g: 250.

38. Weber 1946g: 246.

39. Michael Herzfeld approaches the same point in his comparison of the import of *filotimo*, "honor," in three Greek communities. See Herzfeld 1980: 339ff.

40. On gossip, see for example du Boulay 1976: 389–406. Ethnographers have not generally been so bold, in print, as to label Greeks "paranoid" per se. One can nevertheless find in the tactics of patronage and clientelism the grounds for a psychology of suspicion that sometimes tends to take on a reality sui generis.

41. Cf. Paul Rabinow's introductory remarks in *French Modern* (1989: esp. 10).

42. See Cavounidis 1983: 322 for the relevant percentages and a report of long-term trends.

43. The *Europa World Year Book* reports that 27.2 percent of the Greek labor force was employed in industry in 1988. See *Europa World Year Book* 1991: 1203.

44. The statistics are provided by Verghopoulos 1978: 77.

45. See Vermeulen 1983: 114.

46. Yannitsis 1986: 256; cf. Vermeulen 1983: 94, which reports that fully half of all industrial investments in Greece between 1960 and 1966 were made by multinational corporations; and that one-third of the Greek industrial sector was still foreign-controlled in 1970.

47. See Allen 1986: 188.

48. See Allen 1986: 190.

49. Allen 1986: 188–98. Cf. Tsoukalas 1986a: 164ff. and Herzfeld 1991: 147ff.

50. Allen 1986: 191.

51. Cf. Allen 1986: 191. See also Friedl 1968. On the persistence of the dowry among urbanites, in spite of the Papandreou administration's efforts to discourage it, see Hirschon 1985: 19–20; cf. Hirschon and Thakurdesai 1970: 196. On the changing conception of the dowry, see du Boulay 1983: 260–70.

52. See Allen 1986: 187.

53. See Tsoukalas 1982: 164ff. Tsoukalas, one of the most devoted and one of the harshest native scholars of Athens, himself proposed the contrastive terms.

54. See the first and second parts of Tsoukalas's 1982 monograph.

55. Tsoukalas offers an extensive analysis of the "foreign" and "hidden" sources of the early nineteenth- and early twentieth-century Athenian economy (1982: 227–66). About 8.3 million tourists visited Greece in 1988, the lot of them generating about $2,400,000 in national income. In 1990, tourists spent about $2,570,000 during their visits. See the *Europa World Year Book* 1991: 1203.

56. The data are provided by Unger 1981: 370.

57. Cf. Tsoukalas 1982: 141–46.

58. See also Allen 1986: 192, citing Germidis and Delivanis 1975.

59. See Tsoukalas 1982: 227–39.

60. Mouzelis 1978: 17; and cf. Tsoukalas 1982: 213–14.

61. Greece signed a treaty of accession to the European Community in May 1979; it became a full member of the community in January 1981.

62. Manesis 1986: 16.

63. Tsaousis 1983: 17.

CHAPTER FIVE
"EVERYTHING IS POSSIBLE": NOTES ON THE GREEK MODERN

1. Thus one of the central arguments and the title of Robert Bellah's collection of essays on the sociology of religion. See Bellah 1970.

2. Cf. Greisman 1976: 496.

3. See Habermas 1984: 157–287; 1988: 303ff.

4. Cf. Habermas 1984: 212–13.

5. Weber 1946d: 328.

6. Weber 1946d: 328.

7. Habermas 1987: esp. 110.

8. Weber 1946d: 328.

9. Weber 1946e: 147.

10. Weber 1946e: 147.

11. Weber 1946e: 139.

12. Weber 1958b: 117; cf. also 1958b: 24.

13. Weber 1958b: 117.

14. Weber 1958b: 117.

15. Weber 1946c: 252–62.

16. Foucault 1979a: esp. 135–37.

17. Weber 1958b: 121.

18. Weber 1958b: 121.

19. Weber 1958b: 163.

20. Weber 1946a: 215–16.

21. Weber 1968: 24.

22. And cf. Weber 1946a: 215.

23. Weber 1946e: 142.

24. Weber 1946e: 321.

25. Weber 1946a: 216.

26. Weber 1946a: 199.

27. Weber 1958b: 176.

28. Weber 1946f: 270.

29. Weber 1946e: 156.

30. Cf. Weber 1946g: 250.

31. Cf. Herzfeld's remarks on "statism" in *Anthropology through the Looking-Glass* (1987).

32. Habermas 1987: 315–16.

33. On the body as a ground for modern identity, see Friedman 1992: 839. On the "regulative ideals" of one welfare state, cf. Rabinow 1989: esp. 25–27 and 231–32. Cf. also Foucault on "governmentality" (1979b: 5–15).

34. Cf. Weber 1946c: 254–55.

35. Find the point in Appadurai 1981: 201–19.

36. See *The Savage Mind* (Lévi-Strauss 1966: 217–44).

37. See Sahlins 1985: esp. 29–31 and Geertz 1973: 360–411. It should be noted that Rosaldo rejects the claims of *The Savage Mind* as well as those Sahlins and Geertz later put forward. His justification for rejecting them is, I would submit, worthy of suspicion. But see R. Rosaldo 1980: 26.

38. See Blumenberg 1983: 251ff.

39. Koselleck 1985: 33.

40. Koselleck 1985: 33.

41. Blumenberg 1983: 137.

42. Blumenberg 1983: 35.

43. Koselleck 1985: 33–35.

44. Cf. Herzfeld 1992: 163.

45. There is perhaps one aspect in which the proceduralist welfare state is definitively historicizing, even so: precisely in its enculturation of risk and its institutionalization of assurantiality. Consider Koselleck's remarkable observation on the transformation of political thought during the Age of Revolutions: "Daily encounters with . . . uncertainty emphasized the need for enhanced foresight, and Richelieu's claim that it is more important to think of the future than of the present assumes its proper meaning only when viewed in this light. One might suggest that this is the political forerunner of life insurance, which has gained ground, along with the calculability of life expectancy, since the turn of the eighteenth century" (1985:13).

46. Cf. Herzfeld 1987: esp. 23–25.

47. Bellah et al. 1985: 33.

48. Bellah et al. 1985: 34.

49. Bellah et al. 1985: 34.

50. Bellah et al. 1985: 34.

51. Cf. Jeffreys 1983: 42.

52. See Clogg 1983: 20.

53. Cf. Jeffreys 1983: 51.

54. Cf. Clogg 1983: 20.

55. Clogg 1983: 20.

56. Jeffreys 1983: 52.

57. Thus, at least, the epic's written version has it. But the *Akritis* sometimes appears in oral tales with his parentage reversed. See Herzfeld's discussion (1987: 101–9).

58. I can suggest *istorikos kataskevasmos*: intelligible, no doubt, but not at all familiar.

NOTES TO CHAPTER SIX 263

59. Paul Rabinow locates an abiding "French difference" in social thought and social planning, which he calls the "French modern." But the French modern rests not in a specific practice; it rests rather in a certain ethos, which Rabinow follows Hans Blumenberg in calling an ethos of "missionary and didactic pathos" (cf. Rabinow 1989: 14).

60. Much of the same analysis appears in Faubion 1991.

61. See Slesin, Cliff, and Rozensztroch 1988: 38–45.

62. Not to say that it is thus "beyond the modern." For a brilliant discussion of the sense in which "postmodernism" can be read as a (quite modern) historicization of "high modernism," see Jameson's "Foreword" to Lyotard's *Postmodern Condition* (Jameson 1984: esp. xv–xviii).

63. Cf. Friedman 1992: 838–41.

64. Bloom 1982: 43.

65. Bloom 1982: 43.

66. Cf. Geertz 1973: 208–29.

67. Foucault 1981: 305.

68. For a definitive critique of the stereotype of the Greek "fatalist," see Herzfeld 1987.

69. See Blumenberg 1983: esp. 139.

70. The preceding and this paragraph are substantially reproduced in Faubion 1991.

71. The perspective is urged in Geertz, Geertz, and Rosen 1979.

CHAPTER SIX
THE SELF MADE: DEVELOPING A POSTNATIONAL CHARACTER

1. From Filias's "Prologue" (1984: 7–11) to *Tradition and Modernity in the Cultural Activities of the Greek Family* (Gizelis et al. 1984). My translation.

2. Such a string of ideal-typifying terms is just that; on the ground, one usually finds hybrids. Early Greek historicism, for example, is countermythological and perhaps "protomodern," but Hellenistic Gnosticism, if also countermythological, is nevertheless countermodern in its preservation of the ethically ordered cosmos. Contemporary fundamentalisms, especially millenaristic fundamentalisms, are unquestionably countermodern, but also tend to be counterclassical in admitting no "gap" between the real and the ideal world. Whatever else they may be, these terms are not designations of "cultures" and they are not imbedded in "cultures," either. They designate qualities of regimes of signification that now more than ever are directly at odds not simply over what is valuable but over what is meaningful as well.

3. See *The Critique of Pure Reason* 1933: 237–38.

4. Cf. Blumenberg 1983: 137.

5. Cf. Geertz 1973: 98–101.

6. It is worth noting that Robert Bellah, in his essay on religious evolution, labels the world religions "pre-modern," a label I think accurate. See Bellah 1970.

7. See Rabinow's discussion in *French Modern* 1989: 7–8 and 10–13.

8. Cf. Rabinow 1989: esp. 89–91. Cf. also Foucault 1979a: 89ff. 205–6 for particular examples of this modern, or modernizing, striving.

9. See Foucault 1979a: 257ff.

10. Foucault metaphorizes this inconsistency, which he thinks central to the very

existence of "Man," of a creature both the subject and the object of his own knowledge, with his well-known image of the "empirico-transcendental doublet" (1973: 318–22). The allusion is to Kant, but the image may well make of Kant and his own "inconsistencies" more than they merit. The "inconsistency" of a being at once subject to nature's laws and a law unto itself has a naturalist resolution, a principle that might be called the first principle of any "legitimate" modernity: namely, that "reason" is at once worldly and endowed with its own, "proper" causality. Contemporary empirical realisms and causal theories of mind show some promise of making sense of that principle, which is not transcendentalizing per se.

11. Marcus and Fischer 1986: 46.
12. See Kluckhohn and Leighton 1946.
13. Marcus and Fischer 1986: 48–49.
14. See Crapanzano 1980.
15. See Obeysekere 1981.
16. See Levy 1973.
17. See M. Rosaldo 1980.
18. See L. Abu-Lughod 1986.
19. Cf. Bateson 1958: 113.
20. Cf. Herzfeld's discussion (1987: esp. 37–38).
21. Dorrine Kondo has found the selves of modern Japanese workers to be at once mutable and fragmented; her explanation focuses less, however, upon the sort of reflexive realization that I am concerned with here than on the constant renegotiation of identity from one interactive setting to another. See Kondo 1990: esp. 26–33.
22. A notable exception can be found in Scheper-Hughes 1982: ix–x.
23. See Geertz 1973: 15.
24. The most substantial exception is *Mothering in Greece*. See Doumanis 1983. See also Dubisch 1991.
25. The best-placed exception is Maria Dhamanaki, current leader of Sinaspismos, the leftist coalition that has superseded the "New Left." Melina Mercouri, who served as Andreas Papandreou's Minister of Culture, is the most famous one. Mercouri, however, is "exceptional" in two very important respects: she is an international celebrity; and she is descended from one of Athens's most celebrated mayors, Spiros Mercouris. She narrowly lost the election for the mayorship of Athens in 1990.
26. Of the classist cast of the junta, see above all Mouzelis 1978: 128ff. and Tsoukalas 1982: 178–93.
27. See n. 26 for references.
28. So Koselleck has argued (1985: 21–38).
29. Dubisch 1986b: xii.
30. Friedl noted long ago the temporal gap between urban and provincial style in Greece, a gap noticeable as well between the "true urbanites" and "country bumpkins" or *vlakhi* of Athens itself (1968). For observations on the lagging provincial emulation of urban architecture and interior design, see Pavlides and Hesser 1986: 83–84. It should be added, however, that sexual roles and sexual behavior are somewhat less subject to fashion than attire and shelter. As in France (cf. Bourdieu 1984: 382–85), as elsewhere in the Circum-Mediterranean, so too in Greece, the lower social classes tend to maintain a more extreme rhetoric of sexual difference and a more strict division of sexual labor than the upper classes. In Athens, the sexual style

of the lower classes has been less influential in the long run than the style of the upper. In rural villages, the opposite appears to be the case.

31. Though practices of segregation vary in detail from one place to the next, most ethnographers of rural Greece report that men dominate the *platia*, even if they are not always its exclusive inhabitants. See, for example, Herzfeld 1985: 66 and Friedl 1986: 43–44. For a more recent overview of research on the themes and variations of gender roles in Greece, see Loizos and Papataxiarchis 1991a and 1991b; see also Dubisch 1991.

32. Such, at least, is the impression that might be gained from Fekete 1966.

33. Herzfeld 1985: esp. 36–37 devotes considerable attention to the male life of the *kafenio* in his study of the Cretan village of "Glendi." See also Papataxiarchis 1991. Herzfeld's and Papataxiarchis's reports are broadly representative of "traditional" Greece as a whole. I suspect that the collapse of the exclusivity of the *kafenio* in Athens is still far more the exception than a national rule. On the other hand, the *kafeteria* or coffee shop appears to be a place where the sexes might mingle not just in Athens but in many other Greek cities as well. See Cowan 1991.

34. Jill Dubisch has pointed out to me that the Athenian advent of the motor scooter has given modern young couples an excuse to embrace in public.

35. I have no statistics of my own to support these impressions, and the statistics to which I have access are at least a decade out of date. On the other hand, distributional patterns of employment are remarkably consistent in Greece over time, and the recent past seems not at significant variance with the present. On the distribution of the sexes in the agricultural and industrial sectors, see Cavounidis 1983: 322–36. Psacharopoulos reports that only some 31.5 percent of "economically available women" were participating in the Greek labor force, "one of the lowest . . . rates among Western European and other countries" (1983: 341). Both Cavounidis and Psacharopoulos report that women earn in absolute terms far less than men (see especially Psacharopoulos 1983: 345).

36. Ethnographers are consistent in their observations on this syndrome from Campbell forward. It is known beyond Greece; it is known beyond the Christian Mediterranean as well. Brandes 1980 offers some comparative analysis. See also Jane Schneider 1971: 19–21.

37. See Herzfeld's discussion (1987: 117).

38. Again, see Jane Schneider 1971: 19–21. Du Boulay offers a recent analysis of the Greek case (1986: 139–141).

39. Dubisch 1986a: 33.

40. Cf. Papataxiarchis 1991.

41. Bourdieu's phrase for those well endowed with "symbolic capital" but not with material resources.

42. The term, meant to suggest that curators, artists, musicians, actors, and the like are also members of the proletariat, was apparently introduced into Greece's more official discourses by Melina Mercouri.

43. See Bloom 1975: 95.

44. Tsaousis 1983: 18.

45. Bloom 1975: 101.

46. In other contexts, the accusation of *efthinofovia* is perhaps more appropriate. Cf. Herzfeld 1987: 34–35.

47. On the falsity of metaphor, see Davidson 1979.

48. The Library of General Education in Greece in fact published a collection of essays addressing the relative marginality of psychoanalysis only a few years ago (see Tsavaras, 1984).

CHAPTER SEVEN
THE WORKS OF MARGHARITA KARAPANOU: LITERATURE AS A
TECHNOLOGY OF SELF-FORMATION

1. "I am the wound and the knife! / I am the slap and the cheek! / I am the limbs and the wheel, / and the victim and the hangman!"

2. Herbert Phillips has addressed this point briefly in the introduction to his study of Thai literature. See Phillips 1987.

3. See Richard Altick 1962, which reviews the class origins of English writers from 1800 through 1935. France's aristocracy produced a few distinguished novelists. America's upper classes have produced virtually none, perhaps because, as Paul Fussell put it, they "do not have any ideas."

4. Possibly the best known is Nikos Dhimou, a commentator for the respected weekly, To Vima, host of the Greek equivalent to the Dick Cavett Show, but also a published essayist and poet.

5. The U.S. Department of State's "Background Notes" indicate in 1985 that 96 percent of Greek men and 89 percent of Greek women can read and write (United States Department of State 1985: 1). The figures, the derivation of which is not clear, may be somewhat high, and do not acknowledge definite rural-urban variations.

6. See Aghrafiotis, Papaghounos, and Khiridhakis 1985: 150.

7. The survey is cited in Aghrafiotis, Papaghounos, and Khiridhakis 1985: 167.

8. Aghrafiotis, Papaghounos, and Khiridhakis 1985: 162.

9. Aghrafiotis, Papaghounos, and Khiridhakis 1985: 169.

10. Lambropoulos notes the exceptional degree to which the poet, in modern Greece, is still considered a "hero" (1988: 158).

11. Keeley and Sherrard have made the same point in their introduction to Seferis's collected works. See Keeley and Sherrard 1981: ix–x.

12. Phillips 1987: 9.

13. See Lambropoulos on the "politics" of literary evaluation (1988: 157–81).

14. Cf. Hans Blumenberg's discussion in *The Legitimacy of the Modern Age* (1983: 423–24).

15. Bourdieu 1984: 3.

16. See Bourdieu's discussion of "inherited and acquired capital" (1984: 80–92).

17. The Onassis family, for example, was and remains extremely wealthy and very "worldly," but by no means "cultivated."

18. See Lévi-Strauss's discussion in the "overture" to *The Raw and the Cooked* (1969b: 17–18).

19. Kant first pointed out and raised to the status of an epistemological first principle the universality of the "I think": "It must be possible for the 'I think' to accompany all my representations: for otherwise something would be represented in me which could not be thought at all, and that is equivalent to saying that the representation would be impossible, or at least would be nothing to me" (1933: 152–53).

20. See Joseph Alsop's vast study of the "rare art traditions" (1982). Alsop finds in these traditions a "developed historical sense" (1982: 294), a cultivated collective concern with "the how and the why, the circumstances and ultimate consequences" of real events in real time (1982: 295). But he also finds at the base of them a market economy developed enough to inspire artists to venture out on their own and offer their creations for public sale (1982: esp. 43–45). All such traditions—from that of Hellenistic Greece or Imperial China to that of the twentieth-century Occident (and Orient)—treat art works as signed.

21. Foucault 1979c: esp. 159–60. Daniel Defert suggested to me that Foucault had in part abandoned the position toward which he tended in the essay's concluding paragraphs.

22. Cf. Barthes 1977: 155–64.

23. See Barthes 1977: 142–48. It was Barthes, not Foucault, who announced the author's modern "death" (cf. Barthes 1977: 148). The Foucault of "What Is an Author?" was clearly attracted by that claim, though he stopped just short of making it himself.

24. Canonization is of course an exceedingly complex process, and I do not even begin to address its complexities here. For one treatment, see Ohmann 1987.

25. Writers who have risen to great stature sometimes win the privilege of being taken seriously as critics. Nabokov is one contemporary example.

26. Every and any work can be treated as if it were signed—any work is indeed signed by implication. The Bible, for example, "becomes" literature only when the implication is in force.

27. See Foucault on the ethical and political implications of this. He writes: "texts, books, and discourses really began to have authors (other than mythical, 'acralized' and 'sacralizing' figures) to the extent that authors became subject to punishment, that is, to the extent that discourses could be transgressive" (1979c: 148).

28. Greek editions are typically published in batches of four to six thousand (Aghrafiotis, Papaghounos, and Khiridhakis 1985: 166); the numbers are small, but so, inevitably, is the Greek-language literary market.

29. Keeley and Sherrard 1981: ix.

30. See Robinson's analysis of Palamas in *Greece: The Modern Voice* (Robinson 1975: esp. 64).

31. Cf. Sherrard's discussion of Sikelianos (Sherrard 1975: esp. 91–95).

32. Nadia Seremetakis has found a contemporary parallel among the women of Mani. See Seremetakis 1991.

33. Bien 1972: 18–19.

34. On Cavafy, see Keeley 1975; on Kazantzakis, see Bien 1974.

35. Lambropoulos notes at once the familiarity of such literary cosmopolitanism and its tension with a more "nationalist" canon of Greek literature in *Literature as National Institution* (1988: 34).

36. Bloom 1973. Bloom explores revisionism further primarily in two other works: *A Map of Misreading* (1975) and *Agon: Towards a Theory of Revisionism* (1982).

37. Bloom 1975: 3.

38. Bloom 1975: 9–10.

39. Citations are from the fifth edition, published in 1986. Translations are my own. For the published English version, see Karapanou 1974.

40. The citation is from the third edition of *Dhiskoles Nikhtes* (1977). My translation.

41. It was, in fact, Yiorghos Theotokas who coined the generational label. On the generation, see Vitti 1972 and Mirasyezi 1982, 2:399–543. See also Doulis 1977: 151–79.

42. On the Generation of 1897, see Gerasimos Augustinos's *Consciousness and History* (1977).

43. Cited in Mirasyezi 1982: 496–97.

44. Mirasyezi 1982: 498.

45. Elytis 1984: 10.

46. Citations are taken from the second printing, published in 1986. Translations are my own. It is regrettable that Karapanou's multilingual play is largely lost when *The Sleepwalker* is brought into English. Much of that play is conducted in English.

47. The most intelligent and judicious discussion of the junta available in English to date can be found in Mouzelis 1978 and Tsoukalas 1969.

48. Anghelaki-Rooke notes a remarkably similar principle at work in one of the poems of Lefteris Poulios, who must also be counted among the Generation of 1974. See Anghelaki-Rooke 1975: 21.

49. The preceding discussion of Karapanou's *Sleepwalker* is substantially reproduced, though differently contextualized, in Faubion 1991.

50. Geertz 1983: 99.

CHAPTER EIGHT
MEN ARE NOT ALWAYS WHAT THEY SEEM:
FROM SEXUAL MODERNIZATION TO SEXUAL MODERNITY

1. From an article in *Ta Nea* (The News) (26 January 1987: 7).

2. *Ta Nea* 28 January 1987: 24–25.

3. *Ta Nea* 27 January 1987: 5.

4. *Ta Nea* 27 January 1987: 5.

5. *Ta Nea* 27 January 1987: 5. A note about the speaker is in order. The author of *The Third Wedding Wreath*, one of the most widely acclaimed of Greek neorealist novels, Taktsis had a certain notoriety as a member of the homosexual and transvestite underworld. He once responded to an interviewer's query by characterizing his politics as "sex-revolutionary." He occasionally treated "homosexual" and quasi-sexual themes in his literary work. But no one identified him to me as a "homosexual activist." During my stay, he lived reclusively in a ramshackle part of Athens. He died, apparently a victim of murder, in the summer of 1988.

6. *Ta Nea* 28 January 1987: 24.

7. *Ta Nea* 28 January 1987: 25.

8. *Ta Nea* 31 January 1987: 9.

9. Roussos 1987: 9.

10. Roussos 1987: 9.

11. Cf. Pandelidhis 1982: 85.

12. Foucault 1985: 95.

13. See Foucault 1985: 194ff. Cf. Marrou 1965: 65ff. and Dover 1978: esp. 91.

14. Foucault 1985: 30.

NOTES TO CHAPTER EIGHT 269

15. The words are Lévi-Strauss's. See Lévi-Strauss 1969a: 62.

16. Thus a corroboration of Ortner and Whitehead's thesis (1981) on the correlation between gender distinctions and the organization of "ideal power." Cf. also Friedl 1986: 44 on the correlation in the more segregated setting of Vasilika.

17. Herzfeld 1985: 124.

18. Cf. Herzfeld 1985: 11.

19. Cf. du Boulay 1986: 152.

20. Attalides 1982: 26. Such a traditional conception is also vividly figured in Costas Taktsis's *Third Wedding Wreath*. See Taktsis 1985.

21. The topic of the sexual expression of male friendship is no longer "casual" in Greece, and perhaps no longer "polite." I did not broach it with any of my male acquaintances. I know, however, of one contemporary literary treatment of it. Yannis Ritsos, in his intimate and "Romaic" *Isos Na'ne ki' Etsi* (1985: 10–11), portrays a masturbatory liaison between two young soldiers, to the apparent compromise of neither their private nor their public masculinity. It begins with this invitation: "What do you say, pal, our pride, our manhood, our little part; even more than bread and wine and a cigarette":

. . . Shall we play with them [*tis pezoume*]; you mine and mine yours? That'll be more fun.
No. It's not like me. It's a sin.
What sin? Don't you ever play with yours?
Yeah, but alone, in private [*sta krifa*].
Ridiculous. What alone? What someone else? And we, we're friends.

22. Pandelidhis 1982: 87; citing Ghardhikas 1952.

23. Herzfeld observes that such a woman is a "transgressor" (1985: 136), but may also be "impressive" (1985: 146), at least in rural contexts.

24. In Sioubouras 1980: 224.

25. Again, see Herzfeld 1985: esp. 146. The indignity of the mere woman and the attribution of masculinity to her bolder or more heroic counterpart is, however, not simply an aspect of the rural present. Topping finds it well entrenched even in the earliest of Orthodox imagery: "Always in patristic writings the male provides the sole measure of worth, virtue and excellence. Celibate women were lauded for their *andriki poni* (manly labors) . . . ; holy women for their *andrikos loyismos* (manly attitude); women martyrs for enduring persecution and torture *andrikos* (in the manner of men). To become like a man (*andrizesthe*) represented for women the only possible escape from the inferiority of her sex. . . . The words *yini* (woman) and *thilis* (feminine) acquired such pejorative connotations that in the eulogy for his remarkable sister, St. Macrina, St. Gregory of Nyssa confessed that he hesitated to call her 'woman' since she had gone 'beyond the nature of a woman' (Topping 1983: 10–11).

26. Once again, in corroboration of Ortner and Whitehead's thesis (1981).

27. For a somewhat different estimation of the *malakas*, see Loizos and Papataxiarchis 1991b: 226–27.

28. See Brandes 1981: 227–30. Cf. Brandes 1980: 88–91ff.

29. On *poniria*, see Herzfeld 1986. Indeed, *poniria* has its "feminine" connotations only because it is the archetypical craft of the dominated: of women in the ordinary course of things; of men who find themselves subject to the will of another.

30. Du Boulay 1986: 157.

31. For one attempt to come to terms with some aspects of the spatial expression of contemporary Greek territoriality, see Hirschon and Gold 1982: 63–73.

32. Sioubouras 1980: 13.

33. *Kalliardha* may be wrought by a loose analogy with *malliari*, the language of the radical demoticists of the late nineteenth and early twentieth centuries. *Kallos* is the ancient term for "beauty," though not necessarily the term from which *kalliardha* derives. Etymology here is decidedly obscure.

34. Sioubouras 1980: 9.

35. Sioubouras 1980: 9.

36. The Greek press persistently denied that AIDS was a "homosexual" disease. What few data were available on the disease's Greek course by 1987 lent local support, at least, to their contentions. But whether affirmed or denied, the putative link between AIDS and the "homosexual" was on virtually everyone's mind.

37. Sioubouras 1980: 10.

38. Kolovou 1987: 59.

39. Patsalidhou 1982: 46.

40. Patsalidhou 1982: 53.

41. Patsalidhou 1982: 46.

42. Patsalidhou 1982: 48.

43. Patsalidhou 1982: 48.

44. Patsalidhou 1982: 50.

45. The management of Athens's "gay bars" relaxes its prohibitions during Carnival.

46. Cf. Manesis 1986: 33.

47. Theodhorakopoulos 1982: 184.

48. See Schneider, Schneider, and Hansen 1972.

49. Theodhorakopoulos 1982: 184.

50. Theodhorakopoulos 1982: 184.

51. Offe 1987: 69ff.

52. Cf. Weber 1946b: 194–95.

53. Cf. Offe 1987: 69–70.

54. Theodhorakopoulos 1982: 184.

55. Cf. Sioubouras 1980: 164–65.

56. See Sioubouras 1980: 159.

57. In Sioubouras 1980: 162.

58. Theodhorakopoulos 1982: 169.

59. Foucault 1985: 5.

60. Foucault provides us, in *Discipline and Punish* (1979a) and in the first volume of his *History of Sexuality* (1978) still with the best account of that characterology's emergence and its effects.

61. *Amfi* 3 (1 May 1987): 5.

62. *Ta Nea* 4 February 1987: 14.

63. See the first volume of Martin Bernal's *Black Athena* (1987).

64. Marinatos n.d.: 44.

BIBLIOGRAPHY

About, E.
   1854 *La Grèce contemporaine*. Paris: n.p.
Abu-Lughod, J.
   1980 *Rabat: Urban Apartheid in Morocco*. Princeton: Princeton University Press.
Abu-Lughod, L.
   1986 *Veiled Sentiments: Honor and Poetry in a Bedouin Society*. Berkeley: University of California Press.
Aghrafiotis, Dh.
   1983 *Politistikes Anadhiplosis*. Athens: Theoria.
   1987 *Politistikes Asinekhies*. Athens. Ipsilon.
   1989 *Neoterikotita, Anaparastasi*. Athens: Ipsilon.
Aghrafiotis, Dh., Papaghounos, G., and Khiridhakis, Kh.
   1985 *Cultural Policy in Greece*. Athens: UNESCO Studies and Documents on Cultural Policy.
Alizivatos, N.
   1983 "Ethnos" kata "Laou" meta to 1940. In *Ellinismos, Ellinikotita*, edited by D. G. Tsaousis, 79–90. Athens: Estias.
Allen, P. S.
   1986 Positive Aspects of Greek Urbanization: The Case of Athens by 1980. *Ekistics* 54 (318–19): 187–94.
Alsop, J.
   1982 *The Rare Art Traditions*. New York: Harper and Row.
Altick, R. D.
   1962 The Sociology of Authorship: The Social Origins, Education and Occupation of 1,100 British Writers, 1800–1935. *Bulletin of the New York Academy of Sciences* 66: 6.
Andrews, K.
   1967 *Athens*. Stamford, Conn.: Oak Tree Press.
   1979 *Athens Alive, or The Practical Tourist's Companion to the Fall of Man*. Athens: Hermes.
Anghelaki-Rooke, K.
   1975 The Greek Poetic Landscape: Recent Trends in Greek Poetry. In *Greece: The Modern Voice*, edited by P. A. Mackridge, 13–26. Jamaica, N.Y.: St. John's University Press.
Appadurai, A.
   1981 The Past as a Scarce Resource. *Man* 16: 201–19.
Athens Center of Ekistics
   1980 HUCO: The Human Community in Athens. *Ekistics* 47 (283): 232–63.
Attalides, M.
   1982 Omofilofilia: Kinoniko-Istorika Plesia. In *Omofilofilia*, 9–35. Omilies ke sizitisis pou eyinan sto seminario "I Omofilofilia," 20–21 Martiou 1982.

Augustinos, G.
1977 *Consciousness and History: Nationalist Critics of Greek Society, 1897–1914.*
East European Monographs 32. New York: Columbia University Press.
Axioti, M.
1977 *Dhiskoles Nikhtes.* 3d ed. Athens: Kedros.
Bacon, E. N.
1967 *Design of Cities.* New York: Viking Press.
Banfield, E.
1958 *The Moral Basis of a Backward Society.* Glencoe, Ill.: Free Press.
Barth, F., ed.
1969 *Ethnic Groups and Boundaries.* Boston: Little and Brown.
Barthes, R.
1977 *Image/Music/Text.* Translated by S. Heath. New York: Hill and Wang.
Bateson, G.
1958 *Naven.* 2d ed. Palo Alto, Calif.: Stanford University Press.
1972 *Steps to an Ecology of Mind.* New York: Ballantine Books.
Baudrillard, J.
1976 *La Société de consommation.* Paris: Gallimard.
Bellah, R.
1970 *Beyond Belief: Essays on Religion in a Post-Traditional World.* New York:
Harper and Row.
1985 *Tokugawa Religion.* Paperback edition. New York: Free Press.
Bellah, R., et al.
1985 *Habits of the Heart: Individualism and Commitment in American Life.* Berkeley: University of California Press.
Bendix, R.
1967 Tradition and Modernity Reconsidered. *Comparative Studies in Society and
History* 9 (2): 292–346.
Bernal, M.
1987 *Black Athena: The Afroasiatic Roots of Classical Civilization.* Volume 1: *The
Fabrication of Ancient Greece, 1785–1985.* New Brunswick, N.J.: Rutgers University Press.
Bien, P.
1972 Introduction. In *Modern Greek Writers,* edited by E. Keeley and P. Bien,
4–22. Princeton: Princeton University Press.
1974 The Mellowed Nationalism of Kazantzakis' "Zorba the Greek." *Review of
National Literatures* 5(2): 113–36.
Bigot, C.
1886 *Grèce, Turquie, le Danube.* Paris: Paul Ollendorff.
Bloch, M.
1975a Property and the End of Affinity. In *Marxist Analyses and Social Anthropology,* edited by M. Bloch, 203–22. New York: Wiley.
Bloch, M., ed.
1975b *Political Language and Oratory in Traditional Society.* New York: Academic Press.
Bloom, H.
1973 *The Anxiety of Influence.* New York: Oxford University Press.

1975 A Map of Misreading. New York: Oxford University Press.
1982 Agon: Towards a Theory of Revisionism. Oxford: Oxford University Press.
Bloomer, K. C., and Moore, C. W.
1977 Body, Memory, and Architecture. New Haven: Yale University Press.
Blumenberg, H.
1983 The Legitimacy of the Modern Age. Translated by R. M. Wallace. Cambridge, Mass.: MIT Press.
Boardman, J.
1985 The Parthenon and Its Sculptures. Austin: University of Texas Press.
Boissevain, J.
1979 Toward a Social Anthropology of the Mediterranean. Current Anthropology 20 (1): 81–93.
Bourdieu, P.
1968 Outline of a Sociological Theory of Art Perception. International Social Science Journal 20: 589–612.
1977 Outline of a Theory of Practice. Translated by R. Nice. Cambridge: Cambridge University Press.
1980 The Logic of Practice. Translated by R. Nice. Stanford, Calif.: Stanford University Press.
1984 Distinction: A Social Critique of the Judgment of Taste. Translated by R. Nice. Cambridge, Mass.: Harvard University Press.
Brandes, S.
1980 Metaphors of Masculinity: Sex and Status in Andalusian Folklore. Philadelphia: University of Pennsylvania Press.
1981 Like Wounded Stags: Male Sexual Ideology in an Andalusian Town. In Sexual Meanings: The Cultural Construction of Gender and Sexuality, edited by S. Ortner and H. Whitehead, 216–39. Cambridge: Cambridge University Press.
Braudel, F.
1972 The Mediterranean and the Mediterranean World in the Age of Phillip II. 2 vols. Translated by Sian Reynolds. New York: Harper and Row.
Burgel, G.
1975 Athènes, étude de la croissance d'une capitale méditerranéenne. Paris: Librairie Honoré Champion.
1986 Changes in the Geography of Mediterranean Settlements. Ekistics 53 (316–17): 69–73.
Burke, K.
1945 A Grammar of Motives. New York: Prentice-Hall.
Butor, M.
1986 The Spirit of Mediterranean Places. Translated by Lydia Davis. Marlboro, Vt.: Marlboro Press.
Calvino, I.
1974. Invisible Cities. Translated by W. Weaver. New York: Harcourt Brace Jovanovich.
Campbell, J. K.
1964 Honour, Family, and Patronage: A Study of Institutions and Moral Values in a Greek Mountain Community. Oxford: Clarendon Press.

Caro Baroja, J.
  1966 Honor and Shame: An Historical Account of Several Conflicts. In *Honor and Shame: The Values of Mediterranean Society*, edited by J. Peristiany 79–137. Chicago: University of Chicago Press.
Cavounidis, J.
  1983 Capitalist Development and Women's Work in Greece. *Journal of Modern Greek Studies* 1 (2): 321–38.
Çelik, Z.
  1986 *The Remaking of Istanbul: Portrait of an Ottoman City in the Nineteenth Century*. Seattle: University of Washington Press.
Clogg, R.
  1983 Sense of the Past in Pre-Independence Greece. In *Culture and Nationalism in Nineteenth Century Eastern Europe*, edited by R. Sussex and J. C. Eade, 7–30. Columbus, Ohio: Slavica Publishers.
  1986 *A Short History of Modern Greece*. 2d ed. Cambridge: Cambridge University Press.
Comaroff, J.
  1975 Talking Politics: Oratory and Authority in a Tswana Chiefdom. In *Political Language and Oratory in Traditional Society*, edited by M. Bloch, 141–61. New York: Academic Press.
Condominas, G.
  1968 Introduction à une étude sur l'émigration grecque à Madagascar. In *Contributions to Mediterranean Sociology*, edited by J. Peristiany, 215–34. Paris: Mouton.
Couloumbis, T. A., Petropoulos, J., and Psomiades, H.
  1976 *Foreign Interference in Greek Politics: An Historical Perspective*. New York: Pella Publishing Company.
Couloumbis, T. A., and Yannis, P. M.
  1983 The Stability Quotient in Greece's Post-1974 Democratic Institutions. *Journal of Modern Greek Studies* 1 (2): 359–72.
Cowan, J.
  1991 Going Out for Coffee? Contesting the Grounds of Gendered Pleasures in Everyday Sociability. In *Contested Identities: Gender and Kinship in Modern Greece*, edited by P. Loizos and E. Papataxiarchis, 180–202. Princeton: Princeton University Press.
Crapanzano, V.
  1980 *Tuhami: Portrait of a Moroccan*. Chicago: University of Chicago Press.
Dakin, D.
  1977 The Formation of the Greek State: Political Developments until 1923. In *Greece in Transition*, edited by J.T.A. Koumoulides, 21–63. London: Zeno.
Danforth, L.
  1982 *The Death Rituals of Rural Greece*. Princeton: Princeton University Press.
  1984 The Ideological Context of the Search for Continuities in Greek Culture. *Journal of Modern Greek Studies* 2 (1): 53–86.
Davidson, D.
  1979 What Metaphors Mean. In *On Metaphor*, edited by S. Sacks, 29–46. Chicago: University of Chicago Press.

Davis, J.
1977 *People of the Mediterranean: An Essay in Comparative Social Anthropology*. London: Routledge and Kegan Paul.

de Certeau, M.
1984 *The Practice of Everyday Life*. Translated by S. F. Rendall. Berkeley: University of California Press.

de Ste. Croix, G.E.M.
1981 *The Class Struggle in the Ancient World: From the Archaic Age to the Arab Conquests*. Ithaca: Cornell University Press.

Devlin, P.
1977 Morals and the Criminal Law. In *Philosophical Issues in Law*, edited by K. Kipnis, 54–64. Englewood Cliffs, N.J.: Prentice-Hall.

Dimakis, J.
1977 The Greek Press. In *Greece in Transition*, edited by J.T.A. Koumoulides, 209–35. London: Zeno.

Dimitras, E.
1968 Relations entre communautés rurales méditerranéennes et centres urbains des pays industriels européens par les migrations. In *Contributions to Mediterranean Sociology*, edited by J. Peristiany, 235–43. Paris: Mouton.

Doulis, T.
1977 *Disaster and Fiction: Modern Greek Fiction and the Asia Minor Disaster of 1922*. Berkeley: University of California Press.

Doumanis, M.
1983 *Mothering in Greece: From Collectivism to Individualism*. New York: Academic Press.

Dover, K. J.
1978 *Greek Homosexuality*. New York: Vintage Books.

Dubisch, J.
1983 Greek Women: Sacred or Profane? *Journal of Modern Greek Studies* 1 (1): 185–202.

1986a Introduction. In *Gender and Power in Rural Greece*, edited by J. Dubisch, 3–41. Princeton: Princeton University Press.

1986b Preface. In *Gender and Power in Rural Greece*, edited by J. Dubisch, ix–xii. Princeton: Princeton University Press.

1990 Pilgrimage and Popular Religion at a Greek Popular Shrine. In *Religious Orthodoxy and Popular Faith in European Society*, edited by E. Badone, 113–39. Princeton: Princeton University Press.

1991 Gender, Kinship, and Religion: "Reconstructing" the Anthropology of Greece. In *Contested Identities: Gender and Kinship in Modern Greece*, edited by P. Loizos and E. Papataxiarchis, 29–46. Princeton: Princeton University Press.

du Boulay, J.
1976 Lies, Mockery, and Family Integrity. In *Mediterranean Family Structures*, edited by J. Peristiany, 389–406. Cambridge: Cambridge University Press.

1983 The Meaning of Dowry: Changing Values in Rural Greece. *Journal of Modern Greek Studies* 1 (1): 243–70.

du Boulay, J.
1984 The Blood: Symbolic Relationships between Descent, Marriage, Incest Prohibitions and Spiritual Kinship in Greece. *Man*, n.s., 19: 533–56.
1986 Women—Images of Their Nature and Destiny in Rural Greece. In *Gender
and Power in Rural Greece*, edited by J. Dubisch, 139–68. Princeton: Princeton
University Press.
Dumont, L.
1970 *Homo Hierarchicus*. Chicago: University of Chicago Press.
1977 *From Mandeville to Marx*. Chicago: University of Chicago Press.
1986 *Essays on Individualism*. Chicago: University of Chicago Press.
Durkheim, E.
1951 *Suicide*. New York: Free Press.
Eisenstadt, S.
1987 Introduction: Historical Traditions, Modernization and Development. In
Patterns of Modernity. Vol. 1: *The West*, edited by S. N. Eisenstadt, 1–11. New
York: New York University Press.
Elias, N.
1978 *The History of Manners*. Vol. 1: *The Civilizing Process*. New York: Pantheon.
Elytis, O.
1984 The Retina of John Veltri. In *The Greeks*, edited and translated by K. Friar,
9–11. Garden City, N.Y.: Doubleday.
Evenson, N.
1966 *Chandigarh*. Berkeley: University of California Press.
Europa World Year Book
1991 Greece. In *Europa World Year Book* 1991. Vol. 1. 32d ed, 1201–19. Europa
Publications Ltd.
Fairweather, W.
1901 *Origen and Greek Patristic Philosophy*. Edinburgh: T. & T. Clark.
Faubion, J.
1988 Possible Modernities. *Cultural Anthropology* 3 (4): 365–78.
1991 Absent *Ikonostasia*: Orthodoxy, History, and the Religiosity of Greece's Cultural Elite. *Comparative Social Research* 13: 225–48.
Fekete, I.
1966 *Athens*. London: Lutterworth Press.
Filias, V.
1984 Prologhos. In *Paradhosi ke Neoterikotita stis Politistikes Dhrastiriotites tis
Ellinikis Ikoyenias: Metavallomena Skhimata*, by G. Gizelis et al., 7–11. Athens:
Ethniko Kendro Kinonikon Erevnon.
Filippidhis, Dh.
1982 Urbanisme colonial en Grèce. *Urbi* 6: 25–30.
1983 Singkhroni Elliniki Arkhitektoniki ke Ellinikotita. In *Ellinismos, Ellinikotita:
Idhioloyiki ke Viomatiki Axones tis Neoellinikis Kinonias*, edited by
Dh. G. Tsaousis, 217–22. Athens: Estia.
Finley, M.
1983 *Politics in the Ancient World*. Cambridge: Cambridge University Press.
Fletcher, R.
1977 Cultural and Intellectual Development, 1821–1911. In *Greece in Transition*,
edited by J.T.A. Koumoulides, 153–72. London: Zeno.

Foucault, M.
   1973 *The Order of Things*. A translation of *Les Mots et les choses*. New York: Random House.
   1978 *The History of Sexuality*. Vol. 1: *An Introduction*. Translated by R. Hurley. New York: Random House.
   1979a *Discipline and Punish: The Birth of the Prison*. Translated by A. Sheridan. New York: Vintage Books.
   1979b On Governmentality. *Ideology and Consciousness* 6: 5–21.
   1979c What Is an Author? In *Textual Strategies: Perspectives in Post-Structuralist Criticism*, edited by J. V. Harari, 141–60. Ithaca: Cornell University Press.
   1981 Truth and Power. In *French Sociology: Rupture and Renewal since 1968*, edited by C. C. Lemert, 293–307. New York: Columbia University Press.
   1984 What Is Enlightenment? Translated by C. Porter. In *The Foucault Reader*, edited by P. Rabinow, 32–50. New York: Pantheon Books.
   1985 *The History of Sexuality. The Use of Pleasure*. Vol. 2: Translated by R. Hurley. New York: Pantheon.
Franghoudhaki, A.
   1986 *Ekpedheftiki Metarrithmisi ke Fileleftheri Dhianououmeni*. 3d ed. Athens: Kedhros.
Frazee, C.
   1977 Church and State in Greece. In *Greece in Transition*, edited by J.T.A. Koumoulides, 128–52. London: Zeno.
Friedl, E.
   1959 The Role of Kinship in the Transmission of National Culture to Rural Villages in Mainland Greece. *American Anthropologist* 51: 30–38.
   1963 Some Apsects of Dowry and Inheritance in Boeotia. In *Mediterranean Countrymen: Essays in the Social Anthropology of the Mediterranean*, edited by J. Pitt-Rivers, 113–35. Paris: Mouton.
   1968 Lagging Emulation in a Post-Peasant Society: A Greek Case. In *Contributions to Mediterranean Sociology*, edited by J. Peristiany, 93–106. Paris: Mouton.
   1976 Kinship, Class, and Selective Migration. In *Mediterranean Family Structures*, edited by J. Peristiany, 363–87. Cambridge: Cambridge University Press.
   1986 The Position of Women: Appearance and Reality. In *Gender and Power in Rural Greece*, edited by J. Dubisch, 42–52. Princeton: Princeton University Press.
Friedman, J.
   1992 The Past in the Future: History and the Politics of Identity. *American Anthropologist* 94 (4): 837–59.
Fuller, M.
   1988 Building Power: Italy's Colonial Architecture and Urbanism, 1923–1940. *Cultural Anthropology* 3 (4): 455–87.
Fustel de Coulanges, N. D.
   1956 *The Ancient City*. Garden City, N.Y.: Doubleday.
Geertz, C.
   1973 *The Interpretation of Cultures*. New York: Basic Books.
   1983 *Local Knowledge: Further Essays in Interpretive Anthropology*. New York: Basic Books.

Geertz, C., Geertz, H., and Rosen, L.
  1979 *Meaning and Order in Moroccan Society: Three Essays in Cultural Analysis.*
    Cambridge: Cambridge University Press.
Gellner, E.
  1977 Patrons and Clients. In *Patrons and Clients in Mediterranean Societies*, ed-
    ited by E. Gellner and J. Waterbury, 1–6. London: Duckworth.
  1983 *Nations and Nationalism.* Ithaca: Cornell University Press.
Germidis, D., and Delivanis, M.
  1975 *Industrialisation, Employment and Income Distribution in Greece: A Case
    Study.* Paris: Organization for Economic Cooperation and Development.
Ghardhikas, K.
  1952 Englimata kata ton Ithon. *Pinika Khronia.* Vol. 2.
Gilmore, D.
  1977 Patronage and Class Conflict in Southern Spain. *Man*, n.s., 12: 446–58.
Giner, S., and Salcedo, J.
  1978 Migrant Workers in European Social Structures. In *Contemporary Europe:
    Social Structures and Cultural Patterns*, edited by S. Giner and M. S. Archer,
    94–123. London: Routledge and Kegan Paul.
Gizelis, G., et al.
  1984 *Paradhosi ke Neoterikotita stis Politistikes Dhrastiriotites tis Ellinikis
    Ikoyenias: Metavallomena Skhimata.* Athens: Ethniko Kendro Kinonikon Erev-
    non.
Gottman, J.
  1977 The Role of Capital Cities. *Ekistics* 44 (264): 240–43.
  1983 Capital Cities. *Ekistics* 50 (299): 88–93.
Gregory, D. D.
  1983 The Meaning of Urban Life: Pluralization of Life Worlds in Seville. In
    Urban Life in Mediterranean Europe: Anthropological Perspectives, edited by
    M. Kenny and D. I. Kertzer, 253–72. Urbana: University of Illinois Press.
Greisman, H. C.
  1976 Disenchantment of the World: Romanticism, Aesthetics, and Sociological
    Theory. *British Journal of Sociology* 27: 495–507.
Gutenschwager, M.
  1971 Nea Aeolia: Persistence and Tradition in an Urban Greek Community.
    Ph.D. diss. University of North Carolina, Chapel Hill.
Habermas, J.
  1984 *The Theory of Communicative Action.* Vol. 1. Translated by T. McCarthy.
    Cambridge, Mass.: MIT Press.
  1987 *The Philosophical Discourse of Modernity.* Translated by F. Lawrence. Cam-
    bridge, Mass.: MIT Press.
  1988 *The Theory of Communicative Action.* Vol. 2. Translated by T. McCarthy.
    Boston: Beacon Press.
Hansen, E. C., and Parrish, T.
  1983 Elites versus the State: Towards an Anthropological Contribution to the
    Study of Hegemonic Power in Capitalistic Society. In *Elites: Ethnographic Is-
    sues*, edited by G. Marcus, 257–77. School of American Research. Albuquerque:
    University of New Mexico Press.

Hart, L. K.
    1991 *Time, Religion, and Social Experience in Rural Greece.* Lanham, Md: Rowman and Littlefield.
Herzfeld, M.
    1980 Honour and Shame: Problems in the Comparative Analysis of Moral Systems. *Man*, n.s., 15: 339–51.
    1982 *Ours Once More: Folklore, Ideology, and the Making of Modern Greece.* Austin: University of Texas Press.
    1985 *The Poetics of Manhood: Contest and Identity in a Cretan Mountain Village.* Princeton: Princeton University Press.
    1986 Within and Without: The Category of "Female" in the Ethnography of Modern Greece. In *Gender and Power in Rural Greece*, edited by J. Dubisch, 215–33. Princeton: Princeton University Press.
    1987 *Anthropology through the Looking-Glass: Critical Ethnography in the Margins of Europe.* Cambridge: Cambridge University Press.
    1990 Icons and Identity: Religious Orthodoxy and Social Practice in Rural Crete. *Anthropological Quarterly* 63 (July): 109–21.
    1991 *A Place in History: Social and Monumental Time in a Cretan Town.* Princeton: Princeton University Press.
    1992 *The Social Production of Indifference: Exploring the Symbolic Roots of Western Bureaucracy.* New York: Berg.
Hirschon, R.
    1976 The Social Institutions of an Urban Locality of Refugee Origin in Piraeus, Greece. Ph.D. diss., University of North Carolina, Chapel Hill.
    1983a Under One Roof: Marriage, Dowry and Family Relations in Piraeus. In *Urban Life in Mediterranean Europe: Anthropological Perspectives*, edited by M. Kenny and D. Kertzer, 299–323. Urbana: University of Illinois Press.
    1983b Women, the Aged and Religious Activity: Oppositions and Complementarity in an Urban Locality. *Journal of Modern Greek Studies* 1 (1): 113–30.
    1985 The Woman-Environment Relationship: Greek Cultural Values in an Urban Community. *Ekistics* 52 (310): 15–21.
Hirschon, R., and Gold, J. R.
    1982 Territoriality and the Home Environment in a Greek Urban Community. *Anthropological Quarterly* 55 (2): 63–73.
Hirschon, R., and Thakurdesai
    1970 Society, Culture, and Spatial Organization: An Athens Community. *Ekistics* 30 (178): 187–96.
Hitchcock H.-R.
    1977 *Architecture: Nineteenth and Twentieth Centuries.* Pelican History of Art. New York: Penguin.
Holden, D.
    1972 *Greece without Columns: The Making of the Modern Greeks.* London: Faber and Faber.
Holston, J.
    1989 *The Modernist City: An Anthropological Critique of Brasilia.* Chicago: University of Chicago Press.

Ioannidhis, A.
1984 Tekhni ke Idheoloyia sti Nazistiki Yermania. *Anakinosis, Proto Simposio yia tin Tekhni*, 143–51. Telloghlio Idhrima. Thessaloniki: Aristotelio Panepistimio Thessalonikis.

Jameson, F.
1984 Forward. In *The Postmodern Condition: A Report on Knowledge*, by J.-F. Lyotard, v–xxi. Translated by G. Bennington and B. Massumi. Minneapolis: University of Minnesota Press.

Jeffreys, M.
1983 Adamantios Korais: Language and Revolution. In *Culture and Nationalism in Nineteenth-Century Eastern Europe*, edited by R. Sussex and J. C. Eade, 42–55. Columbus, Ohio: Slavica Publishers.

Jenkyns, R.
1980 *The Victorians and Ancient Greece*. Cambridge, Mass.: Harvard University Press.

Kant, I.
1933 *Critique of Pure Reason*. Translated by N. K. Smith. London: Macmillan Press.

Karapanou, M.
1974 *Cassandra and the Wolf*. Translated by N. Germanacos. New York: Harcourt Brace Jovanovich.
1986a *I Kassandhra ke o Likos*. Athens: Ermis.
1986b *O Ipnovatis*. 2d ed. Athens: Ermis.

Keeley, E.
1975 Cavafy's Hellenism. In *Greece: The Modern Voice*, edited by P. Mackridge, 66–89. Jamaica, N.Y.: St. John's University Press.

Keeley, E., and Sherrard, P.
1981 Foreward. In *Collected Poems*, by G. Seferis, vii–xv. Translated, edited, and introduced by E. Keeley and P. Sherrard. Expanded edition. Princeton: Princeton University Press.

Kenny, M., and Kertzer, D.
1983 Introduction. In *Urban Life in Mediterranean Europe: Anthropological Perspectives*, 3–21. Urbana: University of Illinois Press.

Kerofilas, Y.
1984 *I Athina tou Mesopolemou*. Athens: Filoppoti.
1985 *I Athina tis Bel Epok*. Athens: Filoppoti.

Khatzimikhali, E.
1986 O Adherfos mou. *Andi* 2 (338): 52–53.

Kluckhohn, C., and Leighton, D.
1946 *The Navaho*. Cambridge, Mass.: Harvard University Press.

Kolovou, I.
1987 Dhialeghondas ton Idhio Filo. *Ena* 13 (26 March): 59–66.

Kondo, D.
1990 *Crafting Selves: Power, Gender, and Discourses of Identity in a Japanese Workplace*. Chicago: University of Chicago Press.

Koselleck, R.
1985 *Futures Past: On the Semantics of Historical Time*. Translated by K. Tribe. Cambridge, Mass.: MIT Press.

Kuhn, T.
1970 *The Structure of Scientific Revolutions*. 2d ed. Chicago: University of Chicago Press.
Lagopoulos, A. Ph.
1971 Rank-Size and Primate Distribution in Greece. *Ekistics* 32 (192): 380–86.
Lambiri, I.
1968 The Impact of Industrial Employment on the Position of Women in a Greek Country Town. In *Contributions to Mediterranean Sociology*, edited by J. Peristiany, 261–68. Paris: Mouton.
Lambropoulos, V.
1988 *Literature as National Institution: Studies in the Politics of Modern Greek Criticism*. Princeton: Princeton University Press.
Legg, K.
1969 *Politics in Modern Greece*. Palo Alto, Calif.: Stanford University Press.
1977 The Nature of the Modern Greek State. In *Greece in Transition*, edited by J.T.A. Koumoulides, 283–96. London: Zeno.
Le Goff, J.
1980 *Time, Work, and Culture in the Middle Ages*. Translated by A. Goldhammer. Chicago: University of Chicago Press.
Lerner, D.
1958 *The Passing of Traditional Society: Modernizing the Middle East*. Glencoe, Ill.: Free Press.
Lévi-Strauss, C.
1966 *The Savage Mind*. Chicago: University of Chicago Press.
1969a *The Elementary Structures of Kinship*. Rev. ed. Edited by R. Needham. Translated by J. H. Bell, J. R. von Sturmer, and R. Needham. Boston: Beacon Press.
1969b *The Raw and the Cooked: Introduction to a Science of Mythology*. Vol. 1. New York: Harper and Row.
1973 Social Structure. In *High Points in Anthropology*, edited by P. Bohannon and M. Glazer, 373–409. New York: Alfred A. Knopf.
Levy, R.
1973 *Tahitians: Mind and Experience in the Society Islands*. Chicago: University of Chicago Press.
Lipset, S.
1987 Historical Traditions and National Characteristics: A Comparative Analysis of Canada and the United States. In *Patterns of Modernity*. Vol. 1: *The West*, edited by S. N. Eisenstadt, 60–87. New York: New York University Press.
Loizos, P.
1975 *The Greek Gift: Politics in a Cypriot Village*. Oxford: Oxford University Press.
Loizos, P., and Papataxiarchis, E.
1991a Gender and Kinship in Marriage and Alternative Contexts. In *Contested Identities: Gender and Kinship in Modern Greece*, edited by P. Loizos and E. Papataxiarchis, 3–25. Princeton: Princeton University Press.
1991b Gender, Sexuality, and the Person in Greek Culture. In *Contested Identities: Gender and Kinship in Modern Greece*, edited by P. Loizos and E. Papataxiarchis, 221–34. Princeton: Princeton University Press.

Luhmann, N.
   1980 *Gesellschaftsstruktur und Semantik*. Vol. 1. Frankfurt.
   1982 *The Differentiation of Society*. Translated by S. Holmes and C. Larmore. New York: Columbia University Press.
Manesis, A.
   1986 I Exelixi ton Politikon Thesmon stin Elladha: Anazitondas mia diskoli nomopiisi. In *I Elladha se Exelixi*, 15–59. Athens: Exandas.
Marcus, G., and Cushman, D.
   1982 Ethnographies as Texts. *Annual Review of Anthropology* 11: 25–69.
Marcus, G., and Fischer, J.
   1986 *Anthropology as Cultural Critique*. Chicago: University of Chicago Press.
Marinatos, N. n.d.
   Santorini: Archaeology—History—Religion. Athens: D. and I. Mathioulakis.
Marrou, H. I.
   1965 *Histoire de l'éducation dans l'antiquité*. 6th ed. Paris: Editions du seuil.
Mavrogordatos, G.
   1983a O Dhikhasmos os Krisi Ethnikis Oloklirosis. In *Ellinismos, Ellinikotita*, edited by Dh. G. Tsaousis, 69–80. Athens: Estia.
   1983b *Stillborn Republic: Social Coalitions and Party Strategies in Greece, 1922–1936*. Berkeley: University of California Press.
Meletzes, S., and Papadakis, H.
   1967 *Acropolis Museum*. Munich: Schnell and Steiner.
Mirasyezi, M.
   1982 *Neoelliniki Loghotekhnia*. Vol. 2. Athens: n.p.
Mousourou, L. M.
   1983 To Elliniko Kratos ke O Ellinismos tou Exoterikou. In *Ellinismos, Ellinikotita*, edited by Dh. G. Tsaousis, 165–79. Athens: Estia.
Mouzelis, N.
   1978 *Modern Greece: Facets of Underdevelopment*. London: Macmillan.
   1986 Paradhosi ke Allayi stin Elliniki Politiki: Apo ton Eleftherio Venizelo ston Andhrea Papandhreou. In *I Elladha se Exelixi*, 149–62. Athens: Exandas.
Nozick, R.
   1974 *Anarchy, State, and Utopia*. New York: Basic Books.
Ober, J.
   1989 *Mass and Elite in Democratic Athens*. Princeton: Princeton University Press.
Obeysekere, G.
   1981 *Medusa's Hair: An Essay on Personal Symbols and Religious Experience*. Chicago. University of Chicago Press.
Offe, C.
   1987 Challenging the Boundaries of Institutional Politics: Social Movements since the 1960s. In *Changing Boundaries of the Political*, edited by C. S. Maier, 63–106. Cambridge: Cambridge University Press.
Ohmann, R.
   1987 *Politics of Letters*. Middletown, Conn.: Wesleyan University Press.
Ortner, S., and Whitehead, H.
   1981 Introduction. In *Sexual Meanings: The Cultural Construction of Gender and*

Sexuality, edited by S. Ortner and H. Whitehead, 1–28. Cambridge: Cambridge University Press.

Pandelidhis, A. E.
 1982 I Omofilofilia ke to Piniko Dikeo. In *Omofilofilia*, 85–94. Omilies ke sizitisis pou eyinan sto seminario "I Omofilofilia," 20–21 Martiou 1982.

Panofsky, E.
 1957 *Gothic Architecture and Scholasticism*. New York: New American Library.

Papacosma, S. V.
 1977 The Military in Greek Politics: A Historical Survey. In *Greece in Transition*, edited by J.T.A. Koumoulides, 173–89. London: Zeno.
 1981 The Republicanism of Eleftherios Venizelos: Ideology or Tactics? *Byzantine and Modern Greek Studies* 7: 168–202.

Papataxiarchis, E.
 1991 Friends of the Heart: Male Commensal Solidarity, Gender, and Kinship in Aegean Greece. In *Contested Identities: Gender and Kinship in Modern Greece*, edited by P. Loizos and E. Papataxiarchis, 156–79. Princeton: Princeton University Press.

Parke, H. W.
 1977 *Festivals of the Athenians*. Ithaca: Cornell University Press.

Parsons, T.
 1960 *Structure and Process in Modern Societies*. New York: Free Press.

Patsalidhou, N.
 1982 I Omofilofilia stin Kipriaki Kinonia: Kinoniki Prosengisi. In *Omofilofilia*, 43–55. Omilies ke sizitisis pou eyinan sto seminario "I Omofilofilia," 20–21 Martiou 1982.

Patton, C. V., and Sophoulis, C. M.
 1983 Great Expectations: Illegal Land Development in Modern Greece. *Ekistics* 50 (301): 259–64.

Pavlides, E., and Hesser, J.
 1986 Women's Roles and House Form and Decoration in Eressos, Greece. In *Gender and Power in Rural Greece*, edited by J. Dubisch, 68–96. Princeton: Princeton University Press.

Pentzopoulos, D.
 1962 *The Balkan Exchange of Minorities and Its Impact upon Greece*. Paris: Mouton.

Petsemeris, P.
 1986 Growth, Distribution and Rank Stability of Urban Settlements in Greece. *Ekistics* 53 (316–17): 54–62.

Phillips, H. P.
 1987 *Modern Thai Literature*. Honolulu: University of Hawaii Press.

Pickard-Cambridge, A. W.
 1988 *The Dramatic Festivals of Athens*. Oxford: Clarendon Press.

Pitt-Rivers, J.
 1966 Honor and Social Status. In *Honor and Shame: The Values of Mediterranean Society*, edited by J. Peristiany, 19–77. Chicago: University of Chicago Press.

Pollitt, J. J.
 1972 *Art and Experience in Classical Greece*. Cambridge: Cambridge University Press.

Prevelakis, G.
   1990 Center-Periphery and the Urban Crisis of Athens. *Ekistics* 57 (340–41): 35–43.
Price, R.
   1983 *First-Time: The Historical Vision of an Afro-American People.* Baltimore: Johns Hopkins University Press.
Psacharopoulos, G.
   1983 Sex Discrimination in the Greek Labor Market. *Journal of Modern Greek Studies* 1 (2): 339–58.
Rabinow, P.
   1989 *French Modern: Norms and Forms of the Social Environment.* Cambridge, Mass.: MIT Press.
Rawls, J.
   1971 *A Theory of Justice.* Cambridge, Mass.: Harvard University Press.
Ricoeur, P.
   1984–88 *Time and Narrative.* 3 vols. Translated by K. McLaughlin and D. Pellauer. Chicago: University of Chicago Press.
Ritsos, Y.
   1985 *Isos Na'ne ki'Etsi.* Athens: Kedhros.
Robinson, C.
   1975 Greece in the Poetry of Costas Palamas. In *Greece: The Modern Voice,* edited by P. Mackridge, 41–65. Jamaica, N.Y.: St. John's University Press.
Rosaldo, M.
   1980 *Knowledge and Passion: Ilongot Notions of Self and Social Life.* New York: Cambridge University Press.
Rosaldo, R.
   1980 *Ilongot Headhunting, 1883–1974: A Study in Society and History.* Stanford, Calif.: Stanford University Press.
Rossiter, S.
   1981 *Blue Guide: Athens and Environs.* London: Ernest Benn.
Roussos, Kh.
   1987 *Filakes Alikarnassou—Filakes Kerkiras, Vasanismi Kratoumenon.* Athens: Ekdhosi periodhikou "tis filakis."
Saccopoulos, C. A.
   1986 Roadside Monuments in Greece. *Ekistics* 54 (318–19): 144–48.
Safilios-Rothschild, C.
   1976 The Family in Athens: Regional Variation. In *Regional Variation in Modern Greece and Cyprus,* edited by M. Dimen and E. Friedl, 410–18. New York: New York Academy of Sciences.
Sahlins, M.
   1985 *Islands of History.* Chicago: University of Chicago Press.
St. Clair, W.
   1972 *That Greece Might Still Be Free: The Philhellenes in the Greek War of Independence.* London: Oxford University Press.
Salamone, S. D., and Stanton, J. B.
   1986 Introducing the Nikokyra: Ideality and Reality in Social Process. In *Gender and Power in Rural Greece,* edited by J. Dubisch, 97–120. Princeton: Princeton University Press.

Scheper-Hughes, N.
1982 *Saints, Scholars, and Schizophrenics: Mental Illness in Rural Ireland*. First paperback edition. Berkeley: University of California Press.
Schneider, J.
1971 Of Vigilance and Virgins: Honor, Shame, and Access to Resources in Mediterranean Societies. *Ethnology* 10: 1–24.
Schneider, P., Schneider, J., and Hansen, E.
1972 Modernization and Development: The Role of Regional Elite and Non-Corporate Groups in the European Mediterranean. *Comparative Studies in Society and History* 14: 328–50.
Seferis, G.
1981 *Collected Poems*. Translated, edited, and introduced by E. Keeley and P. Sherrard. Expanded edition. Princeton: Princeton University Press.
Seremetakis, C. N.
1991 *The Last Word: Women, Death, and Divination in Inner Mani*. Chicago: University of Chicago Press.
Sherrard, P.
1975 Anghelos Sikelianos and His Vision of Greece. In *Greece: The Modern Voice*, edited by P. Mackridge, 90–112. Jamaica, N.Y.: St. John's University Press.
Sicilianos, D.
1960 *Old and New Athens*. Translated by Robert Liddell. London: Putnam.
Simmons, J.
1979 *Moral Principles and Political Obligations*. Princeton: Princeton University Press.
Sioubouras, F.
1980 *Pezodhromio*. Athens: Ekdhosis "Kaptos."
Skiotis, D., and Gagaoudaki, C. G.
1977 Photochemical Smog in Athens. *Ekistics* 44 (260): 23–26.
Slesin, S., Cliff, S., and Rozensztroch, D.
1988 *Greek Style*. New York: Crown Publishers.
Smith, M. G.
1984 The Nature and Variety of Plural Unity. In *The Prospects for Plural Societies*, edited by D. Maybury-Lewis, 146–86. 1982 Proceedings of the American Ethnological Society. Washington, D.C.: American Ethnological Society.
Spicer, E.
1971 Persistent Cultural Systems: A Comparative Study of Systems That Can Adapt to Contrasting Environments. *Science* 74: 795–800.
Stasinopoulos, E. K.
1973 *Istoria ton Athinon: apo tin Arkheotita os tin Epokhi mas*. Athens: n.p.
Stavroulakis, N.
1986 *Cookbook of the Jews of Greece*. Port Jefferson, N.Y.: Cadmus Press.
Stewart, C.
1991 *Demons and the Devil*. Princeton: Princeton University Press.
Svoronos, N.
1984 Ta Kiria Provlimata tis Periodhou 1940–1950 stin Elliniki Istoria. In *I Elladha sti Dhekaetia 1940–1950: Ena Ethnos se Krisi*, edited by M. Moskhonas, 21–38. Athens: Themelio.
1987 *Analekta Neoellinikis Istorias ke Istorioghrafias*. Athens: Themelio.

Taktsis, C.
　　1985 *The Third Wedding Wreath*. Translated by J. Chioles. Athens: Hermes.
Tambiah, S.
　　1989 Ethnic Conflict in the World Today. *American Ethnologist* 16 (May): 335–49.
Theodhorakopoulos, L.
　　1982 Omofilofilia ke Pnevmatiko Dhimiouryia. In *Omofilofilia*, 167–87. Omilies ke sizitisis pou eyinan sto seminario "I Omofilofilia," 20–21 Martiou 1982.
Topping, E. C.
　　1983 Patriarchal Prejudice and Pride in Greek Christianity—Notes on Origins. *Journal of Modern Greek Studies* 1 (1): 7–17.
Tsaousis, Dh. G.
　　1983 Ellinismos ke Ellinikotita. In *Ellinismos, Ellinikotita*, edited by Dh. G. Tsaousis, 15–26. Athens: Estias.
Tsavaras, Th., ed.
　　1984 *Psikhanalisi ke Elladha: Stikhia, Thesis, Erotimata*. Vivliothiki yenikis pedhias 16. Athens: Eteria Spoudhon tis Skholis Moraiti.
Tsoukalas, K.
　　1969. *The Greek Tragedy: From the Liberation to the Colonels*. London: Penguin.
　　1981 *I Elliniki Traghodia: Apo tin Apeleftherosi os tous Sindaghmatarkhes*. Athens: Nea Sinora.
　　1982 *Exartisi ke Anaparaghoyi: O Kinonikos Rolos ton Ekpedheftikon Mikhanismon stin Elladha (1830–1922)*. Athens: Themelio.
　　1983 Paradhosi ke Eksingkhronismos: Merika yenikotera erotimata. In *Ellinismos, Ellinikotita*, edited by Dh. G. Tsaousis, 37–48. Athens: Estias.
　　1986a Erghasia ke Erghazomeni stin Protevousa: Adhiafanis, Erotimata, Ipothesis. In *I Elladha se Exelixi*, 163–241. Athens: Exandas.
　　1986b *Kinoniki Anaptixi ke Kratos: I Sinkrotisi tou Dhimosiou Khorou stin Elladha*. Athens: Themelio.
　　1991 "Enlightened" Concepts in the "Dark": Power and Freedom, Politics and Society. *Journal of Modern Greek Studies* 9: 1–22.
Tziovas, D.
　　1985 The Organic Discourse of Nationistic Demoticism: A Tropological Approach. In *The Text and Its Margins: Post-Structuralist Approaches to Twentieth-Century Greek Literature*, edited by M. Alexiou and V. Lambropoulos, 253–77. New York: Pella Publishing Company.
Unger, K.
　　1981 Greek Emigration to and Return from West Germany. *Ekistics* 48 (290): 369–74.
United States Department of State
　　1985 *Greece: Background Notes*. Washington, D.C.: U.S. Department of State, Bureau of Public Affairs.
Urla, J.
　　1988 Ethnic Protest and Social Planning: A Look at Basque Language Revival. *Cultural Anthropology* 3 (4): 379–94.
Veremis, Th.
　　1986 O Stratos stin Politiki meta ton Polemo. In *I Elladha se se Exelixi*, 135–48. Athens: Exandas.

Verghopoulos, K.
1978 *Ethnikismos ke Ikonomiki Anaptixi.* Athens: Exandas.
Vermeulen, H.
1983 Urban Research in Greece. In *Urban Life in Mediterranean Europe: Anthropological Perspectives,* edited by M. Kenny and D. Kertzer, 109–32. Urbana: University of Illinois Press.
Vitti, M.
1972 Family and Alienation in Contemporary Greek Fiction. In *Modern Greek Writers,* edited by E. Keeley and P. Bien, 217–33. Princeton: Princeton University Press.
Vlakhos, E.
1968 *The Assimilation of Greece in the United States.* Athens: National Center of Social Research.
von Grunebaum, G.E.
1954 The Concept of Cultural Classicism. In *Modern Islam: The Search for Cultural Identity,* edited by G. E. von Grunebaum, 691–707. New York: Vintage Books.
Weber, M.
1946a Bureaucracy. In *From Max Weber: Essays in Sociology,* edited by H. Gerth and C. Wright Mills, 196–244. New York: Oxford University Press.
1946b Class, Status, Party. In *From Max Weber: Essays in Sociology,* edited by H. Gerth and C. Wright Mills, 180–95. New York: Oxford University Press.
1946c The Meaning of Discipline. In *From Max Weber: Essays in Sociology,* edited by H. Gerth and C. Wright Mills, 253–64. New York: Oxford University Press.
1946d Religious Rejections of the World and Their Directions. In *From Max Weber: Essays in Sociology,* edited by H. Gerth and C. Wright Mills, 323–59. New York: Oxford University Press.
1946e Science as a Vocation. In *From Max Weber: Essays in Sociology,* edited by H. Gerth and C. Wright Mills, 129–56. New York: Oxford University Press.
1946f The Social Psychology of the World Religions. In *From Max Weber: Essays in Sociology,* edited by H. Gerth and C. Wright Mills, 267–322. New York: Oxford University Press.
1946g The Sociology of Charismatic Authority. In *From Max Weber: Essays in Sociology,* edited by H. Gerth and C. Wright Mills, 245–52. New York: Oxford University Press.
1958a *The City.* Translated by D. Martindale and G. Neuwirth. New York: Collier Books.
1958b *The Protestant Ethic and the Spirit of Capitalism.* Translated by T. Parsons. New York: Charles Scribner's Sons.
1968 *Economy and Society.* Edited by G. Roth and C. Wittich. 3 vols. New York: Bedminster Press.
1975 *Roscher and Knies: The Logical Problems of Historical Economics.* Translated by Guy Oakes. New York: Free Press.
White, H.
1973 *Metahistory: The Historical Imagination of Nineteenth-Century Europe.* Baltimore: Johns Hopkins University Press.
1978 *Tropics of Discourse.* Baltimore: Johns Hopkins University Press.

Wolff, R. P.
   1970 *In Defense of Anarchism*. New York: Harper and Row.
Woodhouse, C. M.
   1948 *The Apple of Discord*. London: Hutchinson.
   1977 *Modern Greece: A Short History*. London: Faber and Faber.
Working Group on the Preservation of the Acropolis Monuments
   1978 The Acropolis: Problems, Measures to Be Taken. *Ekistics* 45 (271): 295–97.
Yannitsis, T.
   1986 Elladha: I Ekviomikhanisi se Krisi. In *I Elladha se Exelixi*, 245–66. Athens: Exandas.
Yanoulopoulos, Y.
   1977 Greece: Political and Constitutional Developments 1924–1974. In *Greece in Transition*, edited by J.T.A. Koumoulides, 64–91. London: Zeno.

INDEX

Benakis, I., 87
Benakis Museum, 87, 95
Bendix, R., 9, 114, 257n.30
Benedict, R., 162, 163
Berlin, 74, 79, 189
Bernal, M., 240
Bien, P., 197
Bigot, C., 53
Biris, K. E., 78–79
bisexuality, 237
Bismarck, 10
Blanchot, M., 193
Bloch, M., 6
blood, 5, 54, 59, 74, 91, 126
Bloom, H., xx, xxi, xxii, 82, 83, 84, 85, 119,
  150, 154, 179, 181, 198–99, 249n.23
Blumenberg, H., 17, 18, 147, 148, 155
body, 217; and capitalism, 149; heroization
  of, 145; morality of, 145; as substance of
  valuation, 145, 149, 180
bohemianism, 39, 109
Bourdieu, P., xii, xiii, xiv, xv, 12, 19, 20, 54,
  80, 189, 247, 249n.11
bourgeoisie, 9, 18, 58, 125, 178, 180, 182, 204,
  219; Athenian, 176, 222; grand, 56, 59, 98,
  120, 127, 184, 190; old, 74; petty, 56, 59,
  110, 119, 171, 190, 247
Brandes, S., 223
Brasilia, 81
Braudel, F., 25
Breton, A., 204
bricolage, xix
British Museum, 33
Brussels, 215
Budapest, 68, 73
Bulgakov, M., 198
bureaucracy, 4, 10, 16, 106, 115, 141, 142, 148
bureaucratization, 80; spatial, 80
Burke, K., 83
business, 38, 108, 222, 237; family, 47, 134,
  174–75; regulation of, 53; schedules of, 52–
  53, 63, 94; schedules of, foreign, 54; touris-
  tic, 53
Butor, M., 101
Byron, Lord G., 55, 89, 90, 91
Byzantine Museum, 87
Byzantium, 56, 71, 87, 128, 181

Cairo, 82, 129
calculability, xvi, 115, 140, 141, 142, 144;
  norm of, 10, 115, 141
Calcutta, 134

Calvin, 141
Calvinism, 140
Calvino, I., 23
Campbell, J., 95, 107, 132
canon, 198; Greek, 207; neo-Hellenic, 151–52
canonization, 152, 184, 194, 195, 211; as antipopulist, 194; vs. subjectification, 194
capital, 20; cultural, 54, 189; material, xiii, 60,
  110; maximization of, xiv, xv; social, 189;
  symbolic, 19, 60, 110
capitalism, xviii, 7, 9, 10, 11, 49, 54, 55, 59,
  110, 115, 122, 141, 142, 149, 245; and the
  body, 149
capitals, 101, 131, 135; cultural, 79; historical,
  83; of history, 83
Carnival, 45, 53, 208, 209
Cassandra, 196, 198, 200, 201, 202, 206
catastrophe: creative, 14, 154, 166, 195–96
Catholicism, 44, 140
cats, 50, 51, 52, 57
Cavafy, C., 89, 196, 197
censorship, 79, 171, 196, 226; spatial, 79
center, 15, 55, 195; city, 27, 38, 70; Department of Transportation's, 38; Kolonaki as,
  39; of literary intelligentsia, 191; the local
  district as, 39; of Occident, 124, 133; Omonia Square as, 38–39; "real," 38; Syntagma
  Square as, 39; touristic, 39; of world system, 246
Center of Social Research, 23
centralism, 54
centralization: administrative, 4
Chandigarh, 81
change, 103, 119, 164, 242, 245; cultural, xx,
  159, 163; economic, 101; political, 101; sociocultural, 20
chaos, xviii, 8, 83, 155, 179, 198; metaphysics
  of, xviii
characterology, 160, 164–65; modern, 162
charisma, 11, 127, 128, 130, 131, 132, 133,
  136, 143, 149, 238, 245; of blood, 5, 59, 74,
  126; of office, 5, 59, 126; as revisionary,
  154; and sovereignty, 126
charity, 50
Charyn, J., 195
Chateaubriand, 90
chauvinism, 47, 62; civic, 46
Chicago, 64
Chile, 216
choice, 115, 118, 125, 164, 176, 233, 237; of
  ends, 10; of traditions, 198
Christianity, xviii, 25

Great Divide, 6, 160
Great Idea (*Meghali Idhea*), 71, 72, 204
Great Powers, 18, 123, 127
Greco-Turkish War (1897), 71, 128, 137, 204
Greek modern. *See* modernity: Greek
Greek Penal Code, 217, 221, 222
Gregory, D., 256n.79
Guatemala, 216
guestworker, xviii, 76
gypsies, 71

Habermas, J., 11, 115, 139, 140, 144, 145, 149, 156
habitus, xii, 156; depersonalized, 141; elite vs. nonelite, 19; functional, 144; rationalization of, 141
Hadrian, 93
Halikarnassos, 215, 216
Hansen, E., 106, 234
health, 79, 119, 130, 180, 215, 235; politics of, 11
Hecataeus, 160
Hegel, W.G.F., 16, 125, 147
hegemony, 188, 124
hellenes, 56, 57, 58, 72, 76, 90; ancient, 240
Hellenic-American Union, 62
Hellenicity, 14, 16, 55, 56, 57, 58, 74, 76–77, 83, 87, 90, 91, 94, 96, 182, 197, 205, 211, 242; metaphorical, 98; problematics of, 211
Hellenism, 16, 138
Hellenists, 56, 206; British, 37
Hellenization, 75, 77–78, 79
Hellenizers, 75
Hellenomania, 90
hermeneutics, 11, 12, 20, 81, 85, 105, 147, 148–49, 193, 199, 220, 223–24, 225
Hermes (literary press), 186
Hermes Avenue, 15, 55, 66, 88, 174
hero, 17, 64, 92, 188
Herodes Atticus, 86, 92
Herodotus, 46
heroism, 50
heroization, 90, 145, 187
Herzfeld, M., xvii, xviii, 12, 13, 45, 75, 79, 105, 122, 219, 221, 263n.68, 260n.39, 265n.33
Hesiod, 89, 92
Hesiod Avenue, 55
heterosexual, 220
hierarchy, 24, 41, 42, 97, 125, 189, 237
Hilton Hotel, 153
historians, 68, 72, 80, 90, 148, 166

historicity, xix, 192; cold, xi, xviii; hot, xi, xii, 192
historiography, 23, 104; rhetoric of, 80–81
history, xi, xvii, xix, xxi, xxii, xxiii, 17, 18, 37, 65, 75, 78, 80, 86, 91, 94, 110, 117, 138, 146–49, 153–54, 241, 242, 245; American, 88; *arkhi* of, 93; cessation of, 242, 245 conceptual, 17; as concreta of past and present, 11; consciousness of, 159, 165; as ethical concern, 12; hermeneutics of, 147; knowledge of, 92–93; life, 166; local, xviii; as *magistra vitae*, 173; making of, 245; as moral burden, 12–13; neutralization of, 148; as object of social re-creation, 13; personal, 165; philosophy of, 156; pragmatics of, xix, 16, 19, 94; selective and exemplary, 91; significative priority of, 93; as substance of valuation, 146, 149; temporalization of, 146–47, 148; truth of, 160
Hitchcock, H.-R., 68
Hitler, A., 11, 72
Hobbes, T., 125
holidays, 45, 53
holism, 15, 19, 24
homeostasis, 80, 133
Homer, 50, 92, 187
Homer Avenue, 15, 55, 88
homogeneity, 74, 136
homogenization, 136, 245
homosexual, 14, 76, 191, 208, 213, 216–17, 222, 224–41, 244–45; active, 220, 221, 222, 227; as figure, 225–26, 230–32; vs. gay, 237, 239–41; liberation of, 236–37; masculine, 228–29; passive, 222, 227, 228, 231, 233; theory of the, 226–29; as third sex, 226; as trope, 229
homosexuality, 14, 217, 226–30, 232, 234, 235–36, 237; active, 228; passive, 228
honesty, 226, 232
honor, 42, 60, 91, 132–33, 218, 221, 222
Horkheimer, M., 148
Hugo, V., 89, 92
Humphreys, S., 13
Hydra, 185
hyperbole, xxi, 84, 88, 104, 147, 202, 210, 231
hypergamy, 61

Iatropoulou, K., 214–15
identity, 149, 167, 180, 181, 200; collective, xix, 137; crisis of, xxi, 10, 138, 144, 181, 195; cultural, 41; ethnic, rhetoric of, 163–64; heterosexual, 237; individual, xix; na-

planning, 16, 39, 68, 76, 78, 82, 83, 87, 92; of
Athens, 66, 68–69, 76; modernist, 64;
moral, 140
Plato, 13, 23, 47, 140, 146, 151, 240
play, 117
pluralism, 70, 71, 73, 80, 83, 244; ethnic, 94;
and racism, 75; religious, 94
poetics, xxiii, 85; of ancient cities, 80; of
Athens, 85–92; countermodern, xxii; of
ethnographic description, 80; Hellenizing,
205; modern, xxii; modernist, 204; practical, xx, 85; of reform, xxi, 20; of restoration,
xxi; romantic, 83, 84; of urban form, 80–85
poetry, 149, 150, 181, 185; Greek, 187, 196–
97
poets, 171, 184, 187, 198–99, 204; metaphysical, 241
poiēsis, 150, 153, 181, 199; historically constructivist, 151, 155, 165, 183, 245; of originality, 245
police, 108, 117, 128, 210, 213, 214, 230, 231,
233, 235, 237
politicians, 5, 121, 227–28
politics, 7, 19, 37, 50, 58, 74, 97, 101, 109,
110, 122, 125, 126–31, 167–68, 171–73,
175, 184, 225; class, 129; of crisis, xxi; of
distinction, 54; of fiction, 155; of health,
11; humanist, 233; of identity, 137, 175; localist, 110; noninstitutional, 234; occidentalist, 110; of opinion, 155; orientalist, 110;
postjunta, 238; of profit, 53; regulative,
125, 136; of sex, 218, 221, 222, 229, 233; of
signification, 226; sovereign, 10, 126, 128,
133, 172, 183, 187, 245; of truth, 154;
women in, 170. See also democratization;
left: political; parties, political; right: political
pollution, 64, 65, 211; air, 8, 25, 34, 38, 49;
political, 66; spiritual, 64
polyglossia, 59, 170, 190, 238
Polynesia, 146
Polytechnic Day, 46, 172
Polytechnic Institute, 46
poniria, 223
population, 54, 68, 72, 73; exchange of, 72,
74; minority, 70–71; welfare of, 133
populism, xiii, 8, 16, 39, 58, 120, 130, 168
Portland, 64
positivism, xix, 7
postmodernism, 116
Pound, E., 204
poustis, 223, 224, 229, 230, 231

poverty, 25, 57, 178, 205, 219
power, 5, 123, 172, 215, 220, 238; Nazi aesthetics of, 73; social, 59; symbolic, 59; will
to, 132
practice, xiv, xix, xx, xxiii, 114, 116, 117, 146,
151, 163, 182, 197, 219, 224, 240; comportmental, 62; countermodern, xv–xvii, xxi;
criminal, 221; economic, 143; ethical, 150;
ethnography of, 80; heterosexual, 236; historically grounded, 13; homosexual, 236;
insider's, 62; iterability of, xiv–xv; logic of,
xix; metacultural, xxiv; modern, xiv, xvii,
xxiv; revisionary, 155; of the self, 218; of
self-formation, 150; sexual, 218; stratifying,
247; tactical, 122
practitioners, xiii, 12
pragmatics, xix, 16, 19, 94, 156
praxis, xii, 193, 241
Praxiteles, 217
praxology, xxiv, 5, 19; vs. ethnography, xxiv
present, xi, xix, xxi, xxii, 11, 16, 18, 60, 85,
87–88, 98, 146, 151, 152, 166, 189, 197,
198, 242; contestation of, 94; cultural, 181;
the Greek, 106; invention of, 65; local, 15;
new, 121; orientalized, 18; past in the, 104;
and past, contrariety of, 83; and past,
mélange of, 94; pasts of Athens's, 91; sensibility of, 87; validity of Greek, 103–5
preservation, 65, 152; of meaning, rhetoric
and, 159; of tradition, 120
prestige, 54, 132, 175, 187, 221; sexually indexed, 218
Prevelakis, G., 257n.16
Priam, 196
Price, R., xi
primitive, 115, 185; romanticization of, 247
primitivism, 216
primitivity, 105
prison, 213–16
privatism, 27, 68, 233
problematic, 6, 114, 116; of Hellenicity, 211
proceduralism, 10, 141, 148, 149–50, 156
production, 47, 53, 155, 192; artistic, 13, 193,
212; of ideas, 192; industrial, 133; material,
59, 136
professionals, 5, 109, 187
progress, 88, 103, 146, 147, 152, 164, 246; as
ethical norm, 164; hermeneutics of, 147;
infinitalization of, 147; infinite, 17, 18, 148,
160; myth of, 152
progressivism, 47, 65, 102, 103, 117, 119, 150,
152, 235, 238, 242

Skeptics, 6
Smyrna Street, 69
socialism, 97; scientific, 7; secular, 44
socialization, 163
Society of the Friends of the Muses (Filo-
    mouson Eteria), 37
sociology, 7, 193
Socrates, 25, 92
sodomy, 222, 230
solidarity, 7
Solomos, D., 152, 197
Solon, 47
Solon Avenue, 88
Sophia, 91, 92
sophists, 6, 160
Sophocles, 42, 92
Sophocles Avenue, 15, 55, 89
Sotiriou, D., 204
South Africa, 216
Soutsos, A., 92
Soutsos, P., 69, 89, 92
Soutsos Street, 15, 69, 89
sovereigntism, 10, 18, 136
sovereignty, 10, 18, 50, 122–38, 143, 144, 149,
    167, 188, 190, 191, 218, 220, 224, 230, 238,
    245; and charisma, 126; vs. egalitarianism,
    126; legitimate, 132, 136; politics of, 126,
    128, 136, 172, 183, 187; radical, 132; sexual,
    220, 223, 224; tactics of, 125–26, 132, 136,
    187
Soviet Union, 84, 109, 129
Spain, 108
Split, 71–72, 73, 91, 128
stadium, 86, 214
Stadium Avenue, 38, 55, 66
Stalin, J., 129
state, xvii, 19, 42, 59, 95, 104, 125, 126, 135,
    136, 142, 148, 171, 187–88, 189; and
    church, separation of, 43; modern, 59; par-
    allel, 128, 129, 130; welfare, 60, 145
statehood, romantic ideology of, 18
status, 15, 24, 41, 70, 80, 117, 167, 176, 185,
    190, 234; and talent, 188
stereotypes, 55, 75, 103, 110, 223; of foreign-
    ers, 49, 173, 174; of peasants, 61; of prole-
    tarian, 61; of women, 175
Stewart, C., 18, 76, 251n.33
Stoa of Attalos, 79
Stoics, 6
stranger, 23, 74, 86, 130
strategy, xiii, xiv, 61, 80, 106, 111, 181, 215,
    218, 234; of individualization and totaliza-

tion, 162; of legitimation, 37; military, 9;
    modern, 162; significative, 159
structuralism, xx
structuration, 163
structure: social, 9, 114
style, xvi, xix, 41, 65, 94, 167, 177–79, 191,
    241; American, 150; architectural, 77; folk,
    178; Greek, 152–53; Hellenic, 55; high, 39,
    77; of life, 80, 137, 190; minimalist, 108;
    modernist, 153; monumental, 142; Phanar-
    iotic, 94; populist, 178; primitive, 152; rus-
    tic, 152; urban, 174; vernacular, 77
subculture, xxii
subjectivism, 155–56; vs. historical relativism,
    155–56; substantive, 145
subjectivity, 14, 178, 186, 192, 194
sublime: romantic, 84
submission: vs. dominance, 218
substance: ethical 145–46, 149
substitution: tropological, xxi
Supreme Court, 214
Sweden, 208
symbol: key, 50, 119
symbolism, 118, 119, 232
synchronicity, 80
syncretism, 68, 137, 179, 188; cultural, 83; ro-
    mantic, 204
synecdoche, xxi, 80, 83, 229
Syntagma Square, 90, 95, 204; as center, 39
synthesis, xviii, xix, 16, 18, 34, 76, 90, 113,
    120, 121, 151, 152, 154, 155, 161, 202; ar-
    chitectural, 98; historical, 19, 153; of tradi-
    tion, 152
system, 12, 53, 80, 155; economic, 101; edu-
    cational, 163; formalistic, 145; incommen-
    surability of the Greek, 9; interactive,
    111; life as a, 140; modern, xii, 7, 9, 101,
    142; political, 101, 104, 131; sovereign,
    125–26, 127, 131, 132, 133, 136, 143, 144,
    149, 172, 187; synchronic, 64; tactics,
    133, 236, 238; world, 59, 70, 136, 143, 187,
    246

Taktsis, C., 214, 268n.5
talent, 5, 155, 187, 188, 194, 196, 207, 216,
    221; and class, 188; and status, 188
Tambiah, S., 250n.17
taste, xiii, 19, 55, 74, 76, 110, 118, 137, 170,
    180; architectural, 82; Hellenic, 55, 180;
    and imperialism, 110; middle-class, 65; for
    multiplicity, 76; Romaic, 180
taste-makers, 77

taxation, 134

technocracy, 17, 19, 60, 65, 68, 246

technology, xviii, 103, 112, 119, 234; disciplinary, 145; of display, 225; of domination, 149–50; modern, 141; of self-formation, literature as 14, 184, 193–95, 197–203, 204–5, 206–12

teleology, xiv, xx, xxiii, 17, 114

telos, telē. See ends

Temple of Olympian Zeus, 55, 89, 93

temporality, 94, 146–49, 153–54; modern, 148

temporalization: of history, 146–47, 148

terror, 129

terrorism, 46, 135, 244

Terzakis, A., 204

testability, 167, 168

text, 193, 198

Thatcher, M., 131

theater, 50, 133; feline, 50; political, 133; of regulation, 133

Theatrical Museum, 87

Themistocles, 92

Themistocles Avenue, 88

Theodhorakopoulos, L., 234, 235, 236

Theodorakis, M., 214

theology, 183, 193

theosis, 183, 237–38

Theotokas, Y., 204–5, 211

Theseus Street, 69

Thesprotia, 135

Thessaloniki, 54, 62, 72, 128, 169, 170, 215, 216

Thessaloniki Festival, 216

thisworldliness, 150, 151

Thrace, 71–72

Thucydides, 23, 46, 88

time, xi, 53, 93, 146, 153, 210; and canonization, 194; naturalistic basis of, 146, 147; as substance of valuation, 180

Times Square, 39

Tinos, 176

tolerance, 14, 77, 96, 156, 206, 233; religious, 42

topography, 15, 27, 93

toponymy, 15, 91, 93, 94

Topping, E., 269n.25

torture, 46, 130, 172, 209, 216

totalization, xix, 152

tourism, xvii, 15, 23, 27, 45, 48, 49, 50, 53, 54, 61, 65, 82, 86, 87, 90, 112, 163, 174, 175, 242, 244; and seasonality, 52

tradition, xvii, 24, 41, 60, 78, 79, 84, 102, 103, 105, 107, 108, 112, 119, 120, 139, 181, 196–98; American, 12; commodification of, 49, 116; consumption of, 49; contents of, 144; cosmos of, 8, 17; demotion of, 122; and the ethically oriented cosmos, 116; legitimacy of, 116; little, 58; malleability of, 229; meaning of, 105–6, 116; and modernity, 15; national, 194–95; preservation of, 120; revision of, 207; synthesis of, 152; transcendence of, 121

traditionalism, xviii, xxi, 34, 58, 111, 114, 116, 119, 139, 150, 153–54

traditions, xviii, 60, 64, 65, 116, 119, 152, 168, 197–98, 236; consumption of, 48

traffic, 25, 69

transcendence, xvi, 7, 8, 34, 116, 141, 142, 147, 192; of tradition, 121

transcendentalism, 150, 151, 211

transition, 106, 170, 179, 180; to modernity, 114; social, 159; women in, 171

transvestism, 208, 213, 222, 225, 228, 231–32, 233, 238; segregation of, 225; as technology of display, 225

Treaty of Lausanne, 72

triangle: commercial, 38, 39, 69, 92

trope, xxiii, 112, 154, 159, 166, 198, 202, 207; as defense, 84–85; homoxexual as, 229; key, 119; of limitation, xxi, 82, 179, 181, 229; master, 80, 83, 84, 196, 204; and metatrope, 98; of representation, xxi, 181, 229

tropology, xxi, xxii, 81, 84, 85, 117, 119, 120, 230, 242; moral, 112; of self, 181; temporal vs. spatial, 166

truth, 156, 159, 160, 186, 192, 194, 196, 202, 203, 204, 226; politics of, 154; regime of, 154

Tsaldharis, 93

Tsaldharis Street, 69

Tsolakoghlou, General, 72

Tsoukalas, K., 59, 104, 135, 172

Turkey, 4, 72, 168, 178, 204, 239

Turks, 70, 71, 77, 79

typicality, 162

typification, 165, 166–68

Tzanio Hospital, 213, 214, 215, 239

Tziovas, D., 254n.36

unemployment, 25, 134

universalism, 124; moral, 102

universities, 54, 59, 129, 189–90, 199

University of Athens, 54, 56, 88, 127, 169, 189, 214